REBIRTH, REFORM, AND RESILIENCE

REBIRTH, REFORM
AND RESILIENCE
Universities in Transition
1300-1700

Edited by
James M. Kittelson
and Pamela J. Transue

OHIO STATE UNIVERSITY PRESS:
COLUMBUS

Frontispiece from
Gregor Reisch, *Margarita Phi / / losophica noua. . . .*
(Ex Argentoraco veteri, J. Grüningerus; 1515),
sig. Av. 324 leaves. 4o in eight.
Reproduced by permission of Special Collections,
The Ohio State University Libraries.

Copyright © 1984 by the Ohio State University Press
All Rights Reserved

Library of Congress Cataloging in Publication Data
Rebirth, reform, and resilience.
Includes bibliographical references and index.
1. Universities and colleges—Europe—History—
Addresses, essays, lectures.
I. Kittelson, James M. II. Transue, Pamela.
LA621.3.R43   1984   378.4   83-25095
ISBN 0-8142-0356-6

CONTENTS

JAMES M. KITTELSON: OHIO STATE UNIVERSITY

Introduction: The Durability of the Universities of Old Europe 1

HEIKO A. OBERMAN: UNIVERSITY OF TÜBINGEN

University and Society on the Threshold of Modern Times: The German Connection 19

LEWIS W. SPITZ: STANFORD UNIVERSITY

The Importance of the Reformation for Universities: Culture and Confession in the Critical Years 42

EDWARD GRANT: INDIANA UNIVERSITY

Science and the Medieval University 68

WILLIAM J. COURTENAY: UNIVERSITY OF WISCONSIN

The Role of English Thought in the Transformation of University Education in the Late Middle Ages 103

JOHN M. FLETCHER: UNIVERSITY OF ASTON IN BIRMINGHAM

University Migrations in the Late Middle Ages with Particular Reference to the Stamford Secession 163

PAUL W. KNOLL: UNIVERSITY OF SOUTHERN CALIFORNIA

The University of Cracow in the Conciliar Movement 190

GUY FITCH LYTLE: UNIVERSITY OF TEXAS

The Careers of Oxford Students in the Later Middle Ages   213

JAMES H. OVERFIELD: UNIVERSITY OF VERMONT

University Studies and the Clergy in Pre-Reformation Germany
254

M. A. SCREECH: UNIVERSITY COLLEGE, LONDON

Two Attitudes toward Hebrew Studies: Erasmus and Rabelais 293

JOHN M. FLETCHER and JULIAN DEAHL:
UNIVERSITY OF ASTON IN BIRMINGHAM

European Universities, 1300-1700: The Development of Research,
1969-1979, with a Summary Bibliography   324

Notes on Contributors   359

Index   361

INTRODUCTION:
THE DURABILITY OF THE UNIVERSITIES
OF OLD EUROPE

James M. Kittelson

niversities are one of the few institutions that are a direct contribution of medieval Latin Christendom to contemporary Western civilization. Being an export wherever else they are found, they are also unique to Western culture. To be sure, all cultures have had their intellectuals: those men and women whose task it has been to learn, to know, and to teach. But only in Latin Christendom were scholars—the company of masters and students—gathered together into the *universitas* whose entire purpose was to develop and disseminate knowledge in a continuous and systematic fashion with little regard for the consequences of their activities. When professors and students today study and write about universities, they are therefore engaged in more than group therapy in the midst of troubled times for what is now ambiguously called "higher education." They are analyzing an essential element in the culture that has come to dominate the entire globe.

The studies in this volume, which was preceded by a conference on the theme in 1979, treat the history of universities from the late Middle Ages through the Reformation; that is, following their secure founding and through the challenges of humanism and confessionalism, but before the knowledge explosion that is associated with the advent of modern science and the Enlightenment. The collective approach of these essays must be characterized as thoroughly eclectic. The first two are rather general in character. Together Professors Oberman and Spitz challenge the notion that

1

the fifteenth and sixteenth centuries were especially difficult times for universities, but they do so from very different perspectives. Professor Grant then describes the important place that scientific education had in the medieval curriculum, and Professor Courtenay provides a wide-ranging reinterpretation of the development of "nominalism" as a more or less agreed upon intellectual stance during the fourteenth century. There follow four essays that may be viewed under the heading "university and society." Professor Fletcher challenges the longstanding view that migrations were an important force in creating new universities; Professor Knoll uncovers the roles that the University of Cracow played between Polish royal policy and the turbulent forces that were unleashed in the Western Schism. Professor Lytle treats the career patterns of English university men; Professor Overfield demonstrates that there may well have been something to the complaints of German humanists during the first decades of the sixteenth century that the secular clergy was poorly educated. Professor Screech then returns to the world of high culture by suggesting that solitary figures such as Erasmus and Rabelais could have important effects upon universities even while steadfastly maintaining their independence from them. Finally, and appropriately, Professors Fletcher and Deahl provide a valuable aid to future work with their bibliography and analysis of research during the past decade.

From the very outset, the eclectic approach that marks this volume has been intentional for the simple reason that the subject and the status of research demand it. The very term *universitas* suggests as much. At base it conveys the sense of the "aggregate" or the "whole" or the "entirety" of something. It carries with it therefore the notion of an integral unit that is complete unto itself. This fundamental meaning was summed up during the Middle Ages in terming a genuine university a *studium generale*. The idea itself is startling, for within it lies the assertion that here—at Paris, or Cambridge, Prague, Bologna, or even "little Wittenberg," as Dr. Martin Luther called it when he learned he was to teach there— one could study all subjects of importance and acquire knowledge that was universal and transferable. This idea was in fact asserted

2

boldly whenever universities conferred the *ius ubique docendi*, the right to teach anywhere; and this right was sanctioned, at least initially, by Pope and Emperor, the two figures with claims to universality in the medieval world.

It must be granted that then as now individual scholars attracted students and controversy to particular institutions by the brilliance (and sometimes the mere eccentricity) of their ideas or style. Nonetheless, the university was and remains something quite different from the trade school, the monastery, or the solitary scholar, all of whose contributions were limited to particular subjects, particular ideas, and frequently enough the work of particular individuals. The university as a whole, complete unto itself, was therefore vastly greater than any of its parts. When, for example, the theologians at Paris, Louvain, and Cologne condemned the teachings of Luther, they did so with the weight of their entire universities. Perhaps this very claim to universality of knowledge and the right to corporate judgment explains why artists, literati, and professors of special wisdom have always been uncomfortable in universities, and universities with them. Without doubt the same claim is also reflected in the fact that from their very inception universities and university people have possessed their own technical language, whether it be the dialectic of the Middle Ages or the academic jargon of the twentieth century.

Consequently, universities must be studied from within, so to speak. They must also, however, be studied from without, from the point of view of the rest of society of which they are a part. To return to the term *universitas*: the notion of an integral unit, complete unto itself, certainly assumes relationship with other units. In just this sense, our frontispiece pictures the place of learning as a tower in the context of other units of the *civitas humana* and not in a certain splendid isolation more suitable to hermits or solitary sages. Indeed, the very idea of this "universal company of masters and scholars" is inconceivable outside the corporate society of twelfth-century Europe that spawned it.[1] Like knights, townsmen, clerics, and kings, the learned were an estate within all society. During the conciliar movement university men claimed even the position of a special *ordo* within the church alongside priests, monks, bishops, and cardinals.[2] The titles themselves of university people were borrowed from their corporate world. The "master of arts" is an analogue to the master of a craft, and at base the highest degree, the doctorate, is a license to teach whose acquisition carried with it an oath to promote the truth and to confute error.

University people were therefore always firmly within society, whatever their occasional pretensions even today to being above it. However much universities claimed separateness, they were forced to make accommodations with everyone else. Like guildsmen they could serve at least as a court of first instance in governing their own members, and indeed it was just this claim that led to the first charters for the University of Paris. But they had also to be subject to higher or nearby authorities, whether Pope, Emperor, Duke, or townsmen who then as now paid the bills and wished some profit from the enterprise. As much may be seen in the condemnation of "Ockhamism" at Paris by Bishop and Pope in the mid-fourteenth century and in the foundation of new universities by princes and townsmen in the Empire during the fifteenth and sixteenth centuries. Indeed, the exact relationship between universities and the larger society remains an unresolved and sometimes vexing problem today, even in authoritarian states.

Our intention to approach the history of universities both from within and from without has, therefore, quite naturally yielded the eclectic character of this volume and of the conference that preceded it. In addition, the merest glance at the concluding essay and its accompanying bibliography reveals that in its eclecticism this volume reflects the general character of research in the contemporary renaissance of university studies. The recent volume edited by Ijsewijn and Pacquet also shares this free-wheeling approach in which the broadest and most detailed works coexist, side-by-side in the same volume, rather like the profusion of tropical fish in a particularly splendid aquarium. Variety is clearly the fashion of the day and for good reason: when the old broad syntheses have begun to break down, the new structure must be built from the ground up with no limitations regarding subjects or methods.

Nonetheless, such eclecticism has its disadvantages if left utterly to itself. In the first place, research can begin to take on something of the character of navel gazing, which yields little more than the observation that the possessors and creators of high culture and their institutional setting have always led a troubled existence in Western civilization. Secondly, by concentrating research on individual problems with no overarching interpretive framework, scholars can easily slip into committing the "wholistic" fallacy, according to which if only each part is carefully identified, the whole will surely have been discovered as well. Finally, even though the fact that universities were connected to society is clearly demonstrated, the detailed researches that have led to this conclusion have also tended to abstract universities away from the broader historical developments that they influenced and that influenced them. To summarize, the burgeoning of university studies, with its attendant and recently established international association, has tended, willy-nilly, to make of the history of universities a separate field of study and therefore to raise the real danger of tunnel vision. Of such a development, the same warning must be put that John of Salisbury, a preuniversity scholar, leveled at dialectic: "that if left by itself, it lies bloodless and barren and does not yield the fruit of philosophy."

Consequently, even at this early point in modern research, some general conclusions should be put forward, however tentatively. First, it is obvious that universities and society have always worked somewhat at cross purposes. The motives of Professor Lytle's careerist students and those of their professors were scarcely the same, no matter how much university people contributed to church, government, and society by way of educated leadership. In just this regard, the dismal fate of the Conciliar Movement strongly suggests that there was a difference between a professor's serving society on its terms and his seeking to remold it according to his own image, as Professor Knoll's presentation of the humiliation of Cracow's professors well illustrates. Moreover, the troubles of the arts professors at Paris, and of Aquinas himself before them, suggest that even remaining purely a teacher and intellectual and not dabbling in the affairs of the world could be offensive to powerful people. Seeking some vision of the truth without regard to the consequences of the search comports ill with politics, religion, and business, and it always has.

Yet, surely this truth is so general that in one form or another it could apply to almost any of society's constituent groups, some of which have simply disappeared or at least had their station vastly reduced over time. By contrast, universities have shown a truly remarkable durability. Indeed, the essays that follow speak univocally, albeit not always directly, to just this point. Whatever the criticisms, whatever humiliations professors suffered at the hands of the post-Schism Papacy, however dependent they were upon the good will of princes, universities endured as the principal repositories of high culture.

This point is in fact made so clearly that it would be easy to draw from it the further inference that somehow, no matter the noise level, universities were not truly under serious attack from the mid-fourteenth through the mid-sixteenth centuries. Nothing could be further from the truth. The most startling fact about the criticism of universities is that it came from within the larger world of learning itself. The list of critics in this period is jammed not so much with ever-parsimonious patrons and grasping politicians, as would be so later, but with names drawn from the very front ranks of European thinkers. Petrarch, Valla, Erasmus, Rabelais—these were jewels in the crown of intellect, and every one of them stridently criticized university men, and in particular those in the higher faculties. Even Philip Melanchthon, who was a theologian, nonetheless resisted Luther's entreaties, refused to take the doctorate in theology, and steadfastly remained on the arts faculty at Wittenberg.[3] Additionally, when Pius II condemned conciliar thought in the bull *Execrabilis*, he condemned a specifically university movement and university way of thinking. Coincidentally, this Pope was Aeneas Silvius Piccolomini, one of the better known among those very humanist critics of universities.

To be sure, the wit and irony with which these humanists criticized university men, with their dialectic and dependence upon

6

Aristotle, could be so biting as to suggest mere envy and jealousy.[4] In about 1335, Petrarch wrote a friend,

> You tell me of an old dialectician who has been violently annoyed by my letter, as though I had condemned his profession. He is raging in public, you say, and threatens to assail our field in a letter of his, and you have been waiting for this letter in vain for months. Do not expect it any longer. Believe me, it will never come. That much good sense is left of him. He is evidently ashamed of his stylistic capacities, or else his silence is a confession of his ignorance. . . . So tell you old man that I do not condemn the liberal arts, but childish old people. For as there is nothing more disgraceful than "an old man in a first-grade class," as Seneca says, so there is nothing so ugly as an old man who is a dialectic debater.[5]

Petrarch gave his learned opponents, real or imagined, the back of his hand. Valla preferred a mild form of slander:

> I would prefer . . . that other Christians and, indeed, those who are called theologians would not depend so much on philosophy or devote so much energy to it, making it almost an equal and sister (not to say patron) of theology. For it seems to me that they have a poor opinion of our religion if they think it needs the protection of philosophy. The followers of the Apostles, truly columns in the temple of God . . . used this protection least of all. In fact, if we look carefully, the heresies of those times, which we understand were many and not insignificant, derived almost entirely from philosophic sources, so that philosophy not only profited our most sacred religion little but even violently injured it. But they of whom I speak consider philosophy a tool for weeding out heresies, when actually it is a seedbed of heresy.[6]

Among them, Petrarch, Valla, and the humanists in general reduced dialectic, the chief tool of university learning, to the plaything of both fools and knaves. Changes in both method and sources were in order.[7]

Yet the humanist critique of universities did not stop there. They also declared that a university education, and one from the higher faculties in particular, was so useless and harmful that it should be replaced by different objectives as well as different methods and sources. On one occasion, Petrarch characterized the teaching of biology at universities and added, after doubting the truth of it all,

"And even if [the facts] were true, they would not contribute anything to the blessed life. What is the use—I beseech you—of knowing the nature of quadrupeds, fowls, fishes, and serpents and not knowing or even neglecting man's nature, the purpose for which we were born, and whence and whereto we travel?"[8] Similarly his attack on the "Old Dialectician" turned on the alleged failure of his university antagonist to proceed from dialectic to higher studies. In this he was much like an earlier critic of universities, John of Salisbury. Valla was of the same mind. Quoting Paul's remark about his "thorn in the flesh" at 2 Corinthians 12:7, he commented, regarding the question of predestination, "Let us not wish to know the height, but let us fear lest we become like the philosophers who, calling themselves wise, are made foolish; who, lest they should appear ignorant of anything, disputed about everything . . . Among the chief of these was Aristotle, in whom the best and greatest God revealed and at length damned the arrogance and boldness of not only this same Aristotle but of the other philosophers as well. . . . Let us then shun knowledge of high things."[9] For the humanists the purpose of learning was most decidedly *not* to develop new or more precisely formulated propositional knowledge of a universal character, but to inculcate true wisdom and right living.

This fundamental critique had its consequences for universities. As recounted below by Professor Screech, the career of Noel Beda, syndic of the theological faculty of the University of Paris, and satirized by both Erasmus and Rabelais, was certainly not one to be envied. Whether justly or not, the humanists also damaged universities as such. Through the Reuchlin Affair and countless other university-centered disputes, they called the moral authority of university faculties deeply into question by appealing outside the university to the larger community of scholars. When the Indulgence Controversy broke out, Luther extended this practice to include the literate public in general, and, by using the vernacular, included those who could not read Latin. Can there be any wonder then that the condemnations of Luther by Paris, Cologne, and Louvain should go unheeded in many quarters, while Elector Frederick the Wise sought the counsel of a nonuniversity figure such

8

as Erasmus?[10] The fifteenth and sixteenth centuries were genuinely troubled times for universities.

Yet, granted that universities endured, one question naturally poses itself: "What abiding impact did the humanists have upon the universities of Old Europe whose work they so criticized?" Intriguingly, they did not condemn universities as such. To be sure, for the most part they found their educational homes in institutions outside the university, such as the Royal Lecturers at Paris or the *Colleqium Trilinque* at Louvain, much as natural scientists were to do somewhat later. What they had was a reform program, the signs of which abound in such things as Melanchthon's and Luther's reform of Wittenberg, Ulrich Zasius's legal studies at Freiburg, and the gradual incursion of Agricola's *De inventione dialectica* into the curriculum of German universities.[11] Additionally, the positive content of their program is, thanks to recent scholarship, fairly accessible. In the realm of theology, it has already been pointed out that they criticized their university colleagues not so much for teaching false doctrine as for teaching too many doctrines. Negatively, this criticism amounted to a mildly skeptical tendency that inclined the humanists to doubt either the knowability or usefulness of general propositions in whatever field.[12] Positively, it inclined them to emphasize the specific, the concrete, and personal behavior in the here-and-now. To remain in the realm of theology, Erasmus was more concerned with enlightened piety than true doctrine; in law a figure such as Zasius championed the principle of ἐπίεικεια or equity in applying the law according to its spirit rather than its letter. In both cases universal knowledge of a propositional nature was the loser.[13] The humanists had, therefore, a concrete educational program that had applications not only at the primary or secondary levels but also in the professional faculties. Consequently, it ought to be possible to evaluate the impact of humanist educational ideals upon the traditional university in an equally concrete way.

It would, however, be far beyond the scope of this essay to trace changes in the form and content of university curricula in general even during the sixteenth century alone. Nonetheless, a case study may provide a potentially telling shortcut to determining some of

9

the likely outside limits to the impact of humanism upon the traditional university. Fortunately, a useful case is at hand in the form of what was initially the Academy and finally the University of Strasbourg.[14]

Several factors make Strasbourg a particularly revealing case study for present purposes. In the first place, the Academy was a new foundation; therefore its creators were free to establish exactly the sort of educational program they preferred without deference to long-standing traditions or procedures. Although it was founded by Protestant reformers, these men also had strong humanistic backgrounds and therefore sought to provide students with both a humanistic education and the fundamentals of Protestant doctrine.[15] As proof of their intentions, these men – Wolfgang Capito, Martin Bucer, and Caspar Hedio notably – prevailed upon Johannes Sturm to come to Strasbourg as rector of their Academy. Thirdly, and most tellingly for present purposes, the Academy had a quasi-theological faculty from the very beginning to train pastors and teachers for the new church. Here the purpose was to teach true doctrine in some depth. Finally, by the mid-1560s both the ministerial candidates, who followed lectures in the Academy as well as in theology, and the professors of theology, who were also pastors, were under the theoretical jurisdiction of both the Academy and the Company of Pastors. Consequently, from the very outset the Academy pursued the objectives of both the new humanistic educational program and of the most traditional part of the traditional university, namely the theological faculty. The question is, how did these two objectives, together with their institutional expressions, coexist?

The answer is, not very well. Initially, in the persons of Peter Martyr Vermigli and Giralomo Zanchi, the theological faculty in this Lutheran town harbored professors with distinct Reformed learnings.[16] In time they, and Zanchi in particular, quite naturally drew fire from the Company of Pastors, which by 1552 was lead by Johannes Marbach, who was also a theology professor and whose doctoral disputation Luther himself had chaired. As the result of a sharp dispute that lasted from 1561 to 1563, Martyr and Zanchi left

Strasbourg so that the theological faculty, like the Company of Pastors, became securely Lutheran both in its professors and in its stated intention to teach according to the unaltered Augsburg Confession.[17]

Six years of harmony followed this housecleaning of the theological faculty. During this period, Sturm, as rector of the Academy, and Marbach, as the city's chief theologian and pastor, worked together to secure an Imperial license that would recognize the Academy's right to offer the Master of Arts degree. Emperor Maximilian II did grant just such a privilege in 1566, and there followed a period of growth during which the Academy in fact functioned as a university to the point that it was finally recognized as such by Ferdinand II in 1621.[18]

This process of institutional development had many ramifications, but for present purposes it was marked by one central fact — the placing of distinct limitations upon the extent to which the humanistic educational program of Sturm and the arts faculty would be allowed to penetrate the training of professional theologians and pastors. Sturm himself initiated the controversies that led to this decision, and to his own eventual dismissal, on 19 December 1569, when he requested a vote of confidence from the *Scholarchen*, or lay commissioners for the school. Here he charged Marbach and the theologians with undermining his entire program. From the very outset, therefore, the real issue was who was to control theological education and what were to be its purposes and nature.

This conclusion is most evident in reform proposals Sturm put forth during the following three years. In the first place, he wished the faculty of the entire Academy to be consulted on appointments to any part of it, a procedure that, by virtue of numbers, would give the arts faculty control over the faculty of theology. He sought also the authority to censor what could and could not be proper subjects for theological disputations with an eye to avoiding doctrinal discussions. But his chief target was the two preachers' colleges that housed the ministrial candidates and theology students. Indeed, the heart of his reform proposal was that "the two colleges

. . . be subject to the Academic Assembly. For it is from these two colleges that barbarism insinuates itself into our school."[19]

Clearly Sturm had a very different vision of the school and of theological education from what prevailed generally in the university world. In fact, the plan of study with which he came forth in June 1572 was so weighted toward the typical humanistic curriculum – and away from dogmatic theology – that it included Luther's catechism only in the eighth and ninth classes. In just this regard, his reasoning as to why the arts professors should be admitted to the deliberations of the theologians and pastors is most revealing: he declared that "we other professors" are "excluded from their Theologians' Assembly" because "we are considered by them to be such unlearned people, who know nothing about the business, and so inept and uncomprehending that we do not understand such matters and cannot judge and consider them."[20]

Here Sturm was perfectly correct. In late 1574 or early 1575 Marbach and the other pastors and theologians presented a lengthy document to the commission charged with judging the affair in which they argued that the theologians should not be made subject to the school as a whole. To them it was "unheard of" for theologians not to meet as a faculty to manage their own affairs, as did the faculties of law, medicine, and the arts. Nowhere, Marbach added, are "theological issues and matters of faith given over for grammarians and philosophers to judge and consider."[21]

Marbach nonetheless lost this round in spite of his forthright defense of the perogatives of the traditional theological faculty within the traditional university. In brief, he was eventually replaced both as Dean of the Academy and as inspector of the two preachers' colleges with the latter task being assumed by a committee of the Academic Assembly. Finally, in 1575, the Senate and XXI, Strasbourg's highest governing council, forced a peace treaty upon Marbach and Sturm according to which they were to leave one another alone in the exercise of their offices and "entirely and in every respect" forgive and forget. Even copies of all the writings the affair spawned were to be handed over to the government.[22] In the process theological training was defined as a humanistic educational activity, one whose chief purpose was most decidedly not to teach true doctrine.

This new situation is perhaps best revealed in the beginnings of yet another controversy, and one that decisively turned the tables on Sturm. The struggle originated over the Lutheran Formula of Concord and in particular the *Condemnamus* portion of the document, according to which subscribers condemned all opinions contrary to orthodox Lutheranism.[23] In March 1578 Johann Pappus, a member of the theological faculty who was to become Marbach's successor as president of the Company of Pastors, published and defended certain theses on whether in principle the church could condemn false teachings *without* contravening the law of love. Upon hearing of it, Sturm charged Pappus with failing to secure the required approval from the Dean of the Academy two weeks before publishing and defending his theses. He added that they would never have been approved, had normal procedures been followed, because they were contentious and badly-timed.[24]

Pappus of course denied Sturm's allegations and, as was common to the sixteenth century, the controversy quickly degenerated into a roaring and ugly argument over the Formula itself and over whether Sturm and the arts faculty were "Calvinist Sacramentarians" in a Lutheran city. Yet, Sturm's primary concern, and that of the pastors, remained the judging of doctrines as such and therefore pressed directly upon the conflict between humanistic educational ideals and the perogatives of the traditional theological faculty. "What will transpire?" Sturm asked in 1580. "Will not the same be forthcoming as so unfortunately occurred at Heidelberg, Jena, Leipzig, and Wittenberg," where opposing professors were driven from their posts after their princes subscribed to the Formula? Clearly, Sturm deplored making doctrinal judgments at all among non-Catholics, and he certainly opposed granting this authority to a class of professional theologians. The other side also held to its position. Pappus himself was relatively silent, but he received support from the University of Tübingen, which had granted him his own doctorate in theology. Against Sturm, Lucas Osiander declared that "to explicate religious controversies reliably and to interpret sacred letters does not belong to all people." Sturm might freely study the orations of Cicero and Demosthenes but in seeking also to judge religious doctrines he was, to Osiander's mind, exceeding his grasp with his reach. This was the work of professionals.[25]

The most intriguing aspect of this entire affair, and one that needs explanation, is that on this occasion the Senate and XXI came to agree with Pappus and the theologians. To be sure, there was no rewriting of the Academy's constitution and no overt repudiation of Sturm's creation, as there was of Sturm himself. But in discussions regarding a successor to Marbach, who died on 18 March 1581, all the responsibilities that had once been Marbach's were placed in Pappus's hands. In the decisive session late that year, the Senate and XXI finally named Pappus president of the company of Pastors and specifically charged him with supervising both the education and the personal lives of the young theologians. In coming full circle, and in fine historical irony, the commission that recommended Pappus's appointment noted that it was precisely his possession of the doctorate in theology that qualified him for the job and overrode his relative youth and inexperience.[26] Theological education in Strasbourg was thereby placed firmly in the hands of the church and the theological faculty, and there it remained. Symbolically at least, the doctorate, i.e., the right to teach true doctrine, carried the day over the humanists' educational program. As a result, however much the *studia humanitatis* were now prerequisite to theology, the dream of Petrarch and Valla, Erasmus and Rabelais did not become a reality, even in the one university designed specifically to embody it.[27]

At least one element is nonetheless still missing. After all, the story has been told largely from within the fledgling University of Strasbourg in spite of abundant evidence that forces from without also played a role. The Senate and XXI was in fact the decisive voice in all these controversies. More importantly, they decided the issues before them without respect to their educational or intellectual merits. In the case of the Sturm/Marbach dispute, Sturm's educational program was not even discussed. Rather, he was simply ordered to bring forth proposals for reform.[28] In the instance of Sturm vs. Pappus, the government decided to dismiss Sturm not because he was wrong educationally – again this issue was not discussed – but because he had criticized the Elector Palatine in print and had thereby become a political liability.[29] Throughout, therefore, it is apparent that the government was not making educational decisions as such. Rather, the University's patrons expected it to govern itself except in the most extreme instances. Both from within and from without the universities of Old Europe were indeed remarkably durable institutions. Moreover, their sponsors wished them to be so.

The essays that follow, although agreeing on this point, also offer some intriguing hints as to why universities endured through such a time of turmoil, criticism, and change. In the first place, Professors Spitz and Oberman point out that the German universities and their professors did adapt themselves to the demands and fashions of a changing world. As Oberman argues and Strasbourg also illustrates, the doctorate continued to be held in extraordinarily high regard, but space was also made for the *studia humanitatis*, albeit not necessarily in the higher faculties. Spitz demonstrates that, by adopting these same *studia humanitatis*, the reformers made of universities powerful agents of the new confessionalism, while developing the arts faculty into not merely a preuniversity faculty but eventually one that could claim equal standing with the professional faculties of law, medicine, and theology. Universities are thus pictured in both studies as not merely creators of but also responders to the demands of the wider culture about them. In just this regard, one may pose a counterfactual, and admittedly ahistorical, question to Professor Screech: "What is the likelihood that the University of Paris would have endured as a principal center of learning had it not eventually responded to the position of figures like Erasmus and Rabelais on the value of Hebrew studies?" It is not only, therefore, that Erasmus and Rabelais were cultural heroes and agents of change but also that the institution did in fact respond, however slowly and reluctant. In this very resilience lies a factor that led to durability.

One other factor that may account in part for the durability of universities appears at first glance to contradict the point just made about their adaptability. In brief, universities retained throughout their own integrity and insisted upon their own methods of pursuing their own objectives. Professor Courtenay, in tracing the arrival of English thought in continental universities, certainly demonstrates that changes in the content of teaching and curricula were wrought by university people themselves. Such fundamental cultural changes occurred as the result of solitary scholars' deciding to pursue their studies in a manner that seemed most convincing to them. The result was a depth of human conviction that changed, but did so slowly and thoughtfully. To be sure, this situation could create anomalies, as Professor Grant's treatment of science in the medieval universities well illustrates. The deeply entrenched, carefully refined, and massive scientific content of the curriculum not only drove real science, the science of Galileo, out of the university but also posed and discussed all the questions upon which real science is based. Nonetheless, the unwillingness of professors to whore after the latest intellectual fashion proved on balance a source of strength to the universities of Old Europe. In just this regard, it is intriguing that Cracow's professors, hopelessly out of step with royal policy on the conciliar issue by 1430, nonetheless insisted upon consulting their colleagues at other universities before bowing to reality. This Professor Knoll reads as a sign of independence, and rightfully so. It may also be taken as a sign of the *integritas* of the *universitas*.

Finally, the universities' very connection with society may also be taken as a source of their durability. As Professor Fletcher demonstrates, the development in a particular locale of what are now called "support services," that is, libraries, housing, lecture halls and the like, made it extremely unlikely that a university could simply move, bag and baggage, from one place to another. It also gave those closest to this ragtag batch of masters and students a clear interest in retaining them and therefore put undoubted limits upon the extent to which tense town-gown relations would be allowed to do genuine damage to the university. In fact, as Professors Lytle and Overfield demonstrate, society itself, for whatever reasons, did value those with a university education. Those who did not have such training, and according to Overfield many secular clergy in Germany on the eve of the Reformation did not, came into opprobrium, and those who did, according to Lytle, became by that fact figures of authority in their communities. In sum, the universities of Old Europe were socially useful institutions. Herein lies another part of the explanation for their durability.

Given the present state of research it is unfortunately not possible to go much beyond these very general and tentative conclusions. It is not even possible to assay how much universities may have changed internally while retaining their external structure and status during these years. For example, in all the work that has been done on universities and university people during the last decade, precious little has gone to elucidate even what students may have been taught during their years of study. (Dare one ask what they may have learned?) As a consequence, finally, it is impossible to determine what positive or negative role universities may have played during these centuries upon the dominant themes in the development of Western civilization, and surely this is the most important question of all. As is common, therefore, when the grand syntheses begin to break down, exciting possibilities for new work appear. This volume is dedicated to that end.

1. Marshall Clagett, Gaines Post, and Robert Reynolds, eds., *Twelfth-Century Europe and the Foundations of Modern Society* (Madison, Wis., 1966), esp. pp. 3–55 for the articles by Klibansky, Holmes, and Katzenellenbogen.

2. Brian Tierney, *The Foundations of the Conciliar Movement. The Contributions of the Medieval Canonists from Gratian to the Great Schism* (Cambridge, 1955); Alan Bernstein, *Pierre d'Ailly and the Blanchard Affair. University and Chancellor of Paris at the Beginning of the Great Schism*, vol. 24, Studies in Medieval and Renaissance Thought (Leiden, 1978).

3. Wilhelm Maurer, *Der Junge Melanchthon Zwischen Humanismus und Reformation*, vol. 2, *Der Theolog* (Göttingen, 1967).

4. The position to which P. O. Kristeller, *Renaissance Thought. The Classic, Scholastic, and Humanist Strains* (New York, 1961), pp. 3–23 certainly tends.

5. Ernst Cassirer, P. O. Kristeller, and John Herman Randall, Jr., eds., *The Renaissance Philosophy of Man* (Chicago, 1948), pp. 134–39.

6. Ibid.

7. Lewis W. Spitz, *The Religious Renaissance of the German Humanists* (Cambridge, Mass., 1963), pp. 4–5.

8. Cassirer, *Renaissance Philosophy*, pp. 58–59.

9. Ibid., p. 181.

10. Charles G. Nauert, Jr., "The Clash of Humanists and Scholastics: An Approach to Pre-Reformation Controversies," *Sixteenth-Century Journal* 4 (1973):1–18.

11. Maria Grossmann, *Humanism in Wittenberg, 1485–1517* (Nieuwkoop, 1975); Guido Kisch, *Erasmus und die Jurisprudenz seiner Zeit* (Basel, 1960), esp. pp. 51 ff.; Terrance Heath, "Logical Grammar, Grammatical Logic, and Humanism in Three German Universities," *Studies in the Renaissance* (New York, 1971), 18:9–64.

12. William J. Bouwsma, *Venice and the Defense of Republican Liberty* (Berkeley, Calif., 1968), pp. 1–52.

13. James D. Tracy, *Erasmus, The Growth of a Mind* (Geneve, 1972), pp. 131–32; Kitsch, *Erasmus*, pp. 51 ff. All of this is not to maintain that the humanists refused to accept the actual teachings of their nominalist adversaries. Erasmus in fact did on occasion. See his paraphrase of Romans 1:17, *Erasmi Opera*, 7, 781B, as compared to Gabriel Biel's treatment of the same passage, as discussed by Heiko A. Oberman, *The Harvest of Medieval Theology: Gabriel Biel and Late Medieval Nominalism* (Grand Rapids, Mich., 1967), esp. pp. 71–74.

14. The most recent study is Anton Schindling, *Humanistische Hochschule und Freie Reichstadt. Gymnasium und Akademie in Strassburg, 1538–1621* (Wiesbaden, 1977).

15. Ibid., esp. pp. 33, 106–8, does not do justice to the dogmatic objectives of the school, as such.

16. John Patrick Donnelly, *Calvinism and Scholasticism in Vermigli's Doctrine of Man and Grace* (Leiden, 1976); Otto Gründler, *Die Gotteslehre Giralomi Zanchi und ihre Bedeutung für seine Lehre von der Prädestination* (Neukirchen, 1965).

17. On the dispute, see James M. Kittelson, "Marbach vs. Zanchi: The Resolution of Controversy in Late Reformation Strasbourg," *Sixteenth Century Journal* 8 (1977):31–44.

18. In general and for what follows, see Schindling, *Humanistische Hochschule*, esp. pp. 44 ff. and 113 ff.

19. Archives municipales de Strasbourg. Archivum S. Thomae 327, fol. 124^v–125. Hereafter cited as AST; Marcel Fournier and Charles Engel, eds., *Les statuts et privileges des universités francaises depuis leur fondation jusqu'en 1789. 4/1, Gymnase, Académie, Université de Strasbourg* (Paris, 1894 = Aalen, 1970), pp. 181–82. Hereafter cited as F & E.

20. F & E, pp. 174–79, 165.

21. F & E, p. 188. AST 79, fol. 374–76, 377, 380^v, 383.

22. Schindling, *Humanistische Hochschule*, pp. 131–36. F & E, pp. 198 ff.

23. See Hans-Werner Genischen, *We Condemn. How Luther and 16th-century Lutheranism Condemned False Doctrine*, trans. Herbert J. A. Bouman (St. Louis, 1967).

24. F & E, p. 181 for the rule and pp. 205 ff. for exchanges about it.

25. F & E, p. 218. *Lvcae Osiandri Theologiae Doctoris Antisturmius vnus* (Tubingae, 1579), pp. 31–32.

26. Protocolles des Sénat et XXI, 1581, fol. 111^v–546.

27. For similar tensions in and among Calvinist academies, see Brian G. Armstrong, *Calvinism and the Amyraut Heresy. Protestant Scholasticism and Humanism in Seventeenth-Century France* (Madison, Wis., 1969), esp. pp. 120–57.

28. F & E, pp. 172–77 for discussions in the Senate and XXI and an early reform proposal.

29. F & E, pp. 219–20 for a complaint from the Elector and Protocolles des Sénat et XXI, 1581, fol. 144–144^v for an early warning to Sturm. The problem was discussed at length during the sessions of April 5, 17, 21, and 29, 1581.

UNIVERSITY AND SOCIETY
ON THE THRESHOLD OF MODERN TIMES:
THE GERMAN CONNECTION

Heiko A. Oberman

he second clause in the title of this chapter is intended to suggest that, just as in the criminal world heroin used to reach its American consumer market via Marseilles, so universities in early modern Germany served as the clearinghouse for medieval academic and cultural goods into modern times. The first part of this study deals with the duality between the words in the title, "University and Society"; the second with the events and developments surrounding the double-edged term, "Modern Times"; the third part with "the German Connection," where it will be argued that this phrase can help to explain both the new cultural climate in the German Empire and the new social role of the German universities. Throughout it will become apparent that, far from being purveyors of irrelevancies and errors from the past, German universities drew upon their own strengths and traditions to perform the vital work of a clearinghouse.

UNIVERSITY AND SOCIETY

Ever since there have been historians, history and historiography have gone separate ways. Their paths were nearest when scholars stayed in specialized fields with immediate sources; they drastically diverged when scholars tried to extract progress either from time or from man and society, as in the traditions of Augustine, Joachim of Flora, and Hegel. A study of the history of universities portrays this bifurcation in striking detail.

19

Studies of single universities have appeared in impressive number during that productive century between 1860 and 1960. From Bologna to Oxford, from Cracow to Cologne, from Louvain to Leiden, the matriculation records have been published, the constitutions and the attendance rates carefully registered. As long as we lived in a society in which the university was placed at the top of the social ladder and in which, accordingly, the professor in any given field was esteemed as the true master of arts—indeed, as the wise and leisured master of the art of living—there was no specific need to raise the questions of the relationship between the university and the "outside world." To the extent that some of us still live in that kind of society, the university reflects, incorporates, and symbolizes society, just as the universal (*ante rem* or *in re!*) of the *via antiqua* fused metaphysics and epistemology and simultaneously embodied the highest level of being and the highest goal of knowledge.

The frontispiece of this volume—taken from a pre-Reformation bestseller, Gregor Reisch's *Margarita Philosophica*—powerfully illustrates this vision in the tradition of the thirteenth-century university and of the later *via antiqua*. The mythological female wizard with the alphabet in hand offers access to the world within the cloister walls where the *trivium* under the guidance of Aristotle, Cicero, and Boethius underlies the *quadrivium*, of which only arithmetic is not shown. On this foundation natural and moral philosophy are studied, and the whole edifice is topped off by Peter Lombard (d. 1160), the Master of the Sentences, with whom, as it had been put so well, scholasticism ceased its "revolt against authority."[1]

For our later reference to the innovation of the *via moderna* over against the *via antiqua*, we should take special note of the identity of theology and metaphysics as the apex of knowledge, here still presupposed in the phrase, *theologia seu metaphysica*. At this point, however, we should observe the cloister walls and the inscription across the access door: *congruitas*. The university claims to be a microcosm of the real world outside, a world that it represents, orders, and encompasses. Surely here is a view of academia that was no longer uncontested already in the fourteenth century and in modern times is more tenaciously held on the Continent than across the Channel and on the other side of the Atlantic.

It is not by chance that university research in the English-speaking tradition coined the term "town and gown" and began to discuss the dimension of social strife and political tension in "the world outside" that was evoked by these new institutions called "universities." Men like Hastings Rashdall and his revisors Sir Maurice ɪowicke and A. B. Emden were much closer to society than their German colleagues.[2] In their world a professor never achieved the Continental heights of an infallible prophet; he was never more than a senior tutor or a don. But even there, in the struggle between "town and gown," the town is all too often of interest only as it reflects the envy evoked by the stupendous dimensions of papal and imperial privileges, or of the exemptions conferred upon the *studium generale*. Thanks to Pearl Kibre we can trace the history of the *authentica habita* or *privilegia scholastica* since the reign of Frederick I (1152-90) and note the decline in the privileges of the university masters, whom she rightly views as "products of the social needs of their time."[3] And thanks to Astrik Gabriel we can look carefully at daily life in the University of Paris.[4] From the numerous contributions of this one conscientious scholar on that great alma mater of the ample German offspring, one could start to write a history of the interaction between Paris and a new class of European nobility, noble no longer by birth but now by "Brief" and soon by books.

When we reach the threshold of modern times, however—somewhere in the period between 1500 and 1700—historians begin to ignore the university to a striking extent. They prefer to focus instead on the countryside, describing the preliminaries to the so-called "German Peasant War" of 1524-25, or on the town, by high-lighting the function of the cities for the Italian Renaissance and the German Reformation. Three very different explanations can be given that will help account for this mysterious tendency to bypass the university with a polite salute at best.

First, the history of universities is regarded as the domain of medievalists, rather than of scholars of early modern Europe. The latter field, in its search for new objects of research that promise access to "reality" through society (thus to overcome the division between history and historiography), has overlooked the universities almost entirely. Libraries, monasteries, the Curia, the Imperial and lesser courts, and currently the town (preferably the life of Imperial Cities as recorded in tax records and property lists) seem to offer far more touch with "reality."

The second reason is a curious one, because it is a distortion due to well-established knowledge. The one disadvantage of the strength of the very important field of Renaissance studies is that, insofar as this field reached into sixteenth-century Germany, it tends to reduce the whole story to one fifteen-year period between the Reuchlin affair and the dramatic confrontation between Erasmus and Luther. Scholars of the Renaissance intend more or less explicitly and more or less consciously to show how the progressive forces of that era had to assail the conservative ambiance of the stubbornly medieval universities. The *Letters of Obscure Men* against the *Magistri Nostri* of Cologne seem to require as little comment as the campaign for liberty of that truly European Dutchman, Erasmus, who, himself unshackled by university statutes, moved freely from Paris to London and from Louvain to Basel and Freiburg and stood up against a typical medieval man – a Wittenberg University professor who liked to invoke the authority of his doctor's degree. The contribution of Lewis Spitz to the *Festschrift* dedicated to Paul Oskar Kristeller has already called this view into question by its sheer weight of source references.[5] But, as is common knowledge, the path from *Festschrift* to textbook and thence to the classroom is paved by many good intentions and even more forbidding obstacles.

Though we will have to return to the question of the relation between the northern Renaissance and the German universities, it may help at the outset to place the *Letters of Obscure Men* in perspective by quoting a similar protest agains the proud "Masters." This one, however, is dated around the high days of the medieval university and belongs to the genre of the *Carmina Burana*:

> Iam fit magister artium
> qui nescit quotas partium
> de vero fundamento:
> habere nomen appetit,
> rem vero nec curat nec scit,
> examine contento.
> Iam fiunt baccalaurii
> pro munere denarii
> quamplures idiotae:
> in artibus, et [ab] aliis
> egregiis scientiis
> sunt bestiae promotae.[6]

To take such parodies as evidence is not unlike quoting a *bon mot* inserted in the *Sapientia Commentary* of Robert Holcot (d. 1349) as the disappointing result of an intelligence test of European royalty in the mid-fourteenth century:

> Rex illitteratus
> quasi
> asinus coronatus.[7]

Rather, the warning that "an illiterate King is a crowned ass" should alert us to the fact that not merely politics but also a lengthy medieval tradition of so-called *Fürstenspiegel* underlay the later initiatives of so many German rulers to found a university in their own principalities.

The third reason for taking the pulse of the times everywhere *but* in the university is perhaps the most formidable one. The best of university historians themselves have argued that on the threshold of modern times the universities deserted their social obligations and were driven into an internal crisis that lamed them at precisely the moment they were most needed. Or—to invert cause and effect—the universities are presented as having been written out of court and paralyzed by the challenge of northern humanism, the Reformation movement, and the resulting confessionalism.

There is indeed evidence for a thoroughgoing crisis in the fifteenth century that is too clear to be overlooked. Howard Kaminsky, for example, has made a convincing case for Prague that

23

cannot be refuted. After Tabor's defeat in 1434 that university "was only a ghost of itself."[8] And Jacques Verger dared an overall evaluation of all French universities, which he views as having been in the grips "of a crisis generated by diverse abuses."[9] He interprets – as he should – by relating the crisis of the universities to the political and social problems that engulfed and confused the French university world.

Yet, when we look at Germany this is exactly the period during which a fresh wave of new foundations rolled through the country from Ingolstadt to Tübingen and Wittenberg. This fact in itself cautions us against generalizing about *the* crisis and *the* decline of *the* university in Europe.

But were these new foundations themselves not merely external monuments to regional chauvinism that mark little more than an advanced state of ossification of the university ideal itself? Some of the best German scholars have indeed argued this way and thus brought Germany in line with what is held to be the situation in countries to the south and west of the Empire. Gerhard Ritter, for one, used Heidelberg to illustrate the general state of the later medieval German university and diagnosed a sickness unto death due to the crisis of the scholastic method itself. This method made the authority of Aristotle absolute at the expense of experience and adulated the authority of logic at the expense of graspable, concrete truth. In a posthumously published article of the highly gifted young scholar, Jürgen Bücking, Ritter's line of argument is extended to the sixteenth century. According to Bücking, humanism and the Reformation considerably accelerated the crisis of the late medieval German university. By highlighting the university's desolate situation – and without presenting an alternative – humanism and the Reformation created a spiritual vacuum "that, driven by necessity, called the civil powers into the picture."[10]

In other words, due to internal strife, external bias, and criticism from humanists and reformers, the German university lost out to the state and was transformed from an independent corporation into a state department for education. The verdict of the greatest living authority on the University of Erfurt, Erich Kleineidam, is unambiguous: "For the University of Erfurt, the Reformation meant a catastrophe."[11] Kleineidam would be the first to grant that the sharp decline of Erfurt, which had been a leading transregional university since its foundation in 1389, is to be seen in connection with the Thirty Years' War, the steep rise in popularity of Wittenberg, and the competition of Marburg, newly founded in 1527 without papal permission, but, significantly, granted imperial privileges in 1541. Nonetheless, Kleineidam's analysis of the withering of one university supports the sweeping summary of Alfred Müller-Armack, who declared without hesitation or qualification that the Lutheran princes were responsible for the German universities' losing their medieval breadth and universality in the process of being "transformed" into factories for civil servants.[12] The immediate relevance of such an interpretation is obvious. As a matter of fact, Müller-Armack's article was intended to warn the "Princes" of our day, the *Kultusminister*, the governmental departments of education, and the modern German parliament not to repeat the tragic mistakes of the sixteenth-century Reformation.

With this sample of contemporary 'relevance,' we have arrived at the end of part 1 and are back to the point of departure, namely the bifurcation of history and historiography. If we refuse to look beyond the sheltered realm of internal university research, we allow a vacuum to emerge, by virtue of the failure of the professional university historians to claim the full and complete theme, "university *and* society." Then the ideologists, like Müller-Armack, march in, fill out the space left and occupy the unprotected no-man's-land under the always impressive but fundamentally unclear flag of "crisis." It is true that history without vision—or, if we so prefer, without ideology—is reduced to a recording of past events, does not deserve a place in any historiography, and is not worthy to be remembered by later generations of scholars. Hence, any alternative view will be shaped by a vision. But we should feel called upon to display clearly the breathtaking treasures of knowledge gathered in a century of university research so that the story of the emergence of early modern times is told without bypassing or manipulating the complex yet crucial history of the universities.

To be true, this story has to deal with the dismal failings *and* with the recreative resilience that carried the institution of the *universitas literarum* through the period of intellectual rebirth, dreams, and confusions that we appropriately associate with the threshold of modern times.

ON THE THRESHOLD OF MODERN TIMES

This is not the place to discuss the problem of "epochs" and prolong the seemingly endless debate about the content of that most elusive word "modern." For all we know, in a hundred years a totally Chinese or Islam-dominated world may well hold that we have not yet reached that state even today. Rather, in this second part, I want to recall and call attention to a series of external and internal social and political contributions that the medieval university made and by which it advanced or at least accelerated the appearance of what is here humbly called the "threshold" of modern thought and institutions. None of these will be uncontested with respect to their long-term impact and perennial value, but all of them deserve to be recounted.

Vern L. Bullough has argued that "the establishment of the university was one of the most significant, if not the most significant, factor in western intellectual achievement."[13] I think he is correct, even though he chooses to prove his thesis by means of a quantification of academic achievements that is not unlike the achievement-test procedure in college entrance examinations. Indeed, one must be awed by his industry and gifts of calculation; he did come up with some interesting results, for example, his finding that for a career in eighteenth-century Scotland the length of schooling was far more significant than social class origins. But computer analysis provided him with probability statistics at once too exact and too exacting: "X^2 = 29.89 with 9 degrees of freedom, $p < 0.001$; Pearson's contingency coefficient = 0.3001"[14] Pondering the extent to which the computer is programmed to look for repetition, indeed for the emergence of the 'natural laws of history,' the contingency coefficient is more likely to be close to zero!

26

Well before Mr. Bullough moves smoothly back in time and space to fourteenth-century Florence, it becomes clear that no amount of quantification can help to objectify the initial decision as to the meaning given to the term "achievement." Although I do not claim my nonmathematical argument to be proof of the "achievements" of the universities, at least it is based on sundry samples taken from such widely varying value systems that their telling power may well reach beyond a single ideological school.

Assuming that the Conciliar Movement is to be regarded as a significant chapter in European history—most clearly in parliamentary history and in the history of the late medieval refashioning of the *corpus christianum*—it deserves to be pointed out that universities, and initially the University of Paris in particular, played a major role in the inception, growth, and diffusion of conciliarism.[15] This conciliarism ranged from the cautious use of earlier legal conciliar theory to the daring political conciliar ideals of Basel (1431-49), which were truly revolutionary in comparison with the early days of the Great Schism (1378-1415). The older work by L. Dax and H. Keussen, as complemented today by J. Gill, P. R. McKeon, and especially by Anthony Black has not only established the high proportion of *doctores* among those who promoted the conciliar case from the *via cessionis* to the *via concilii*, but also the extent to which the independence of the corporate *studium generale* was translated into the idea of a *concilium generale*, for which it became in turn the shining model.[16] Although the *doctores* already formed a numerically strong lobby at Pisa (1409), represented as they were by 105 colleagues, the decision of Constance (1414-18) to vote according to nations was patterned after the organization of the University of Paris. The decision of the Council of Basel to accept the "one man-one vote" rule necessarily heightened the impact of those licentiates in theology and canon law who had before served as *periti* and advisors but now constituted some 30 percent of the vote.

It is not, however, without significance for our further argument to correct Black's research on one crucial point, namely that at Basel "most of the university support for the conciliar programme came from secular masters."[17] On the contrary, the Friars from Observant Wings of the mendicant orders—Dominicans, Franciscans, and Augustinians alike—*all* tenaciously supported Felix V long after his cause had ceased to be politically viable. They stood and could stand with the secular masters partly because they themselves defended reform by a measure of corporate independence and almost without exception insisted upon a rigorous *reformatio im membris et in capite.* The history of the Observant Movement in the later Middle Ages is yet to be written, but its failure to support Rome at Basel and its close cooperation with the secular authorities[18]—be they princes or city magistrates—strikingly parallels the loyalty of the secular masters to the territorial princes who founded and endowed the new German universities.

On the eve of the Reformation and before humanism settled north of the Alps, Observantism in piety and in learning, the pursuit of wisdom, and the drive for knowledge—had been seeking the protection and support of the new patrons: the territorial estates. Hence, the territorialization of the universities was not an unwanted result but a desired goal and intended accomplishment, which is to be located on the medieval side of this threshold and to be interpreted not as crisis but as achievement. To take but three examples: Ingolstadt (1472), Tübingen (1477), and Wittenberg (1502) admittedly requested the traditional accreditation from Pope and Emperor—though not always in that order (Wittenberg!)—and the chancellor whose seal and approval was required for the *licentia ubique docendi* was still to be a high prelate. Yet in all three cases there can be no doubt that these young German universities were territorial foundations meant to serve a function in territorial politics: in the case of Duke Ludwig the Rich for Bavaria, of Count Eberhart the Bearded in the interest of Württemberg, and of Prince Frederick for electoral Saxony.

Moreover, not for all young universities does Heinz Scheible's correct observation hold, that "the University of Wittenberg is a purely princely foundation without 'ständische,' ecclesiastical or municipal cooperation."[19] The older University of Louvain had been acknowledged by Pope Martin V in 1425 on the joint request of the Duke of Brabant and the town magistrates. And in the time of the Reformation we find examples of at least an attempt at purely municipal universities in Strasbourg, Basel, and Geneva. Indeed, the Reformation movement in southern Germany and Switzerland preferred a citizen's university, trusting "townhall" rather than princely overseers. Nonetheless, we may say in general that, during the fifteenth century when a true founding wave swept through Germany, the establishment of a university was one of *the* characteristics of the development so conveniently called "territorialization." That is, it was part of the emancipation of the territorial princes from the Empire and increasingly from the Popes as well.

Once again, in a striking parallel to conciliar practice in its evolution from the Council of Constance to the Council of Basel, the concept of organizing according to nations was also widely abandoned by the new universities. The statutes of Ingolstadt, Tübingen, and Wittenberg no longer allowed for separate nations as organizational units. Rather, in an effort to establish a cohesive republic of learning, they introduced instead into the faculty of arts the scholarly more relevant and too often inappropriately disparaged alternatives of the *via antiqua* and the *via moderna*.

These universities were to assume the social role of providing the territorial princes with a newly required class of councillors, judges, ambassadors, lawyers, and in general with civil servants for the rapidly expanding state departments. The eminent historian of the Council of Basel, Juan de Segovia, was himself such a fervent conciliarist that it cannot surprise us that he designated the doctors as "*ordinem . . . quasi precipuum*" in the church.[20] The German princes were intent upon making full use of this new mobility by establishing them also as *precipuum* in the state. On the eve of the Reformation, the doctoral office had therefore achieved a new height of respectability and authority, well after the Conciliar Movement had collapsed and at the very time its one seemingly lasting fruit, the Gallican Freedoms and the establishment of a national French Church, had been crushed by the Concordat of 1516 between Rome and Paris.

As the new class of civil servants, the *doctores* had been riding high with the tide of conciliarism, but did not have to share its dismal descent. One incident is instructive in just this regard. Almost to the day three years before Martin Luther nailed his 95 Theses to the doors of the All Saints Church at Wittenberg, Dr. Johann Eck, alumnus of Tübingen, professor and vice-chancellor at Ingolstadt, and future opponent of Luther, posted his theses to defend the propriety of taking interest at five percent; and he did so while knowing full well that the Council of Vienna (1311-12) had condemned the mere intention of taking interest on a loan as heresy! Dr. Eck called for ending the ecclesiastical farce of condemning officially what was allowed to be practiced daily, but furtively, in disguise, and therefore unsupervised. Five percent, after all, was a mere third of the going rates of the Fuggers in Augsburg and their competitors.

The Nuremberg humanists around Christoph Scheurl, later known as the *Sodalitas Staupitziana*, accused Eck of being in the pay of the Fuggers, and evidence available today gives them the nod. They succeeded in convincing Gabriel von Eyb, *ordinarius loci* and Chancellor of Ingolstadt, to cancel the disputation. Hitherto unknown documents reveal an intriguing turn in the debate away from the issue of usury and toward the authority of the university and its *doctores*.[21] Briefly, Eck had the University of Mainz confirm in an official *Gutachten* of 10 January 1515 that a sworn doctor has the right to announce and carry through a disputation irrespective of the approval of his bishop. Eck, in his ecclesiology on a middle road between conciliarism and curialism, defended and articulated the independence of the doctoral office that had been propagated in the years between Constance and Basel and that was to provide Martin Luther three years later with the platform and authority to send Archbishop Albrecht of Mainz his 95 Theses in which he called for the immediate reversal of Albrecht's indulgences policy on the basis of his, Luther's doctoral findings.

We may conclude this second part with the observation that far from being paralyzed by inner strife and far from being doomed to social irrelevancy by introspection and self-contentment, the youngest sprouts of the Parisian alma mater produced self-conscious leaders in sundry sensitive fields reaching all the way from economics to pastoral theology. They were prepared to invoke their ancient papal and imperial prerogatives as a platform for a reform that reached well beyond the hallowed walls of the university and went to the roots of society and the public life of their age. It is high time, therefore, that we free ourselves from an overall interpretation that is based upon the perspective of the *Letters of Obscure Men*. Intended by their authors as caricature and parody, they are unfortunately taken too often as factual evidence, as if sworn to under oath in a court of law.

THE GERMAN CONNECTION

In the 1970 issue of *Daedalus*, dedicated to "The University's Dilemma," McGeorge Bundy wrote a fascinating article under the title, "Were Those the Days?"[22] In this essay he dares to answer the question of what he thought we were doing in the 1950s before his own White House years of service under Presidents Kennedy and Johnson and while he was dean of Harvard's Faculty of Arts and Sciences.

There is no need here to recount his answer in any detail. I want to point first of all to the beloved—yet spurious—contrast between the going caricature of the early modern German territorial university with Nathan Pusey's Harvard, for which Mr. Bundy claims, "It was not under the sway of Washington—neither the federal dollar nor the seductions of political power had Harvard in thrall." The German doctors, I submit, would have been able to claim exactly the same and yet would have obeyed the bidding of their *Landesherr* to speed to the capital—as fast as McGeorge Bundy himself did when Kennedy called. The moral of this story is simple: what is glorified as "public service" in our time is too easily interpreted as the subservience of a prince's lackey when it comes to the fifteenth and sixteenth centuries.

One more element of the *Daedalus* article is worthy of being underlined. Mr. Bundy tried—and, I may add, successfully—to catch the Harvard spirit of the decade we call the fifties of our century. This decade had characteristics all its own in comparison with the forties and the sixties. Yet, as soon as we historians turn to the transitions between 1350 and 1650, we are all too easily trapped by the assumption that a century in that time did not last one hundred years and did not equal ten decades of change. I cannot rid myself of the suspicion that the theories of crisis and decline that were presented in part 1 and discussed in part 2 paint on too large a canvas with strokes of whole centuries, which on closer consideration results from looking at the past from too large a distance to do justice to our theme—a theme that calls for regional as well as social differentiation with all of these to be provided a clear time index.

In having chosen as a point of departure the intertwining of the history of conciliarism and of academic foundations, I am necessarily reminded of the crucial importance of such a time index. Well before the Reformation and about the time the Italian Renaissance began to make its first converts north of the Alps, the ideal of a *concilium generale* lost much of its earlier appeal. For our understanding of the ensuing period, it ceases to be a suitable backdrop or yardstick for the *studium generale*.

All of us are prepared to grant that we have not yet begun to measure the impact or rather the repercussion of the failure of the conciliar movement after the middle of the fifteenth century. The conciliar reform ideal did not die nor did it, like the famous old soldier, fade away. The very shock widely experienced by Luther's challenge of the infallibility of the Council of Constance during his debate with Eck in the summer of 1519 is witness to the fact that at least some forms of conciliarism were merely dormant and by no means dead. As a matter of fact, Luther initiated a new epoch of hope and political activity directed towards a future general council, hope for the reform of church and society. But in the later part of the fifteenth century, we see that even the last loyal supporters of conciliarism, the reformed or observant wings of the mendicant friars, no longer expected a council to bring about the intended reformation.

It was a university professor, John of Paltz (d. 1511)—since 1483 doctor and professor at the University of Erfurt, and for a short time attached to the same monastery as his fellow Augustinian Luther—who made himself the spokesman of the mendicant reform movement around 1500. To quote from his widely read *Supplementum Coelifodinae*, first published in Erfurt, 1504: "Many mendicant friars badly need to be reformed. This is no insurmountable problem, for such goes on every day with the help of princes and city governments, authorized by the Pope. However, this task is nearly impossible in so far as it concerns the secular clergy, unless a miracle happens and God Almighty himself intervenes."[23] What rings of despair in a general reformation is belief in a reform *pars pro toto* for the whole *corpus christianum* by the Observant Mendicants, and what seems to have bypassed the universities did not in fact do so. The old university professor is a member of the reformed Augustinians who emphasized in their *Constitutiones* the special importance of their *studium generale* in Erfurt and Wittenberg.[24]

There is a second development that is entitled to our attention. The *devotio moderna*, so appropriately demythologized by R. R. Post and divested of its glorious association with the Christian Renaissance, did indeed begin as an antiintellectual movement of the *petite bourgeoisie* and craftsmen in the small merchant cities of the Ijsseldelta in Holland.[25] But in a development of some ten decades of reaching out to Paris and southern Germany, it sought and managed to attain academic status. After the death of its founder Geert Groote in 1384, it moved up to the Rhine valley to provide the first three generations of academic teachers after Gabriel Biel (d. 1495) fused this movement of popular piety with the *via moderna* and established it firmly at the University of Tübingen. The once antiacademic *devotio moderna* reached the pinnacle of society within the walls of a university and held its own through 1517; its disciples were removed from their teaching positions only after the Battle of Lauffen on 13 May 1534 allowed Duke Ulrich to "reform" the University.

But again the time index should be noticed. What we called

"firmly established" in fact covered less than four decades. With the publication in 1521 of the final section of Biel's *Collectorium* in Paris, the University of Tübingen seemed to have broken into international prominence. Biel's compend was indeed the harvest of centuries of medieval thought. Yet the preface by Johannes Brassikan the Younger (d. 1539), which hitherto has escaped attention, unmistakably announced that a new era had arrived: "I thank God that he has made me in his own image—a poet." And indeed, not only a poet, but even more, "a German." Brassikan, proud student of the *bonae litterae* and Bebel's successor as professor of rhetoric, was prepared to salute the loving care, dedication, and toil of the scholastics, but he made quite clear, "happily, our age is a new one, the epoch of Erasmus."[26]

Brassikan's preface paid homage to the past. But such reverance had already become unusual. Scholasticism came under siege from the liberal arts, and biting judgments were delivered in a far from polite style by these students of polite letters. Labelled the faint ghost from an era long dead, scholasticism was repudiated as the embodiment of medieval barbarism and obscurantism. Humanist pride joined forces with the new confessional fervor of the Reformation to construct a caricature of late medieval scholasticism that has not yet been overcome by modern scholarship. Yet, the pre-Reformation achievements of the Tübingen masters, which need not be listed here, establish this university as a significant "German Connection": a reform movement of great vitality on the threshold of modern times.

About a second German Connection it is possible to be brief. Over against all the current theses of crisis and decline of the universities, it must be remembered that Luther's Reformation movement started in a university. To put the matter differently, and more strongly, Luther's Reformation is inconceivable without the institutional framework and protection of his university. In a little-noticed document, the Rector and Senate of Wittenberg stood up for Luther in response to the charge of heresy by the Dominicans and certified publicly at the time the curia had opened its case against Luther as a heretic that the disputation on the 95

Theses had taken place in keeping with academic constitutions that guaranteed the right of the *doctores* to investigate matters of truth in exactly this way.[27] Moreover, the succeeding disputations in Heidelberg (May 1518) and in Leipzig with Eck (July 1519), as well as Luther's effort to transform the interrogation by Cardinal Cajetan into a disputation (October 1518) by pitching his authority as a doctor against that of a prelate, mark the decisive early stages in which Luther's stand was clearly based upon academic footings. Finally, the silent, but stubborn and effective protection by Frederick the Wise was not granted to Luther as a person but as an eminent member of his favorite *Landesuniversität*.

The *Devotio Moderna* and the *Reformatio Moderna*, so different in their programs for the reform of piety and of theology, both owed much of their success to the fact that they gained a solid foothold in the one institution outside the existing monastic orders that was able to provide them a durable base for operations, namely the university. Reform humanism in the tradition of the Northern Renaissance was less fortunate in its burgeoning stages. Unaccountably, the usual *Festschriften* written on the occasion of a centenary of one's own university have produced on this point, next to much valuable information, a misleading impression, for nearly all of them have at least one chapter about the "great impact of humanism" upon their beloved alma mater. The truth is, however, that the *literati, poetae,* and *theologi* before and contemporary with Erasmus at first tried to gain admission to the universities and then had to form their own local or regional *sodalitates*, the predecessors of the learned academies of arts and sciences to be established much later in the wake of the Enlightenment. Temporarily successful efforts were made, as in the case of Celtis and Reuchlin in Ingolstadt, but the Mutianus circle did not succeed in forcing its way into the hallowed halls of Erfurt, and Melanchthon left Tübingen for Wittenberg, disappointed because he was not allowed to teach advanced students and had been reduced to the role of a grammar school teacher training mere schoolboys.[28] Here again a look at the frontispiece is instructive. The lowest three levels there, presented under the names of Cicero, Donatus, and Priscianus, illustrate well that the traditional curriculum allowed the new humanists at best only a place in undergraduate teaching, closer to our modern junior high school than to what we would call a university. What the students of Erasmus wanted was to scale the heights above the elementary studies in the *trivium* and *quadrivium*.

Further evidence of the humanists' tenuous position comes from a recent critical edition of the proceedings of the Dominicans in Lower Germany. In 1531 they decided not to admit to the order students who specialized in "studiis ut vocant humanitatis aut bonis literris." Not surprisingly, no one was allowed to read any of the works of Erasmus, with of course two exceptions: "magistris nostris et inquisitoribus duntaxat exceptis."[29] It would be an error, however, to conclude that this decision was solely an overreaction to Wittenberg that shortsightedly lumped Erasmus and Luther together, as would be the case throughout the century. As early as 1516, Cologne, the sister university of Louvain, had already voted against granting students permission to attend lectures in poetry well before Luther appeared on the scene.[30] Louvain's own Collegium Trilingue had still a long way to go before it was mentally and spiritually incorporated into the university; and its godchild, the Parisian College of Royal Lecturers, was founded and favored not by the old masters but by a capricious French monarch. By contrast, it is the much criticized German state university, tyrannized, as it is often suggested, by the absolutist territorial prince, to whom we owe the great debt of having opened – sometimes by persuasion and often by decree – the doors of the universities to the *studia humanitatis* on a higher than mere undergraduate level.

The confessionalization of the university in the sixteenth century, again often seen as both cause and effect of the *Verstaatlichung* of the universities, is rather due to another dual development. On the one hand, the city universities as conceived in Strasbourg and Basel, attempted for a time in Tübingen and executed in Calvin's Geneva, were more patterned after their medieval predecessors than their own instigators would have been willing to admit.[31] Granted, at the apex of learning Lombard was replaced by Holy Scripture, but the equation of theology and metaphysics was retained—just as before in the *via antiqua* theology was to be the Queen of the Sciences. The progress made in the *via moderna* was thwarted; the move from metaphysics to physics and its programmatic distinction between the realm of faith and the realm of experience and experiment—its greatest advance—was ignored. Moreover, exactly the same development as in reformed urban universities took place in the Jesuit institutions of higher learning that did so much to stem the tide of the Reformation in Europe. Here again Peter Lombard was replaced, after some hesitation, with Thomas Aquinas (d. 1274); yet the same identification of theology and metaphysics obtained, and again the *studia humanitatis* were permitted only as propaedeutics to scriptural studies and spiritual exercises. Whatever else their diverse merits inside and outside European society, the Calvinists and Jesuits formed a double phalanx that limited the scope of free inquiry and investigation to a considerably larger extent than did the German territorial universities of the time.

One final word is necessary to lay to rest the idea of the disintegration and irrelevancy of the German universities in the sixteenth and seventeenth centuries. The contenders in the many confessional wars of these years themselves had no doubts about the strategic significance of these well-established institutions of learning. A virtually unknown document, preserved in the Vatican Archives to be dated about 1540, presents a vivid picture of the emergency plans laid for the Dominican order in view of the loss of so many universities to the 'heretics.'[32] It did so at about the same time that Luther proudly enumerated the institutions of higher learning that had been won for the Reformation.[33] The crucial role of the universities is attested to also on the other side of the confessional demarcation line. We call attention to an anonymous report to be dated about 1620 of an unofficial papal nuncio to Germany who requested support for the new Jesuit "university" in Dillingen because "Tübingen, Leipzig, Jena, Wittenberg, Marburg, Helmstedt, Rostock, Frankfurt-an-der-Oder, Strasbourg, Altdorf, Heidelberg, and Basel" were no longer in Catholic hands. The report concludes with the sentence: "It is advisable to send to these universities some well-trained Catholic missionaries in disguise who should act as if they seriously study law and medicine, since in these two fields the Lutherans are preeminent, so that Catholics are practically forced to study there."[34]

I cannot and do not claim to have told the whole story, or as it is put to the witness in an American court, "the truth, the whole truth, and nothing but the truth." We have only begun to unravel the transitions in the universities on the threshold of modern times. But some of our working assumptions will have to be radically revised, and many more surprises will await us once we dare to advance on the wide field of "the university and society" and leave behind us long-treasured confessional and ideological certainties.

1. Hastings Rashdall, *The Universities of Europe in the Middle Ages*, 3 vols., 2d ed. (Oxford, 1936), 1: *Salerno, Bologna, Paris*, p. 60. Hereafter cited as *The Universities of Europe*.

2. The first edition was published in London, 1895.

3. Pearl Kibre, *Scholarly Privileges in the Middle Ages. The Rights, Privileges, and Immunities, of Scholars and Universities at Bologna, Padua, Paris and Oxford*, Mediaeval Academy of America Publication, 72 (Mediaeval Academy of America, London, 1961), p. 325. For the precarious nature of the *licentia docendi* due to the competition between the curia, the university (chancellor!) and the local hierarchy, particularly in Paris, see Jürgen Miethke, "Der Zugriff der kirchlichen Hierarchie auf die mittelalterliche Universität. Die institutionellen Formen der Kontrolle über die universitäre Lehrentwicklung im 12. bis 14. Jh. (am beispiel von Paris), *Kyrko-historisk årsskrift* 77 (1977), 197–202. Cf. Arno Borst, "Krise und Reform der Universitätten im frühen 14. Jahrhundert," *Mediaevalia Bohemica* 3 (1970):123–47.

4. A. L. Gabriel and G. C. Boyce, eds., *Auctarium Chartularii Universitatis Parisiensis* VI: *Liber Receptorum Anglicanae Nationis* (*Alemanniae*), (Paris, 1964). See also A. L. Gabriel, *The College System in the Fourteenth Century Universities* (Baltimore, n.d. [1962]).

5. Lewis W. Spitz, "The Course of German Humanism," *Itinerarium Italicum. The Profile of the Italian Renaissance in the Mirror of its European Transformations*, dedicated to Paul Oskar Kristeller on the occasion of his 70th birthday, ed. H. A. Oberman and T. A. Brady, Jr., *Studies in Medieval and Reformation Thought* 14 (Brill, 1975), pp. 371–436. For the Reuchlin case, see James H. Overfield, "A New Look at the Reuchlin Affair," *Studies in Medieval and Renaissance History* 7 (1971): 165–207; Overfield, "Scholastic Opposition to Humanism in Pre-Reformation Germany," *Viator* 7 (1976):391–420.

6. M. Edélestand Du Méril, *Poésies populaires latines du moyen âge* (Paris, 1847), p. 153, cited in Rashdall, *The Universities of Europe* 1:290. Content and metrical form suggest the deletion of 'ab' between 'et' and 'aliis.'

7. *Super libros sapientiae* (Hagenau, 1494; reprint Frankfurt a.M., 1974), Lectio LIIII D. Df. Alexander Neckam, *De naturis rerum. Libri duo*, ed. T. Wright (London, 1886). Lib. 2, cap. 21, p. 141.

8. "Tabor was defeated at the Battle of Lipany in 1434, and soon after that the conservative Hussites got what they had been fighting for . . . and Emperor Sigismund was finally received as the legitimate King of Bohemia. By this time . . . the university [of Prague] was only a ghost of its old self, but 'the masters' were still on hand, their ranks thinned by death and weakened by age" (Howard Kaminsky, "The University of Prague in the Hussite Revolution: The Role of the Masters," *Universities in Politics. Case Studies from the Late Middle Ages and Early Modern Period*, ed. J. W. Baldwin and R. A. Goldthwaite [Baltimore/London, 1972], pp. 79–106, esp. 105f. Cf. Arno Borst, "Krise und Reform der Universitäten im frühen 14. Jahrhundert," *Mediaevalia Bohemica* 3 (1970):123–47).

9. Jacques Verger finds in the fifteenth-century French universities a sentiment "non d'une décadence, mais d'une crise, géneratrice d'abus divers," yes, even "le sentiment d'hommes en proie à l'incertitude, sinon aux contradictions, devant les problemes intellectuels, politiques et sociaux qui se nouaient autour de la crise de l'université ("Les universités française au XVᵉ siècle; crise et tentatives de réforme," *Cahiers d'Histoire* 21 (1976):43–66, esp. 66f.)

10. Jürgen Bücking, "Reformversuche an den deutschen Universitäten in der frühen Neuzeit," *Festgabe für Ernst Walter Zeeden*, ed. H. Rabe, H. Molitor, H.-Ch. Rublack, Reformationsgeschichtliche Studien und Texte, Supplementband 2 (Münster i. W, 1976), pp. 355–69, esp. 357. Cf. Gerhard Ritter, *Via antiqua und via moderna auf den deutschen universitaten des XV. Jahrhunderts* (Heidelberg, 1922; reprint Darmstadt, 1975), p. 145f.

11. Erich Kleineidam, "Augustinus Gibbon de Burgo OESA und die Wiederrichtung des theologischen Studiums der Augustinereremiten an der Universität Erfurt," *Analecta Augustiniana* 41 (1978):67–112, esp. 68.

12. Alfred Müller-Armack, "Holzwege der Universitätsreform. Aus Stätten wissenschaftlicher Bildung werden höhere Schulen," *Frankfurter Allgemeine Zeitung* 105 (6 May 1977), 9f.

13. Vern L. Bullough, "Achievement, Professionalization, and the University," *The Universities in the Late Middle Ages*, ed. J. IJsewijn and J. Paquet, Mediaevalia Lovaniensia Series 1, Studia 6 (Leuven; 1978), pp. 497–510, esp. 503.

14. Ibid., p. 502.

15. For further literature, see Brian Tierney, *Foundations of the Conciliar Theory. The Contribution of the Medieval Canonists from Gratian to the Great Schism* (Cambridge, 1955; reprint 1968); Hubert Jedin, *A History of the Council of Trent*, vol. 1 (St. Louis, 1957); G. H. M. Posthumus Meyjes, *Jean Gerson. Zijn Kerkpolitiek en Ecclesiologie* (Nijhoff, 1963); Francis Oakley, *The Political Thought of Pierre d'Ailly. The Voluntarist Tradition*, Yale Historical Publications Miscellany, vol. 81 (New Haven, London, 1964); August Franzen, "The Council of Constance. Present State of the Problem," *Historical Problems of Church Renewal*, Concilium, vol. 7 (Glen Rock, N. J., 1965), pp. 29–68; Isfried H. Pichler, *Die Verbindlichkeit der Konstanzer Dekrete. Untersuchungen zur Frage der Interpretation und Verbindlichkeit der Superoritätsdekrete Haec Sancta und Frequens* (Vienna, 1967). Cf. my Introduction to Brian Tierney, *Ockham, The Conciliar Theory, and the Canonists*, Facet Books, Historical Series, vol. 19 (Philadelphia, 1971), pp. vii–xxi. For the Council of Basel, see esp. the rich bibliography of Joachim W. Stieber, *Pope Eugenius IV, the Council of Basel, and the Secular and Ecclesiastical Authorities in the Empire: The Conflict over Supreme Authority and Power in the Church*, Studies in the History of Christian Thought, vol. 13 (Leiden, 1978), pp. 449–84. Cf. the review article for the whole period of conciliarism by Giuseppe Alberigo, "Il movimento conciliare (XIV–XV sec.) nella ricerca storica recente," *Studi Medievali*, 3ª Serie, 19 (1978), 913–50.

16. Lorenz Dax, *Die Universitäten und die Konzilien von Pisa und Konstanz* (Freiburg i. Br., 1910), hereafter cited as *Die Universitäten und die Konzilien*; Hermann Keusen, "Die Stellung der Universität Köln im grossen Schisma und zu den Reformkonzilien des 15. Jahrhunderts," *Annalen des Historischen Vereins für den Niederrhein* 115 (1929), 225–54; J. Gill, "The Representation of the *universitas fidelium* in the Councils of the Conciliar Period," *Councils and*

Assemblies, ed. G. J. Cuming and D. Baker, Studies in Church History 7 (Cambridge, 1971), pp. 171–95. L. Dax has argued that the doctores had received a right to vote already at Pisa in *Die Universitäten und die Konzilien*, p. 16f; P. R. McKeon, "Concilium generale and studium generale: The Transformation of Doctrinal Regulation in the Middle Ages," *Church History* 35 (1966):24–34; Anthony Black, *Monarchy and Community: Political Ideas in the Later Conciliar Controversy 1430–1450*, Cambridge Studies in Medieval Life and Thought, 3d ser. (Cambridge, 1970), 2:23f.

17. Anthony Black, "The Universities and the Council of Basel: Collegium and Concilium," *The Universities in the Late Middle Ages*, pp. 511–23, esp. 516. See the contrary conclusions of J. W. Stieber, *Pope Eugenius IV*, pp. 104, 107, 109.

18. See Theodor Kolde, *Die deutsche Augustiner-Congregation und Johann von Staupitz. Ein Beitrag zur Ordens- und Reformationsgeschichte* (Gotha, 1879), pp. 108f., 134f. Cf. Adalbero Kunzelmann, OSA, *Geschichte der deutschen Augustiner-Eremiten*, V: *Die sächsische-thüringische Provinz und die sächsische Reformkongregation bis zum Untergang der beiden*, Cassiciacum, 26/V (Würzburg, 1974), pp. 391, 447f.

19. Heinz Scheible, "Gründung und Ausbau der Universität Wittenberg," *Beiträge zu Problemen deutscher Universitätsgründungen der frühen Neuzeit*, Wolfenbütteler Forschungen (Bremen, Wolfenbuttel, 1978), 4:131–47, esp. 134.

20. Black, "The Universities and the Council of Basel," p. 519.

21. See Heiko A. Oberman, *Werden und Wertung der Reformation. Vom Wegestreit zum Glaubenskampf*, Spätscholastik und Reformation, 2, 2d ed. (Tübingen, 1979), esp. pp. 328f.; cf. pp. 188ff.

22. McGeorge Bundy, "Rights and Responsibilities: The University's Dilemma," *Daedalus* 99 (1970): 531–67, esp. 535.

23. "Multi mendicantes sunt irreformati, ergo merito reformandi. Quod est facile possibile in mendicantibus et fit cotidie per principes et civitates auctoritate summi pontificis. Sed hoc est quasi impossibile in sacerdotibus saecularibus, quod reformentur stantibus rebus ut nunc, nisi forte magna potentia dei descenderet et ecclesiae suae etiam in talibus subveniret" (Leipzig, 1510), fol. xl^v–2^r.

24. Johann von Staupitz, *Sämliche Schriften 5: Constitutiones Fratrum Eremitarum sancti Augustini ad apostolicorum privilegiorum formam pro reformatione Alemanniae*, Spätmittelalter und Reformation. Texte und Untersuchungen, 17 (Berlin, in preparation).

25. R. R. Post, *The Modern Devotion: Confrontation with Reformation and Humanism*, Studies in Medieval and Reformation Thought (Leiden, 1968), 3:676–80.

26. Dedicatory epistle to Wendel in Steinbach's *Grabielis Byel Supplementum in octo et viginti distinctiones ultimas Quarti Magistri Sententiarum*, ed. G. Müller (Paris, 1521).

27. *D. Martini Lutheri, Opera Latina. Varii Argumenti* 2 (Erlangen and Frankfurt A.M., 1865), p. 426.

28. Robert W. Scribner, "The Erasmians and the Beginning of the Reformation in Erfurt," *Journal of Religious History* 9 (1976):3–31.

29. "Inhibemus omnibus partribus et fratribus nostrae provinciae, ne habeant aut legant quoscunque libros Erasmi, magistris nostris et inquisitoribus duntaxat exceptis. Quod si iuventutem ornata dictio delectat, legat Tullium, Quintelianum aut e nostris divum Hieronymum, Lactantium, Cyprianum, Augustinum et reliquos.

Nolumus etiam, quod recipiantur Lovanii quincunque studentes, qui relictis studiis consuetis intendunt solum studiis ut vocant humanitatis aut bonis litteris, sed neque permittantur ibidem aut alibi quicunque fratres praetextu studii in oppido commorari. Quod si pertinaciter restiterint, includantur, invocato etiam, si opus sit, auxilio brachii secularis" (Chapter 1531. *Acta Capitulorum Provinciae Germaniae inferioris ordinis fratrum praedicatorum ab anno MDXV usque ad annum MDLIX*, Sec. Codicem Parisiensem Arch. Nat. LL, 1530, ed. S. P. Wolfs O.P. [The Hague, 1964], p. 112, ll. 166–76).

30. The early resistance in Cologne against the *studia humanitatis* is documented by a recommendation of 1516 that barred poetry lectures from the curriculum. Hermann Keussen, *Die alte Universität Köln. Grundzüge ihrer Verfassung und Geschichte* (Cologne, 1934), p. 196. Quoted by Laetitia Boehm, "Humanistische Bildungsbewegung und mittelalterliche Universitätsverfassung: Aspekte zur frühneuzeitlichen Reformgeschichte der deutschen Universitäten," *The Universities in the Late Middle Ages.* ed. J. IJsewign and J. Paquet (Leuven, 1978), pp. 315–46, esp. p. 325, note 18.

31. For further bibliographical data, see *Les Universités Européenes du XIVᶜ au XVIIIᶜ Siècle. Aspects et Problèmes.* Actes du Colloque International à l'occasion du VIᶜ Centenaire de l'Université Jagellonne de Cracovie 6–8 Mai 1964, Études et documents 4, Commission Internationale pour l'Histoire des Universités 1 (Geneva, 1967). Cf. *Werden und Wertung der Reformation*, pp. 357–63.

32. *Vier Documente aus römischen Archiven. Ein Beitrag zur Geschichte des Protestantismus vor, während und nach der Reformation* (Leipzig, 1843), pp. 84ff. Republished in *Die Kirche im Zeitalter der Reformation*, ed. H. A. Oberman, Kirchen- und Theologiegeschichte in Quellen, 3, no. 113 (Neu Kirchen-Vlayn: NeuKirchener Verlag, 1980).

33. Cf. the list with inclusion of Deventer and Zwolle: "feine particularia, quae fere respondent universitatibus." *D. Martin Luthers Werke. Kritische Gesamtausgabe* (Weimar: Böhlau), pp. 1883ff.; *Tischreden* 4. 529, 21–23, no. 4809 (June, 1542).

34. *Geschichte der Moralstreitigkeiten in der römische-katholischen Kirche seit dem sechzehnten Jahrhundert mit Beiträgen zue Geschichte und Charakteristik des Jesuitenordens*, ed. I. von Dollinger and Fr. H. Reusch, (Nördlingen, 1889), 2:390–93.

THE IMPORTANCE OF THE
REFORMATION FOR THE UNIVERSITIES:
CULTURE AND CONFESSIONS
IN THE CRITICAL YEARS

Lewis W. Spitz

artin Luther, in *An Appeal to the Ruling Class of German Nationality as to the Amelioration of the State of Christendom*, addressed himself to the problem of the universities (Section 25). "The universities need a sound and thorough reformation," he wrote; "I must say so no matter who takes offence. Everything that the papacy has instituted or ordered is directed solely towards the multiplication of sin and error. Unless they are completely altered from what they have been hitherto, the universities will fit exactly what is said in the Book of Maccabees: 'Places for the exercise for youth, and for the Greekish fashion. . . .' Nothing could be more wicked, or serve the devil better, than unreformed universities."[1] He went on to attack the supremacy of that "defunct pagan" Aristotle, to specify which of his books should be retained and how they were to be used, emphasized the utility of rhetoric, demanded the teaching of the three languages (Latin, Greek, and Hebrew), the mathematical disciplines, and history. "For Christian youth, and those of our upper classes, with whom abides the future of Christianity, will be taught and trained in the universities." The magisterial Reformation was born in the university, was opposed by the universities, triumphed with the help of universities, and, in turn, had a profound impact upon the universities for centuries thereafter.

There is more concern with education today than at any other time in Western history with the possible exception of the period of the Renaissance and Reformation when education on all levels was

42

passionately examined and major changes were made. Now that we have resurrected such subjects as the generations' conflict and the urban Reformation, have exploited humanism and reform, and have developed late scholasticism into the leading major growth industry in academia, we do right to turn attention to the history of universities in early modern times. There is no work for our period that compares with the grand syntheses on the medieval university by Rashdall and Denifle, but the rich source materials provide a wealth of unexplored documentation that would be the envy of the medievalists.

It is tempting to propose a wave theory (*Wellentheorie*) for the history of universities. Such a theory would be analogous to Otto von Gierke's socioeconomic theory of the pendular swing between individualism and collectivism, or in educational and philosophical history, the three great ages of the *trivia* and the swing to and fro between rhetoric, grammar, and dialectic in western thought. Antiquity had in effect failed to develop institutions of higher learning clearly defined, well organized, perpetuated, incorporated. The medieval universities have for a long time held the attention of historians as one of the most original creations of Western civilization in that epoch. For more than three centuries they assumed a quasi-monopoly on a certain type of teaching and, to a large extent, on general culture. Historians, then, have seen the universities of the Renaissance as in a period of decline and the early Reformation years as disastrous. A period of new vitality and significance to society was followed by decline in influence during the second half of the seventeenth century and the eighteenth century followed by a nineteenth century rise to new importance on the Continent with the French reorganization of higher education and the age of the German professoriate. The university in the twentieth century is being weighed in the balance. We have seen a surge of new universities on the Continent and of red-brick universities on the island and the rise of the American universities from their nineteenth century college status to institutions of world importance. This story of the rise and fall of the universities through the centuries is one of epic proportions and grandeur.

Historiographically, the story of the universities is bracketed between volumes such as Charles Homer Haskins, *The Rise of the Universities*, and such titles as Max Weber, *On Universities*, and Fritz Ringer's *The Decline of the German Mandarins; the German Academic community, 1870-1933*, Paul Gerbod's *La Condition universitaire en France au XIXe siècle*, or Stephen Potter's *The Muse in Chains*, including a chapter on "The fall of Oxford." Histories of the universities largely have been histories of the teaching of theology, law, medicine, or the sciences. But other approaches are possible. For example, scholars could consider the history of universities as the history of human groups placed into a given historical social context. The influence of the *Annales* school is evident in this new approach. Jacques Verger, *Les Universités au Moyen Age* (Paris, 1973), explores the history of universities in terms of the concept of "intellectual work" and *mentalité*. Sven Stelling-Michaud has distinguished between treating the *"histoire interne" and the "histoire externe"* of the universities. One might also use the distinction of *idéologique* (the production of ideas and learning) and *professionel* (the formation of men) in the universities. We need not merely follow the time-honored pattern of rise, apogee, and decline, but should study each moment of that history in a societal context. At the end of the Middle Ages and the beginning of early modern times, the universities had their own proper character, their specific roles to play. They merit study for their own sake, for they represent a new phase of equilibrium that was neither perfect nor defined. Their historic evolution and the dialectic of their internal problems cumulated telling effects that provoked new crises and a profound mutation.

There are two points of view concerning the universities at the end of the Middle Ages, during the Renaissance, on the eve of the Reformation. The one interpretation perceives the universities during the second half of the Quattrocento as exhausted by internal contradictions and caught in a period of intellectual currency inflation and the cultural operation of Gresham's law. This decline resulted from several causes: the very great gap between university theology and the exigencies of real religious sentiment, the aristocratization of the university millieu, and the development of learned academies not associated with the universities. Meanwhile, the traditional autonomy that was officially maintained in fact floundered under the blows of the states; the development of colleges ruined the very principles of scholastic pedagogy and the success of humanist ideas discredited the concept of the professoriate as the highest calling. Before long, the divorce was complete between the cutting edge of learning and university teaching.[2]

Another point of view is that the universities of the Renaissance were far from decadent, but were instead dynamic and in transition to a new phase. This positive evaluation may be associated with the name of Paul Oskar Kristeller who set forth his ideas some four decades ago and has held to them with admirable consistency.[3] From the contradictions and difficulties a new mutation arose in the universities of the Renaissance. University graduates such as Pomponazzi (not, as often asserted, a stoic, but a neo-Aristotelian), Versalius, Luis de Leon (1527-91), a mystic and translator of the Vulgate), Copernicus, Galileo, and many others are sufficient witnesses of the persistent dynamism of the universities. We tend to think of such patrons of arts and letters as Giangalleazzo Visconti and Lorenzo di Medici as Maecenases for individual humanists and artists, but they were equally interested in the support of the universities. The Renaissance saw the founding or revival of important universities including Piacenza, Pavia, Arezzo, Rome, Perugia, Florence, and Ferrara. Piacenza was founded by papal charter on 6 February, 1248. Pavia was moved there in 1398 by Giangalleazzo Visconti and endowed with twenty-seven professors of civil law, including the famous postglossator Baldus, twenty-two professors of medicine, and professors of philosophy, astrology, grammar, and rhetoric, as well as lecturers on Seneca and Dante. When Giangalleazzo died in 1402, to the relief of Florence (death, as Machiavelli noted, being his country's best ally), the university folded within two years. It was resurrected in 1412 with a full *studium generale* of all four faculties, and through the rest of the fifteenth century it had the most brilliant professors, with only Padua as a rival for excellence. When Pisa closed in 1406, it was Lorenzo di Medici who intervened and reopened it, combining it with the University of Florence in 1473, and it lasted until 1850. In Ferrara the d'Estes founded a university which in 1474 had fifty-one professors and various humanists on the faculty. Italian professors were sought after by northern universities in humanistic disciplines as well as in mathematics and science, a story not yet adequately told as part of the reception of the Italian Renaissance, the *Itinerarium Italicum*. The pattern of princely patronage anticipates a process that we shall see operative in the North during the Reformation era. The momentum for change lay in this movement and influence, and its critical importance must not be obfuscated by preoccupation with intellectual forces such as scholasticism, which although far from dead had lost initiative, creativity, and the power to control the intellectual and religious destiny of Europe, which was entering a period of radical crisis.

THE REFORMATION AND THE UNIVERSITY WORLD

The magisterial reformation was a university movement in its inception and early development. Nevertheless, historians have been prone to see the role of the university in the movement as essentially negative. Despite the fact that the *initia Lutheri* and the *initia Reformationis* lie in the theological faculties of two universities, Erfurt and especially Wittenberg, the role of the universities is seen in the light or rather in the darkness of the condemnation of Luther by Louvain and Cologne and the equivocation of the Sorbonne. In turn, the effect of the Reformation on the universities has also been seen as negative, since enrollments plummeted for a decade as a result of the disturbances and controversies, the confessional differences, and threat of war (along with harvest failures and plagues).[4] The decades that followed are portrayed in either shades of grey or all black, with universities being dominated by dogmatic theological faculties and torn by confessional strife more vicious than the battle of the *Viae* or the struggle between humanism and scholasticism.

An extensive revision of this traditional picture is in order. The period between the founding of the University of Wittenberg and Frankfurt-on-the-Oder, the last of the medieval German universities, the one to serve electoral Saxony and the other Brandenburg, and the foundation and prospering of Halle and Göttingen in 1693 and 1736 respectively, should be seen as a creative period in university history with the reformation of old universities and the formation of new ones, Protestant and Catholic, most of which are alive and vital to this very day.[5]

It will be instructive to review the phases of the founding of the universities within the Empire and the ecclesiastical-political context of their founding in order to appreciate more fully the interplay of reformation and culture[6] After the establishment of the University of Prague (1348) and of Vienna (1365), two decades passed before the founding of the next medieval German universities.[7] The impetus of legal reform within the Empire and of church reform, developing into the conciliar movement, contributed to their founding. These were the Universities of Heidelberg (1386), Cologne (1388), and Erfurt (1392). There followed offshoots or affiliates. Leipzig (1409) was formed by dissident German faculty and students from Prague. Rostock (1419) was kind of branch of Erfurt and Leipzig. The Würzburg school (1402) soon closed again. It is interesting to observe how easily the university faculties that had played a significant role in church reform and the conciliar movement adjusted to the reassertion of papal supremacy during the course of the fifteenth century. The universities became the bulwarks of orthodoxy against all heretical deviation.

A period of nearly four decades elapsed before the establishing of new universities during the second half of the fifteenth century. They followed in rapid order: Greifswald (1456), Basel and Freiburg (1460), Ingolstadt (1472), Trier (1473), Mainz and Tübingen (1477). The University of Copenhagen (1479) owed much to Cologne by way of precedent and faculty-student patronage. Then, after another cesura of more than two decades, came the last two pre-Reformation universities: Wittenberg (1502) and Frankfurt-on-the-Oder (1506). All of these institutions were medieval and ecclesiastical in their essential purposes and received authorization from the papacy. But these universities also received privileges from the emperor and were founded and supported by the secular governments, the cities, and the territorial princes. The cities established Cologne, Erfurt, and Basel, and the rest were founded and maintained by princes. The reasons were basic: the prestige of the city or princedom, the need for better educated churchmen, the growing demand for public servants, especially in law, to man the burgeoning bureaucracies of the state, and, especially in the case of Wittenberg and Frankfurt-on-the-Oder, the cultural quickening inspired by the Renaissance spirit and humanist presences at the courts. The more powerful and ambitious princes, the seven electors, spiritual and secular, in particular felt the need to have a university within their own domains. With Wittenberg and Frankfurt, the electors of Ernestine Saxony and Brandenburg had their universities at last. Perhaps the fact that Wittenberg received papal confirmation only after it had already opened was symbolic of the growing independence of universities from papal control, although not too much should be read into this fact for the papacy favored its foundation.[8] In view of the fact that some historians stress the role of the secular governments in the founding of universities during the Reformation period, it is necessary to stress the fact that these pre-Reformation universities were largely founded under the aegis of the state, urban or princely.[9] The urban and territorial universities of the Reformation period had direct lineage and precedent in the medieval universities in that respect, just as the territorial churches grew naturally out of the proprietary church structure of the Middle Ages.

The second half of the fifteenth century and the first two decades of the sixteenth constitute a phase of university history under the rising star of humanism. To be sure, the battle of the *viae* continued in its dreary way, generating no fresh ideas, a fact that must be recognized despite all revisionist efforts to depict the *viae* as the culmination of medieval thought. Some universities, such as Cologne, managed to accommodate both *viae* under the same university roof. With the coming of humanism, tamed and modified as northern humanism was for the most part, a new intellectual movement introduced a significantly different challenge to the universities.[10] The conflict of humanism and scholasticism has been overdramatized, to be sure, for the accommodation of the scholastics to the new classical interest was greater than formerly assumed by historians.[11] The harbingers of humanism were half scholastic and half humanist in mid-*quattrocento*. But the momentum was with humanism and that determined the nature of the intellectual and institutional struggles in the universities on the eve of the Reformation. The princely courts, episcopal as well as secular, were colored by Renaissance affectations. The impulse to promote humanists at the universities came from such patrons and was initially imposed upon the universities from the outside, against the will of scholastic doctors.

The pattern of university reception of humanism varied from one university to another. The older universities in the south were the first to entertain humanists and in each case the secualr courts encouraged this development. In Vienna, Maximilian I established the College of Poets and Mathematicians alongside the university, with the German arch-humanist, Conrad Celtis, as the star poet. At Ingolstadt and at Heidelberg individual humanists served as lecturers in poetry and rhetoric. Rudolph Agricola, the father of German humanism, and members of the Rhenish or Danubian sodalities, along with wandering Italian and French humanists, served as extracurricular professors. Although Vienna established a permanent lectureship in poetry in 1493 and Tübingen in 1497, in general it was not until the second decade of the sixteenth century that humanism became institutionally secure and professorships were provided for the humanist disciplines in the universities.[12] The universities of Erfurt, known as *omnium novorum portus*, and Leipzig became lively centers of humanist learning.[13] At Erfurt the circle of the gotha canon Mutianus Rufus was influential within the university. At Leipzig a series of transient humanist orators and poets were followed by the appointment of humanists such as Peter Mosellanus, a young Erasmian. A humanistic reform of Erfurt and Leipzig was not achieved until 1519.[14] New humanist translations of Aristotle were to replace the medieval Latin texts.

Instruction in classical Latin, poetry, rhetoric, lectures on Cicero and Virgil, and the study of Greek were added to the curriculum. Rostock, originally an offshoot of Erfurt and Leipzig, effected a reform in 1520 and Greifswald the following year. University reform in favor of the humanistic disciplines was effected in Heidelberg in 1522 and in Tübingen in 1525. Even Cologne, ridiculed in the *Epistolae Obscurorum Virorum* and depicted as the strongest citadel of scholasticism by historians, yielded to the influence of humanism. Cologne was among the half dozen German universities that sought to appoint Erasmus, prince of the humanists, to its faculty. It is important to note that the actual structural changes in these institutions all came after the inception of the Protestant Reformation. In fact, the leader in effecting decisive curricular change in favor of humanism in the arts and reform in theology was the university that was to become the cradle of the Reformation, the University of Wittenberg—*Leucoria*.

The University of Wittenberg, the creation of Elector Frederick the Wise, played a special role in humanism as in reform. In a frontier village on the Elbe, built on a white hill that Luther called "the sandbox of the Empire," far from the oldest centers of learning, the university was unencumbered by long-standing traditions. Humanism received its first impetus from Herman von Busche, Nicolaus Marschalk, and Peter of Ravenna and was after them championed by Christoph Scheurl, Otto Beckmann, and Jodocus Trutvetter.[15] The *Dialogus* of Andreas Meinhardi, published in 1508, provided a utopian description of Wittenberg and its university and stressed the modernity of its humanist lecturers. Nicolaus Marschalk in 1503 delivered an oration at Wittenberg on the occasion of the first graduation of twenty-four baccalaureates. He spoke in praise of the muses and of the laurel crown of the poets.[16] Marschalk's student Johannes Lang exercised an important influence on Luther between the years 1512 and 1517. Along with representatives of both *viae* on the arts faculty, three teachers of the *humanae litterae* were appointed at the very outset. They did not have the right to give examinations, and attendance at their lectures was not obligatory. But they served as a bridgehead for later occupation of academic territory and expansion. The Elector played an important role in developing the university. It was his fortunate decision to appoint Philipp Melanchthon to the arts faculty, rather than Peter Mosellanus, whom Luther favored. Just as Duke George paid for Mosellanus as a poet and rhetorician at Leipzig, so Frederick the Wise endowed professorships at Wittenberg. The story of the reform of the University of Wittenberg is very well known, but a brief sketch may serve to bring to mind the results of recent scholarship that has added clearer lines to the picture.

Although no humanist theologically speaking, Luther was, nevertheless, a protagonist of the humanist curriculum on the arts level.[17] He understood that the reform of theology in the advanced faculty of theology would be impeded and perhaps even impossible if the students' arts training was exclusively in traditional dialectic and Aristotle in Latin commentaries and if they lacked education in poetry, rhetoric, languages, and history, subjects he deemed necessary for Biblical exegesis and the theological disciplines. He took an active role in promoting these subjects with the Augustinian colleagues and especially with Melanchthon after his arrival in 1518. Melanchthon's draft of the statutes for the Faculty of Liberal Arts in 1520 eliminated everything that had referred to scholasticism.[18] Melanchthon's inaugural oration, *De corrigendis adolescentia studiis*, was programmatic for Wittenberg, decrying the loss of learning, the ignorance of Greek language and culture, and the schoolmen's dialectic, and urging the university to turn to the *studia humanitatis* for new light.[19] The various reform statutes adopted between 1533 and 1536 merely rounded out the work begun by Luther, Melanchthon, and their colleagues between 1518 and 1520 and completed the symbiosis of humanism and Reformation. Melanchthon, *praeceptor Germaniae*, labored for a reform of education from top to bottom. His role in the educational reform of the secondary schools was of critical importance. He took the initiative in encouraging the establishment of *gymnasia* in Nuremberg and many other cities, and his influence reached through Johannes Sturm in Strasbourg to Roger Ascham in England and Claude Baduel in Nimes.[20]

There was a natural relation between humanist learning and

51

evangelical theology, for the three sacred languages, the drive *ad fontes* to the biblical and patristic sources, and the utility of rhetoric for the preaching of the Word were compelling reasons for abandoning dialectic, except for apologetic purposes at a later phase, and rejecting Aristotle, whose *Nicomachaean Ethics* intruding into theology had gone so far in reinforcing scholastic semi-Pelagianism expressed in the well-known formula *facientibus quod in se est, deus non denegat gratiam.* A year before Melanchthon's famous oration, Luther had written against scholastic theology (*Disputatio contra scholasticam theologiam*), and in thesis forty-four he boldly declared that only without Aristotle does one become a theologian! He repeated the assertion in the Heidelberg Disputation before the Augustinians in 1518 and thereafter consistently contrasted the *theologia crucis* of St. Paul and Augustine to the *theologia gloriae* of the Aristotelian theologians, the scholastics. Shortly after Heidelberg Luther wrote to his former teacher Trutvetter (9 May 1518): "I believe that it is simply impossible to reform the church, if the canons, the decretals, scholastic theology, philosophy, logic, as they are now taught are not eliminated from teh ground up and other studies established" (Enders, *Br.,* 1, 188). He had in mind the study of the Scriptures and church fathers. The *inintia reformationis* are to be found in university theology. The Reformation, in turn, had a tremendous impact upon the universities throughout the Empire and, indeed, in all Europe.

Between the years 1520 and the death of Melanchthon in 1560, the Reformation effected great changes in the universities. Once again the older institutions are seen to adjust to a new social, religious, and cultural need, some reacting with hostility, others accommodating themselves to the evangelical-humanist reforms. Once again new universities are founded to serve the new cause directly. The initial effect of the Reformation upon the universities was a loss of enrollment as the disturbances of the early years inhibited student travel. Wittenberg, Erfurt, and indeed all the German universities experienced a sharp drop in enrollment.[21] The social unrest and peasant-artisan revolts of 1525 had a further adverse effect upon the universities. Luther's *Babylonian Captivity of the Church* (1520) divided the humanist spirits, the older, in general, turning against his radical theology and many of the younger rallying to him. Reverberations of this strife were felt also within the humanist circles of the universities. The question of the persistence of students once matriculated to the completion of their degrees needs closer examination in any case, for even before the Reformation at the University of Leipzig, for example, only one third as many students received degrees as enrolled at the university.

Just as Wittenberg reached the nadir of its fortunes, Prince Philipp of Hesse established the first Lutheran university at Marburg (1527). Once again Melanchthon played a key role, and his correspondence with Philipp of Hesse reveals the extent to which he influenced the organization of the new evangelical university, which like reformed Wittenberg was to become the prototype of other new foundations. The university was given an imperial charter in 1541, but received no church sanction, of course. The endowment for faculty support was taken from the confiscation of Dominican holdings, and the library was made up of the expropriated books of the Fanciscans and Augustinians. The Landgrave took a personal interest in the appointment of the professors and in the curriculum. Two theologians were appointed to teach the Old and the new Testaments, three jurists were to deal with Roman law, and canon law was to be omitted. The medical professor lectured on the physics of Aristotle as well as on Hippocrates, Galen, and Avicenna. The Arts faculty was staffed with ten professors who were to teach Hebrew, Greek, classical Latin, rhetoric (to be taught by two professors), dialectic, natural science, Latin poetry, and history, astronomy, and grammar. Luther had advocated the study of history in the university, and this new foundation introduced history as an academic subject along with the works of specific classical historians, including Orosius' *Historiarum adversus paganos septem libri*, a generous interpretation of the concept of classical history. The Word of God was to serve as the guiding principle for all instruction. The professors were to be *docti* and *pii*, learned in the humanistic disciplines as well as faithful to evangelical teachings. A pedagogical department, an embryonic school of education that was attached to the university, was to have two masters who were to teach Greek, Hebrew, and music as well as dialectic and rhetoric based on Melanchthon's textbooks. Church prebends were to be replaced by salaries paid for by various cities at the direction of the Landgrave.[22] Once again the social and ecclesiastical need for the university was evident for the university was designed to educate government officials, pastors, and teachers. This dual role was in line with Melanchthon's consistent stress on higher education's purposes, to train students to serve the *res publica*, or the commonwealth and the church.

Since Wittenberg and Marburg served as models for new Protestant universities that followed, it is important to note that when Wittenberg's official reform was completed in 1536, the university took on a more conservative caste as well. Academic degrees were reestablished, the disputations were reintroduced, canon law (decretals) was taught in the law school, four professors lectured on the Bible and on Augustine's *De spiritu et littera*, Lombard's *Sentences* were banned forever, and Aristotle was given new recognition, though not in theology. Luther became increasingly interested in history, and Melanchthon incorporated history officially into the curriculum. Melanchcthon revised *Carlton's Chronicle* to serve as a textbook for the teaching of universal history and followed Cicero in rhetoric and Aristotle in dialectic, physics, politics, and ethics. In this respect he was perhaps more "medieval" than the Italian Renaissance universities which in general arranged for the lectures on Aristotle's metaphysics and ethics to be given on Thursday, a day reserved for electives, and only the dialectic and natural science treatises were given on regular days. Melanchthon was less discriminating. In 1537 he called himself a *homo peripateticus.* Luther at first indulged Melanchthon and then gradually let himself be persuaded of the utility of Aristotle in various areas of learning, though not in religion or ethics. The stress on natural science and astronomy is impressive and helps to explain why, despite Melanchthon's stress on the ancient authorities which had a retrogressive effect, Lutheran areas produced excellent iatrochemists, botanists, astronomers, and other scientists during the sixteenth and seventeenth centuries. Melanchthon's educational achievement was to systematize the teaching of humanistic disciplines and to work out a synthesis of classical learning and evangelical theology that gave to the Protestant universities and academies a program and way of approach to learning that in turn gave them great vitality and influence.

The universities in the Protestant lands were now reorganized and new ones established based largely on the model of Wittenberg. Basel was reformed in 1532, and in the fall of 1536 Melanchthon introduced university reform to Tübingen.[23] That prolific second generation reformer Joachim Camerarius drew up the new statutes for the university arts faculty. This same Camerarius in 1543 completed the reform of the University of Leipzig begun in 1539 after the principality of Luther's old enemy Duke George of Saxony had turned evangelical.[24] In 1539, Greifswald and the University of Copenhagen were reformed on the model of Wittenberg. In 1540 Melanchthon's son-in-law led the reform of the University of Frankfurt-on-the-Oder. The second Lutheran university to be established was the University of Königsberg, patterned after Wittenberg.[25] Albert I, duke of Prussia, founded it in 1544 as a "purely Lutheran" place of learning. The University of Jena was established in a time of troubles, for when John Frederick of Saxony was captured during the Schmalkald War by the Emperor and was deprived of the electoral title and certain lands, he conceived the plan for Jena in order to have an orthodox university in his territories. His three sons carried out his wish, obtained a charter from Ferdinand I, and inaugurated the university in 1558. Melanchthon remained at Wittenberg, and thus Jena and Wittenberg became rivals for the theological leadership of Lutheranism and generated acrimonious strife. Finally, the ancient University of Heidelberg was also reorganized in 1557 and 1558 under the supervision of Melanchthon. By 1564 the University of Rostock had been reorganized along evangelical lines. Then Duke Julius of the house of Brunswick-Wolfenbüttel founded the Lutheran University of Helmstedt. This "Academia Julia" received its charter from Maxmilian II in 1575. It was richly endowed, attracted many students from the aristocracy, and proved to be a very influential institution until it was finally suppressed in 1806 during the Napoleonic period. It became a center for the study of church and secular history and progenitor of the Göttingen school of history.

From the death of Melanchthon until the end of the Thirty Years' War, the universities became increasingly agents of confessionalism. Jena had been established expressly to oppose the Philippism of Wittenberg. Melanchthon's student David Chytraeus, on the other hand, exercised a great influence in making Helmstedt a school favoring a more irenical and moderate position. The seventeenth century saw the establishment of Giessen (1607), Rintel (1621), Strasbourg (1621), and Altdorf (1622). Melanchthon's influence continued throughout this period in terms of educational philosophy despite the disputes that swirled about his name from the time of his compromises during the interim and long after his death. Not only did the rivalry of the orthodox Lutherans and the Philippists or Melanchthonians lead to the founding of new universities and strife between older ones, but as Calvinism arose as a rival to Lutheranism and infiltrated certain faculties, counter-Calvinist universities were founded. Giessen was established to counteract Marburg, which under the reformed territorial prince became Calvinistic. From the 1560s on, Heidelberg had become a Calvinist center and similarly the University of Frankfurt-on-the-Oder received a Calvinist caste because of John Sigismund of Brandenburg's confessional change. These changes in the confessional position of established universities were particularly significant since Calvinism was not to receive official recognition and tolerance in the Empire until the Peace of Westphalia and could not therefore receive imperial credentials for new universities. The Calvinists contented themselves with establishing academies along the lines of the Genevan and Strasbourg academies; for example, at Heborn and Bremen in 1584, at Burgsteinfurt in 1591, and at Neustadt-an-der-Haardt in 1578, although the latter went defunct in 1584. These schools were embryonic universities with an arts curriculum, but they lacked degree-granting powers and the advanced faculties of theology and law.

56

At the Protestant universities, the faculties of theology, usually reflecting the confession of the prince patron, became the arbiters of orthodoxy, replacing the prerogatives formerly held by pope and councils. The princes and the people took their religious faith very seriously so that, although the universities became increasingly state institutions in terms of support and control, they were nevertheless religious and not secular in their orientation. In 1583 the chancellor of Tübingen declared in an address: "*Pietas cuius causa praecipue academiae constitutae sunt.*"[26] Moreover, the universities continued to have a great deal of internal self-regulation and autonomy in governing their own affairs. The law faculties gained in prestige with their increasingly important role of supplying functionaries for the burgeoning territorial government bureaucracies. Thus, although the universities were subjected to greater state control, they also gained in power and importance in the social scheme of things. Although professors were no longer the guild of clerics of the medieval *universitas* or corporation, living off student stipends or ecclesiastical prebends, they gained security and status in a more compactly organized institution.

Confessionalism also played an important role in the development of education in the Catholic Reformation. In addition to the universities of Paris, Louvain, and Cologne, which were quick to condemn Luther, such lesser universities as Leipzig, Mainz, and Ingolstadt played a prominent role in the Catholic effort from the very beginning. Ingolstadt was an early center of humanist studies, starring Johannes Reuchlin and Johannes Eck, a scholar of considerable classical and patristic learning. Ingolstadt in particular developed into a center of counterreformation activities. Theologians and canon lawyers were invited to the Council of Trent from these universities that had remained faithful to the church. The Council in turn confirmed all the ancient privileges of the universities (Session 25, Cap. 6, Concilium Tridentinum, Acta 4, 2). The role played by university professors at Trent, however, remained modest compared with the leadership of Gerson, d'Ailly, and others in the councils of the fifteenth century.[27]

The role of the Jesuits in founding academies and manning the older and newly founded universities was of critical importance.

They combined in their *ratio et institutio studiorum* humane disciplines within a scholastic structure. The pattern of Jesuit relationship to the Catholic universities varied. At Ingolstadt the Jesuits, and Canisius himself for a time, developed their program within the well-established Catholic university. At Dillingen the Jesuits were installed by the founding grant of Cardinal Otto Truchsesz von Waldburg, the bishop of Augsburg. At Fulda, a Jesuit college existed into the eighteenth century without ever achieving full university status. Würzburg had precisely the same organization as Fulda, but there the school very quickly developed into a *studium generale*.[28] The Jesuits valued highly the *Humaniora* in academies or gymnasia and for membership in their own order. In their university curricula, they restored Aristotle to his canonical status and followed Trent in exalting Thomas Aquinas to supreme status in theology, the *Summa Theologica* serving as the basic statement of religious teaching. Their faculties were international and moved from one institution to another, perhaps too frequently, in accordance with the policy of the order, even against the regulations of some universities. Thus the Spanish Jesuit Gregor of Valencia taught at Dillingen 1573 to 1575 and then in Ingolstadt until his death in 1603. He was held to be the main representative of baroque scholasticism in achieving the harmonious union of humanism and a sound scholasticism.[29] The heart of Jesuit education was "*res litteraria studiumque pietatis*". The goal was "*docte simul et religiose educandi.*"

One intriguing development that affected both Protestant and Catholic universities was a result of the stress of Melanchthon and of the Jesuits on the need for *gymnasium* secondary or preparatory education before students were admitted to the university. There developed the tendency to push language study and other humanistic subjects back into that secondary level. The result for the universities was for the fourth faculty, the arts faculty, to develop more and more into a philosophical faculty on a par with the faculties of theology, law, and medicine, rather than preparatory for those faculties. This development is still a feature of the modern university, of course, with ambivalent educational results.

HUMANISM AS A CRITICAL DETERMINANT FOR UNIVERSITY HISTORY

In tracing the course of German humanism through individual literati, one is impressed with the continuity and vitality of the humanist tradition through the sixteenth and well into the seventeenth century.[30] One aspect of this important continuum is the correlation between humanism and reform, both Catholic and Protestant, among educators on the *gymnasium* and *lycée* levels as well as in the arts faculties of the universities. The percolation of an "arts and humanism mentality" into the theological faculties occurred just as it had been deliberately designed and planned by Luther, Melanchthon, Calvin, and the magisterial reformers. It is an area that calls for further research, but I present here some preliminary explorations and suggestions. It would be of value to distinguish "arts humanism" in a sense recognizable to an Italian humanist of the quattrocento, from what Ernst Wolf calls "evangelical humanism" or Ernst Schwiebert has dubbed "Biblical humanism." For in that way the impact of classical or Renaissance humanism on the universities during that reformation epoch can be more accurately examined and convincingly presented. Biblical humanists specialized in exegesis; arts humanists were found predominantly in the arts faculties and gymnasia. Following classical models and Italian precedents, they introduced new methods into the trivium and taught subjects such as poetry, moral philosophy, and history. Melanchthon's pioneering effort in introducing universal history into the curriculum was but a reflection of an attitude toward history characteristic of the Italian Renaissance.

Humanism also continued as a powerful influence within the Catholic institutions in the Habsburg dynastic holdings to the mid-seventeenth century and beyond. Whereas the initial impact of the Reformation produced a state of upset leading to decline in the standards of excellence, as the Reformation proceeded, the influence of humanism engendered a spirit of critical learning and intellectual speculation that reinvigorated the universities down to the Thirty Years War. By 1650 the Church had regained control of educational institutions, mostly through the work of the Jesuits, throughout the Habsburg-dominated area. The role of the secular rulers in this Catholic area was also very powerful.[31] The fact that in Protestant universities a kind of new scholasticism developed in theology should not obscure the important continuity of classical humanist learning and the humanistic disciplines. Humanism continued to play a leavening and critical role in both Catholic and Protestant areas into the seventeenth century.

CONCLUSIONS

It is bold to venture upon such a vast subject for what must at best be a brief discussion. It is equally daring to undertake drawing general conclusions based upon such a rapid survey. Yet, it was no one less than Erasmus who in his *Praise of Folly* declared: "There are two main obstacles to the knowledge of things, modesty that casts a mist before the understanding, and fear that, having fancied a danger, dissuades us from the attempt." A few concluding observations are in order on the impact of the Reformation on the universities and on the history of universities during the early modern period in general.

1. The Reformation on balance had a significant and a positive influence upon universities. They played a more important role in the sixteenth and early seventeenth centuries than they did during most of the preceding century after the collapse of the conciliar movement and than they were to do during the eighteenth century, when the academies and scientific societies assumed much of the intellectual leadership in European culture.

The negative aspect of the picture had been very much exaggerated in the literature for polemical or antireligious reasons. Thus the increased role of the secular powers in founding, maintaining, and controlling the universities is criticized. Universities were said to have become territorial and parochial instead of international. And a degeneration from humanism to reformation to confessionalism is said to have precipitated the decline of the European university. But a survey such as this underlines the fact of continuity from the medieval through the Reformation period of many developments, including secular control of many nominally ecclesi-

60

astical institutions. Moreover, the careful study of the matriculation books, and much work remains to be done on this question,
indicates that the universities of the sixteenth century were not so
local as has been asserted. Before the Reformation some had a
limited international appeal. Now in many cases it was precisely
their confessional position that attracted like-minded students
from afar.[32] Thus students from an area like Steyer divided between
study at Wittenberg or Ingolstadt according to their religious pref-
erence. Moreover, a very good argument can be made for the
vitality of post-Reformation Lutheranism, whose so-called scholastic orthodox theologians not only wrote clearly in theology and
were conscientious about matters of faith, but were also classical
and patristic scholars, not mere polemicists, and sometimes poets,
historians, authors of devotional materials, and pastors.

Moreover, there were many positive aspects to confessionalism in
this era. When compared with the schools and universities of the
medieval period, and especially the late Middle Ages, the schools
and universities of the confessional period experienced a much
greater intensity of both discipline and intellectual life. It should
also be emphasized that the continuity of humanism as an intellectual force, although somewhat domesticated, was still vital. In fact,
the knowledge of classical culture had a broader and deeper base
than in the preceding century and demonstrably prepared the way
for Enlightenment culture. The symbiosis of evangelical religion
and humanist culture in the case of the Protestants, as well as of
scholastic structure and humanist substance in the case of the
Jesuits, was a winning combination that gave to humanism
strength as well as longevity. The *orbis academicus* was kept international as a world of learning through the continued influence of
humanism. When the Dutch universities assumed the intellectual
leadership of Protestantism from the second quarter of the seventeenth century, the importance of the humanist tradition was evident in their relative tolerance and world outlook. By the end of
the seventeenth century, confessionalism relaxed, and in important ways universities lost some of their sense of direction and
reason for being.[33]

2. All through their history, universities have been founded for

three reasons: the development of new badly needed subjects (such as civil law), new methods superior to those practiced in older institutions however renowned, and new societal demands. Territorial and confessional universities of the sixteenth century were not really out of line with the medieval tradition, for there had been a growing tendency to an organization that accompanied the development and consolidation of European nationalities. Moreover, Italian Renaissance universities had reflected the special interests of territorial or city states, from Frederick II with his University of Naples to those of the Visconti, Medici, or d'Estes. What is more, medieval universities had not been innocent of confessionalism. The University of Toulouse had been founded as a check on the Albigensians, and the papacy had restrained the founding of theological faculties in the interest of the Sorbonne especially in Italy, where there were only four theological faculties—at Pisa, Florence, Bologna, and Padua—set up for the convenience of the regulars, all around the mid-fourteenth century. Confessional lines were not so sharply drawn in Reformation universities as has often been imagined. Ferdinand II and Rudolf II chartered most of the new Lutheran universities, although the Calvinists had more trouble getting imperial sanction and had to settle for lesser titled institutions.

3. The *translatio literarum* or *Musarum* led to new universities that usually had greater vigor and few inhibiting regulations and traditions, from Wittenberg and Marburg to Halle and Göttingen. In a similar fashion, new commercial cities such as Antwerp and Amsterdam replaced Bruges and Ghent.

4. Universities with a strong liberal arts tradition, such as Altdorf, Leiden, Helmstedt, and the more debatable Strasbourg, Nîmes, and others tended to a moderate and more free tradition. These were, in fact, even commissioned to bestow the laurel wreath on poets!

Bern, Lausanne, and Geneva emerged from academies to university status later. They were derived from *gymnasia* and lycées or Calvinist academies. The story of the Jesuits in French education and somewhat in the smaller Catholic German universities is instructive and reinforcing of this thesis to a point. Similarly, individual reformers such as Melanchthon, with his humanist component, were more flexible than Amsdorf, who had not had the privilege of a serious encounter with the arts.

5. Solid endowment and financial support coupled with a curial or regent's style of administration or supervision were major factors in the advance and predominance of certain universities during our period of investigation. But, as in the case of relatively moderately supported Altdorf, which was long one of the most eminent though not richly endowed universities, support is not the sole criterion of success. The intellectual tradition, including arts humanism, was very important. On the other extreme invidious patronage could also spell the ruination of a university for a long period, as in the case of Louvain.

6. Universities are tough, resilient institutions capable of surviving dormant periods, hostile forces, and even then of emerging as revitalized centers of new learning. The confessional universities nearly all survived the Thirty Years War and have remained a force to be reckoned with beyond the Napoleonic period and Nazi decades down to the present time.

1. Martin Luther, *Selections from His Writings*, ed. John Dillenberger (Garden City, N.Y., 1961), pp. 470-71. For the interplay of Luther and the University of Wittenberg, see the excellent article by Helmar Junghans, "Wittenberg und Luther–Luther und Wittenberg," *Freiburger Zeitschrift für Philosophie und Theologie* 25, nos. 1-2, 104-19 (1978). I am grateful to the Institute for Advanced Study, Princeton, for providing the leisure time for the revision of this article.

2. Jacques Verger, *Les Universités au Moyen Age* (Paris, 1973), p. 5. Verger believes the critical period for universities to have been the second half of the fifteenth century, when the universities were exhausted by contradictions, pp. 204-5. Kurt Müller, "Zur Entstehung und Wirkung der Wissenschaftlichen Akademien und Gelehrten Gesellschaften des 17. Jahrhunderts," in Hellmuth Rössler and Günther Franz, eds., *Universität und Gelehrtenstand 1400-1800* (Limburg/Lahn: 1970), pp. 128-129, 142, argues that in the seventeenth and eighteenth centuries many leading scholars and scientists such as Leibniz, Newton, Huygens, Boyle, and Tschirnhaus refused any association with universities and stayed with academies for which the *Académie des sciences* (1666) and the *Royal Society* (1662) served as models. The academies drew talent away from the universities so that it was only with the founding of universities in Uppsala (1710), St. Petersburg (1725), and Göttingen (1751) that the closer ties of academies and universities were established that were later advocated programmatically by Wilhelm von Humboldt.

3. Paul Oskar Kristeller, *Die italienischen Universitäten der Renaissance, Schriften und Vorträge des Petrarca-Instituts Köln* 1 (Krefeld, [1957]), 30 pp. Rudolf Pfeiffer, *History of Classical Scholarship from 1300 to 1850* (Oxford: 1976), pp. 55–56, writes: "Despite the development we have just described at Bologna, the old Italian universities did not play a decisive part in promoting the teaching side of Renaissance scholarship; as we shall see, more was achieved by new transalpine foundations. But there were important teaching institutions in Italy outside the universities. One of the earliest of these was the so-called 'Studio' in Florence, founded in 1321." Pfeiffer is mistaken in repeatedly referring to the *Studium* as though it were not the university in Florence. A typical negative assessment of the effect of the Reformation on the universities is that of Klaus Conermann, "Doctor Faustus: Universities, the Sciences and Magic in the Age of the Reformation," in Douglas Radcliff-Umstead, ed., *The University World: A Synoptic View of Higher Education in the Middle Ages and Renaissance* (Pittsburgh, 1973), pp. 104–6.

4. F. T. Bas, *Luther in Het Oordeel van de Sorbonne* (Amsterdam, 1974) on the *Determinatio* of 1521; K. Blockx, *De ver oordeling van Maarten Luther door de theologische faculteit van Leuven in 1519* (Brussels, 1958); D. S. Hempsall, "Martin Luther and the Sorbonne, 1519–1521" (Brussels, 1958); D. S. Hempsall, "Martin Luther and the Sorbonne, 1519–1521," *Bulletin of the Institute of Historical Research* 48 (1975):28–40. See also the narrative account in Daniel Olivier, *The Trial of Luther* (St. Louis, 1978), pp. 104–11.

5. Among the classic accounts are Georg Kaufmann, *Geschichte der deutschen Universitäten*, 2 vols. (Stuttgart, 1888–96); Stephen d'Irsay, *Histoire des Universités Françaises et Etrangères des Origines a Nos Jours*, 2 vols. (Paris, 1933–35), badly biased against Protestantism, hereafter cited as *Histoire des Universités Françaises*. Friedrich Paulsen's work has held up well, *Geschichte des gelehrten Unterrichts auf den deutschen Schulen und Universitäten vom Ausgang des Mittelalters bis zur Gegenwart*, 2 vols. (Leipzig, 1919–21). Two chapters of special interest are Ludwig Petry, "Die Reformation als Epoche der deutschen Universitätsgeschichte. Eine Zwischenbilanz," *Festgabe Joseph Lortz* 2 (Baden Baden, 1958): pp. 317–53, by a good Catholic scholar who reviews the older literature, and Max Steinmetz, "Die Konzeption der deutschen Universitäten im Zeitalter von Humanismus und Reformation," in *Les Universités Européennes du XIVᵉ au XVIIIᵉ siecle* (Geneva, 1967). Steinmetz is a leading East German Marxist.

6. The lively interest in the history of the universities is in evidence from the growing bibliography and a new commission and journal for the history of European universities. See the *Bibliographie internationale de l'histoire des universités*, 2, A. Moreira De Sa et al., eds. Geneva, 1976), and *Bibliographie zur Universitätsgeschichte. Verzeichnis der im Gebiet der Bundesrepublik Deutschland 1945–1971 veröffentlichten Literatur*, Erich Hassinger, ed. (Freiburg/Munich, 1974). The International Commission for the History of Universities has begun the publication of *The History of European Universities: Work in Progress and Publications*, John M. Fletcher, general editor (The University of Aston in Birmingham).

7 . See Paul Uiblein, "Zu den Beziehungen der Wiener Universität zu anderen Universitäten im Mittelalter," in *The Universities in the Late Middle Ages*, Jozef IJsewijn and Jacques Paquet, eds.(Louvain, 1978), pp. 169–89; A. Lhotsky, *Die Wiener Artistenfakulät 1365–1497* (Graz/Vienna/Cologne, 1965).

8. See the excellent overview provided by Gustav Adolf Benrath, "Die deutsche evagelische Universität der Reformationszeit," in Rössler and Franz, *Universität and Gelehrtenstand* pp. 63–83, used extensively here. The venerable volume by Theodor Muther, *Aus dem Universitäts und Gelehrtenleben im Zeitalter der Reformation. Vortrage* (Erlangen, 1866; reprint edition, Amsterdam, 1966), contains material of considerable interest on the constitutions of German universities and the like.

9. D'Irsay, *Histoire des Universités Françaises* pp. 313–19, so emphasizes the subjugation of

the universities to civil authorities in the Reformation as to be blinded to the role of cities and princes prior to the Reformation. His confessional bias shows in his kind acknowledgement of princely protection and contributions to the universities and academies of the counterreformation.

10. Two recent publications of special interest are Gerhart Hoffmeister, "The Pagan Influence of the Italian Renaissance on German Life and Letters, 1450–1520," in his collection *The Renaissance and Reformation in Germany. An Introduction* (New York, 1977), pp. 51–67; Eckhard Bernstein, *Die Literatur des deutschen Frühhumanismus* (Stuttgart, 1978).

11. James H. Overfield, "A New Look at the Reuchlin Affair," *Studies in Medieval and Renaissance History* 8 (1971): 165–207, and in his unpublished Princeton dissertation makes a telling argument for a revisionist point of view regarding scholastic opposition to humanism in pre-Reformation Germany. Charles Nauert has encouraged a more favorable assessment of the "obscure men" of Cologne in various articles, "The Clash of Humanists and Scholastics: An Approach to Pre-Reformation Controversy," *Sixteenth Century Journal* 4 (April, 1973):1–18; "Peter of Ravenna and the 'obscure men' of Cologne: a Case of Pre-Reformation Controversy," *Renaissance Studies in Honor of Hans Baron*, Anthony Molho and John Tedeschi, eds. (DeKalb, Ill., and Florence, 1971), pp. 609–40.

12. See the outstanding article by Laetitia Boehm, "Humanistische Bildungsbewegung und mittelalterliche Universitätsverfassung: Aspekte zur frühneuzeitlichen Reformgeschichte der deutschen Universitäten," in Jozef IJsewijn and Jacques Paquet, *Universities in the Late Middle Ages*, pp. 315–46.

13. Erich Kleineidam, *Universitas Studii Erffordensis. Überblick über die Geschichte der Universität Erfurt im Mittelalter 1392–1521, Teil 2: 1460–1521* (Leipzig, 1969), pp. 271–356. The old classic by F. W. Kampschulte is still surprisingly useful: *Die Universität Erfurt in ihrem Verhältnisse zu dem Humanismus und der Reformation, aus den Quellen dargestellt*, 2 vols. (Trier, 1858–60).

14. Herbert Helbig, *Die Reformation der Universität Leipzig im 16. Jahrhundert* (*Schriften des Vereins für Reformationsgeschichte*, no. 171) (Gütersloh, 1953).

15. Ernst Schwiebert, *Luther and His Times* (St. Louis, 1950), p. 272.

16. Edgar C. Reinke, ed. and trans., *The Dialogus of Andreas Meinhardi. A Utopian Description of Wittenberg and its University, 1508* (Ann Arbor, Michigan, 1976); Edgar C. Reinke and Gottfried G. Krodel, eds. *Nicolai Marscalci Thurii oratio habita albiori academia in alemania iam nuperrima ad promotionem primorum baccalauriorum numero quattuor et viginti anno domini mcccccii* (Valparaiso, 1967).

17. See the outstanding article by Helmar Junghans, "Der Einflusz des Humanismus auf Luthers Entwicklung bis 1518," *Luther-Jahrbuch* 37 (1970):37–101.

18. Kurt Aland, "Die Theologische Fakultät Wittenberg und ihre Stellung im Gesamtzusammenhang der Leucoria während des 16. Jahrhundert," in *450 Jahre Martin-Luther-Universität Halle–Wittenberg* 1 (Halle, Saale, 1952):163ff; Ernest G. Schwiebert, "New Groups and Ideas at the University of Wittenberg," *Archive for Reformation History* 49 (1958):71ff.

19. Robert Stupperich, ed., *Melanchthons Werke in Auswahl, 3, Humanistische Schriften* (Gütersloh, 1961), pp. 29–42; selections translated in Robert M. Kingdon, ed., "On Improving the Studies of Youth," *Transition and Revolution. Problems and Issues of European Renaissance and Reformation History* (Minneapolis, Minn., 1974), pp. 164–71. Hereafter cited as *Transition and Revolution*.

20. See for example, Melanchthon's *In laudem novae scholae*, 1526, in Stupperich, *Melanchthons Werke in Auswahl*, pp. 63–69, translated in Kingdon, *Transition and Revolution* pp. 171–75: "The Oration of Philipp Melanchthon *In Praise of a New School*, delivered at

Nuremberg in an Assembly of Very learned Men and nearly the Entire Senate (1526)." On Baduel, see Kingdon, *Transition and Revolution*, pp. 179–82. On Roger Ascham, see Lawrence V. Ryan, *Roger Ascham* (Stanford, 1963), pp. 127–28, passim. On Johannes Sturm and the Strasbourg academy, see the recent volume by Anton Schindling, *Humanistische Hochschule und Freie Reichsstadt. Gymnasium und Akademie in Strassburg 1538–1621* (Wiesbaden, 1977).

21. An interesting article on the background of university students is Hermann Mitgau, "Soziale Herkunft der deutschen Studenten bis 1900," in Rössler and Franz, *Universtät und Gelehrtenstand*, pp. 233–68. It would be valuable to use the matriculation books of the Reformation period to do a similar study, though admittedly the data would be more difficult to come by than for the eighteenth to the twentieth centuries.

22. Benrath, "Deutsche evangelische Universität", pp. 69–74.

23. Richard L. Harrison, Jr., "Melanchthon's Role in the Reformation of the University of Tübingen," *Church History* 47, no. 3 (September, 1978): 271–78. See also Harrison's dissertation, "The Reformation of the Theological Faculty of the University of Tübingen, 1534–1555" (Vanderbilt, 1975).

24. Frank E. Baron, ed., *Joachim Camerarius (1500–1574). Beiträge zur Geschichte des Humanismus im Zeitalter der Reformation* (Munich, 1978).

25. Max Steinmetz and the collective, *Geschichte der Universität Jena 1548/1558*, 2 vols. (Jena, 1958).

26. Benrath, "Deutsche evangelische Universität", p. 75.

27. D'Irsay, *Histoire des universités*, pp. 342–43. See also Th. Kurrus, "*Bonae artes*: Über den Einflusz des Tridentinums auf die philosphischen Studien an der Universität Freiburg im Breisgau," *Festgabe für A. Franzen: Von Konstanz nach Trient; Beiträge zur Geschichte der Kirche von den Reformkonzilien bis zum Tridentinum*, ed. Remigius Bäumer (Munich, 1972), pp. 603ff. On Ingolstadt, see H. Dickerhof, "Universitätsreform und Wissenschaftauffassung: Der Plan einer Geschichtsprofessur in Ingolstadt 1624," *Historisches Jahrbuch* 88 (1968): 325ff.; W. Kausch, *Geschichte der Theologischen Fakultät Ingolstadt im 15. und 16. Jahrhundert (1472–1605)* (Berlin, 1977); Laetitia Boehm and Johannes Spörl, eds., *Die Ludwig-Maximilians-Universität in Ihren Fakultäten*, 2 vols. (Berlin, 1972–78).

28. On the role of the Jesuits, see Ernst Schubert, "Zur Typologie Gegenreformatorischer Universitätsgrüdungen: Jesuiten in Fulda, Würzburg, Ingolstadt und Dillingen," Rössler and Franz, *Universität und Gelehrtenstand*, pp. 85–105.

29. Schubert, "Zur Typologie Gegenreformatorischer Universitätsgründungen," p. 99.

30. The argument for the continuity of humanism through the Reformation period is made in Heiko A. Oberman and Thomas A. Brady, Jr., eds., *Itinerarium Italicum. The Profile of the Italian Renaissance in the Mirror of its European Transformations* (Leiden, 1975), pp. 414–36. Studies of interest for humanist continuity are Werner Kaegi, *Humanistische Kontinuität im Konfessionellen Zeitalter* (Basel, 1954); W. Kölmel, "*Scolasticus literator*: Die Humanisten und ihr Verhältnis zur Scholastik," *Historisches Jahrbuch* 93 (1973): 301ff., critical of both Kristeller and Baron's reading of humanism; E. Trunz, "Der deutsche Späthumanismus um 1600 als Standeskultur," *Zeitschrift für geschichte der Erziehung und des Unterrichts* 21 (1931): 17ff.

31. R. J. W. Evans, "Humanism and Counter-Reformation at the Central European Universities," *History of Education* (Great Britain) 3(2) (1974): 1–15.

32. Evidence for the continued international character also of confessional universities, as well as of the special importance of the Dutch universities is to be found in the following studies: Robert van Roosbroeck, "Die Beziehungen der Niederländer und der Niederlädischen Emigraten zur deutschen Gelehrtenwelt im XVI. Jahrhundert. Eine Ubersicht," Rössler und Franz, *Universität und Gelehrtenstand* pp. 107–25; Heinz Schnepen, *Niederländische*

Universitäten und deutsches Geistesleben von der Gründung der Universität Leiden bis ins späte 18. Jahrhundert (Münster/Westfalen: Aschendorff, 1960); Gerhard Krause, *Andreas Gerhard Hyperius. Leben-Bilder-Schriften* (Tübingen, 1977), a Dutch professor at Marburg who wielded great influence.

33. Benrath, "Deutsche evangelische Universität," p. 78. For a retrospective view see also Hanns Rückert, "Die Stellung der Reformation zur mittelalterlichen Universität," *Vorträge und Aufsätze zur historischen Theologie* (Tübingen, 1972), pp. 65–95.

SCIENCE AND THE MEDIEVAL UNIVERSITY

Edward Grant

rior to the monumental research on medieval science by Pierre Duhem in the first two decades of this century,[1] the title of this article would have evoked laughter and/or scorn. Any juxtaposition of the terms "science" and "medieval" would have been thought a contradiction in terms. Since Duhem's time, however, and largely because of him and a series of brilliant successors, we have grown accustomed to the concept of medieval science, which has even developed into a significant research field. But now that historians of science have grown accustomed to the idea that there was indeed science in the Middle Ages, the time has come to risk laughter and/or scorn once again by proposing the *prima faciae* outrageous claim that the medieval university laid far greater emphasis on science than does its modern counterpart and direct descendant. It is no exaggeration or distortion to claim that the curriculum of the medieval university was founded on science and largely devoted to teaching about the nature and operation of the physical world.[2] For better or worse, this is surely not true today. This paper will attempt to describe not only the origins of this incredible development, but to present the details that will substantiate the claim that the medieval university provided to all an education that was essentially based on science.

That science became the foundation and core of a medieval university education is directly attributable to the unprecedented translation activity of the twelfth and early thirteenth centuries.[3]

From approximately 1125 to around 1230, a large portion of Greco-Arabic science had been translated from Arabic and Greek into Latin. Prior to this activity, only a miniscule portion of Greek science had ever been made available in Latin. From the Roman Empire period to the twelfth century, western Europe subsisted on a meager scientific fare that had been absorbed into handbooks and encyclopedic treatises associated with the names of Chalcidius, Macrobius, Martianus Capella, Boethius, Isidore of Seville, Cassiodorus, and Venerable Bede. When not merely repetitive, the sum total of science embedded in these treatises was frequently inaccurate, contradictory, and largely superficial. Nothing illustrates the sorry state of affairs better than the virtual absence of Euclid's *Elements*. Without the most basic text of geometry, the physical sciences of astronomy, optics, and mechanics were impossible. Although a cosmological picture of the world was available in Chalcidius' partial translation of Plato's *Timaeus*, the latter treatise in and of itself did not provide a detailed natural philosophy with adequate physical and metaphysical principles. Despite the lack of geometry and technical science and an inadequate natural philosophy, twelfth century scholars at Chartres, such as Adelard of Bath, Bernard Silvester, Thierry of Chartres, William of Conches, and Clarenbaldus of Arras, had begun to interpret natural phenomena, and even biblical texts, with critical objectivity.[4] Whether, if given sufficient time, this bold intellectual venture would have generated new insights and theories about the physical world will never be known. For the influx of Greco-Arabic science into western Europe had already begun and would soon overwhelm the incipient rational science that had been evolving within the context of the old learning.

   The achievements of the international brigade of translators that labored in Spain, Sicily, and northern Italy were truly monumental. Within a period of approximately 100 years, they made available in Latin the works of Aristotle and the commentaries of Averroes, which together would dominate scientific thought for the next four hundred years; Euclid's *Elements*; Ptolemy's *Almagest*, the greatest astronomical treatise until the *De revolutionibus* of

Copernicus; Alhazen's *Optics*, the *Algebra* of al-Khwarizmi; and the medical works of Galen, Hippocrates, and Avicenna.[5] Many lesser scientific works were also rendered into Latin. And if we push into the 1260s and 1270s, we must add the approximately forty-nine translations from Greek into Latin by William of Moerbeke, which included the works of Archimedes and his commentator Eutochius, Proclus, and the Greek Aristotelian commentators, Simplicius, Themistius, Alexander of Aphrodisias, and John Philoponus, as well as works by Hero of Alexandria and Ptolemy.[6] To improve the quality of the texts of Aristotle, Moerbeke translated almost the whole of the Aristotelian corpus from Greek to Latin.

When compared to the paucity of scientific texts prior to the age of translation, the achievements of the translators of the twelfth and thirteenth centuries are truly staggering. It enabled two things to occur that might not otherwise have happened. First it laid the true foundation for the continuous development of science to the present day, and secondly it provided a powerful and comprehensive subject matter that enabled the university to emerge as a fundamental intellectual force in medieval society.

The first of these consequences of the translations of the twelfth and thirteenth centuries is not the subject matter of this paper, but will be mentioned again, since its importance cannot be overestimated. It is, however, the second momentous consequence of the translations that shall be the primary concern. With the introduction of Aristotelian science and philosophy and the numerous other works that came along with it, the basis for an extensive curriculum became available and it is hardly surprising that by 1200, two of the three greatest universities of Christendom, Oxford and Paris, were already in existence with curricula based on the new science. To substantiate the claim that the medieval universities taught an essentially science curriculum, it is necessary to distinguish two aspects of medieval science. The first, and most important, was natural philosophy, or natural science, which consisted of the "natural books" (*libri naturales*) of Aristotle and formed one of the major subdivisions under what was usually called the

Three Philosophies, which also embraced moral philosophy and metaphysics.[7] Along with Aristotelian logic,[8] natural philosophy constituted the most significant part of the arts curriculum of every medieval university and will receive emphasis here.

Before turning to it, however, we must describe and discuss the second aspect of medieval science, which was concerned with the exact sciences of arithmetic, geometry, astronomy, and music. Here indeed you will recognize the old *quadrivium* of the venerable seven liberal arts. When compared with the quadrivium as represented in the curriculum of the monastic and cathedral schools prior to the translations, it is readily apparent that the exact sciences as taught in the medieval universities shared little more than the name "quadrivium" with what was dispensed under that rubric in the early Middle Ages.[9] The emphasis on the exact sciences was not, however, of equal breadth and scope in all medieval universities. Although they formed an integral part of the curriculum at Oxford from the thirteenth century onward, they received much less emphasis at Paris and other places. For example, mathematics was not regularly taught at Paris in the thirteenth century and only sporadically in the fourteenth. At Paris it was more usual for masters to offer mathematical instruction privately during feast days. Mathematics and the other quadrivial sciences were thus rarely part of the regular course of instruction. Such courses were offered by interested masters to students who probably had special interests in the exact sciences and were presumably well motivated.[10]

It was Oxford that served as the model for regular instruction in the exact sciences. From lists compiled by Father James Weisheipl, we can obtain a good sense of the books used in the quadrivial courses.[11] At the heart of the exact science curriculum was geometry and Euclid's *Elements*. Of the thirteen genuine and two spurious books of the medieval Latin version of the *Elements*, only the first six were formally required.[12] Practical, or applied, geometry was also stressed.[13] In this category, use was made of the *Treatise on the Quadrant* (*Tractatus quadrantis*) of Robertus Anglicus, which described the use of an astronomical instrument known as the quadrant; the *Treatise on Weights* (*Tractatus de ponderibus*) associ-

71

ated with the name of Jordanus de Nemore and concerned with the subject of statics;[14] and treatises on perspective or optics drawn from works by Ptolemy, Alhazen, John Pecham, Roger Bacon, and others.[15]

Although medieval technical astronomy was based on the famous *Almagest* of Ptolemy, which appears on curriculum lists, it is implausible to suppose that anything more than the descriptive sections of the first book could have served as a text. Since the objective of astronomical instruction was "to enable students to understand the position of the planets and to calculate the variable feast days of the ecclesiastical year,"[16] two elementary thirteenth-century texts came to serve the first of these goals, namely, the understanding of the planetary positions. The most famous of these is surely the *Sphere* (*De sphaera*) of John of Sacrobosco, which provided a general cosmological and astronomical sketch of the different components of the finite, spherical universe accepted by all during the Middle Ages.[17] From Sacrobosco's introduction we learn that he has divided the treatise into four chapters, "telling first, what a sphere is, what its center is, what the axis of a sphere is, what the pole of the world is, how many spheres there are, and what the shape of the world is. In the second we give information concerning the circles of which this material sphere is composed and that supercelestial one, of which this is the image. . . . In the third we talk about the rising and setting of the signs, and the diversity of days and nights which happens to those inhabiting diverse localities, and the division into climes. In the fourth the matter concerns the circles and motions of planets, and the causes of eclipses."[18] The treatment of the planets in the fourth book was, however, so meager that an unknown teacher of astronomy composed another treatise, *The Theory of the Planets* (*Theorica planetarum*),[19] that consisted of numerous definitions describing all aspects of planetary motion. Along with Sacrobosco's *Sphere*, the anonymous *Theory of the Planets* served to introduce generations of students to the basic elements of planetary astronomy and to provide them with a skeletal frame of the cosmos.

To achieve the second objective and enable students to compute the variable feast days in the ecclesiastical calendar, *compotus* treatises, representing practical astronomy, were employed, most notably those written in the thirteenth century by Robert Grosseteste and John of Sacrobosco.[20]

Only in arithmetic and music was there a continuation with the quadrivial tradition of the early Middle Ages. In these subjects, Boethius' *Arithmetica* and *Musica*[21] served as the basic links. But even here treatises translated in the twelfth century or newly composed in the thirteenth and fourteenth augmented the Boethian texts. Arithmetic, which in its Boethian tradition was of a largely theoretical nature, was supplemented by books 7 to 9 of Euclid's *Elements*, which treated of number theory.[22] To this was added a strong practical component in the form of treatises that described and exemplified the four arithmetic operations for whole numbers, as, for example, Sacrobosco's enormously popular *Algorismus vulgaris*,[23] and fractions, the latter usually under titles such as *Algorismus minutiarum* or *Algorismus de minutiis*.[24] In music, the traditional treatises of Boethius and St. Augustine (*De musica*) were supplemented by the early fourteenth-century treatises of Johannis de Muris (John of Murs). Of some four or five musical treatises, most significant were his *Musica speculativa secundum Boetium*, a commentary on the *Musica* of Boethius, and his *Ars nove musice* (*The Art of the New Music*).[25]

The significance attached to the exact sciences in the university curriculum does not emerge from curriculum lists, which are at best sporadic and spare of detail. We can best infer their importance from the attitudes of different scholastic authors who were also university teachers. Geometry was no longer valued merely for its practical use in measurement or even as a vital aid for philosophical understanding. Roger Bacon and Alexander Hales extolled its virtues as a tool for the comprehension of theological truth.[26] Geometry was essential for a proper understanding of the literal sense of numerous passages, descriptions, and allusions in Scripture, as, for example, Noah's ark and the temple of Solomon. Only by interpreting the literal sense with the aid of geometry could the higher spiritual sense be grasped. But it was not spiritual truth alone that was at issue in the study of geometry. Robert Grosseteste, in his treatise *On Lines, Angles, and Figures,* conceived of geometry as essential to natural philosophy.[27] Since the universe was constituted of lines, angles, and figures, it could not be properly understood without geometry. Indeed, geometry was required for comprehending the behavior of light, which was multiplied and disseminated in nature geometrically, as were most physical effects.[28]

Arithmetic was equally valued and was often placed first among the mathematical sciences, although in an imaginary debate between geometry and arithmetic, Nicole Oresme implies that the former ranks higher than the latter.[29] In that interesting and unusual dialogue, arithmetic presents itself as the firstborn of all the mathematical sciences and the source of all rational ratios and therefore the cause of the commensurability of the celestial motions and the harmony of the spheres. Moreover, prediction of the future depends upon exact astronomical tables, which must be founded on the precise numbers of arithmetic. In a fascinating rebuttal, geometry claims greater dominion than arithmetic since it embraces both rational and irrational ratios. As for the beautiful harmony allegedly brought into the world by the rationality of arithmetic, geometry counters by noting that the rich diversity of the world could only be generated by a combination of rational and irrational ratios, which it alone can produce. Geometry and arithmetic were both valued because they were essential to penetrate the workings of nature and to describe the great variety of motions and actions in the physical world. The medieval emphasis on geometry and arithmetic may come as a surprise to those who are wrongly convinced that medieval Aristotelian natural philosophers and theologians were hostile to mathematics.[30]

The science of astronomy, which included astrology,[31] was also regularly lauded as an essential instrument for the comprehension of the macrocosm. It could predict, though not determine, future events. Bacon judged it essential for church and state, as well as for farmers, alchemists, and physicians;[32] Grosseteste considered it invaluable for many other sciences, including alchemy and botany.[33] The significance of astrology and astronomy for medicine, which Bacon and many others routinely emphasized, was manifested at the University of Paris in the 1360s by the foundation of the College of Maître Gervais,[34] which was endowed with books and instruments by King Charles V and subsequently approved by Pope Urban V. So strong was the interest in astrology that in 1366 candidates for the license in arts were required to read "some books in mathematics," which probably included books on astrology since the latter subject was also implied by the term "mathematics."[35]

Music was also accorded high status. It was significant in medicine since physicians could employ it as part of the overall regimen of health. As a factor in stirring the passions in war and soothing them in peace, the study of the mathematical structure of music was deemed helpful and worthwhile. It was even important for the theologian, as Roger Bacon emphasized. Since musical expressions and instruments are mentioned frequently in Scripture, the wise theologian would do well to learn as much about music as possible.[36]

One as yet unmentioned but significant component of the science curriculum of the medieval university is medicine. As one of the three separate higher faculties, medicine was taught only to those who chose to matriculate for a medical degree. It was not an arts subject as were all of the sciences considered thus far. Prior to its institutionalization in the major medieval universities, especially Bologna and Paris, medicine had been taught during the thirteenth century at specialized centers such as Salerno and Montpellier.[37] With its installation as a higher faculty in the medieval university, medicine became a profession and was therefore the first science to achieve professional status.[38] Prior to the emergence of universities, medicine had been accorded a modest, and even lowly, place in the hierarchy of the arts and sciences.[39] Its orientation was toward the practical with theories that were rather specific to medicine. With its acceptance into the university, it was soon amalgamated with the newly arrived Aristotelian natural philosophy and developed into a highly theoretical and speculative discipline.[40] Except for Italy, an undesirable consequence of the emphasis on theory was the exclusion of surgeons and surgery from medieval medical schools.[41]

That Italian medical schools generally avoided the divorce of surgery and medicine may perhaps provide a small clue toward the explanation of the reemergence of the practice of human dissection at the University of Bologna after a lapse of approximately one thousand years.[42] Although the first recorded anatomical dissection at Bologna was that of Bartolommeo da Varignana in 1302, the practice probably began in the latter part of the thirteenth century. Human dissection in the medical schools undoubtedly intensified interest in the study of human anatomy. Because of its extraordinary role in medical education, human dissection was occasionally worthy of mention by those who witnessed one or more of them in the lecture hall. The famous surgeon, Guy de Chauliac (1298–1368), has described how his master, Bertuccio, proceeded through a dissection in four stages, or cuts, anatomizing first the "nutritive" members, then the "spiritual" members, then the "animal" members, and finally the "extremities."[43] Lacking refrigeration, anatomical dissections were performed only in winter and, for obvious reasons, were done as quickly as possible. When bodies with internal organs and soft parts were unavailable, anatomies were performed on skeletal remains. Without dissections— and bodies were not easy to come by—Henri de Mondeville (d. ca. 1326) resorted to colored anatomical illustrations, a practice that was probably not widespread.[44]

The anatomies performed in the medical schools of medieval universities were not, however, intended for research but were solely for instructional purposes. Despite the use of so vivid a visual aid, the parts of the body and their relationships were seen through the texts of the great medical authorities such as Galen and Avicenna. Traditional errors were usually perpetuated and new knowledge was minimal. In time, anatomy professors even ceased to teach directly from the cadavers they dissected and instead confined themselves to formal lectures while an assistant actually illustrated the body.[45]

Unfortunately for our knowledge of the quadrivial sciences, no dramatic counterpart to human dissection emerged to prompt an occasional remark on classroom procedure and teaching technique. Although the exact sciences of the quadrivium were judged useful for the study of physical nature and Scripture, the texts representing the different sciences appear on required curriculum lists from time to time and we can even occasionally learn the length of time devoted to a particular text, the sources have thus far been silent on the manner in which these subjects were actually taught in the classroom. Did the students memorize some or most texts, which may have been prohibitively expensive?[46] Did they solve problems? Were visual aids used in teaching astronomy and geometry? Was the abacus used in practical arithmetic? Were Arabic numerals employed for computations?[47] On these and other vital matters we are largely ignorant.

Teaching aids were not unknown, although the specific information available seems confined to the early Middle Ages prior to the universities. Gerbert of Aurillac (946–1003), who became Pope Sylvester II, was reputed to have used visual aids in his teachings. His pupil, Richer, describes globes and spheres designed and constructed by Gerbert solely for instructional purposes. One of these simulated the motions of the constellations, where the latter were shaped and represented by means of wires fixed to the sphere, the axis of which was made from a metal tube through the center of the globe.[48] Thus did Gerbert fix the shapes of the different stellar configurations on the minds of his pupils and also show them how all rotate relative to one another. During the eleventh and twelfth centuries, the game of *rithmomachia*, mentioned by John of Salisbury and Alan of Lille, may have been used as a teaching aid and has been described as "the great medieval number game."[49] It was played upon a table or board divided into a series of squares, and by means of its rules a student could become familiar with arithmetic, geometric, and harmonic proportions, as well as with numerical progressions and the different numerical ratios used in the Middle Ages, such as multiple, superparticular, and superpartient. The educational value of the game lay in its stress on the rules of proportion defined and discussed in the *Arithmetica* of Boethius which, as we saw, was used as an arithmetic text throughout the Middle Ages. Played at first with Roman numerals and later with Arabic, it would undoubtedly have proved useful in the study of music, geometry, and astronomy, since facility with numbers was important in all of the quadrivial subjects. Although rithmomachia texts do not appear in the curriculum lists, they may have been used nonetheless.

Aside from the possible use of teaching aids in the quadrivium, the manner of teaching the exact sciences in the medieval university is virtually unknown. Perhaps it was much the same as the teaching of natural philosophy from the natural books, or *libri naturales*, of Aristotle about which we know much more and to which we must now turn.

The natural books of Aristotle, which formed the core of the curriculum in natural philosophy at all medieval universities, consisted of the *Physics*, the *De caelo* (*On the Heavens*), *On Generation and Corruption*, *On the Soul*, *Meteorology*, *Parva Nauralia* (*The Small Works on Natural Things*), as well as the biological works such as *The History of Animals*, *The Parts of Animals*, and the *Generation of Animals*. Here then were the treatises that formed the comprehensive foundation for the medieval conception of the physical world and its operations. Although some students at medieval universities were content to acquire only a bachelor's or master of arts degree and others subsequently entered the higher faculties of law, medicine, and theology, all studied the natural books of Aristotle. More than anything else, it is that shared experience that enables us to characterize medieval education as essentially scientific. That Aristotle's scientific books should have formed the basis of university education for some four centuries comes as a surprise when one contemplates the intense and bitter resistance those books met when initially introduced into the University of Paris in the thirteenth century.[50] For the first time in the history of Latin Christendom, a conceptually rich and methodologically powerful body of secular learning posed a threat to theology and its traditional interpretations. Although many theologians and almost all masters of

78

arts eagerly embraced the new Aristotelian learning, there was a growing uneasiness among certain traditionally-minded theologians. With its emphasis on the eternity of the world, the unicity of the intellect, and its naturalistic and deterministic modes of explanation, the Aristotelian world system was not easily reducible to the status of a theological handmaiden, as abortive attempts to ban and then expurgate the texts of Aristotle in the first half of the thirteenth century at Paris bear witness. By the 1260s and 1270s, an intensive effort was made to control the new learning and bring it into conformity with the aims and objectives of traditional theology. This time, however, the weapons employed were not the ban or expurgation, but the outright condemnation or restriction of a whole range of ideas deemed dangerous and reprehensible. The modest Condemnation of 1270 and the massive one of 219 propositions in 1277 by the bishop of Paris and his advisers were an attempt to curb the pretensions of Aristotelian natural philosophy by emphasizing the absolute power of God to do whatever He pleased short of a logical contradiction, even if that meant the invocation of hypothetical and real divine actions that were impossible in the natural world as conceived by Aristotle and his followers.[51]

Despite the effect all this had on the interpretation of Aristotelian natural philosophy, the natural books of Aristotle remained the heart of medieval university education. There was never any serious attempt to dislodge them after 1250. It was because of a world view derived from Aristotle's natural books that C. S. Lewis could declare that "the human imagination has seldom had before it an object so sublimely ordered as the medieval cosmos."[52] The primary purpose of a medieval university arts education was to enable students to comprehend and interpret the structure and operation of that sublime cosmos.

The manner of achieving this laudable objective was made to depend on lectures and disputation. Lectures were at first largely sequential section-by-section expositions or commentaries on each required text. Here the master read a passage of the text and explained its meaning to the students. When he had finished read-

79

ing and explaining a number of passages or sections (*textus*) of an Aristotelian work, it became customary to pose a question on those passages and to present the pros and cons of it followed by a proposed solution.[53] These questions frequently formed the basis of the master's *Questiones* on that particular Aristotelian work. In time, however, the questions previously posed toward the end of a lecture came to displace the commentary on the text itself. Thus the mode of teaching came eventually to concentrate on specific questions (*questions*) or problems that followed the order of the required text and developed from it.[54] The written forms of this pedagogical technique that have survived are usually associated with the names of well-known masters who presumably gave some version of the surviving written text in their lectures.

In its public oral version, arts and theology masters were concerned with questions (*questiones disputate*) either in the form of ordinary or magisterial disputations where the master himself posed and answered the questions or in the form of extraordinary or quodlibetal disputations where the questions were raised by the audience and ultimately resolved by the master.[55] In all of these sessions, the undergraduate and/or bachelor was expected to participate either as a respondent (*respondens*) to objections posed during the dispute or as the one who resolves or determines a question under the supervision of a master.[56] Responding to questions and determining them was thus an integral and vital part of the training and education of all who would eventually become masters of arts. For the masters themselves it was a regular feature of intellectual life.

Whatever the roles of masters and students in the disputed questions at the medieval universities, it is clear that the question form of scholastic literature lay at the heart of the educational system. Science, which constituted the core of the curriculum, was thus taught by the analysis of a series of questions posed by a master and eventually determined by him. Many of these *questiones* on the different works of Aristotle, and other texts as well, were written down and published through university auspices. Each question followed a fairly standard format. The enunciation of the question was always followed by one or more solutions supporting either the affirmative or negative position. If the affirmative position was initially favored, the reader could confidently assume that the author would ultimately adopt the negative position; or conversely, if the negative side appeared first, it could be assumed that the author would subsequently adopt and defend the affirmative side. The initial opinions, which would subsequently be rejected, were called the "principal arguments" (*rationes principales*). Following the enunciation of the principal arguments, the author might then describe his procedure and perhaps further clarify and qualify the question or define and explain particular terms in it. He was now ready to present his own opinions, usually by way of one or more detailed conclusions or propositions. Often, in order to anticipate objections he would raise doubts about his own conclusions and subsequently resolve them. At the very end of the question, he would respond to each of the "principal arguments" enunciated at the beginning of the question.

By its very nature, the *questio* form encouraged differences of opinion. It was a vehicle *par excellence* for dispute and argumentation. Medieval scholastics were trained to dispute and consequently often disagreed among themselves.[57] Far from a slavish devotion to Aristotle, they were emboldened by the very system within which they were nurtured to arrive at their own opinions. The system would have been very different indeed had it simply provided them with a conclusion and then merely supplied a rationale and defense of that conclusion. But medieval scholasticism always posed at least two options and often many more. In principle, one was expected to evaluate arguments critically and by a process of elimination arrive at truth. Scholastic ingenuity was displayed by introducing subtle distinctions that, upon further development, might well yield new opinions on a given question. It is thus hardly surprising that centuries of disputation should have produced a variety of opinions on a very large number of questions. Hundreds of questions drawn from Aristotle's natural books formed the basic substance of natural sciences as taught and studied at the medieval university.[58] Not only were they concerned with the nature and behavior of the noble and near perfect celestial region and the less perfect generable and corruptible elemental and compound bodies of the sublunar realm, but they also inquired about the eternity of the world and whether other worlds, or an infinite space, might lie beyond ours. The nature of the celestial region, or heaven, was of major concern and elicited such questions as whether it was light or heavy and whether it had absolute directions, such as up and down, front and behind, and right and left. Was celestial matter similar to terrestial matter and therefore subject to the Aristotelian categories of change in substance, quantity, quality, and place? Or was it immutable, in which event the very conception of a celestial "matter" was called into question. Since medieval scholars were almost unanimous in their belief that the planets and stars were carried around on physical spheres, a variety of questions were posed about the nature and motion of those spheres. What is their total number and how are they moved — by angels? forms? souls? or perhaps by some inherent principle? Are the celestial movers integral to the orbs they move, or distinct from them? Do those movers experience fatigue and exhaustion? Does God move the *primum mobile*, or first movable sphere, directly and actively as an efficient cause, or only as a final and ultimate cause? Are all the orbs of the same specific nature? Are they concentric with the earth as center or is it necessary to assume real eccentric and epicyclic orbs? The causative influences of the celestial region on the terrestrial were also of great interest and concern for astrology and natural philosophy, evoking numerous questions about the nature of the forces involved in this unidirectional relationship. Are the celestial and terrestrial regions continuous or discontinuous? How are the various phenomena of the upper terrestrial region, such as comets, the Milky Way, and the rainbow, formed, and what are they made of? Questions were also posed about the nature of the terrestrial region that was deemed so radically different from the superior and more perfect celestial region. Here the focus was on elements and compounds and their interrelationships and motions. Do elements remain or persist in a compound? Are there only four elements? Is there any pure element? Can one element be generated directly from another? Does a compound or mixed body consist of all four elements? What is the cause of the natural motions of light and heavy bodies? Is there something absolutely heavy and something absolutely light? Finally, questions were also posed about the earth and its relation to the cosmos: Is the earth spherical? Is it always at rest in the center of the world? Is its size as a mere point in comparison to the heavens?

Science at the medieval universities consisted of responses and solutions to questions of the kind just described. Generation after generation of masters of arts taught and wrote on such questions, and generations of students were considered to have been properly educated if they could absorb and master the diverse and often conflicting responses to these seemingly innumerable problems. To understand the nature and content of medieval natural science as taught at the medieval university one must become familiar with the vast *questiones* literature.[59]

The *questiones* on the Aristotelian natural books may have represented the scientific fare of the masters of arts and the hordes of undergraduates and bachelors of arts whom they taught, but it is only one aspect of the natural philosophy and science of the medieval university. Our description would be incomplete and defective without mention of the relevant scientific discussion in the theological faculty. Here masters and bachelors in theology were regularly confronted with problems about the nature of the physical world and its creation. Not only were traditional commentaries produced on the creation and structure of the world as described in *Genesis*, but even more important were the commentaries and *questiones* on the *Sentences* of Peter Lombard, a theological treatise written around 1150 and divided into four books devoted, respectively, to God, the Creation, the Incarnation, and the Sacraments.[60] As the standard text on which all theological students had to lecture and comment for some four centuries, the second book on creation afforded ample opportunity to reflect on the origin and operation of the physical world.[61] In considering the six days of creation, medieval theologians, most of whom were also masters of arts thoroughly trained in the natural philosophy of Aristotle and the medieval disputes embedded in the *questiones* literature, injected much contemporary physical theory into their theological deliberations. Problems lurking in the creation account made this almost inevitable, as is evident when they tried to distinguish the heaven, or firmament, created on the first day from the heaven created on the second day; or when they sought to explain the differences, if any, between the light mentioned on the first day and the visible, familiar light associated with the sun and the other celestial luminaries created on the fourth day; or when they were compelled to explain the distinction, if any, between the waters above the firmament and the waters below. But it was not the creation account alone that encouraged theologians to inject science into their explanations, but also problems such as the whereabouts of God and the motions of angels discussed in the first book of the *Sentences*. God's location served as a point of departure for discussions about the possible existence of an infinite extracosmic space; the motion and the positions of angels raised problems about space, place, and the continuum when it was found necessary to distinguish the ways in which angels moved and occupied places from the way bodies did.[62] But theologians also eagerly introduced logic and mathematics into their responses to purely theological problems in the *Sentences*.[63] The amounts of grace, merit, sin, and reward that might be dispensed by God were often discussed in a context of the intension and remission of forms and were expressed in the language of proportions and proportionality relations that had been evolved in natural philosophy. Problems of infinity and continuity in a logicomathematical context were frequently introduced into discussions as to whether God's power was capable of producing infinitely intensive qualities and attributes.[64] The widespread acceptance of the doctrine of God's absolute power to do whatever He pleased short of a logical contradiction generated innumerable speculations *secundum imaginationem* in which God was imagined to perform some act according to some given proportional relationship.[65] Many of the acts that God was imagined to perform were couched in logicomathematical terms and concepts imported from natural philosophy or were contrary to traditional Aristotelian conceptions of the physical world.

Theologians played a significant role in developing the character and content of natural philosophy and science in the medieval university. It is no accident that the greatest medieval figures in science were also theologians, as the names of Albertus Magnus, Thomas Aquinas, Duns Scotus, William Ockham, Thomas Bradwardine, Nicole Oresme, Theodoric of Freiberg, and Henry of Hesse, to name only a few, bear witness. Theologians were, of course, not inherently more brilliant in such matters than masters of arts who remained as teachers and scholars in the arts faculty. Theologians were simply better trained than their counterparts in the arts faculty. Not only were they thoroughly versed in Aristotelian science and philosophy, but they were the recipients of some eight or nine years of rigorous training in the subtleties of theology. Since theology and theological considerations played a vital role in many questions of natural philosophy, theologians had a considerable advantage over arts masters. But if that were not enough, masters of arts, who were untrained in theology, were forbidden at the University of Paris to discuss "any question which seems to touch both faith and philosophy" unless they resolved the question in favor of the faith. Required to take an oath to this effect beginning in 1272, masters of arts were intimidated by the theologians and generally omitted theological considerations from their deliberations, even where these might have been relevant.[66] An illustration of the manner in which arts masters might have felt frustrated and intimidated by theologians is available from the works of John Buridan, probably the greatest natural philosopher among the Parisian arts masters in the fourteenth century. Considering the possibility of the existence of vacuum in his *Questions on the Physics* which, according to Buridan himself, touches faith and theology more than any other question, Buridan felt that despite his oath, he had to introduce theological considerations or avoid entirely a range of arguments in opposition to his own position that were yet essential to the whole question.[67] It is clear from the context that Buridan felt constrained to introduce no theological material into the argument, even though this meant that he could not treat the question honestly. Elsewhere, Buridan shows much deference to the theologians, as when he declares, for example, with Aristotle, that no body exists beyond the world, but immediately informs his reader that "you ought to have recourse to the theologians [in order to learn] what must be said about this according to the truth of faith."[68]

The oath of 1272 required at the University of Paris of all masters of arts throughout the fourteenth and perhaps most, if not all, of the fifteenth century clearly raises the question of freedom of scientific inquiry at the University of Paris. To the oath of 1272 must, of course, be added the Condemnation of 1277, which was also in effect throughout the fourteenth century and perhaps the fifteenth as well. Many of the articles condemned forbade approval, under penalty of excommunication, of Aristotle's fundamental conviction of the eternity of the world; they compelled arts masters to accept the possibility that God could create other worlds, or that He could move our world with a rectilinear motion despite the vacuum that would be left behind, even though these hypothetical situations were judged impossible within Aristotelian natural philosophy.[69] We must inquire, therefore, whether these and other restrictions contained in the Condemnation of 1277, as well as the denial to masters of arts of the right to discuss purely theological questions, seriously curtailed freedom of inquiry in natural philosophy and restricted investigation of scientific problems.

Despite a degree of intimidation where theological issues might have been relevant to the proper discussion of a scientific question (as with Buridan above), the pursuit of natural philosophy was not really hampered or restricted by theologians, by university authorities, or by church or state. The conflict between philosophy and faith in the thirteenth century produced a situation in the fourteenth in which the arts masters were willing to leave theology to the theologians and hoped, though in vain, that the theologians would leave philosophy and natural science to the arts masters.[70] Although all had to accept the truth of basic Christian doctrine, propositions contrary to those truths could be discussed speculatively under the guise of "speaking philosophically" or "speaking naturally" (*loquendo naturaliter*).[71] By accepting doctrinal truth on faith and confining themselves to the domain of natural philosophy or science, arts masters could avoid almost all consideration of the miraculous in nature.[72] As a representative of this approach, John Buridan was probably typical of the arts masters in the fourteenth century. Rather than become preoccupied with supernatural possibilities, which could pose theological difficulties for a master of arts, Buridan devoted himself to the analysis and comprehension of the behavior of natural powers.[73] He sought to defend Aristotelian science as the best means of understanding the physical world, although he disagreed on numerous significant points with Aristotle. Readily conceding that God could interfere at any time and alter the natural course of events, as was demanded by the Condemnation of 1277, Buridan, nevertheless, assumed that "in natural philosophy, we ought to accept actions and dependencies as if they always proceed in a natural way." Should conflict arise between the Catholic faith and Aristotle's arguments, which, after all, are based only on sensation and experience, it is not necessary to believe Aristotle, as, for example, on the doctrine of the eternity of the world. And yet, if we wish to confine ourselves to a consideration of natural powers only, it is appropriate to accept Aristotle's opinion on the eternity of the world, *as if it were true*. As with most arts masters, Buridan was primarily interested in arriving at truths about the regular operations of the physical world in the "common course of nature" (*communis cursus nature*) and little concerned with all the hypothetical natural impossibilities that God might perform but which He probably hadn't performed and very likely would not perform.

The basis for a "common course of nature" could be established, in Buridan's view, by formulating laws and principles from inductive generalizations aided by reason. Such laws need not be absolute but empirical, "accepted because they have been observed to be true in many instances and to be false in none." Since Buridan's methodology of science was predicated on the "common course of nature," God's intervention in the causal order, which all acknowledged possible, became irrelevant. Thus could Buridan proclaim that "for us the comprehension of truth and certitude is possible." Using reason and experience, Buridan sought to "save the phenomena" in accordance with the principle of Ockham's razor—that is by the simplest explanation that fit the evidence.

Despite the theological condemnation of 1277 and their sworn oath not to dispute theological questions, arts masters were remarkably free to pursue their investigations and to arrive at whatever opinions they pleased. The enormous *questiones* literature with its hundreds of problems demonstrates this beyond any reasonable doubt. The majority of questions taken up in the natural books of Aristotle produced at least two opposing opinions and occasionally more. Some of these alternatives won a consensus among the masters, others did not. Without an atmosphere of intellectual freedom, such diversity could not have been achieved.[74]

In fact, the most famous (or perhaps infamous) of medieval theological condemnations, that of 1277, may have served to stimulate intellectual and scientific curiosity even as it sought to inhibit and curtail academic inquiry. By emphasizing God's absolute power to do anything short of a logical contradiction, the Condemnation of 1277 encouraged numerous invocations and applications of God's absolute power to a variety of hypothetical physical situations.[75] The supernatural alternatives that scholastics at the University of Paris considered in the wake of the condemnation conditioned them to consider possibilities outside the ken of Aristotelian natural philosophy and usually in direct conflict with it, as, for example, the conditions that would obtain if God created a plurality of worlds, or moved the world with a rectilinear motion leaving a vacuum behind, or created an accident without a subject. So widespread was the contemplation of such hypothetical possibilities in the late Middle Ages that it is no exaggeration to view them as an integral feature of late medieval thought. Encouraged to pursue the consequences of hypothetical situations that were naturally impossible in Aristotelian science, scholastics showed that alternatives to Aristotelian physics and cosmology were not only intelligible but even plausible. Although such speculations did not cause the overthrow of the Aristotelian world view, they did challenge some of its fundamental principles and made many aware that things could be otherwise than was dreamt of in Aristotle's philosophy. Freedom of inquiry into the physical operations and principles of the world was little hindered and obstructed by theology and theologians during the Middle Ages. To the contrary, theological restrictions may actually have stimulated the contemplation of plausible (and even implausible) physical alternatives and possibilities far beyond those that Aristotelian natural philosophers might otherwise have considered.

Free though it was to pursue almost any lines of inquiry, science at the medieval university remained largely a bookish tradition based primarily on the works of Aristotle and Averroes and the technical treatises associated with the exact sciences of the quadrivium. With a few notable exceptions (e. g., Theodoric of Freiberg's *On the Rainbow* and perhaps Peter Peregrinus' *Letter on the Magnet*),[76] science in the medieval university was neither experimental nor truly empirical. Despite occasional glimmerings of a concept of scientific progress, such an idea was essentially alien to medieval thought.[77] Scientific knowledge and an understanding of nature's operations and structure were derived primarily from the study of established authors. By careful analysis of such venerable texts, it was possible to gain new insights and to develop further the traditional wisdom. Occasionally, original contributions were even made and the *moderni* were sometimes consciously aware that they had developed a new technique for the treatment of an old or new problem. Moreover, there were always opportunities to conjure up daring and novel imaginative hypothetical physical situations by appeal to God's absolute power. But in its fundamental features, medieval science was essentially a rational inquiry based on the world view embedded in the natural books of Aristotle. Although scholastic natural philosophers produced numerous alternative solutions to most of the problems or *questiones* with which they were regularly concerned, they had no mechanisms for choosing among them. As the primary vehicle for the development and expression of scientific ideas and conclusions, the scholastic *questio* form contained within itself the strengths and weaknesses of medieval science as practiced and taught at medieval universities. By enunciating problems in the form of a question rather than as an already derived conclusion, the scholastic *questio* encouraged the presentation of the pros and cons of an argument. Each question contained all of the worthy arguments for and against it. Authors not only argued for their own conclusions, but were always expected to refute the contrary positions. In this way careful analysis was encouraged and a reasonably complete picture of all the relevant arguments and conclusions was available to subsequent readers who might then make yet further additions and alterations. At its best, the scholastic *questio* was a thorough method for the analysis of scientific problems.

But there were serious deficiencies in medieval scholastic procedure. Although the multiplication of opinions is a sign of free inquiry, there was no means of deciding most issues other than by consensus, which, often enough, was lacking. For how could one determine the true number of invisible celestial spheres; whether they formed a continuum or were merely contiguous; or what was the true cause of the natural motion of elemental bodies; or whether there was an internal resistance in compound bodies, as some believed? The *questio* form of scientific inquiry suffered from another grave deficiency. As the major form of scholastic literature for the pursuit of science and natural philosophy, the *questiones* produced an atomization of Aristotle's physical treatises into sequences of particular questions and problems that focused attention on the independent question and, as a consequence, tended to sever each question from its connections and associations with other related issues treated in the same work or elsewhere in the Aristotelian corpus.[78] Not only were related topics unintegrated, but even single topics were left in the form of a series of specific questions that were not organized into a larger, coherent, integrated whole. In this way, serious deficiencies and weaknesses of Aristotelian and contemporary science went undetected or overlooked. Primacy of the independent question in medieval Aristotelian physics and cosmology prevented, or at least seriously inhibited, any larger synthesis that might have revealed glaring

90

inconsistencies within the intricate Aristotelian world view. As long as Aristotelian science dominated the medieval university, the *questio* form of inquiry was its most characteristic feature, with the straightforward commentary also of importance. Even Galileo, while a young professor at the University of Pisa around 1590, found occasion to write *questiones* on Aristotle's *De caelo* and *On Generation and Corruption*.[79] By the late sixteenth century, however, Jesuit scholars developed the *cursus philosophicus*, which largely abandoned the formal procedure of the *questio* in favor of a more developed and integrated narrative account. The subject matter, however, remained much the same. Although the medieval university with its largely Aristotelian curriculum continued into the seventeenth century, its intellectual dominance was by then at an end. A new science based on a heliocentric astronomy and cosmology and a different physics had come into being. With its emergence, science moved outside its traditional university setting where Aristotelianism continued to reign and control the curriculum. The medieval university was now an anachronism and embarrassment. In time, the new science would reenter the university, but only as one of a number of subjects, where it now had to fight for its place in the curriculum. Never again would science achieve the exalted and almost exclusive status it held in the medieval university.

It is now time to assess the role of medieval science as it was institutionalized in the medieval university. Or to put it another way, what was the significance of the medieval university with its almost exclusive concern with the science of its day? What was its legacy to Western civilization? To understand and appreciate the medieval contribution, we must begin with the massive translations of the twelfth and thirteenth centuries. Near the beginning of this paper were mentioned two consequences of this extraordinary phenomenon. The translations of Greco-Arabic science, with Aristotle's natural books forming the core, laid the foundation for the continuous development of science to the present and also provided a curriculum that made possible the development of the university as we recognize it today.

Without the translations, which furnished a well articulated body of theoretical science to Western Europe, the great scientists of the sixteenth and seventeenth centuries, such as Copernicus, Galileo, Descartes, and Newton, would have had little to reflect upon and reject, little that could focus their attention on significant physical problems. Many of the burning issues of puzzling scientific problems that were resolved in the Scientific Revolution of the seventeenth century entered Western Europe with the translations or were brought forth by university-trained medieval natural philosophers who systematically commented upon that impressive body of knowledge. The overthrow of one world system by another does not imply a lack of continuity. Medieval science, based on the translations of the twelfth and thirteenth centuries, furnished the physicists and natural philosophers of the seventeenth century with issues, theories, and principles that had to be rejected in order for significant advances to be made. That what emerged was radically different should not blind us to the essential continuity of inquiry between medieval and seventeenth century science. Although solutions differed, many fundamental problems were common to both. With the introduction of Greco-Arabic science during the twelfth and thirteenth centuries, Western Europe began an unprecedented and uninterrupted concern for the nature and structure of the physical world. To its everlasting glory, the medieval university was the fundamental instrumentality for this epoch-making and still continuing chapter in the history of Western civilization.

1. An emiment physicist, Duhem not only published hundreds of papers in physics, but also wrote fifteen volumes on medieval science embraced within three works: *Les Origines de la Statique*, 2 vols. (Paris, 1905–6); *Etudes sur Léonard de Vinci ceux qu'il a lus et ceux qui l'ont lu*, 3 vols. (Paris, 1906–13); *Le Système du monde: histoire des doctrines cosmologiques de Platon à Copernic*, 10 vols. (1913–59), the last five volumes of which were published posthumously. For many topics, these works still form an indispensable point of departure. A brief biographical sketch of Duhem (with primary and secondary bibliography) by Donald G. Miller appears in the *Dictionary of Scientific Biography*, 16 vols, ed. Charles C. Gillispie (New York, 1970–1980), 4:225–33.

2. Walter J. Ong has perceptively observed that "because of the university curriculum, a distinctive feature of late medieval civilization was an organized and protracted study of physics which was more intense and widespread than ever before. Greek or Roman civiliza-

tions had seen nothing on this scale" (*Ramus: Method, and the Decay of Dialogue from the Art of Discourse to the Art of Reason* [Cambridge, Mass., 1958], p. 144). By "physics" Ong means "natural science" (p. 142) or natural philosophy. He notes further (pp. 144–45) that the medieval study of Aristotle polarized around a "logic-and-physics" context rather than one of "metaphysics-and-theology."

3. For a recent valuable and informative article on the translations, see David C. Lindberg, "The Transmission of Greek and Arabic Learning to the West," in David C. Lindberg, ed., *Science in the Middle Ages* (Chicago, 1978), pp. 52–90. Although translations of scientific works from Arabic to Latin actually began during the tenth and eleventh centuries, the works that would be fundamental to the university arts curriculum, especially those of Aristotle, were only translated during the twelfth and thirteenth centuries.

4. See M. D. Chenu, *Nature, Man, and Society in the Twelfth Century, Essays on New Theological Perspectives in the Latin West*, selected, edited, and translated by Jerome Taylor and Lester K. Little (Chicago, 1968; original French version published in 1957), p. 33; on "The Discovery of Nature," see pp. 4–18; Brian Stock, *Myth and Science in the Twelfth Century, A Study of Bernard Silvester* (Princeton, 1972), pp. 271–73. For the strongest claims on the critical objectivity of twelfth-century scholars, see two articles by Tina Stiefel: "Science, Reason and Faith in the Twelfth Century: the Cosmologists' Attack on Tradition," *Journal of European Studies* 6 (1976): 1–16; "The Heresy of Science: A Twelfth-Century Conceptual Revolution," *Isis* 68 (1977): 347–62.

5. Many of these were translated by a single prolific translator, Gerard of Cremona, whose translations are listed and discussed by Michael McVaugh in Edward Grant, ed., *A Source Book in Medieval Science* (Cambridge, Mass., 1974), pp. 35–38; see also Richard Lemay, "Gerard of Cremona," *Dictionary of Scientific Biography*, vol. 15, (Supplement 1), pp. 173–92.

6. For a list of these translations, see Grant, *Source Book in Medieval Science*, pp.39–41.

7. The *libri morales* consisted of Aristotle's *Nichomachean Ethics, Politics and Economics*; the *Metaphysics* consisted primarily of the books of Aristotle's *Metaphysics*. The *libri naturales* will be detailed below. For the lists of books studied under the three philosophies, see James A. Weisheipl, O.P., "Curriculum of the Faculty of Arts at Oxford in the Early Fourteenth Century," *Mediaeval Studies* 26 (1964): 173–76, hereafter cited as "Curriculum at Oxford"; for more on the *libri morales*, see Nancy G. Siraisi, "The *libri morales* in the Faculty of Arts and Medicine at Bologna: Bartolomeo de Varignana and the Pseudo-Aristotelian Economics," *Science, Medicine and the University: 1200–1500, Essays in Honor of Pearl Kibre, Part 1, Manuscripta* 20 (1976): 105–18.

8. Logic was one of the subjects of the *trivium*. For a list of the works studied in logic during the thirteenth and early fourteenth centuries at Oxford, see Weisheipl, "Curriculum at Oxford," pp. 169–70. Although Weisheipl observed that logic at Oxford "occupied about half of the actual curriculum," it will not be considered further here since it was a tool of analysis rather than a science in its own right. Its importance in medieval university education was, however, enormous.

9. The term "quadrivium" was rarely used in university statutes (see Pearl Kibre, "The *Quadrivium* in the Thirteenth Century Universities [with Special Reference to Paris]," in *Arts libéreaux et philosophie au moyen âge: Actes du quatrième congrès international de philosophie médiévale, Université de Montréal, Canada, 27 août–2 septembre 1967* [Montreal: Institut d'études mediévalés; Paris, Librairie philosophique J. Vrin, 1969], p. 175) and does not seem to occur in curriculum lists. Hereafter cited as *Arts libéraux et philosophie au moyen âge*. The explanation may lie in the fact that the four traditional quadrivial sciences were not conceived as part of a liberal arts education. Indeed the seven liberal arts, though transmitted to the Middle Ages by the Latin Encyclopedists (Martianus Capella, Isidore of Seville,

Boethius) were not taught as such in the medieval universities. Thus, although all the subjects of the seven liberal arts were usually represented in the university curriculum, they were absorbed into a larger whole in which natural philosophy, metaphysics, and moral philosophy were the major components (See Philippe Delhaye, "La place des arts libéraux dans les programmes scolaires du xiiie siecle," in *Arts libéraux et philosophie au moyen âge*, pp. 169, 172). Moreover, the disciplines of the traditional quadrivium had undergone a transformation. Arithmetic, geometry, and astronomy, which were theoretical subjects in the liberal arts tradition, were enlarged in scope during the late Middle Ages to embrace practical and applied knowledge.

10. For the contrast between Oxford and Paris in the study of mathematics and the exact sciences in general, see Guy Beaujouan, "Motives and Opportunities for Science in the Medieval Universities," in A. C. Crombie, ed., *Scientific Change: Historical Studies in the Intellectual, Social and Technical Conditions for Scientific Discovery and Technical Invention, from Antiquity to the Present.* Symposium on the History of Science, University of Oxford 9–15 July 1961 (New York, 1963), pp. 221–22. Arithmetic was also taught outside the university at Oxford and in Italy.

11. Weisheipl, "Curriculum at Oxford", pp. 170–73. For additional curriculum information on the arts and sciences as taught at Bologna, Paris, and Oxford, see Hastings Rashdall, *The Universities of Europe in the Middle Ages*, a new edition by F. M. Powicke and A. B. Emden, 3 vols. (Oxford, 1936): 233–53 (Bologna); 1:433–96 (Paris); 3:140–68 (Oxford).

12. These books were probably in one of the versions attributed to Adelard of Bath in the twelfth century. For the history of the translations of Euclid's *Elements* in the Latin Middle ages, see John E. Murdoch, "Euclid: The Transmission of the Elements," *Dictionary of Scientific Biography*, (New York, 1971): 4:443–48.

13. "Treatises titled *Practica geometriae* (Applied or Practical Geometry) were written by Hugh of St. Victor, Leonardo Fibonacci, and Dominicus de Clavasio, while others, under different titles or anonymously, wrote similar treatises with substantially the same content." In these works, geometry was applied to height measurement (*altimetria*), surface measurement (*planimetria*), and the measurement of solids (*cosmimetria* or *stereometria*). "In each of these parts geometry was applied to determine various measurements in astronomy and optics, as well as to measure heights of mountains, depths of valleys, and in general, lengths, areas, and volumes" (Grant, *Source Book in Medieval Science*, p. 180). Although such works do not appear on the Oxford lists supplied by Weisheipl, they represent the most general treatises on applied geometry and would have been more appropriate than any of the works in this genre cited below. For typical problems translated from the *Practica geometriae* of Dominicus de Clavasio, see Grant, *Source Book in Medieval Science*, pp. 181–87.

14. According to Weisheipl, the text generally used was the *Elementa Jordani de ponderibus*, which, however, does not fit the titles identified by E. A. Moody and Marshall Clagett in their edition of *The Medieval Science of Weights* (*Scientia de ponderibus*), *Treatises Ascribed to Euclid, Archimedes, Thabit ibn Qurra, Jordanus de Nemore, and Blasius of Parma* with English Introductions, English Translations, and Notes (Madison, Wis., 1959).

15. For the manuscripts, printed editions, and translations of the optical works of these authors, see David C. Lindberg, *A Catalogue of Medieval and Renaissance Optical Manuscripts*, Subsidia Mediaevalia IV (Toronto, 1975).

16. Weisheiple, "Curriculum at Oxford," p. 172.

17. For the Latin text and English translations, see Lynn Thorndike, ed. and trans., *The Sphere of Sacrobosco and Its Commentators* (Chicago, 1949), pp. 76–142.

18. Ibid., p. 118.

19. Olaf Pedersen estimates at least 200 extant manuscripts of the *Theorica planetarum* (see

his "The Theorica Planetarum – Literature of the Middle Ages," *Classica et Mediaevalia, Revue Danoise de Philologie et d'Histoire* [1962]: 23:225–26). For Pedersen's introduction to, and translation of, the *Theorica*, see Grant, *Source Book in Medieval Science*, pp. 451–65.

20. Weisheipl, "Curriculum at Oxford," pp. 172–73. University professors wrote numerous treatises on the quadrivial sciences some, or even many, of which may have been used as texts at some time or other. Mere absence from a curriculum list is not an accurate guide as to whether or not a particular work may have served as an actual text. This is true not only because extant curriculum lists are rare in themselves, but even if they were abundant it is probable that many texts would not have appeared on official curriculum lists because they were assigned and required by the professor himself without official university sanction (Weisheipl, "Curriculum at Oxford," p. 168). It does, however, seem plausible to assume that a given treatise served as a text if a large number of manuscripts of it have been preserved. For mention of numerous quadrivial works composed by faculty at the University of Paris, see Pearl Kibre, "The *Quadrivium* in the Thirteenth Century Universities," pp. 175–91.

21. Both treatises have been edited by G. Friedlein, *Boetii De institutione arithmetica libri duo; De institutione musica libri quinque* (Leipzig, 1867). An English translation of parts of the *Arithmetica* appears in Grant, *Source Book in Medieval Science*, pp. 17–24. Boethius' treatise is actually a paraphrase and near translation of Nichomachus of Gerasa's Greek treatise on arithmetic composed around 100 A.D. (For a translation of the latter, see *Nichomachus of Gerasa: Introduction to Arithmetic*, translated by Martin Luther D'Ooge with studies in Greek arithmetic by Frank E. Robbins and Louis C. Karpinski [New York, 1926]).

22. Also more advanced than Boethius was the rather widely used *Arithmetica* by Jordanus de Nemore in the thirteenth century (for translation of a few of its propositions, see Grant, *Source Book in Medieval Science*, pp. 102–6). In the fourteenth century, Thomas Bradwardine composed an *Arithmetica speculativa*, which has been described as "little more than the extraction of the barest essentials of Boethian arithmetic" intended, it seems, "for arts students who may have wished to learn something of the quadrivium, but with a minimal exposure to mathematical niceties" (cited in John E. Murdoch, "Bradwardine, Thomas," article in *Dictionary of Scientific Biography* [New York, 1970]: 2:395; according to Murdoch, "the *Arithmetica speculativa* was first printed in Paris, 1495 and reprinted many times during the fifteenth and sixteenth centuries" [p. 396]).

23. Sacrobosco's treatise, also known by the title *De arte numerandi*, was based on al-Khwarizmi's ninth-century Arabic treatise, which had been translated into Latin before the middle of the twelfth century with the title *De numero indorum* (for the Latin text of this translation, see Kurt Vogel, *Mohammed ibn Musa Alchwarizmi's Algorismus das früheste Lehrbuch zum Rechnen mit indischen Ziffern*, hereafter cited as *Mohammed*. Nach der einzigen [lateinischen] Handschrift [Cambridge Un. Lib. Ms. Ii. 6.5] in Faksimile mit Transkription und Kommentar herausgegeben [Aalen], 1963]). Although other practical arithmetic works describing the basic operations with Arabic numerals and containing the term "algorismus" (an obvious corruption of al-Khwarizmi's name) in their titles were written during the Middle Ages (Vogel, *Mohammed*, p. 42; the popular *Carmen de algorismo*, written around 1200 by Alexandre de Villedieu, was in the form of a poem in 284 Latin hexameters; for an analysis of it and Sacrobosco's treatise, see Guy Beaujouan, "L'enseignement de l'arithmetique elementaire a l'universite de Paris aux xiiie et xive siècles," in *Homenaje a Millas-Vallicrosa*, 2 vols. [Barcelona, 1954, 1956]: 1:93–124), Sacrobosco's was easily the most popular and retained its primacy until the sixteenth century. Hereafter cited as "l'enseignement de l'arithmetique elementaire." Most of Sacrobosco's treatise has been translated in Grant, *Source Book in Medieval Science*, pp. 94–101. The practical arithmetics and algorisms referred to here were probably studied at medieval universities. But the use of Arabic numerals also formed part of the curriculum of medieval business schools. In England,

Oxford was the center for business courses that formed no part of the curriculum for university degrees at Oxford University (see Nicholas Orme, *English Schools in the Middle Ages* [London, 1973], pp. 75-77). It was in Florence, however, where business schools flourished and played a significant role in education. From the fourteenth century, and perhaps earlier, private abacus schools—which, despite the title, made no use of the physical abacus or counters of any kind—taught young children the use of Arabic numerals, the arithmetic operations, and how to solve a large variety of problems, including those that we would call algebraic. Most prominent Florentine Renaissance figures—including Niccolo Machiavelli and Leonardo da Vinci—attended abacus schools as youngsters. According to Giovanni Villani, writing sometime around 1338, some one thousand to two thousand children were learning "the abacus and algorism" in six schools within Florence. My source for the abacus schools of Florence is Warren Van Egmond, *The Commercial Revolution and the Beginnings of Western Mathematics in Renaissance Florence, 1300-1500* (Ph.D. diss., Indiana University, 1976), pp. 7, 68, 73. The vicissitudes of Arabic numerals in Europe and the role of arithmetic in medieval European society are brilliantly described by Alexander Murray, *Reason and Society in the Middle Ages*, Part 2: Arithmetic (Oxford: The Clarendon Press, 1978), pp. 141-210.

24. Apparently, treatises on sexagesimal and vulgar fractions were not introduced into the university curriculum until rather late (Beaujouan, "L'enseignement de l'arithmetique elementaire," p. 123), probably in the fourteenth century. John of Ligneres (Johannes de Lineriis) (fl. in France in the first half of the fourteenth century) composed a popular *Algorismus minutiarum*, which treated both sexagesimal (or physical) and vulgar fractions. See Emmanuel Poulle, "John of Ligneres," *Dictionary of Scientific Biography* (New York, 1973), 7:122-28; for literature on the *Algorismus minutiarum*, see pp. 127-28.

25. Emmanuel Poulle observes that John of Murs viewed musical problems mathematically and that "his work reveals the pedagogic qualities that assured his musical writings a wide diffusion until the end of the Middle Ages" ("John of Murs," *Dictionary of Scientific Biography* [New York, 1973], 7:128). The extent to which music was studied in the medieval university is largely unknown. It is not even mentioned in the curriculum lists at Oxford until 1431 (Weisheipl, "Curriculum at Oxford," p. 171). For a description of a treatise in which traditional themes, techniques, and terms from natural philosophy (motion, intension and remission of forms) were applied to the problems of determining the proper subject of "worldly music" (*musica mundana*), see John E. Murdoch, "Music and Natural Philosophy: Hitherto Unnoticed *Questiones* by Blasius of Parma," *Manuscripta* 20, no. 2 (1976): 119-36.

26. For references, see Kibre, "The *Quadrivium* in the Thirteenth Century Universities," p. 184; and David C. Lindberg, *John Pecham and the Science of Optics, "Perspectiva Communis,"* edited with an introduction, English translation, and critical notes (Madison, Wis., 1970), p. 19.

27. See David C. Lindberg's translation in Grant, *Source Book in Medieval Science*, pp. 385.

28. Roger Bacon explains how geometry is essential to the various sciences, including optics. Only by means of geometry can the multiplication and propagation of the species be explained in optics, astronomy, and other relevant sciences. See R. B. Burke, trans., *The "Opus Majus" of Roger Bacon*, 2 vols. (Philadelphia, 1928), 1:131-36. Indeed Bacon's lengthy section on mathematics in the *Opus Magnus* is intended to show its indispensability for science and theology.

29. *Nicole Oresme and the Kinematics of Circular Motion: "Tractatus de commensurabilitate vel incommensurabilitate motuum celi,"* pt. 3, edited with an introduction, English translation, and commentary by Edward Grant (Madison, Wis., 1971), pp. 284-323 for text and translation, pp. 67-77 for analysis (especially 72-73).

30. Mathematics was widely applied to philosophy and theology during the Middle Ages,

especially in the fourteenth century. Problems in motion and the intension and remission of forms were frequently mathematized. For an excellent description and assessment of the significant and extensive role of mathematics in philosophy and theology, see John E. Murdoch, "*Mathesis in philosophiam scholasticam introducta*, The Rise and Development of the Application of Mathematics in Fourteenth Century Philosophy and Theology," *Arts libéraux et philosophie au moyen âge*, pp. 215–54. It was not that Galileo and his successors reintroduced mathematics into physics, but rather that they restricted its scope to what was more properly and appropriately mathematizable (see Edward Grant, *Physical Science in the Middle Ages* [New York, 1971; reprinted by Cambridge University Press, 1977], pp. 58–59)

31. The terms *astronomia* and *astrologia* were used indifferently in the Middle Ages when referring to the "science of the stars" (*scientia stellarum* or *astrorum*). The latter descriptive phrase actually embraced both astronomy and astrology, which were usually taught together; "Astronomy proper, in our sense, came to be called *scientia motus*, or *motuum*, while astrology in our sense was called *scientia iudiciorum*." (Richard Lemay, "The Teaching of Astronomy in Medieval Universities, Principally at Paris in the Fourteenth Century," *Manuscripta* 20, no. 3 [1976]: 198; hereafter cited as "Teaching of Astronomy").

32. See A. G. Little, ed., *Part of the "Opus tertium" of Roger Bacon* (Aberdeen, 1912), pp. 12–14; Kibre, "*Quadrivium* in the Thirteenth Century Universities," p. 190. In Burke, *Opus Majus*, 1:261–70, Bacon defends "true mathematicians," by whom he means astronomers or astrologers (Burke trans., vol. 1, pp. 261–70).

33. Grosseteste, *De artibus liberalibus* in L. Baur, ed., *Die philosophischen Werke des Robert Grosseteste, Bischofs von Lincoln, Beitraäge zur Geschichte der Philosophie des Mittelalters*, (Munster, 1912), 9:4–7; Kibre, *Arts libéraux et philosophie au moyen âge*.

34. In the official statutes, the college was listed as "Collège Notre Dame de Bayeux" (Lemay, "Teaching of Astronomy," p. 201, n. 8).

35. For all this, see Lemay, "Teaching of Astronomy," pp. 200–202, 210. Throughout the Middle Ages, a good physician was thought to be one who could determine the present and future positions of the stars and could use that knowledge for the benefit of his patients. That celestial bodies could affect terrestrial matter, including organic entities, was taken as self-evident. Since it was further assumed that the position and relationships of every star and planet affected the nature and intensity of its influence, it is obvious why physicians were thought to require knowledge of astronomy and astrology. For a brief discussion of medical astrology at institutions other than Paris, see Lemay, "Teaching of Astronomy," pp. 206–9.

36. For various references, see Kibre, "*Quadrivium* in the Thirteenth Century Universities," pp. 186–87.

37. For a brief description of the origins and status of these four medical schools, see Vern L. Bullough, *The Development of Medicine as a Profession* (New York, 1966), pp. 46–73; hereafter cited as *Development of Medicine*. For an interesting and informative summary account of medieval medicine, see Charles H. Talbot, "Medicine," in David C. Lindberg, ed., *Science in the Middle Ages*, pp. 391–428, especially pp. 400–405, 408–13; hereafter cited as "Medicine."

38. Its development into a profession is the fundamental theme of Bullough's book.

39. Talbot, "Medicine," p. 400, who cites Hugh of St. Victor's *Didascalicon*.

40. Talbot, "Medicine," p. 402.

41. Bullough, *Development of Medicine*, pp. 81–82.

42. Why the longstanding prejudice against the practice of human dissection should have been overcome first at Bologna is difficult to explain (Bullough, *Development of Medicine*, p. 62).

43. *La grande chirurgie de Guy de Chauliac*, ed. E. Nicaise (Paris, 1890), pp. 30-31. The passage is translated in Bullough, *Development of Medicine*, p. 64. Three of the four members mentioned by Guy de Chauliac are also cited in *The Anatomy of Master Nicholas* (*Anatomia Magistri Nicolai Physici*) written around 1200 by a Master Nicholas of the Salernitan school. In this treatise, we learn that the animal members are situated above the epiglottis and include the brain, pia mater, dura mater, and the like; the spiritual members lie between the epiglottis and diaphragm and include the heart and lung; the nutritive members are between the diaphragm and kidneys and include liver, spleen, and stomach. By "extremities," perhaps Guy intended the generative members, which, according to Master Nicholas, include the testes and seminal vessels below the kidneys. For Master Nicholas, see *Anatomical Texts of the Earlier Middle Ages*, trans. George W. Corner (Washington, D.C., 1927), pp. 67–70; the translation is reproduced in Grant, *Source Book in Medieval Science*, p. 728.

44. Guy de Chauliac mentions this pejoratively in the passage cited in n. 43.

45. See Grant, *Source Book in Medieval Science*, p. 730, n. 1 by Michael McVaugh. This cooperative procedure of the medical schools is illustrated in numerous woodcuts in early printed texts.

46. The *repetitiones* carried on at most medieval universities seem to have had memorization of lectures as their main purpose. Following the lecture of a master, the students were expected to convene that same afternoon and repeat it as substantially close to the original as possible. According to Weisheipl, Dominican students in the fourteenth century were expected to repeat science and logic lectures on a daily basis and to give a general *repetitio* once a week before the master himself ("Curriculum at Oxford," p. 152). From this we sense that each student was expected to repeat the lecture each day. At Bologna, the master assigned a *repetitor*, "who," according to Rashdall, "attended the lecture and then repeated it to the students afterwards and catechized them upon it" (*Universities of Europe in the Middle Ages*, 1:249). Whether or not the original lecture was first repeated by an officially assigned *repetitor*, it would appear that the students themselves were expected to repeat the lectures in the hope that they would memorize the whole of it in a form as close to the original as possible.

47. Analysis of university texts used in teaching quadrivial subjects may provide significant information and insight about the possible substantive content of medieval lectures, but such analysis is essentially mute about actual classroom procedures. Analysis may suggest, as it did to Guy Beaujouan, ("L'enseignement de l'arithmétique elementaire," p. 105) that the hexameral verses of the *Carmen de algorismo* were memorized and its obscurities then clarified by appeal to Sacrobosco's *Algorismus vulgaris* (or *prosaicus*, as Beaujouan cites it). If medieval students studied arithmetic merely by memorizing the *Carmen de algorismo*, we would have a reasonable idea of classroom practice, which would consist of the memorization and subsequent verbatim repetition of the text itself (we would, however, still remain ignorant of the precise manner in which the text was repeated and what was actually understood by such rote procedures). But what does it mean to say that the *Algorismus* of Sacrobosco was used in the classroom to clarify the *Carmen*? How were these texts interrelated in actual classroom teaching? Inferences from texts and their possible interrelationships offer little basis for reliable descriptions about actual classroom methods employed to convey the contents of those texts to students. Even the knowledge that problem texts were compiled for the study of arithmetic does not enable us to penetrate the veil that obscures actual classroom practice (Beaujouan, "L'enseignement de l'arithmétique elementaire," pp. 115–23). The mere existence of problem texts does not inform us as to their actual use in the classroom, nor how they may have been used if they were an integral part of classroom instruction. Even Siegmund Günther's four hundred page study, which bears the intriguing title "Geschichte des mathematischen Unterrichts im deutschen Mittelalter bis zum Jahre 1525" (*Monumenta Germaniae Paedogogica*, vol. 3 [Berlin: A. Hofmann & Co., 1887]), has

virtually nothing of value to say about classroom instruction in mathematics, not even in a brief section (pp. 192–97) devoted specifically to "Methods of Academic Instruction" ("Methode des akademischen Unterrichts") where we are told (p. 196), presumably on a priori grounds, that among the seven liberal arts the usual disputational method of teaching would be most risky in mathematics. Since Günther's fine book is actually an analysis of the numerous mathematical texts written and available in the Middle Ages, and therefore is more a history of medieval mathematics than a history of mathematical instruction, the title of his work is obviously misleading. In sum, knowledge of titles and content of science texts used at the universities still leaves unanswered numerous questions about the manner in which the content of those texts was actually conveyed to students. But there is yet much of value that can be said about what was learned in the medieval classroom on the basis of a knowledge of the specific texts involved. For example, although a bias against Arabic numerals is occasionally detected at universities in nonteaching matters (see Murray, *Reason and Society in the Middle Ages*, pp. 171–72), the probable use of Sacrobosco's *Algorismus* and similar treatises as university texts strongly suggests that Arabic numerals were taught and regularly used at the medieval university. Since the Arabic number system was based on place value, it not only supplemented but often supplanted the use of the abacus, which also relied on place value (Murray, *Reason and Society in the Middle Ages*, pp. 163–67; Beaujouan, "L'enseignement de l'arithmétique elementaire," p. 95). All this does not, however, rule out the possibility that the abacus may have been used to check the accuracy of computations that used Arabic numerals.

48. For the details and references, see Oscar G. Darlington, "Gerbert, the Teacher," *American Historical Review* 52 (1946–47): 467–70; for the title of Richer's work, see p. 456, n. 2.

49. My remarks on *rithmomachia* are drawn entirely from Gillian R. Evans, "The Rithmomachia: A Mediaeval Mathematical Teaching Aid?", *Janus, Revue international de l'histoire des sciences* 63 (1976): 257–73. For John of Salisbury and Alan of Lille, see p. 257; for the quotation, see p. 262.

50. For a general account of the fate of the Aristotelian corpus at the University of Paris, see Gordon Leff, *Paris and Oxford Universities in the Thirteenth and Fourteenth Centuries* (New York, 1968), pp. 187–238; hereafter cited as *Paris and Oxford Universities*. Much of what follows in this paragraph is drawn from my article, "The Condemnation of 1277, God's Absolute Power, and Physical Thought in the Late Middle Ages," *Viator* 10 (1979): 211.

51. For a brief history and background, see John F. Wippel, "The Condemnations of 1270 and 1277 at Paris," *Journal of Medieval and Renaissance Studies* 7 (1977): 169–201; Roland Hisette, *Enquete sur les 219 articles condamnés à Paris le 7 Mars 1277* (Louvain: Publications Universitaires; Paris, 1977). References to the Latin texts and translations of the Condemnation of 1277 are provided in Grant, "The Condemnation of 1277," *Viator* 10 (1979): 211, n. 1.

52. *The Discarded Image, An Introduction to Medieval and Renaissance Literature* (Cambridge, 1964), p. 121.

53. Weisheipl, "Curriculum at Oxford," p. 154.

54. This was true for lectures in both arts and theology. For the former, see Weisheipl, "Curriculum at Oxford," and for the latter, Mary Martin McLaughlin, *Intellectual Freedom and Its Limitations in the University of Paris in the Thirteenth and Fourteenth Centuries* (New York, 1977), p. 208; hereafter cited as *Intellectual Freedom and its Limitations*.

55. See Leff, *Paris and Oxford Universities*, pp. 167–68. On the quodlibetal disputes, see P. Glorieux, *La Littérature quodlibétique*, 2 vols. (Belgium, 1925 [vol. 1]; Paris, 1935 [vol. 2]).

56. The ultimate determination of all questions disputed in public at official occasions was the right and privilege of masters alone.

57. Talbot has a low opinion of the medical disputations, or "intellectual wrestling

matches," as he calls them ("Medicine," pp. 404–5). "Viewing the subjects of these wrangles with a dispassionate eye and at a distance of some centuries, it is hard to see what all the fuss was about." The medieval disputants, however, took these controversies quite seriously and so must we if we are to understand not only medieval medicine and natural philosophy, but medieval intellectual life in general.

58. For typical questions drawn from *questiones* on Aristotle's *Physics* (by Albert of Saxony), *De caelo* (John Buridan), *On Generation and Corruption* (by Albert of Saxony), and *Meterology* (by Themon Judaeus), see Grant, *Source Book in Medieval Science*, pp. 199–210. Most of the questions cited below are drawn from this lengthy list of some 266 *questiones*. I have discussed some of them in my article, "Cosmology," in David C. Lindberg, ed., *Science in the Middle Ages*, pp. 265–302. In another article, "Aristotelianism and the Longevity of the Medieval World View," *History of Science* 16 (1978): 93–106, I have attempted to assess the impact of the *questiones* form of literature on medieval concepts of the cosmos and to explain the role of that literature in perpetuating the medieval Aristotelian world view. The hundreds of written *questiones* mentioned above were almost certainly not in the original form in which they were first discussed and debated in the university classroom. They represent revised and often polished versions of the classroom lectures and debates and therefore do not provide a sense of the actual "give and take" that may have occurred at the original classroom presentation or at the public dispute. In the absence of first hand descriptions of classroom lectures and debates, student annotations of standard texts are helpful as are the lectures of minor, or little known, teachers who may not have revised their presentations for "publication." These cautions and insights are provided by John E. Murdoch, "Music and Natural Philosophy: Hitherto Unnoticed *Questiones* by Blasius of Parma(?)," *Manuscripta* 20, no. 2 (1976): 134–35.

59. To arrive at a quite reasonable estimate of the number of extant commentaries and *questiones* on the works of Aristotle alone, see Charles H. Lohr, "Medieval Latin Aristotle Commentaries," *Traditio*, vol. 23 (1967), vol. 30 (1974).

60. For the complete text see *Petri Lombardi Libri IV Sententiarum* studio et cura PP. Collegii S. Bonaventurae in lucem editi, 2d ed. (Ad Claras Aquas, 1916). A third edition of the first two books (issued as one volume in two parts) appeared in 1971 with the title: *Magistri Petri Lombardi Parisiensis Episcopi Sententiae in IV Libris Distinctae*, editio tertia (Grottaferrata [Romae]: Editiones Collegii S. Bonaventurae Ad Claras Aquas, 1971).

61. See bk. 2, distinctions 12–15 in vol. 1, pt. 2 of *Magistri Petri Lombardi Parisiensis Episcopi Sententiae in IV Libris Distinctae*. Hereafter cited as *Magistri Petri Lombardi*.

62. All this is found in bk. I, distinction 37: "In what ways is God said to be in things" (*Quibus modis dicatur Deus esse in rebus*, *Magistri Petri Lombardi*, pp. 263–75). Thus Richard of Middleton and Jean de Ripa injected discussions of infinite extracosmic space; Richard and St. Bonaventure considered whether or not angels move with successive motion; and Richard also sought to determine whether an angel is actually in a space. For Richard of Middleton, see *Super quatuor libros Senteniarum Petri Lombardi Quaestiones subtilissimae*, 4 vols. (Brescia, 1591; reprinted Frankfurt am Main by Minerva G.m.b.H., 1963): 1: 325–34; for de Ripa, see, "Jean de Ripa I Sent. Dist. 37: De modo inexistendi divine essentie in omnibus creaturis," edited by André Combes and Francis Ruello, with an introduction by Paul Vignaux in *Traditio* 23 (1967): 231–34; for Bonaventure, see *S. Bonaventurae Opera Omnia*, I, *Commentaria in primum librum Sententiarum* (Quaracchi, 1882), pp. 657–64. Peter Lombard's consideration of angels in bk. 1, distinction 37 was only incidental to his major concern with God. The extensive treatment of angelic nature and behavior is reserved for bk. 2, distinctions 1–11.

63. As confirmation of this tendency, John Major (1469–1550), in the introduction to his own commentary on the second book of the *Sentences* (1528), could declare that "for some

two centuries now, theologians have not feared to work into their writings questions which are purely physical, metaphysical, and sometimes purely mathematical." Although he deplores the practice, Major confesses that he has "not blushed to follow in their footsteps."

64. For a brilliant discussion of these themes and much else, see John E. Murdoch, "From Social into Intellectual Factors: An Aspect of the Unitary Character of Late Medieval Learning," in J. E. Murdoch and E. D. Sylla, eds., *The Cultural Context of Medieval Learning* (Dordrecht-Holland, 1975), pp. 271–348, especially 298–303. Hereafter cited as "From Social into Intellectual Factors."

65. On *secundum imaginationem*, see Murdoch, "From Social into Intellectual Factors," pp. 292, 294, 297, 300, 312, and his "*Mathesis in philosophiam scholasticam introducta. . .*," *Arts libéraux et philosophie au moyen âge*, p. 248; also Grant, *Physical Science in the Middle Ages*, p. 34 and "The Condemnation of 1277," *Viator* 10 (1979): pp. 239–40, 241–42.

66. The oath appears in H. Denifle and E. Chatelain, eds., *Chartularium Universitatis Parisiensis*, 4 vols. (Paris, 1889–97): 1: 499–500 and has been translated by Lynn Thorndike, *University Records and Life in the Middle Ages* (New York, 1944), pp. 85–86. Thorndike's translation has been reprinted in Grant, *Source Book in Medieval Science*, pp. 44–45.

67. The relevant passage appears in Buridan's *Questions on the Eight Books of the Physics of Aristotle*, bk. 4, question 8, and has been translated in Grant, *Source Book in Medieval Science*, pp. 50–51 (the title of the Latin edition appears on p. 50, n. 1).

68. Translated in Grant, *Source Book in Medieval Science*, p. 51, n. 4, from Buridan, *Questions on De caelo*, bk. 1, question 20 (for the Latin text, see *Iohannis Buridani Quaestiones super libris quattuor De caelo et mundo*, ed. E. A. Moody [Cambridge, Mass., 1942], p. 93).

69. These articles are discussed at length in Grant, "The Condemnation of 1277," *Viator* (1979): 211-44.

70. See Mary Martin McLaughlin, *Intellectual Freedom and Its Limitations*, p. 135.

71. Thus Nicole Oresme, after demonstrating that a perfect eclipse of the moon could only occur once through all eternity, explains that "I always understand this 'naturally speaking' (*naturaliter loquendo*) and have even assumed an eternity of motion." Of course, "supernaturally speaking," the world will endure for only a finite time. Hence Oresme qualified his intent and proceeds as if it were natural to suppose that the world is eternal. The passage cited here appears in Oresme's *De proportionibus proportionum*, ch. 4 in Edward Grant, ed. and trans., Nicole Oresme, *De Proportionibus proportionum and Ad pauca respicientes*, edited with introduction, English translations, and critical notes (Madison, Wis., 1966), p. 305.

72. McLaughlin, *Intellectual Freedom and Its Limitations*, p. 312.

73. What follows on Buridan is largely drawn from my article, "Scientific Thought in Fourteenth-Century Paris: Jean Buridan and Nicole Oresme" in *Machaut's World: Science and Art in the Fourteenth Century*, ed. Madeleine Pelner Cosman and Bruce Chandler, *Annals of the New York Academy of Sciences* (New York: The New York Academy of Science, 1978), 314: 108-11.

74. As for the many theologians who also discussed scientific questions, there were virtually no intellectual restrictions other than acceptance of doctrinal truth. And even doctrinal truth was often uncertain and debatable. On the remarkable degree of intellectual freedom available to medieval theologians of the thirteenth and fourteenth centuries, see McLaughlin, *Intellectual Freedom and Its Limitations*, pp. 170–237. During the thirteenth and fourteenth centuries, individuals and ideas were of course censured. For the most part, however, censures were directed against novice theologians lecturing on the *Sentences* and were usually formulated by the members of the theology faculty itself (McLaughlin, *Intellectual Freedom and Its Limitations*, pp. 209–10). Censures by theological commissions were also

frequent enough, as, for example, the one against William Ockham in 1326 when fifty-one articles drawn from his commentary on the *Sentences* were censured, though not condemned (McLaughlin, *Intellectual Freedom and Its Limitations*, pp. 276–77). Generally, it was the university itself—that is, the masters themselves—that exercised control over the intellectual content of lectures and publications; and "if the restrictions imposed were ever effective, it was because they were accepted by the consent of the society, not at the command of an external authority" (McLaughlin, *Intellectual Freedom and Its Limitations*, p. 310). The concluding sentence of Mary McLaughlin's splendid study admirably conveys the powerful sense of free inquiry that prevailed at the medieval university (p. 317): "Masters of the late thirteenth and fourteenth centuries might indeed exercise, with little or no hindrance, that freedom of the teacher, first explicitly asserted by Siger of Brabant and his colleagues, to discuss and to explore his materials and problems, regardless of the truth of the opinions he considers."

75. See Grant, "The Condemnation of 1277," *Viator* 10 (1979): 239–40. What follows is based on my article, where evidence is furnished for the claims made here.

76. Translations of both treatises appear in Grant, *Source Book in Medieval Science*, pp. 368–76, 435–41. Whether Peter Peregrinus was university trained is presently unknown.

77. In his article, "Medieval Ideas of Scientific Progress," *Journal of the History of Ideas* 39 (1978): 561–77, George Molland concludes that his account "has done little to disturb the traditional view that saw few conceptions of scientific progress in the Middle Ages (p. 576). The absence of a sense of scientific progress is perhaps attributable to (p. 576) "the divorce between theory and practice that characterized so much scholastic science." See also Molland's earlier article, "Nichole Oresme and Scientific Progress," *Miscellanea Mediaevalia*, veröffentlichungen des Thomas-Instituts der Universität zu Köln, Band 9: *Antiqui und Moderni* (Berlin/New York, 1974): 206–20.

78. On this point, see my paper, "Aristotelianism and the Longevity of the Medieval World View," *History of Science* 16 (1978): 98–99. My discussion here on the impact of the medieval *questio* has relied heavily on this article.

79. These Latin *Juvenilia*, as they have been called, appear in *Le Opere di Galileo Galilei*, Edizione Nazionale, ed. Antonio Favaro, vol. 1 (1890), and were recently translated by William A. Wallace, *Galileo's Early Notebooks: The Physical Questions, A Translation from the Latin, with Historical and Paleographical Commentary* (Notre Dame, Ind., 1977).

THE ROLE OF ENGLISH THOUGHT IN THE TRANSFORMATION OF UNIVERSITY EDUCATION IN THE LATE MIDDLE AGES

William J. Courtenay

f one were to select the two most discussed influences that shaped intellectual life in the late medieval universities north of the Alps, these would probably be the spread of Ockham's thought from England across northern Europe in the fourteenth century and the advent of humanism from Italy in the fifteenth.[1] Of these two "modern" movements, what is generally called nominalism was the earlier and, unlike humanism, was born within the university. Once considered antithetical, historians now see certain parallel interests and sometimes close friendships between nominalists and humanists, and it has even been suggested that one movement laid the conceptual foundation for the other.[2] Despite the struggle between the *via antiqua* and the *via moderna* in the fifteenth century and the occasional sanctions agains the *nominales*, the heirs to the thought of William of Ockham hold a principal place in the history of European universities on the eve of the Reformation.

The process by which nominalism supposedly captivated and transformed late medieval university life developed in three stages, according to our present understanding.[3] The first stage took place at Oxford, where initial opposition to Ockham's teaching (ca. 1317–24) by John Lutterell, John of Reading, and Walter Chatton, eventually gave way to acceptance and then extremism in Robert Holcot and Adam Wodeham (ca. 1330). After 1334, with the principal exception of Thomas Bradwardine, Ockham supposedly influenced most Oxford thinkers until Wyclif. The second stage occurred at Paris, where again, after a period of opposition culminating in the prohibitions on Ockhamist teaching in 1339 and 1340 and the condemnations of Autrecourt and Mirecourt in 1346 and 1347, a more orthodox form of nominalism developed through the efforts of John Buridan, Gregory of Rimini, and Nicholas of Oresme. From 1360 to 1385 this ideology claimed the allegiance of the majority of Parisian scholars and masters, including Pierre d'Ailly, Henry of Langenstein, Marsilius of Inghen, and Jean Gerson. The third stage began with the dissemination of nominalism on German soil through the exodus of German students and masters from Paris to Germany in the 1380s after the failure to reach an immediate solution to the Great Schism. By most accounts, the universities founded or refounded in Germany and eastern Europe in the wake of the papal schism — Vienna (1384), Heidelberg (1386), Erfurt (1392), and Cracow (1397) — were populated not just by *emigres* from Paris but by masters who were aligned with or influenced by the teachings of Parisian nominalists. Especially influential were Henry Totting of Oyta, Henry of Langenstein at Vienna, Marsilius of Inghen, and Conrad of Geinhausen at Heidelberg. Henry of Langenstein's famous phrase, "O felix schisma," implied not only the beneficial result of improving philosophical and theological teaching in German centers and political conditions that favored the multiplication of universities east of the Rhine, but might be seen as praise for a particular intellectual viewpoint: nominalism.[4]

This dramatic progression from Ockhamism at Oxford to the *via moderna* in Germany, largely a construct of Franz Ehrle, is now suspect at many points. In what follows a different picture will be set forth, one already familiar to those who have contributed to it, perhaps uncomfortably unfamiliar to others. I have intentionally avoided couching the question in terms of the development or dissemination of nominalism as is normally done. Our vision of what was happening in the fourteenth century has been obscured by the presupposition that there was, in that period, a clearly defined nominalist movement and that the terms nominalism, Ockhamism, *moderni*, and *via moderna* can be used interchangeably or have related meaning. These labels, each with a somewhat different meaning, have their place in the history of the fifteenth-century universities.[5] But the assumption that they designate a school of thought that can be traced back into the period before the Great Schism and the Hussite Revolt distorts the intellectual history of the fourteenth century, as has often been noted.[6] The categories of nominalism and Ockhamism, in light of recent studies, have proven far less useful for interpreting the writings of Holcot, Buridan, Autrecourt, Rimini, Oresme, Oyta, Inghen, and others. By abandoning the traditional approach, a new picture emerges. Whatever revolution occurred in the intellectual climate of fourteenth-century universities as a result of English influence was more the result of English thought in the generation after Ockham rather than a direct contribution either of Ockham or of nominalism. Moreover, that transformation began in the 1340s, not only at Paris but in Italy and Germany as well.

THE RECEPTION OF OCKHAM IN ENGLAND

Ockham's philosophy and theology, set forth at Oxford and probably London in the years 1318–24, brought an immediate reaction from Reading, Lutterell, Chatton, and the Pseudo-Campsale. Lutterell, and to a lesser extent Chatton, saw Ockham's thought as a new, interdependent, philosophical/theological system that contained numerous suspect or heretical propositions.[7] It was largely through them that proceedings against Ockham were initiated at the papal court at Avignon. The concerns of Reading and the Pseudo-Campsale were more limited. Reading essentially defended Scotus' metaphysics against Ockham's critique.[8] The Pseudo-Campsale reacted to Ockham's logic and wrote a point-by-point critique of Ockham's *Summa logicae*.[9]

In the years immediately following Ockham's departure for Avignon (1324), the violent reaction to his thought in England declined. Of the initial adversaries, Reading and Lutterell preceded Ockham to Avignon and Chatton remained in England until 1333 as the major voice of opposition. Subsequent theologians, however, were less concerned about Ockham or were to some extent influenced by him. Richard Fitzralph, for whom Ockham was only one of many sources, usually rejected Ockham's opinions; John Rodington blended aspects of Ockham and Scotus.[10] Robert Holcot, who was not a student of Ockham and probably never heard him lecture, was well aware of Ockham's writings and was influenced by his thought. Yet he never sought to defend Ockham's teaching, cited him critically more often than favorably, and was a frequent opponent of Adam Wodeham, with whom his name is usually linked.[11]

The only example we have of a direct follower of Ockham is in fact Wodeham, who was Ockham's student and probably editor of some of his philosophical and theological writings after Ockham left England.[12] Only in Wodeham does Ockham's name appear time and again as part of the solution to a scholastic question. But Wodeham felt himself free to criticize Ockham on a number of points, some of considerable significance.[13] In fact, as we read more of Wodeham, he is appearing as a major figure in his own right and not simply a student of Ockham.

In the years after 1330, Ockham's logic, which remained a point of contention in the arts faculty, began to attract an important following. The defenders of the traditional understanding of simple supposition,[14] such as the Benedictine, Roger Swineshead, and the Mertonian, William Sutton, tried not only to answer Ockham's arguments but to reduce an elaborate discussion to a few major points that could be grasped by the student.[15] Sutton's *textus de suppositionibus* became popular, both in England and on the Continent (particularly in Germany) as an introduction to supposition theory. More popular, however, were the works of William Heytesbury, particularly his *Regulae solvendi sophismata* (ca. 1335) and John Dumbleton's *Summa logicae* (written during the 1340s).[16] Both works accept the major points of Ockham's logic and natural philosophy.[17] Similarly, Richard Billingham's *Speculum iuvenum* (ca. 1350) also reflects a more positive attitude toward Ockham's logic.[18]

The same cannot be said of Ockham's theology. Among English theologians after Wodeham we find only modest use of Ockham:

occasional parallels with or criticisms of positions he held, but rarely the mention of his name. This is true for Kilvington, Halifax, Rosetus, Buckingham, Monachus Niger, Alexander Langeley, and John Stuckele. Where we find a strong reaction to semi-Pelagianism, as in Bradwardine and Halifax, it was probably directed more against Wodeham (and possibly Holcot) than against Ockham.[19] Thus, although Ockham's logic and natural philosophy did eventually win a following at Oxford in the 1330s and 1340s, no similar development took place in the realm of theology with the important exception of Wodeham.

Nevertheless, some fundamental changes did take place in English theology after Ockham, particularly in the decade 1330–40. These changes were related to developments that had occurred or were occurring in the areas of logic, physics, and mathematics, but the transformation of theology did not directly depend upon the areas of philosophy in which Ockham's approach was a point of contention. What was new was not so much Ockham but rather the development of new treatises and new methodological approaches, specifically linguistic and mathematical tools that could be applied to theological problems. If we are to understand what was so attractive about English thought for the universities of continental Europe, we must turn our attention away from Ockham and examine more closely the period 1330–40.

THE SCHOLARLY EXPLOSION

The first thing that strikes one about England in the decade 1330–40 is the impressive number of logicians, mathematicians, and theologians whose works have survived. They represent only a portion of the known English authors of that decade, but the extant works witness to their significance and popularity as well as to an unusually high period of productivity within English scholasticism. Not even Paris in its best years, with its ability to attract talent throughout Europe, could field a similar group of extant authors: Thomas Bradwardine, Simon Bredon, Richard Brinkley, Thomas Buckingham, Walter Burley, Walter Chatton, Crathorn,

William of Collingham, John Dumbleton, Adam of Ely, Thomas Felthorp, Richard Fitzralph, Robert of Halifax, Haveral, William Heytesbury, Robert Holcot, Richard Kilvington, Alexander Langeley, John Maudith, Monachus Niger, Bartholomew of Reppes, John Rodington, Roger Rosetus, Walter Segrave, John Stuckele, William Sutton, Roger Swindshead, John Went, and Adam Wodeham. One might surmise from the sheer level of productivity that something important was going on in England, particularly at Oxford, in this period.

Logica Anglicana: The New Logic[20]

Ockham's rejection of the traditional understanding of simple supposition and his reinterpretation of Aristotle's categories coincided with a period of rapid growth in Oxford logic that altered the arts curriculum.[21] Ockham's nominalism and the reaction of Burley and others played a role in that transformation, yet from another perspective, the structure of his *Summa logicae* is reflective of a broader revision in terminist logic in Ockham's generation. The traditional division between the segments based on the *logica antiqua* (predication, the categories, syllogisms, topics, fallacies) and the *logica modernorum* (signification, supposition, relation, appellation, restriction, distribution, i.e., the logic of the properties of terms) was recast into a simpler progression from terms, to propositions, to syllogisms. Many of the innovations of twelfth– and thirteenth–century terminist logic, such as *copulatio, ampliatio, appellatio,* and treatises *de syncategorematibus* declined and were absorbed into treatises *de suppositionibus.*

The expansion of supposition theory was probably the most important development in Oxford logic in the fourteenth century. Originally supposition concerned only the subject term of the proposition, but gradually in the thirteenth and early fourteenth centuries it came to be applied to other self-significant parts of speech as well. These new categories of supposition were explored in separate treatises that examined the problems and established rules. Thus there were treatises *de relativis* (for the supposition of relative terms), treatises de 'incipit' et 'desinit' (for the supposition of predicate terms in propositions containing those verbs), treatises de maximo et minimo (for the supposition of comparative and superlative adverbs and adjectives), treatises de 'scire' et 'dubitare' (for the supposition of terms whose object was unclear or unknown), and treatises dealing with the supposition of mediate terms implying a privative or positive function, such as scire, credere, dubitare, intelligere, appeto, debeo, possum promittere, possibile, impossibile, contingens, necesse.[22] Gradually the insolubilia, or self-contradictory statements, were handled alongside or within supposition theory, which in turn was equated with Sophismata (originally the difficult problems that formed the material for the disputations in the arts faculty known as de sophismatibus). Other areas of logic developed as well, e.g., treatises De consequentiis (on inferences) and de obligatoriis (rules of inference), but for our purposes those connected with supposition theory are the most significant. Although these developments were influenced by Ockham's logic, they did not depend directly on his nominalism but were the common property, the common achievement of Oxford logicians, particularly in the generation 1320–35.

Many of the newer treatises that began appearing in Oxford logic after 1320 concerned the supposition of terms in propositions about motion and change (motus, mutatio, incipit, desinit), growth and decay or expansion and contraction (augmentatio, diminutio, intensio, remissio, condensatio, rarefactio), measurement (maximum, minimum, latitudo, longitudo, continuum, finitum, infinitum, proportio), and time (tempus, duratio, instans, praeteritum, de futuris contingentibus, and the whole area of tensed propositions). These interests were not totally absent in the logic of the thirteenth century, but they were systematically explored in the fourteenth century in an unprecedented manner. This new logic paralleled and in many cases was blended with what has been called the new physics as reflected in a series of new treatises (derived from the libri naturales of the arts curriculum, principally Aristotle's Physics), on motion, change, measurement, and time. These physical treatises were roughly contemporaneous with the logical treatises, and some of them are, in fact, a blend of the two worlds within the arts curriculum. It is difficult to say whether the exploration of these problems was a development of logic, as would be suggested by the structure and content of Heytesbury's *Regulae solvendi sophismata* (1335),[23] or whether the interests in the new physics determined the content and direction of logic. In any event, what we find by 1335 is a logic particularly suited to the analysis of problems in physics and mathematics and a mathematical physics that depends heavily upon language analysis.

Certain aspects of this development were stimulated by Ockham's *Summa logicae*, *Expositio aurea*, *Expositio super libros Physicorum*, and the *Tractatus de successivis* extracted from the last work.[24] Ockham's extensive analysis of supposition, of relative terms, of propositions *de 'incipit' et 'desinit'*, *de praeterito et de futuro*, *de possibili, impossibili, et contingenti*, his explorations of *mutatio*, *motus, duratio, locus, ubi*, and finally the empiricism of his methodology were all influential in furthering the new logic and the new physics. On the other hand, the blending of logic and physics and the development of mathematical physics were far removed from Ockham's viewpoint and were pursued independent of (and occasionally in opposition to) Ockham's logic and physics.[25] But if one did not make real entities of time, motion, place, measure, or mathematical relations, one could easily wed the new physics, with its stress on quantification, to the philosophy of Ockham. The compatibility of Ockham's logic and physics with Bradwardine's *De proportione velocitatum in motibus* can be seen in the way both Heytesbury and Dumbleton eventually blended the two approaches.[26]

The creation of the new logic and the new physics were well underway by 1330 and drew upon the works of Ockham (especially the *Summa logica* and the *De successivis*), Burley (particularly *De finito et infinito, De insolubilibus, De sophismatibus, De duratione, De intentione et remissione formarum*, and *De primo et ultimo instanti*), Bradwardine (*De insolubilibus, De proportione*, and *De continuo*), and Kilvington's *Sophismata*. This activity continued into the 1330s and 1340s, but by 1330 it had already begun to produce another offspring, a new theology.

Theologia Anglicana: *The New Theology*

Among the many theological bachelors reading the *Sentences* at Oxford in the fall of 1330 were two mendicants whose commentaries quickly became major works in late medieval theology: Robert Holcot and Adam Wodeham. In Holcot's work we find an extensive application of the new logic to theology, and in the context of theology some further refinements in the logic of tensed propositions.[27] In Wodeham's work, particularly in distinctions 1–8 of the first book, one finds an analysis of theological problems in terms of the language of the new physics: *maximum et minimum*, augmentation and diminution, intention and remission of forms, movement and velocity, *incipit et desinit*, proportion, the infinite, and *latitudo*.[28] These two authors herald the beginnings of a new theology at Oxford whose features differ markedly from those of the earlier period.

The first of these features is the striking absence of "school" traditions at Oxford by the end of the first quarter of the fourteenth century. By 1320 Thomism had become such a minor force at Oxford that it is all but invisible in the documentation that has survived. It would not be revived there until the end of the century, and then by Benedictines and Carmelites more than by Dominicans.[29] Similarly, Scotism as a major intellectual current at Oxford disappears with John of Reading, who may be its last representative. Chatton and Rodington cannot be properly so characterized, and one does not encounter Scotists at Oxford in the next two or three decades.[30] Aegidianism, found only among the Austin Friars, similarly disappears after the opening decades of the fourteenth century.[31]

These intellectual affiliations were not replaced by new competing ideologies. As we have already seen, no strong school of Ockhamism developed at Oxford, nor do the Mertonians represent a "school of thought." Anneliese Maier's "Bradwardine-Schule" in which she placed Kilvington and Buckingham is an imaginary construct.[32] The simple fact is that Oxfordians of the second quarter of the fourteenth century were not system-building, be it their own or that of some earlier scholastic. Systematic, metaphysical

111

programs had given way to individual inquiry, analysis, and a more free-enterprise intellectual stance.

The disappearance of "schools" at Oxford after 1320 cannot, I think, be attributed directly to Ockham's influence. As has been shown, Ockham was only moderately influential at Oxford in the next twenty years. Perhaps the type of soil in which the school traditions were rooted was not deep or rich at Oxford. School traditions, to the degree they existed at Oxford in earlier years, did not play so prominent a role as at Paris, nor did the mendicant orders, which tended to foster a school mentality, dominate Oxford as thoroughly as they dominated Paris and Cambridge. The freedom and challenge to investigate new ideas took precedence over any interest to defend the opinions of masters long dead. In fact, that spirit of free inquiry devoid of "school" concerns is one of the distinguishing features of Oxford thought in the 1330s and one of its principal gifts to Paris in the 1340s.

A second feature of the new theology is that *Sentences* commentaries, the major vehicle for scholastic theology, gradually severed their dependence on the structure of Lombard's *Sentences* and concentrated on those questions that were of most interest to the author and his contemporaries. Wodeham was one of the last English scholastics to make an attempt at relating his questions to Lombard's distinctions. The failure of that attempt is clearly revealed by the structure of his Oxford lectures, where the first book ends with the Trinity and the third book begins with future contingents. Despite the enormous length of Wodeham's commentary, the number of theological topics treated has been reduced in comparison to the earlier literature or, more precisely, concentrated around issues of central importance to that age: beatitude and fruition, the Trinity, interrelation of the divine will and human freedom, grace and divine acceptation, future contingents, and questions of penance. Those issues remain at the heart of the new theology well into the 1340s.

The third feature—and this brings us to the content of the new theology—is the degree to which the new logic and the new physics have reshaped the vocabulary and the method of theological analysis. Biblical examples and citations still abound, but just as important are the logical analysis of terms of knowing, believing, loving, and willing (*cognitio, delectatio, dilectio, odium, tristitia, volitio, nolitio*), issues of instantaneous or successive action (*incipit et desinit, simul et subito, de primo et ultimo instanti*), intention and remission of forms (*intensio, remissio, augmentatio, diminutio*), and problems of space, time, motion, infinity, proportion, velocity, and measurement. These concerns were not absent from the earlier literature, but from 1330 on they became major preoccupations, an elaborate methodological apparatus for analyzing and solving theological problems. This metalinguistic approach to theology, with its heavy use of examples from the worlds of mathematics and physics, has been seen by John Murdoch as the application of a new set of linguistic tools, "measure languages," such as that of the intention and remission of forms, proportions, *incipit et desinit, de primo et ultimo instanti, de maximo et minimo*, continuity and infinity, and others.[33] Without question these measure languages lie at the heart of the new theology, but their principal and immediate source is probably more the new logic than mathematics or physics (to the degree these are separable), which enter only because the new logic was deeply concerned with the supposition of terms of motion, growth, and change, as well as processes of the human mind and will.

This approach was not a movement away from theological concerns but was grounded in a firm belief in the unity of knowledge as well as the assumption that some theological problems could only be analyzed and solved in this way. The problem of the Trinity, for instance, received such revived interest in this period largely through the hope that the rapid developments taking place in logic (particularly those concerning *paralogismi*) would ultimately permit theologians to give an adequate account of three persons in one.[34]

On the other hand, methodologies and tools of analysis from logic and natural philosophy were not simply being applied to theological problems; within the theological literature, questions in physics and mathematics were being further developed.[35] The pred-

ilection for theology to contain arguments and insights of philosophical and scientific interest could be illustrated back into the
thirteenth and twelfth centuries, and in that sense the "unity of
learning" is an aspect of medieval thought in general, not just of
the fourteenth century. Yet it was that long-standing habit of
ignoring the boundaries between disciplines (often worrisome to
university authorities who discouraged arts masters from treating
theology and theological masters from being overly fond of philosophy) that permitted theology to respond to the new logic and the
new physics. The new theology was not the result of arts masters
who, after entering theology, could not shake loose from their
earlier training and interests. Many of the works that went to make
up the new logic and mathematics were written by students of
theology, e.g., much [of the work] of Burley, Bradwardine's *De
proportione* and his *De continuo*, and probably Kilvington's *Sophismata*. Moreover, many of those who contributed to the new theology, such as Holcot, Wodeham, Halifax, Rosetus, or Monachus
Niger, were in religious orders, whose philosophical training was
streamlined and propaedeutic, whose ultimate and immediate
goals were always theological, and who taught arts, if at all, only
after completing their theological work.

A final feature of the new theology that only becomes evident
around 1335 is the shortening of *Sentences* commentaries to a
smaller number of basic questions occupying less than half the size
of Ockham's or Wodeham's commentaries. With the exception of
Bradwardine's *Summa de causa Dei* (which is not, strictly speaking,
a *Sentences* commentary), Oxford theological commentaries would
never again reach the dimensions of Wodeham's *lectura*.[36] That
should not be interpreted as a decline in the theological interest,
for the number of commentaries increases and the individual contributions remain of high quality.[37]

These changes in English thought, viz., the entire complex of the
new logic, physics, and theology that make such an exciting body
of literature to study, did not begin to emerge until the late 1320s
and early 1330s, that is, until after the contributions to logic and
natural philosophy of Ockham, Burley, Kilvington, and Bradwardine. Because of that, the new theology as a distinct phenomenon

114

did not really exist until ca. 1330 and thus could not have been exported before that date. This chronology is important as we turn to the topic of *translatio studii*.

THE ADVENT OF ENGLISH THOUGHT AT PARIS

In tracing the spread of Ockham's thought outside England, historians have generally focused their attention on Autrecourt, Remini, and Mirecourt at Paris (active 1339–47), passing over in silence the span of two decades that separates these figures from the period of Ockham's theological and philosophical writing at Oxford and London (1317–24).[38] Considering the close ties between Paris and Oxford before the outbreak of the Hundred Years War and the four-year residence of Ockham at Avignon, where Parisian theologians were also present, why did it take so long for Ockham's thought to make a positive impact on the leading Continental university?

The Reception of Ockham's Thought

At the time Ockham completed his lectures on the *Sentences* at Oxford (ca. 1319), Paris was still the intellectual capital of Europe. The close intercommunication between the two universities remained into the late 1320s. It is not surprising to find, therefore, that Ockham's thought, at least his logic and physics, was known at Paris soon after its appearance in England. Anneliese Maier noted that Francis of Marchia, in lecturing on the *Sentences* at Paris in 1319–20, cited an opinion on "quantity" that is identical with a position put forward by Ockham in his *Sentences* commentary, several of his commentaries on Aristotle, in his *Quodlibeta*, and in *De sacramento altaris*.[39] Francis Mayronis, lecturing at Paris in 1320–21, also cites opinions that are strikingly similar to those of Ockham and which a later editor identified as such in the margin of the printed edition.[40] However, the opinions referred to by Marchia and Mayronis were not exclusively Ockham's, and since his name is not mentioned in their texts, we are not certain that Ockham was the source they had in mind.[41]

We have better evidence for the awareness of Ockham's thought at Paris in the writings of Walter Burley.[42] Burley's earliest and most continuous attack was against Ockham's natural philosophy, although the nominalist presuppositions on which it was based were common to Ockham's physics and logic. Before 1323 Burley, in his *Tractatus de formus*, attacked Ockham's physics, specifically his conception of quantity, time, motion, and change.[43] His attack was continued in his *Physics* commentary, the first sections of which were written between 1323 and 1326.[44] In the same period, particularly after the appearance of Ockham's *Summa logicae* (ca. 1324), Burley extended his attack to include Ockham's view of simple supposition and his view of universals.[45] Although Burley's critique of Ockham continued at least until 1337, long after he had left Paris for Avignon and eventually England, the early stages of his critique (ca. 1321–27) took place at Paris. Burley's knowledge of Ockham's thought could have come to him directly from Oxford, but he was made aware of it at Paris, and his critique of Ockham was delivered initially to a Parisian audience.

We also find references to Ockham's opinions on quantity, time, duration, motion, and change in the *Sentences* commentary of Michael of Massa, read at Paris in 1325–26, in which Ockham is cited by name, perhaps for the first time in a Parisian work.[46] Massa saw Ockham's position in physical theory to be a revival of the ancient oneness-philosophy of the Eliatics, which had been rejected by Plato and Aristotle.[47] One also receives the impression from Michael's commentary that Ockham's natural philosophy had won a following at Paris and that Michael was as much (if not more) concerned over Parisian supporters of Ockham as he was over Ockham himself.[48]

Thus, by the time Ockham was in Avignon awaiting the outcome of the investigation into his orthodoxy, several of his works were available at Paris and some of his views well-known. Parisians watched the proceedings in Avignon with interest, expecting that some definitive doctrinal statements might emerge. Some Franciscans were aware that opinions of Scotus were under investigation as well as those of Ockham.[49]

Ockham's "visibility" at Paris had a particular character that has not been sufficiently noted. First, it was Parisian *theologians* who were concerned about his ideas, for his opinions are cited only in works written by bachelors or masters of theology. Second, these Parisian theologians were concerned primarily about Ockham's natural philosophy and, to a lesser extent, his logic. They appear to have been less concerned over his theological opinions. Third, there is the hint that Ockham's natural philosophy had begun to attract supporters at Paris, whether within the arts or theological faculty is difficult to determine. Massa's *Okanistae* may refer to such a group, or it could also be nothing more than the common scholastic practice of giving a plural label to one person's opinion.[50] Eventually, however, such supporters of Ockham's natural philosophy did exist. The *Tractatus de successivis*, which contains the heart of Ockham's teaching on time, motion, and place, was extracted from his *Expositio in libros Physicorum* by such followers as a concise statement of Ockham's version of the new physics.[51]

Given the revolutionary quality modern historians usually attribute to Ockham's thought, it is perhaps surprising that there was not more mention of him at Paris in this period. Most areas of his thought received no mention, and many Parisian theologians ignored his logic and physics as well. By contrast, the work of Thomas, Scotus, Durand, and Aureol elicited almost immediate attention and, in the case of the latter two, not because a religious order was promoting their work but because the ideas therein evoked quick and widespread response. Why did Paris not view Ockham's work the same way?

Part of the reason may lie with a Parisian pride in their own achievements. Fourteenth-century English scholars who were familiar names to Parisian theologians were masters of theology at Paris: John Duns Scotus, Robert Cowton, Thomas Wilton, William of Alnwick, John Baconthorpe, Walter Burley, and others. They may have looked down on those whose highest degree was from an English *studium generale*. More importantly, however, Paris was at the time gripped in the controversies over Durand and Aureol, which may have left little energy for other concerns. As a *cause célèbre*, the investigation of Ockham at Avignon in 1324–28 was of only minor interest at Paris. The view from the Seine in 1328 noted some aspects of Ockham's thought worthy of comment, but whatever they found in Reading, Chatton, Fitzralph, or Rodington—if they read them at all—could not in their eyes compare with the controversies generated at Paris.

The Dormition of Paris

These features did not change for more than a decade. In the period from 1326 to 1340, Paris theology appeared to be frozen into a conservative, traditional mold that showed few signs of creativity. Not only did the newer developments in English thought go unnoticed, but the exciting aspects of Marchia, Mayronis, Massa, and Odonis were not further explored. The *Sentences* commentary of the Dominican, Bernardus Lombardi (1327–28), was unconcerned with developments later than Durand and showed a movement away from Thomism.[52] Peter of Aquila, who read in 1334 and referred once to Ockham, cited no author more recent than Landulf of Caracciolo (1320–21), and his adherence to Scotism earned for him the title of *Scotellus* ("little Scotus").[53] Thomas of Strasbourg, the Augustinian reading in 1336–37, cited no one more recent than Odonis (1325–26), ignored his fellow Augustinian Michael de Massa completely, and set himself in the school tradition of Aegidianism.[54] As late as 1337 Paris theology seemed principally concerned with the defense of their respective doctors, Thomas, Scotus, and Giles, against the threats primarily of Durand and Aureol.

In the arts faculty, the situation appears more creative. From at least 1328, John Buridan was teaching as a master of arts. Some areas of his thought, specifically his logic and his ethical theory, bear the traces of Ockham's influence, although Buridan can no longer be called a strict disciple of Ockham in his logic.[55] On the other hand, in natural philosophy Buridan was a sharp critic of Ockham.[56] He did not accept Ockham's nominalism with regard to quantity, motion, or time. If there were defenders of Ockham's natural philosophy in the arts faculty in the period 1325–40, Buridan was not among them.

118

If Buridan was aware of Ockham, he does not seem to have been particularly interested in Ockham's contemporaries (save Burley) or in the new group of scholars active at Oxford in the decade after Ockham. One searches in vain in Buridan for traces of influence from Bradwardine or Kilvington, let alone the new theology. Buridan's horizon seems to have been limited to Paris.

Why this traditionalism and isolation at Europe's leading university at a time when Oxford was experiencing the high point of its creativity? A tone of conservatism may have been set by John XXII's campaign against suspect opinions and his hounding of the Spiritual Franciscans. Already in 1326 at Avignon fifty-one opinions of Ockham were put forward for condemnation, and the writings of Peter John Olivi were reproved.[57] Three years later a list of propositions from the writings of Meister Eckhart were similarly condemned.[58] Intellectual initiative and creativity were not being rewarded by the Papacy, the leading ecclesiastical patron, and John XXII's letters to Paris demanding the arrest of the associates of Michael of Cesena and his subsequent campaign against Thomas of Wales, demanding his arrest and imprisonment, furthered a climate of caution and conservatism.[59] Until the University of Paris took and won its stand against Pope John on the beatific vision in 1334, it may not have been possible for a new generation of theologians to look beyond their own immediate, personal concerns.[60]

A second reason lay in the channels of communication between Oxford and Paris in this period. Throughout the thirteenth and early fourteenth centuries close contact was maintained. It was almost an obligation for Oxford to keep abreast of what what going on in the more prestigious university, and it consciously sought to do so. In addition to the rapid acquisition of Parisian-produced works in philosophy and theology, some Parisian masters like Roger Bacon, John Baconthorpe, and Walter Burley returned to Oxford after Paris, bringing fresh, eyewitness impressions of the teaching and disputes there. Paris, by contrast, acquired Oxford material less directly or systematically. The approved list of books available for copying in Parisian bookstores in 1304 almost totally ignores any English contributions to scholastic learning.[61] What Paris received from Oxford came through English scholars who studied or taught at Paris, primarily those in the theological faculty, such as Bacon, Scotus, Burley, and others. In this area the English students and masters in the arts faculty at Paris probably played a minor role, since they did not in most cases have any prior Oxford experience. What they brought to Paris was not Oxford logic and certainly not Oxford theology, but the grammar traditions of their preuniversity education. Whether they remained at Paris for further education or returned to England, they represent an avenue of communication, if at all, only from Paris to England, not from Oxford to Paris. The same is true for the small number of French students in English *studia*, since few had any prior Parisian experience nor did they return to Paris after their English studies.

Just as important as the presence of English students in the higher faculties at Paris was the academic mentality of the religious orders. They maintained a broader, supraprovincial perspective, both in their exchange of students between the provincial *studia* and in their desire to have the libraries of their *studia generalia* stocked with the latest works of their members. Unlike the secular theologians who, upon reaching the *magisterium*, taught within their *alma mater* or moved rapidly into an ecclesiastical career, the religious orders, especially the mendicants, sent their masters as lectors to the provincial *studia*, thus creating a continuous, enriching cross-fertilization.

A number of important changes took place in the channels of contact between Oxford and Paris after 1325. In the late 1320s and early 1330s France and England were moving toward war, which would eventually bring in both countries prohibitions against scholars going abroad for education. The Acts of the English-German Nation at Paris shows a declining English presence, and English theological students at Paris after 1325, such as John Northwode (1329) or the Cistercian, Henry of England (1340), are rare and do not seem to have completed their degree abroad.[62] Over and above the political and military situation, Oxford had finally become not only an acceptable alternative but a preferable one. By 1330 Oxford theology had surpassed Paris and for that reason alone was no longer so dependent on contemporary Parisian thought.

120

The absence of Oxford–trained logicians on the Parisian theological faculty, and more especially the absence of theological students who had already begun their theological studies in an English *studium*, goes far to explain the lack of English influence on the Parisian theology of the 1330s. English theologians at Avignon in the 1330s mingled freely with those of Paris. Lutterell, Burley, Chatton, Fitzralph, and Anthony Bec were for a time resident alongside such Parisian theologians as Palude, Odonis, Peter Roger, and Bernard Olivieri. But as far as we know, neither the Oxford nor the Paris-trained theologians returned to Paris to teach. By then they were involved in ecclesiastical careers for which the university was only preparatory.

It was unfortunate for Paris that its direct contact with English education, particularly with Oxford, all but ceased at the very time Oxford philosophy, science, and theology entered their most expansive and productive period. When Fitzralph went to Paris in 1329, the new type of Oxford thought that so captured the attention of late Parisian theologians was barely in evidence. Ockham was known, but it was primarily his philosophy that had attracted notice, and support for it was probably very minor. The logical and theological contexts were missing that would make Ockham's work more exciting and meaningful, and those did not begin to appear at Oxford until the late 1320s.

The Advent of English Thought

The atmosphere at Paris changed suddenly and radically in the years 1339–43. In September 1339 the arts faculty at Paris decreed that no unauthorized books could be read (i.e., lectured on) publically or privately, mentioning specifically the works of William of Ockham.[63] In November of the following year, Nicholas of Autrecourt, along with five other theologians, was called to Avignon to answer charges of false teaching.[64] In December 1340 the arts faculty renewed its prohibition on the teaching of Ockham's works and put forward a list of propositions that should not, without further clarification, be taught in the schools.[65] Finally, by the fall semester of 1343, in the *Sentences* commentary of Gregory of

121

Rimini, one finds a wealth of new English sources appearing, particularly those of Oxford.[66] Not only is Ockham found there in abundance, but citations from Chatton, Fitzralph, Wodeham, Bradwardine, Kilvington, Heytesbury, Buckingham, Halifax, and Monachus Niger. Although Gregory often placed his own thought over against these English thinkers, his knowledge of them and his willingness to cite them is remarkable. It is one of the striking things about Gregory's commentary that it is the first at Paris to reflect this new interest and may in part be the means by which others were stimulated to look into the important contributions of recent English thought. Almost no *Sentences* commentary at Paris in the next few generations was uninfluenced by those English writings.[67] Already by 1345 Paris was captivated by English thought as if little else existed. Richard de Bury's famous remark, although often discounted as too pro-English, is not far from the truth, as the events after 1340 were to bear out.[68] After a period of inactivity, Paris scholars had become obsessed with the "English subtleties," although they denounced them in public. One might well ask, what happened at Paris toward the end of the 1330s that produced that change, and how are the events of 1339 and 1343 related?

Because of the paucity of documentation, particularly in those critical areas of educational history before individual writers become visible to the historian, many aspects of our picture must remain at the level of conjecture. However, despite the enormous amount of literature generated by the statutes of the arts faculty of the University of Paris in 1339 and 1340 in which scholars have tried to sift out the roles and interrelationships of Ockham, Buridan, Autrecourt, and "nominalism," there are some fundamental misunderstandings in that area that can and need to be corrected.

First and most important, the papal letter of November 1340, citing Nicholas of Autrecourt and several others to Avignon to answer charges of holding suspect opinions, has little to do with the documents of the arts faculty that precede and follow it in the *Chartularium*.[69] Nicholas was a bachelor of theology and had been so for a year or more.[70] The opinions, therefore, for which he was being called before the *curia romana* were the concern of theologians, not masters of arts. The positioning of the documents in the *Chartularium*, which has led to lengthy and interesting comparisons of these statutes of the arts faculty with the writings and attributed opinions of Autrecourt, is purely coincidental.

Moreover, the two statutes of the arts faculty do not condemn the opinions of Ockham. They are rather concerned about the *type of speculation* and the teaching techniques that were going on in the lecture halls of the arts faculty in 1339 and 1340 for which Ockham was one of the sources. The statute of 1339, although in no sense a condemnation of the opinions of Ockham, attempted to block Ockham's *Summa logicae* and perhaps some of his other philosophical works from joining the official reading list of books that could be commented on in public or private lectures.[71] The statute of 1340, by contrast, is concerned with the newer views being put forward by lecturers in arts, under the influence of the writings of Ockham and possibly several other English authors. This second statute is not so much aimed at a particular kind of logic, *de virtute sermonis*, as at a teaching technique that leads students astray by considering only the falsity of certain propositions taken at face value without revealing the truth intended by the author.[72] Only the most superficial reading of Ockham's *Summa logicae* could credit that approach to Ockham, but it is certainly possible the lecturers in arts who wished to limit their analysis of propositions to the meaning *de virtute sermonis* might have claimed Ockham's theory of simple supposition as support for that approach.[73] It must be kept in mind, however, that both statutes concern the arts faculty alone. No similar prohibitions exist for the faculty of theology.

If the arts statutes of 1339 and 1340 were aimed at Ockham only indirectly and probably not at the theologian Autrecourt in any sense, at whom were they directed? The usual answer to this question is "the Ockhamists," cited in the title caption of the 1340 statute and mentioned again in the Register of the English-German Nation.[74] Their identity and relation to Ockham has yet to be determined. In any event, there is little reason to label the 1340 statute "nominalist." Apart from the anachronistic use of a fifteenth-century label, there is little about the statute that concerns either the logic or the natural philosophy of Ockham.[75]

There is one indirect way in which the summons of Autrecourt to Avignon may have been related to the arts statute of 1340. One of the fears expressed in the statute was that a failure to go behind the surface meaning of a statement to make clear the intention of the author might lead to the misinterpretation of the Bible by claiming biblical statements false *de virtute sermonis*, when, on a different level, they were true. It would seem they had in mind passages that were traditionally interpreted spiritually or allegorically and whose literal meaning was unacceptable. This fear would have been the concern of theologians, not masters of arts. It is possible, therefore, that in 1340 there were students in theology who handled biblical and theological propositions *de virtute sermonis* and defended their procedure on the grounds of current practice in the arts faculty. If so, theological masters concerned over the teaching techniques and analytical method of theological bachelors, such as Autrecourt, might well have put pressure upon the arts masters to prohibit these practices at the preparatory stage, i.e., in the arts faculty. If Autrecourt learned his techniques or approach in the arts faculty, it would have been in the late 1320s before he became a student in the theological faculty.

Through what channels did this interest in Ockham and other English theologians enter the arts and theological faculties at Paris? The interest in Ockham among the *Artistae* may have developed naturally out of the presence at Paris of his works in logic and natural philosophy. Ockham's theological ideas, however, were not commented on at Paris before the 1340s. When they received attention, it was in the context of the new English theology. What was taking place, therefore, was not so much the advent of Ockham's thought, which was accessible at Paris for well over a decade, but the advent of the new theology.[76]

One possible avenue for the introduction of the new theology is that English theologians, such as Wodeham and Rodington, who went to Basel for the general chapter meeting of the Franciscans in

1339, may have visited the Paris convent and stimulated interest in the newer work.[77] More likely is the possibility that the newer English thought was already well established in Italian *studia* in the late 1330s and was brought to Paris specifically by Italian scholars, such as Gregory of Rimini. That possibility deserves some amplification.

Throughout the 1330s, in contrast to the small number of French students studying abroad in England, one encounters Italian students in English *studia*, specifically Oxford, London, and Norwich.[78] Most of them belonged to the mendicant orders and, like the Franciscan, Nicholas of Assisi, returned eventually to Italy to teach in one or more of the provincial *studia*. Slowly the libraries of the Italian convents, particularly those of the Franciscans at Assisi, Perugia, and elsewhere, acquired manuscripts of the newer English works,[79] and their use in the classroom would have stimulated interest in those works among the other mendicant orders in centers, like Perugia and Bologna, where the mendicants operated what were for them *studia generalia*, where lectures on philosophy were given and where the *Sentences* were read.[80] In some respects these mendicant *studia generalia*, especially where they coincided with cathedral and collegiate schools, were more important for intellectual formation than the universities, which for the thirteenth and fourteenth centuries have received almost all our attention. It was these *studia* that gave many students their entire philosophical training and much of their preparation in theology. Moreover, it was in these *studia*, by the second quarter of the fourteenth century, that theological students did their early teaching before reading at the university. To them masters returned to teach after their regency or the attainment of the *magisterium*. By comparison the time spent at the university could be much briefer. Unfortunately for us, these mendicant *studia* are not well documented, and the university years, no matter how brief, often produce the best documentation.

Thus the channels of communication between the Continent and England, which had shrunk for Paris in the 1330s, were active for Italy in that same period. Alfonso Maierù speaks of the later

125

stages of this development as a cultural invasion of Italy by English thought, and the date of many of the manuscripts and the biographies of individuals such as Nicholas of Assisi indicates that this invasion took place at least as early as its Parisian counterpart, possibly earlier.[81] In any event, it was that environment that prepared the theological perspectives and training of the first Parisian theologian to reflect the new theology: Gregory of Rimini.

Gregory of Rimini

When Gregory returned to Paris in 1341 or 1342 to undertake his baccalaureate, some portions of his *Sentences* commentary had probably been drafted in the preceding years while lecturing in Italy at Bologna, Padua, and Perugia. Furthermore, the places where Gregory had lived and lectured would have brought him in close contact with the more prominent teaching centers of the other mendicant orders. Bologna was a *studium generale* for the four major mendicant orders, Padua a *studium generale* for the Franciscans, and Perugia a *studium* for logic, natural philosophy, and theology for Dominicans and Franciscans. Also, the close proximity of Perugia with the Franciscan *studium generale* at Assisi, with its contacts with the English *studia*, is an important link when one considers the availability of sources. In any event, before Gregory began his Parisian lectures in 1343, he had acquired most of his knowledge of the newer English sources, either in Italy or through the libraries available to him at Paris.[82]

Whatever the setting, the breadth of Gregory's familiarity with the newer English thought is striking. His extensive knowledge of Burley and Ockham is not so surprising, considering what we know already of Paris.[83] But his interest in Ockham the theologian, not just the logician or natural philosopher, is new. When one adds to those sources Gregory's citations of Kilvington's *Sophismata* and Heytesbury's *Sophismata*, it is apparent that he was familiar with the basic texts of the new logic.[84]

Gregory was also well versed in the new theology. Beyond Chatton and Fitzralph,[85] who are first cited at Paris by Gregory, he was familiar with Wodeham (the Oxford lectures, the London lectures, and the *Lectura secunda*),[86] Bradwardine's *Summa de causa Dei* (at least by the time he completed his *textus ordinarius*, 1346–48),[87] and the *Sentences* commentaries of Kilvington, Buckingham, Halifax, and Monachus Niger.[88] In fact, there are few English theologians from the previous twenty years that Gregory did not know (or at least did not mention).[89] By contrast, he chose not to cite a number of Parisian theologians who were frequently mentioned by others: Alexander of Hales, Bonaventure, Landulf of Caracciolo, Francis Mayronis, Gerard of Siena, Gerard Odonis, and Peter of Aquila. Gregory was as much in dialogue with English theologians as with Parisian.

What effect did Gregory's contact with the newer English thought have on his own work, either his method or his philosophical and theological conclusions? In light of the recent tendency among scholars to see Gregory as a conservative Augustinian theologian opposed to Ockhamism, logic-chopping, and Pelagian theology, one might imagine there was little in English thought beyond Bradwardine's *De causa Dei* that he could view in a positive way.[90] Was his attitude toward these sources one of opposition and their influence, therefore, negative? This is a large and important question, and only a few essential aspects can be examined here.

Gregory's Method: Structure and Content

In contrast to the work of Thomas of Strasbourg, Gregory's not too distant predecessor as Augustinian *Sententiarius* at Paris, the style and mood of Gregory's commentary seems like a different intellectual world. Gone is the heavy dependence on Giles of Rome, the prominent place of metaphysics, the preoccupation with questions of 'being' and 'act.' In its place one finds a greater concern for problems of evidence and certitude, the structure of physical nature, and the interrelation of God and man. This shift has sometimes been ascribed to Gregory's rediscovery of Augustine.[91] It is not simply Gregory's thorough reading of Augustine, however, that marks the new and distinctive character of his commentary (although it is certainly an important feature), but the way in which his reading of recent English theology altered his interests and his approach. Gregory's debt to the metalinguistic, physical, mathematical, and theological interests of recent Oxford thinkers was great, and even some aspects of his Augustinianism may have been informed or shaped by his reading of English theologians.

First, Gregory's interest in the physical world and even his theology utilizes the "measure languages" and the "limit languages" of the new logic and theology.[92] One often encounters mathematical examples and questions that deal with the infinite, eternity, the continuum, time, motion, succession, *primum instans*, velocity, proportion, magnitude, *gradus*, *minimum-maximum*, *magis-minum*, augmentation and diminution, intention and remission, and that favorite topic that embraces so many of the analytical tools mentioned above as well as the psychological antinomies (*velle-nolle*, *amor-odium*, *fruitio-tristitia*): *de contradictorio in contradictorium transire*.[93] Although some of these interests were shared by earlier Parisian theologians (e.g., Marchia, Massa, Odonis) and would become more omnipresent in later ones (e.g., Mirecourt and Ceffons), Gregory's use of this approach is extensive and coincides remarkably with his citations to recent English authors.

Second, many of the questions that receive expanded treatment in Gregory (in contrast to earlier Parisian theologians) are those that had already fascinated English theologians, and again it is the English *auctoritates* that figure prominently in Gregory's discussions. One thinks immediately of his epistemology, his understanding of propositional logic, and the problem of the object of knowledge and belief.[94] But it is also true of his discussions of the acts of the human will and intellect, of *cognitio*, *notitia*, *volitio*, *dilectio*, *delectatio*, and *fruitio*, as well as the questions concerning the interrelation of the divine and human wills, such as grace and justification, future contingents, whether God can lie, and the *de odio Dei*.[95] As with Wodeham, one finds in Gregory a full-scale treatment of the Trinity from the standpoint of logic, *paralogismi*, and relation (*paternitas*, *filiatio*).[96] Gregory even cites recent English opinion on such standard questions in Parisian theology as God's existence, the subject of theology, and divine omnipotence.[97]

128

Adopting a language and a methodology does not imply that one adopts conclusions as well. What influence did English thought have on Gregory's solutions to the questions posed by the literature he inherited? To answer this, one would need to give attention to each English source Gregory used and examine each question for which they are important. Some impressions can be gained by examining Gregory's attitude toward and use of his major (and most controversial) English source: William of Ockham. It was supposedly against Ockham that Gregory formulated the two innovations for which he is most famous: his teaching on the *complexe significabile* and his strongly anti-Pelagian theology of grace.

Gregory and Ockham

Gregorian scholarship has come a long way from the days when Rimini was considered the "standard-bearer of the Nominalists." The present tendency is to polarize Ockham and Rimini. This has created a false picture and obscured some of the legitimate reasons why earlier generations linked the two names.

It is easy to be misled by the fact that when Gregory cites Ockham he usually disagrees with him. Gregory's scholastic style seldom reveals the contemporary or recent authors with whom he is in agreement. He acknowledges his debt to the fathers, especially Augustine, but never his debt to the doctors. Thus he introduces Ockham or Wodeham, as he does Thomas or Scotus, to set up a variety of opinions against which he will demonstrate his own knowledge and ability to provide a solution. On many questions Ockham will appear as an opponent when, in fact, Gregory is essentially adopting Ockham's position and making only minor modifications on it.

When one looks, therefore, not at what Gregory says about Ockham but at what he does in the position he adopts, one recognizes that Gregory shares almost the entire natural philosophy of Ockham as well as much of his logic and epistemology. With slight modifications Gregory adopts Ockham's position on relation,[98] motion,[99] time,[100] and quantity.[101] That is no small point since, as

Weisheipl and others have observed, those positions are important building blocks of Ockham's nominalism and are closely associated with his redefinition of simple supposition.[102] Moreover, it was Ockham's natural philosophy probably more than any other aspect of his thought that angered a generation of Parisian theologians. Rimini's is the first Parisian work in either the arts or theological faculty to adopt Ockham's natural philosophy.

Gregory's epistemology, much of his logic, and his approach to the problem of universals are also heavily dependent on Ockham;[103] but here one must add two important reservations. Gregory did not follow Ockham in his rejection of intelligible and sensible species, nor did he agree with Ockham on the issue of the object of knowledge.[104] For Ockham the object of knowledge was not the *res extra*, but the proposition.[105] For Gregory the object of knowledge was the total *significatum* of the proposition or, more precisely, that which is propositionally signifiable (*complexe significabile*).[106] How important are these two issues in separating Gregory from the tradition of Ockham?

These two particular issues were ones that even the closest of Ockham's followers had difficulty in assimilating. Ockham's rejection of species, whatever its relation to his nominalism or his desire to dispense with unnecessary pluralities, was not unique but drew upon arguments in earlier Parisian theology.[107] By contrast, and it is difficult to find anyone after Ockham who felt that species were unnecessary to the cognitive process,[108] Holcot retained them.[109] Wodeham, Ockham's closest follower, retained them.[110] Given the arguments against Ockham's position that had been raised in English circles between 1320 and 1340 – sources that Gregory knew well – it would be remarkable if Gregory had not retained species.

The case is similar with Ockham's position on the object of knowledge. It did not sit well. It was rejected by Chatton and Crathorn (which one might expect) and modified by Holcot and Wodeham (which one might not expect).[111] Wodeham's modification is the most interesting here. In his lectures on the *Sentences* at London and again in his *Lectura secunda* after Oxford, he modified Ockham's position by creating what amounts to the *complexe signi-*

ficabile.[112] The parallelism of the passages in Wodeham and Gregory, as Gedeon Gál has recently shown, makes clear that Gregory's theory or version of the problem was adopted from Wodeham. The fact that later Parisian authors, such as Jean de Ripa, attribute the idea originally to Gregory is only evidence that they did not know their Wodeham and other English sources as well as did Gregory.

If one lays the philosophy of Rimini, the logic, epistemology, and physics, alongside that of Wodeham, one has an almost one-to-one correspondence. Where Wodeham agreed with Ockham (which is the case most of the time), Gregory also agrees. Where Wodeham departed from or modified Ockham's position, Gregory sided with Wodeham. On the basis of that realization, one cannot set Rimini's philosophy in direct opposition to Ockham's.

Gregory and the Pelagian Crisis

Gregory's theology, particularly his understanding of grace and justification, stands in opposition to that of Ockham and Wodeham. Was this the real break between Gregory and English thought, or did Gregory even here draw some of his vision and argumentation from English sources?

Ockham's teaching on justification and grace was attacked immediately in England as Pelagian;[113] alongside his Eucharistic theology, it was one of the principal areas brought under investigation at Avignon. Interestingly enough, it was not the Dominicans or Augustinians who attacked Ockham on this point, but Franciscans and secular theologians. The first critique came from Chatton in his *Reportatio* of 1321–23.[114] Chatton's attack occurred almost simultaneously with that of Lutterell, who prepared the list of suspect propositions for the Avignon trial.[115] The censured propositions of 1326 did not end the debate. Wodeham (1330–34) defended Ockham's position against Chatton,[116] and Halifax (also a Franciscan, writing ca. 1334–40) attacked Wodeham for being a Pelagian.[117] Thomas Bradwardine entered this controversy in the same period. Probably in his *Sentences* commentary, now dated

131

with reasonable certainty to 1332–33 but no longer extant, and certainly in a treatise on penance written while he was *baccalaurius formatus* (1334–37) Bradwardine attacked the "modern Pelagians" for their view on grace and justification.[118] Bradwardine's *De poenitentia* (now lost) was eventually incorporated into his *Summa de causa Dei*, just as was his *De futuris contingentibus* (written before 1337).[119] We do not know the extent and exact nature of his early version of Bradwardine's attack on the "Pelagians," but his position was known in England before 1340 and possibly on the Continent as well.

Thus throughout the period 1320–40 there was a strong current of anti-Pelagian feeling among certain English theologians. The crucial area of debate was not the necessity or dispensability of grace, *de potentia absoluta*, but the nature and operation of grace *de facto*. Ockham and Wodeham, and even more so Holcot, had designated a large area of positive human achievement apart from grace.[120] Good acts, even the complete love of God above all other things, were within the power of the natural man. But man could not, solely on the grounds of such acts, earn salvation by attaining the acceptation of God that made good acts meritorious. Chatton, Lutterell, Halifax, and Bradwardine saw that position as Pelagian and insisted that the avoidance of sin and the achievement of a good act were just as much the combined product of human free will and divine grace as was the meritorious or acceptable act. Bradwardine's *Summa de causa Dei*, which in its final form appeared in 1344, was not the beginning of an attack on semi-Pelagianism but the final and definitive statement of a position that had been voiced for several decades in England.

When Gregory presented his own attack against the "modern Pelagians" in 1343–44 at Paris, he was familiar with the English theological literature on the question. He was familiar with Chatton, Wodeham, and Halifax, although he may not yet have known Bradwardine's position.[121] Gregory's treatment of the problem had some distinctive characteristics and was not simply derivative from his English sources. His analysis of the question is much more extensive and far better argued than by either Chatton or Halifax.[122] Moreover, unlike Chatton, Gregory combined a strong attack on Peter Aureol and the absolute necessity of grace (in the tradition of Scotus, Ockham, and Wodeham) with a strong defense of the total necessity of grace *de potentia ordinata* (against Ockham and Wodeham). There can be no question that Gregory knew and used the English anti-Pelagian arguments and focused the problem where they had, on the *de facto* operation of grace. It is also true that Gregory, as in so many areas, made the discussion of his own and brought it to a new level.

English Thought and the Condemnation of 1347

In the years after Gregory of Rimini's *Lectura*, it is hard to find a *Sentences* commentary at Paris that is not influenced in some way by the newer English thought. John of Mirecourt, who read the year after Gregory, not only cited numerous English sources but lifted entire sections from Bradwardine, Halifax, Buckingham, and others.[123] Alfonsus Vargas of Toledo, who also read at Paris in 1344–45, followed Gregory's lead in utilizing the newer English thought and added the name of Rodington to the corpus of *Anglici* known at Paris.[124] Similarly, in 1348–49, in the commentaries of Hugolino of Orvieto and Peter Ceffons, one finds the same awareness of and, especially in the case of Ceffons, dependence upon, English authors.[125] Although Hugolino has a smaller list of English authors than did Gregory, he does cite Ockham, Wodeham, Kilvington, Halifax, and Buckingham, and there is reason to think he was aware of Bradwardine as well. Moreover, with Hugolino and Ceffons we find additional English sources joining the Parisian repertory: Robert Holcot, Alexander Langeley, and John Stuckele.

Paris never retreated from the impact of this invasion of English thought. Almost every commentary written at Paris up to the end of the century cites these English authors and is influenced by the issues and approaches contained therein. Some, like Jean de Ripa, rarely reveal the debt, although it can be traced in his work.[126] Others like John Hiltalingen of Basel, Pierre d'Ailly, Henry Totting of Oyta, and even John Capreolus, the *princeps Thomistarum*, are less reticent about the importance of the English contribution.

133

Because English thought was found so inherently interesting by Parisian theologians after 1343, even by such conservative Augustinians as Gregory and Hugolino, one would assume that the new Parisian Articles—derived from a series of propositions condemned between 1347 and 1352—either had little to do with *subtilitates Anglicanae* or were directed at an extremism born of misuse. Yet most historians since Michalski have suspected that the new Parisian Articles were in some way a response to the invasion of English thought into Paris.

The 1347 condemnation has been viewed as a turning point in the history of the Paris theological faculty, the culmination of an almost decade-long controversy over Ockhamism.[127] In that view the new articles blocked the development of Ockhamism at Paris (or deradicalized nominalism) in much the same way the first Parisian Articles of 1277 blocked the growth of Latin Averroism. Others taking a longer view of things saw in 1347 the limitation of speculation *de potentia Dei absoluta* that had been set in motion by the antideterministic tone of the first Parisian Articles, which reasserted the freedom of God over man, nature, and events. On the basis of recent research, what was the relationship between the "English invasion" and the new Parisian Articles?

The first observation is that most of the propositions extracted from Mirecourt's commentary, which form the bulk of the new Parisian Articles, were extracted precisely from those sections in which Mirecourt was citing English texts. Many of them are English theological propositions. The examiners were disturbed by the provocative nature of the propositions themselves as well as Mirecourt's failure (in their view) to resolve questions in a clear, efficient, and decisive manner, thus allowing students to be perplexed or, worse, stumble into false opinion. The authors of the 1347 condemnation were not attacking Ockhamism or some radical form of nominalism; they were attacking a method of theological argumentation that Paris inherited from Oxford, namely the use of theological *sophismata* to test and improve the analytical skills of students in theology.[128] For them, provocative theological propositions that seemed to attribute to God the impossible or impugned the divine nature by making God responsible for sin should be avoided or quickly rebutted, not sophistically analyzed.

A second observation is that the Parisian masters of theology were seriously divided over this issue far more than the Articles reflect. Of the six *Sentences* commentaries that survive from Paris in the decade 1340–50, five are heavily dependent on English theology, although not all adopt the methods of the new theology to the same degree. The two Cistercian commentaries, those of Mirecourt and Ceffons, stand closest to the English method. Those of Alphonsus Vargas and Hugolino are more reserved. The *Sentences* commentary of Gregory stands in between. Contrary to what is sometimes asserted, Gregory was not among the authors of the condemnation.[129] He held at least one opinion that was condemned in 1347 and had left Paris before the condemnation took place.

If the majority of those who were actively writing theology at Paris in the decade 1340-50 show traces of the method and ideas that came under attack in 1347, who were the masters who compiled or signed the Parisian Articles? The testimony of Peter Ceffons suggests that they were older theologians, probably seculars who could remain regent masters for many years in contrast to mendicants, who usually moved out of Paris soon after completing the required regency.[130] But among them may have been younger mendicants as well. The commentary of the Carmelite, Paul of Perugia, who read in the same year as Alphonsus and Mirecourt, shows no English influence, nor do the fragments that survive from the commentaries of the Franciscans, James of Spinalo and Astensius.[131] Despite the fact that Augustinians, particularly Gregory, did make use of English thought, no members of the four major mendicant orders were accused of fantastic opinions or false teaching in the critical period 1340–47. On the contrary, the major opponent of Autrecourt was a Franciscan, Bernard of Arezzo, and Hugolino, whose commentary is less dependent on the English method than Gregory's, made the new Parisian Articles part of the guidelines for the theological faculty created at Bologna (1360–64).[132]

A third observation is that the new Parisian Articles were produced by the university and were not binding outside Paris unless, as at Bologna, they were specifically written into the statutes. Unlike the product of the Avignon commission that investigated Autrecourt and which probably contained some non-Parisian theologians, the new Parisian Articles were not papal or suprauniversity in perspective, nor did they have the international and ecclesiastical authority of the Articles of 1277, which were applied to Oxford as well as Paris and which were issued by the Bishop of Paris and the Archbishop of Canterbury. The Paris theologians chose to break with traditional procedures of academic doctrinal investigation and not transfer the investigation of suspect theological opinions to an outside ecclesiastical agency. In doing so they may have been asserting their right as protector and definer of theological orthodoxy or simply expressing frustration that the investigation of Autrecourt, which probably became a concern of the faculty and turned over to the papacy in 1339, took until 1346 to resolve itself.

One final observation: the movement after 1347 to decentralize theological education and break the Parisian-Oxonian monopoly on the *magisterium* may have been aided by the belief that Oxford and Parisian theology had become too radical and that the mendicants were the voices of caution and orthodoxy. The new faculties of theology established at Prague, Bologna, and attempted elsewhere were initially dominated by mendicant theologians. The program of decentralization was eventually successful, although the new foundations north of the Alps, with the exception of Prague, did not flourish when first founded and had to be renewed at the end of the century.[133]

It is hard to isolate the particular ways in which Parisian theology was changed under the impact of English thought. In contrast to Oxford after 1334, Parisian commentaries did not reduce themselves to five or ten central questions independent from the organization of Lombard's *Sentences*. One continues to find at Paris long commentaries whose structure remains wedded to the distinctions of Peter Lombard. As to content, the interests of Parisian theologians in problems of logic, physics, and mathematics did not begin in the 1340s. One already finds these interests in the commentaries of Marchia, Massa, Odonis, and Aquila, which is probably why the newer English sources eventually did find such an apt audience at Paris. The new element in content is that these mathematical and metalinguistic interests were further stimulated, and the language and much of the method of Oxford theology was adopted.

The one area in which English thought may have had a fundamental shaping effect on Paris lies in the area of school traditions. Coincident with the arrival in Paris of the type of English thought that had ended school traditions at Oxford, we find the rapid eclipse of school traditions at Paris. Between 1340 and the end of the century we do not find Thomists, Scotists, or Aegidians. Instead there is a community of individuals contributing in individual ways to a common body of theological problems. When John of Basel in 1365 used the phrase "*scola nostra,*" he had in mind any doctor among the Austin Friars who lectured in the convent, not a particular *Lehrrichtung*. We do not find the school traditions, the world of the Thomists, Albertists, and terminists returning until the very last years of the fourteenth century, a world fragmented by the Great Schism and on the eve of the Council of Constance. The half-century of school independence that took over Paris in 1340 also produced one of its greatest and most creative periods. That in itself may be the major and most salutory gift of English thought to Paris in this period.

THE ARRIVAL OF ENGLISH THOUGHT ON GERMAN SOIL

There is no question that the ecclesiastical and political events of the early 1380s, especially as they were responded to by the University of Paris and the King of France, ultimately caused a migration of German scholars from Paris and provided German teaching centers with men of high reputation and vision.[134] Despite the temptation to link directly the Parisian exodus of scholars with the dissemination of nominalism, it is unlikely that the philosophical and theological ideas they brought with them, to the degree that these were either Ockhamist or nominalist, were as new to Germany as is sometimes suggested. It is quite possible that the intellectual orientation that developed into the *via moderna* and the *nominales* of the early fifteenth century was established on German soil before the Parisian exodus. It may even be that what is sometimes seen as the predominance of nominalism at Paris in the third quarter of the fourteenth century, as represented by Marsilius of Inghen, Henry of Langenstein, Henry Totting of Oyta, and Pierre d'Ailly, was not a simple and direct Parisian inheritance from the generation of John Buridan, Gregory of Rimini, and Peter Ceffons, but an intellectual orientation influenced by developments that had already taken place in Germany.

The Schools of Medieval Germany

In tracing the intellectual history of late medieval Germany, one sometimes overlooks the fact that German higher education did not begin with the founding (or, in the case of Vienna and Erfurt, refounding) of universities in the late fourteenth century. From at least the end of the thirteenth century, thus well before the founding of the University of Prague in 1347, one could obtain a basic training in philosophy and theology without venturing outside German-speaking lands.

Two types of schools for the study of philosophy and theology existed. First of all, there were schools for the training of the secular clergy, both cathedral schools in episcopal cities and collegiate schools there and elsewhere, especially in the towns along important trade routes.[135] Many of the collegiate chapters were independent, but some belonged to congregations, such as the Austin Canons or the Schottenklöster. Secondly, there were schools for the regular clergy, principally the *studia* of the mendicant orders.[136] Both types of schools were fed by secondary schools, local convents in the case of the mendicants and town schools in the case of the secular clergy, that provided basic training in grammar, logic, and the other liberal arts. The system was not centralized, although it became more so in the course of the fourteenth century.[137]

The most important centers of study in fourteenth-century Germany were those towns in which numerous schools for the secular clergy coincided with major *studia* of the mendicant orders. Of these Cologne was the most important, having numerous collegiate schools and a *studium generale* for each of the four major mendicant orders.[138] By the second quarter of the fourteenth century, Cologne could boast of a teaching heritage that included Albertus Magnus, Thomas Aquinas, John Duns Scotus, and Meister Eckhart. Not only did Cologne attract German students, but it was one of the three *studia generalia* (alongside Paris and Bologna) to which Polish and Hungarian friars could come to complete their education.[139] Magdeburg was a *studium* of philosophy and theology for the Dominicans and Franciscans; Erfurt, a town rich in schools, was a major *studium* for the Dominicans, Franciscans, and Augustinians.[140] Prague was a *studium generale* for the Franciscans and Augustinians, and after 1347 for the Dominicans and Carmelites as well.[141] In Poland the centers that became significant were Wroclaw (Breslau) and Cracow, and in the area of Austria and Hungary Vienna, which had many secular and religious schools, was a *studium generale* only for the Augustinians.[142]

These centers of higher learning were not universities throughout most of the fourteenth century, with the exception of the schools of Prague, which were raised to university status in 1347. They did not grant degrees nor confer the *ius ubique docendi*. They were not open to students from all provinces (again with the exception of Prague and Cologne). They also did not have all four faculties of arts, theology, law, and medicine. And yet they possessed all the features of a university as far as the exchange of ideas and most academic exercises were concerned. The schools of a town were closely interrelated. For example, at Erfurt the four town schools (Marienstift, Severi-Stift, Schottenkloster [St. Jacobus], and the Augustinerchorherren) were united under one rector.[143] The mendicant classrooms at Erfurt and elsewhere were open to those of other orders and to nonregulars as well. The mendicant graduate of one of these *studia* could teach in the convents of the order as *lector* without attaining the *magisterium* of the university. And perhaps most importantly, these centers produced commentaries on Aristotle, works in logic, *Sentences* commentaries, and quodlibetic questions, most of which, unfortunately, were never circulated in manuscripts.

Since these *studia* with one exception were not universities, they did not produce abundant documentation, nor did they have the desire or need to preserve the products of their intellectual activity. Their lectures and debates were preparatory or reflective of the university and, for the most part, did not pretend to claim the level of quality or general appeal that would warrant publication. Thus in looking for the presence and influence of English thought one has fewer sources to examine than for Paris. But one cannot infer that there was consequently less intellectual activity. What evidence there is suggests that the newer English thought was known in German *studia* by the 1340s. Each academic center expressed this through a different type of evidence, e.g., grammar and logic at Erfurt, and theology at Cologne. In light of the close contact and intellectual exchange that existed among the *studia* of each mendicant order and the fact that philosophy and theology were studied at Cologne, Erfurt, and Prague, it would be dangerous to treat those places as isolated centers, each with its own separate intellectual life. The close contacts between Prague and Erfurt are well documented.[144] We should proceed, therefore, as archaeologists, aware that the evidence unearthed at one site may not be unique but may be symptomatic of more widely shared interests and beliefs.

Before turning to the presence and influence of English thought in Germany, we should consider the channels of communication between Germany and educational centers elsewhere. All the centers mentioned above, including the University of Prague, maintained an academic connection with Paris, the principal university on the Continent conferring the doctorate in theology. We must assume that German students returning from Paris as masters of arts or doctors of theology brought with them the fruits of their learning experience—the ideas, methodologies, sources, and manuscripts acquired in their years of study abroad. For the mendicants, as was noted earlier, the years in a provincial *studium* spent in preparation for the university or lecturing after the university would usually outnumber the years actually spent at the university. Thus there would have been a constant flow between the German *studia* and Paris throughout the fourteenth century.

There is no reason to assume, however, that intellectual influences from outside Germany were necessarily mediated through Paris. There were direct ties with Bologna, as is evidenced by the career of Conrad of Ebrach.[145] Moreover, the names of German and Czech students studying at Oxford reveal a contact with English theology that was firsthand and, in the case of late fourteenth-century Prague, particularly influential.[146] In the period from 1340 to 1355, one finds at Oxford secular clerks and theologians such as Master Sifridus and Ebrard Huoprost, the Augustinian John Klenkok, the Franciscans Herman of Cologne and Friedrich of Regensburg, and the Dominican from Prague, Jan Moravecz.[147] They came directly from central Europe to Oxford, and in most cases returned without attending Paris as well. Thus, some of the interest in English thought we find in Germany at mid-century probably came directly from England.

One final channel of communication must be explored. One might expect that some of the newer English sources, particularly the works of Ockham, would have come via the Franciscan convent in Munich, where Ockham was in residence from 1328 until his death in 1347. This was probably not the case. The Franciscan convent at Munich, although it housed at times a number of distinguished theologians, was neither an important teaching convent nor a *studium particulare theologiae*. Ockham's activity in Germany appears to have been directed solely to political thought and ecclesiological problems. By contrast, the textual traditions of his theological and philosophical writings are closely tied with England.

Paris and Oxford remain the two best sources for the dissemination of the newer English thought into the German *studia*. Since there is very little evidence that these sources were significant at

Paris before the 1340s, we can assume that their presence in Germany before 1345 was probably coming directly from England rather than through Paris.

The New Logic in Germany

Interest in English logic and, to a lesser degree, in English natural philosophy can be established for German *studia* well before the 1380s. Among the surviving manuscripts of the works that comprise the new logic and physics at Oxford are a number of German and East European manuscripts of the fourteenth century, some of them remarkably early. For example, at Magdeburg in 1341 the Augustinian friar Conrad of Nipeth made a copy of Ockham's *Summa logicae*.[148] Numerous fourteenth-century manuscripts of the same work copied by German, Czech, or Hungarian scribes have survived.[149] One of these, Munich, Staatsbibl., clm 23 530, is even more reflective of the newer English thought since in addition it contains Bradwardine's *Insolubilia*, Kilvington's *Sophismata*, and various treatises of Heytesbury. One of the few surviving manuscripts of Ockham's *Tractatus de successivis*, copied before 1350, is German.[150] The only surviving manuscripts of Heytesbury's *Insolubilia* are in Italy and Erfurt.[151] And the earliest extant copy of Heytesbury's *Regulae solvendi sophismata*, copied in 1337 two years after its composition, was brought from England to Germany by a Franciscan from Cologne.[152] A large majority of the manuscripts of this last work are Italian or German.[153]

The presence of manuscripts of English logic in Germany in the second and third quarters of the fourteenth century suggests more than the availability of these ideas. It also reveals a strong interest. And we have evidence that English works had an influence in shaping opinion. In a *sophisma* presented at Erfurt in 1332, John Aurifaber adopted a position similar to Ockham in order to criticize the *novi modi significandi* of the grammarians.[154] Aurifaber's work circulated quickly and widely. One surviving copy was made at Deventer in 1333.[155] Its influence was felt even outside Germany and the Low Countries, since it was one of the sources for Pierre d'Ailly's *Destructiones modorum significandi.*[156] We also find the Franciscan Otto of Merseburg at Erfurt, writing a commentary on Porphyry and the *Categories* of Aristotle that is Ockhamist in tone.[157] Similarly, an anonymous commentary containing questions on various works of Aristotle, written at Erfurt between 1350 and 1375, cites Ockham seventeen times.[158]

The works of the new English logic were available and influential in Germany before the 1380s, particularly at Erfurt, but elsewhere as well. How much of a positive impact they made is another question. There is no indication that the logic and natural philosophy of Ockham, for example, were widely adopted in the German schools of this period to the exclusion of other positions. The popularity of Ockham's works probably depended upon the wider interest in the newer English thought. As the teaching of logic developed in the German *studia* of the fourteenth century, it was largely to England that they looked, importing Burley and Sutton as well as Ockham, Kilvington, Heytesbury, and Dumbleton.[159] What they sought was not nominalism or Ockhamism but the new treatises and learning aids that had been developed in England. In the process, however, Ockham's philosophy did get an early foothold and a favorable hearing in the German *studia.*

The New Theology

In a wave parallel to the importation of the new logic, the theological works of Ockham, Holcot, Wodeham, Kilvington, Halifax, and others made their way into Germany before 1380. Manuscripts of Holcot's *Sentences* commentary are well represented in central and eastern Europe.[160] One manuscript, copied at the Franciscan convent in Prague in 1359-60, contains portions of the *Sentences* commentaries of Holcot, Kilvington, and Halifax. The commentary of Halifax, most copies of which are found in Italy and Germany, has survived in Magdeburg, Eichstätt, Frankfurt, and Vienna, the last three from Dominican convents.[161] Frederick of Regensburg, who studied at Oxford around 1354, acquired a copy of the *Sentences* commentary of Monachus Niger, which he carried back to Germany.[162] Also, before 1350 a subredaction of Wodeham's *Ordinatio* was prepared, probably in northern Germany.[163] One copy, dated around 1350, belonged to the Franciscan convent in Lüneburg, and another (not at Erfurt) to the Franciscans at Faldern and Verden.

When we turn from the interest revealed by the surviving manuscripts to actual influence, we have far less evidence to go on. What we have, however, is significant. Surprisingly, we find the presence of Ockham's theological thought at Cologne in the 1340s, mediated by way of Adam Wodeham. Between 1334 and 1348 a student at Cologne read the *Sentences* "secundum Adam."[164] This *Extractio* of Wodeham's *Lectura*, being a reduced version of Wodeham's text with personal comments added by the lecturer, abounds in citations from Ockham and other English authors, as did the original work of Wodeham. Like Cologne, Prague was also aware of the newer English theology. Henry Totting of Oyta, in his lectures at Prague around 1370, before going to Paris, was familiar with Bradwardine.[165] His interest in English theology resulted in his abbreviation of Wodeham's Oxford lectures, probably completed at Paris around 1375.[166]

It would be remarkable that such interest in English theology, particularly in Wodeham, would not also be reflected at Erfurt. And yet the few surviving manuscripts of fourteenth-century Erfurt theology contain few direct references to Ockham.[167] They need to be reexamined with eyes that look not for Ockham alone but for the influence of a broader range of English theology.

Conclusions

The introduction into Germany of the fourteenth-century English contributions to logic, physics, and theology occurred in the second and third decades of the fourteenth century, as it did at Paris and in the *studia* of Italy. The presence of the thought of Ockham and Wodeham in the two major centers of higher education in Germany, Cologne, and Erfurt is sufficient to suggest that these ideas did not penetrate German intellectual circles for the first time in the 1380s. They were available earlier in the German *studia* where German theologians received their basic training in arts or theology. In fact, the strong interest that German theologians and masters of arts had in Ockham at Paris in the period from 1360 to 1380 may suggest that Paris did not give nominalism to Germany but that Germans, already versed in "Ockhamist" thought, helped revive an interest in Ockham and English thought at Paris after more than a decade (1350–65) in which it was rarely cited. The greatest of the Parisian "nominalists" at the end of the fourteenth century, Pierre d'Ailly, may well have owed as much of his nominalism to his German contemporaries and masters as he did to the heritage of Ockham's thought derived from Parisian writers of the 1340s. In any event, by the third quarter of the fourteenth century the curricula in arts and theology in the schools and universities of Europe all bear the traces of the new English influence on scholastic learning.

1. There were other important movements, such as the various forms of realism (Wyclifite, Albertist, or Thomist), or the influence of German mysticism and the *Devotio moderna*, or the developments in logic and physics, but these have not captured the attention of historians to the same degree.

2. In particular, see the work of H. A. Oberman, "Some Notes on the Theology of Nominalism with Attention to its Relation to the Renaissance," *Harvard Theological Review* 53 (1960): 47–76; "The Shape of Late Medieval Thought: The Birthpangs of the Modern Era," *Archiv für Reformationsgeschichte* 64 (1973): 13–33; "Headwaters of the Reformation," in *Luther and the Dawn of the Modern Era*, ed. H. A. Oberman (Leiden, 1974), pp. 40–88; "Reformation and Revolution: Copernicus's Discovery in an Era of Change," in *The Cultural Context of Medieval Learning*, ed. J. E. Murdoch and E. D. Sylla (Dordrecht, 1975), pp. 397–435.

3. The general picture as well as the assembling of the supporting documentation was first achieved by Franz Ehrle, *Die Sentenzenkommentar Peters von Candia, des Pisaner Papstes Alexander V*. Franziskanische Studien, 9 (Münster i.W., 1925). The developments at Oxford and Paris and their interrelationship were worked out by Constantine Michalski in a series of articles between 1920 and 1937, collected together under the title *La Philosophie au XIVᵉ siècle: Six Etudes*, ed. K. Flasch (Frankfurt, 1969). For a revision of aspects of that picture, see N. W. Gilbert, "Richard de Bury and the 'Quires of Yesterday's Sophisms'," in *Philosophy and Humanism: Renaissance Essays in Honor of Paul Oskar Kristeller*, ed. E. P. Mahoney (London, 1976), pp. 229–57. The transfer of nominalism to Germany and Eastern Europe has been dealt with in many works since Ehrle; see particularly A. L. Gabriel, "'Via antiqua' and 'Via Moderna' and the Migration of Paris Students and Masters to the German Universities in the Fifteenth Century," in *Antiqui und Moderni*. Miscellanea Mediaevalia, 9 (Berlin, 1974):

439–83; and Zenon Kaluza, "*Translatio studii*. Kryzys Uniwersytetu Paryskiego w latach 1380–1400: jego skutki," *Studia Mediewistyczne* 15 (1974): 71–108. The earlier picture has become fixed in the textbooks; see, for example, Frederick Copleston, *A History of Philosophy* (London, 1953), 3:122–52, or Etienne Gilson, *History of Christian Philosophy in the Middle Ages* (New York, 1955), pp. 487–520.

4. Henry of Langenstein, Letter to Friedrich von Brixen, ed. Gustav Sommerfeldt, "Zwei Schismatraktate Heinrich von Langenstein," *Mitteilungen des Institut für österr. Geschichtsforschung*, Erg.-Bd. 7 (1904); Letter to Count Ruprecht, ed. G. Sommerfeldt, "Ruprecht III. von der Pfalz und die deutsch Publizistik," *Zeitschrift für Gesch. des Oberrheins* 22 (1907): 311.

5. In the fourteenth century, the terms *via moderna*, *nominales*, and *schola nominalistarum* never occur as labels characterizing a contemporary body of thought or the intellectual orientation of contemporary thinkers. The term *Ockanistae* does occur but had a limited use that will be discussed later. The term *moderni* was also used but meant simply "contemporary" and, until the late fourteenth century, carried no connotation of a particular intellectual persuasion. As the late twelfth century became the dividing line for calling eminent theologians "fathers" or "doctors," so the early fourteenth century became the dividing line for "modern doctors" as opposed to "ancient doctors."

6. Positions in logic, epistemology, and metaphysics that one would call nominalistic attracted many supporters in the fourteenth century, and much of that development can be traced to Ockham. But in saying this, one must keep several things in mind. Nominalism in the philosophical sense of that word was never a movement or programmatic ideology in the fourteenth century. At no time were nominalistic philosophical or theological positions linked together around a few fundamental presuppositions and insights, let alone a philosophical or theological school. What sometimes goes by the name *nominalism* in the present literature is essentially a variety of *pactum*–theology (i.e., a theology in which the relation between God and creation or between God and the Church is conceived in terms of covenants or contractual agreements) that predates Ockham by a century, is predominantly Franciscan, and in its fourteenth-century form owes as much to Scotus as to Ockham. In most cases it has little or nothing to do with philosophical nominalism. The coincidence in the same writer of *pactum*–theology and nominalist philosophical principles, such as in Ockham or Pierre d'Ailly, only means that those ideas were compatible and could, but need not, be part of the same intellectual outlook. On the meaning of *nominales*, *moderni*, and *via moderna*" in the fourteenth century, see W. J. Courtenay, "Nominalism and Late Medieval Religion," in *The Pursuit of Holiness*, ed. H. A. Oberman and C. Trinkaus (Leiden, 1974), pp. 26–59; "Nominalism and Late Medieval Thought," *Theological Studies* 33 (1972): 716–34; Elisabeth Gössmann, *Antiqui und Moderni im Mittelalter* (Müchen, Paderborn, and Wien, 1974); Neal Ward Gilbert, "Ockham, Wyclif, and the 'via moderna'," in *Antiqui und Moderni*. Miscellanea Mediaevalia, 9 (Berlin, 1974), pp. 85–125. On the scholastic background of *pactum*–theology, see Berndt Hamm, *Promissio, Pactum, Ordinatio, Freiheit und Selbstbindung Gottes in der scholastischen Gnadenlehre* (Tübingen, 1977); W. J. Courtenay, "The King and the Leaden Coin: The Economic Background of '*sine qua non*' Causality," *Traditio* 28 (1972): 185–209. The difficulties entailed by a "schools of thought" approach to the fourteenth century has been repeatedly noticed but not proclaimed loudly enough to change our scholarly habits; cf. Jan Pinborg, *Die Entwicklung der Sprachtheorie im Mittelalter* (Münster, 1967), p. 142; H. Schepers, "Robert Holkot contra dicta Crathorn," Teil 2, *Philosophisches Jahrbuch* 79 (1972): 135.

7. On Lutterell's reaction to Ockham, see: A. Pelzer, "Les 61 articles de Guillaume Occam censurée à Avignon en 1326," *Revue d'histoire ecclesiastique* 18 (1922): 240–70; J. Koch, "Neue Aktenstücke zu dem gegen Wilhelm Ockham in Avignon geführten Prozess," *Recherches de Théologie ancienne et médiévale* 7 (1935): 353–80, 8 (1936): 79–93, 168–97; F. Hoffmann, *Die erste Kritik des Ockhamismus durch den Oxforder Kanzler Johannes Lutterell nach der Hs. CCV*

der Bibliothek des Prager Metropolitankapitels (Breslau, 1941); F. Hoffmann, Die Schriften des Oxforder Kanzlers Iohannes Lutterell. Texte zur Theologie des Vierzenhnten Jahrhunderts (Leipzig, 1959); C. K. Brampton, "Personalities at the Process against Ockham at Avignon, 1324–26," Franciscan Studies 26 (1966): 4–25; D. Burr, "Ockham, Scotus and the Censure at Avignon," Church History 37 (1968): 144–59. For Chatton's relation to Ockham, see L. Baudry, "Gauthier de Chatton et son commentaire des Sentences," Archives d'histoire doctrinale et littéraire du moyen âge 18 (1943): 337–69; G. Gál, "Gualteri de Chatton et Guillelmi de Ockham Controversia de Natura Conceptus Universalis," Franciscan Studies 27 (1967): 191–212; G. Gal and S. Brown, in the introduction to William of Ockham, Scriptum in librum primum sententiarum ordinatio (St. Bonaventure, 1967), 1: 26*–31*; N. Fitzpatrick, "Walter Chatton on the Univocity of Being: A Reaction to Peter Aureoli and William Ockham," Franciscan Studies 31 (1971): 88–177; G. Gál, in the introduction to William of Ockham, Summa Logicae (St. Bonaventure, 1974), pp. 47*–56*; G. Etzkorn, "Walter Chatton and the Absolute Necessity of Grace," Franciscan Studies 37 (1977): 32–65; W. J. Courtenay, Adam Wodeham (Leiden, 1978), pp. 66–74. The relationship of Chatton and Ockham was not entirely negative. Chatton did, on occasion (for example in his Reportatio), refer favorably to some of Ockham's arguments, as Baudry pointed out. Similarly, as Gál has shown, Ockham altered his position on universals as a result of Chatton's critique.

8. See F. Longpré, "Jean de Reading et le Bx. Jean Duns Scot," La France franciscaine 7 (1924): 99–109; S. Brown, "Sources for Ockham's Prologue to the Sentences," Franciscan Studies 26 (1966): 36–51; G. Gál, "Quaestio Ioannis de Reading de necessitate specierum intelligibilium, defensio doctrinae Scoti," Franciscan Studies 29 (1969): 66–156; S. Brown and G. Gál, introduction to William of Ockham, Scriptum in librum primum sententiarum ordinatio (St. Bonaventure, 1970), 2:18*–34*.

9. On the Logica reali contra Ockham, once attributed to Richard Campsale, see V. Doucet, "L'oeuvre scolastique de Richard de Conington, O.F.M.," Archivum Franciscanum Historicum 29 (1936): 420, n. 4; E. A. Synan, "Richard of Campsall, an English Theologian of the Fourteenth Century," Mediaeval Studies 14 (1952): 1–18; E. A. Synan, "The Universal and Supposition in a Logica attributed to Richard Campsall," in Nine Mediaeval Thinkers, ed. J. R. O'Donnell (Toronto, 1955), pp. 183–232; E. A. Synan, The Works of Richard of Campsall, (Toronto, 1968), 1:16–17; G. Gal, introduction to William of Ockham, Summa Logicae (St. Bonaventure, 1974), pp. 56*–62*.

10. There is not yet a sufficiently thorough examination of Fitzralph's attitude toward Ockham. See G. Leff, Richard Fitzralph: Commentator of the "Sentences." A Study in Theological Orthodoxy (Manchester, 1963); W. J. Courtenay, Adam Wodeham, pp. 75–81, J. F. Genest, "Le 'De futuris contingentibus' de Thomas Bradwardine," unpublished thesis, Memoire pour le Diplome de l'Ecole pratique des hautes etudes (5ᵉ section) (Paris, 1975), pp. 137–39. On Rodington, see M. M. Tweedale, "John of Rodynton on Knowledge, Science, and Theology," (Ph.D. diss., University of California, Los Angeles, 1965).

11. For a long while, Holcot was assumed to be a disciple of Ockham and a major representative of radical nominalism or Ockhamism at Oxford. A more nuanced view began to appear in 1962; see H. A. Oberman, "Facientibus quod in se est Deus non denegat gratiam. Robert Holcot, O.P., and the Beginnings of Luther's Theology," Harvard Theological Review 55 (1962): 317–42; F. Hoffman, "Robert Holcot: Die Logik in der Theologie," in Die Metaphysik im Mittelalter, 2d International Congress of Medieval Philosophy, Köln, 1962 (Berlin, 1963), pp. 624–39; E. A. Moody, "A Quodlibetal Question of Robert Holcot O.P. on the Problem of the Objects of Knowledge and Belief," Speculum 39 (1964): 53–74; H. Schepers, "Holkot contra dicta Crathorn," Philosophisches Jahrbuch 77 (1970): 320–54; 79 (1972): 106–36; F. Hoffmann, Die theologische Methode des Oxforder Dominikanerlehrers Robert Holcot (Münster i.W., 1972); Courtenay, Adam Wodeham, pp. 95–106.

12. The earlier literature on Wodeham and his relation to Ockham has been summarized in Courtenay, *Adam Wodeham*.

13. Among the issues on which Wodeham criticized or modified Ockham's opinions are: the object of knowledge (see G. Gál, "Adam of Wodeham's Question on the 'Complexe Significabile' as the Immediate Object of Scientific Knowledge," *Franciscan Studies* 37 (1977):66–102; epistemology (see the forthcoming article by Katherine Tachau, "The Problem of *species in medio* at Oxford in the generation after Ockham," in *Mediaeval Studies*); the augmentation of grace (Vat. lat. 1110, fol. 9ʳ; Paris, Univ. 193, fol. 146ʳᵃ).

14. In Ockham's view of simple supposition (as distinct from personal or material) the subject term in a proposition supposits for the *intentio animae* (i.e., the universal concept in the mind) not a universal existing outside the mind and inherent in things.

15. On Swineshead, see: J. A. Weisheipl, "Roger Swyneshed, O.S.B., Logician, Natural Philosopher and Theologian," in *Oxford Studies Presented to Daniel Callus*, O.H.S., n.s. 16 (Oxford, 1964): 231–52; "Ockham and Some Mertonians," *Mediaeval Studies* 30 (1968): 207–13; "Developments in the Arts Curriculum at Oxford in the Early Fourteenth Century," *Mediaeval Studies* 28 (1966): 162–65; J. Coleman, "Jean de Ripa O.F.M. and the Oxford Calculators," *Mediaeval Studies* 37 (1975): 150–52. On Sutton, See J. A. Weisheipl, "Developments in the Arts Curriculum," 158–59, 162; Weisheipl, "Repertorium Mertonense," *Mediaeval Studies* 31 (1969): 219.

16. For Heytesbury and Dumbleton, see C. Wilson, *William Heytesbury: Medieval Logic and the Rise of Mathematical Physics* (Madison, 1956); J. A. Weisheipl, "Developments in the Arts Curriculum," 159–61, 168–73; "Ockham and Some Mertonians," 195–207; "Repertorium Mertonense," 210–17.

17. Ockham rejected a separate ontological existence for categories other than substance and quality. Motion, time, place, and quantity are not absolute things, for Ockham, separate from or in addition to permanent, physical things in motion, in time, or extended in space.

18. Billingham's work is discussed by Weisheipl in "Developments in the Arts Curriculum," 159–60; "Repertorium Mertonense," 176–77.

19. Bradwardine does not identify the "modern Pelagians" against whom he wrote his *Summa de causa Dei*. Halifax, on the other hand, specifically calls Wodeham's position Pelagian. For this aspect of Bradwardine's thought, see G. Leff, *Bradwardine and the Pelagians* (Cambridge, 1957); H. A. Oberman, *Archbishop Thomas Bradwardine. A Fourteenth Century Augustinian* (Utrecht, 1958). On Halifax's critique of Wodeham, see Courtenay, *Adam Wodeham*, pp. 118–20.

20. One must be careful not to confuse this new logic with what was called the *logica nova*, or *ars nova*, that referred to the portion of Aristotle's logic recovered in the twelfth century (the *Prior* and *Posterior Analytics*, the *Topics*, and the *Sophistici elenchi*) and that remained a separate stage of study in the arts curriculum. Similarly, the phrase *logica modernorum* embraces the entire development of terminist logic, which had its roots in the twelfth century. Cf. L. M. De Rijk, *Logica modernorum*, 3 vols. (Assen, 1962–67).

21. Apart from the specialized study by C. Wilson on Heytesbury, the best work on Oxford logic in the fourteenth century are the articles of Weisheipl, "Curriculum of the Faculty of Arts at Oxford in the early Fourteenth Century," *Mediaeval Studies* 26 (1964): 143–85; "Developments in the Arts Curriculum"; and "Ockham and Some Mertonians." The following description is derived largely from the work of Weisheipl; Wilson; P. Boehner, *Medieval Logic* (Manchester, 1952); and E. A. Moody, *The Logic of William of Ockham* (London, 1935; New York, 1965).

22. The new treatises are best represented by Heytesbury's *Regulae solvendi sophismata* and Richard Billingham's *Speculum iuvenum*. See Weisheipl, "Developments in the Arts Curricu-

lum," 159–61. John Murdoch, "From Social into Intellectual Factors: An Aspect of the Unitary Character of Late Medieval Learning," in *The Cultural Context of Medieval Learning*, ed. J. Murdoch and E. Sylla (Dordrecht, 1975), pp. 271–348, has been supposition theory as one of several analytical "languages" used in the fourteenth century. My own impression is that most of the new "languages," even the measure and limit languages, derive from supposition theory or are developed simultaneously.

23. The chapters in Heytesbury's *Regulae* set forth most of the new areas of supposition theory, many having to do with physics and mathematics as well: (1) *De Insolubilibus*, (2) *De 'scire' et 'dubitare,'* (3) *De relativis*, (4) *De 'incip' et 'desinit,'* (5) *De maximo et minimo*, (6) *De tribus predicamentis*. See Wilson, *William Heytesbury*. Equally important in this regard is an earlier work by Richard Kilvington, *Sophismata* (before 1330). A critical edition is being prepared by Norman Kretzmann. See also F. Bottin, "Un testo fondamentale nell' ambito della 'nuova fisica' di Oxford: I Sophismata di Richard Kilmington," in *Antiqui und Moderni*. Miscellanea Mediaevalia, 9 (Berlin, 1974): 201–05; Kretzmann, "Socrates is whiter than Plato begins to be white," *Nous* 11 (1977): 3–14.

24. For a discussion of Ockham's positive contributions to the development of late medieval logic and physics, see H. Shapiro, *Motion, Time and Place According to William Ockham* (St. Bonaventure, 1957); E. A. Moody, *The Logic of William of Ockham* (London, 1935; New York, 1965).

25. The incompatibility of Ockham's logic and the new physics was acknowledged by E. A. Moody, who otherwise was a strong supporter of Ockham's positive influence on the development of science (*The Logic of William of Ockham*, pp. 308–09). Moody later modified his position ("Ockham and Aegidius of Rome," *Franciscan Studies* 9[1949]: 438). Weisheipl, however, assumes a basic opposition between Bradwardine and Ockham, in physics as well as in theology ("Ockham and Some Mertonians")

26. On Bradwardine's physics and its relation to Heytesbury and Dumbleton, see H. Lamar Crosby, *Thomas of Bradwardine. His 'Tractatus de Proportionibus'. Its Significance for the Development of Mathematical Physics* (Madison, 1955); Wilson, *William Heytesbury*; Weisheipl, "Ockham and Some Mertonians."

27. F. Hoffman, "Robert Holcot: Die Logik in der Theologie," in *Die Metaphysik im Mittelalter*, 2d International Congress of Medieval Philosophy (Berlin, 1963), pp. 624–39; E. A. Moody, "A Quodlibetal Question of Robert Holcot O.P. on the Problem of the Objects of Knowledge and Belief," *Speculum* 39 (1964): 53–74; H. Schepers, "Holkot contra dicta Crathorn," *Philosophisches Jahrbuch* 77 (1970): 320–54; 79 (1972): 106–36; F. Hoffmann, *Die theologische Methode des Oxforder Dominikanerlehrers Robert Holcot* (Münster i.W., 1972).

28. This aspect of Wodeham has been touched on by J. Murdoch, "From Social into Intellectual Factors," pp. 271–348, but it needs further investigation.

29. On the early Thomist School at Oxford, see F. J. Roensch, *Early Thomistic School* (Dubuque, 1964), pp. 28–83, 200–265.

30. On Reading, Chatton, and Rodington see above, notes 7, 8, and 10. On Chatton's obliviousness to Scotus's view of divine acceptation and the dialectic of the two powers, see G. Etzkorn, "Walter Chatton and the Controversy on the Absolute Necessity of Grace," *Franciscan Studies* 37 (1977): 32–65.

31. Cf. F. Roth, *The English Austin Friars, 1249–1538*, vol. 1: *History* (New York, 1966); and W. J. Courtenay, "Augustinianism at Oxford in the Fourteenth Century," to appear in *Augustiniana* 30 (1980).

32. A. Maier, *Die Vorläufer Galileis im 14. Jahrhundert* (Rome, 1949), p. 96. There is no evidence that Kilvington studied under Bradwardine, although they did share common interests. Buckingham's references to "doctor noster Bradwardine" do not imply a *Lehrrichtung* but only the simple fact that Bradwardine, like Buckingham, was a fellow of Merton

College. The theological differences between Bradwardine, Kilvington, and Buckingham are too serious for us to place them together, and their common interest in problems of physics and mathematics are by no means unique to those three.

33. Murdoch was the first to spell out the close interrelation and mutual interdependence of logic, physics, mathematics, and theology in the fourteenth century. In particular, see his "Mathesis in philosophiam scholasticam introducta: The Rise and Development of the Application of Mathematics in Fourteenth Century Philosophy and Theology," in Arts libéraux et philosophie au moyen âge (Paris and Montreal, 1969), pp. 215–54; "Philosophy and the Enterprise of Science in the Later Middle Ages," in The Interaction between Science and Philosophy, ed. Y. Elkana (Atlantic Highlands, N.J., 1974), pp. 51–74; "From Social into Intellectual Factors"; "Subtilitates Anglicanae in Fourteenth-Century Paris: John of Mirecourt and Peter Ceffons," in Machaut's World, ed. M. Cosman, Annals of the New York Academy of Sciences (New York, 1978), 341:51–86. Murdoch sees these features as a characteristic of fourteenth-century thought in general. For my part I see development. Although the interest in the application of logic and physics to theology appears at least as early as 1310 at both Oxford and Paris and is probably a more gradual process than our sources suggest, the particular languages and applications develop first at Oxford and are only used at Paris later.

34. This topic has been explored in Hester Gelber, "Logic and the Trinity: A Clash of Values in Scholastic Thought, 1300–1335" (Ph.D. diss., University of Wisconsin, Madison, 1974).

35. This point is documented extensively in the works of Anneliese Maier, especially Die Vorläufer Galileis im 14. Jahrhundert (Rome, 1949, 1966); Zwei Grundprobleme der scholastischen Naturphilosophie (Rome, 1951, 1968); and Metaphysische Hintergründe der spätscholastischen Naturphilosophie (Rome, 1955). More recently, John Murdoch, in the articles cited on page 13. It was the fact that physics and mathematics were not just imported into theology but were actually being done within theology that convinced Murdoch of the unity of philosophy, theology, and science in the fourteenth century.

36. The Euclidian structure of Bradwardine's De cause Dei is another example supporting Murdoch's thesis of the penetration of mathematics into theology.

37. One might well wonder whether theologians were reducing the number of questions to those that already had a logical, physical, or mathematical dimension or whether they were introducing those analytical tools into questions that were more strictly theological in the earlier period. The reduction in the number of questions has already been noted by P. Glorieux, "Sentences," Dictionnaire de théologie catholique 14 (1941): 1860–84; and Murdoch, "From Social into Intellectual Factors," p. 275.

38. Anneliese Maier traced the opposition to aspects of Ockham's thought by Walter Burley, Francis of Marchia, and John Buridan: "Zu einigen Problemen der Ockamforschung," Archivum Franciscanum Historicum 46 (1953): 161–94, also in Ausgehendes Mittelalter (Rome, 1964), 1:175–208; Metaphysische Hintergründe. A positive influence, however, cannot be documented until the 1340s, and very little consideration has been given to the time lag between Ockham and Autrecourt.

39. A. Maier, "Zu einigen Problemen der Ockhamforschung," AFH 174–77 (or AM, 188–95); cf. Metaphysische Hintergründe, pp. 199–209).

40. Franciscus de Mayronis, In Libros Sententiarum (Venice, 1520; reprint Frankfurt, 1966), e.g., fols. 10vb, 13va, 15ra, 16ra, 19va. Ockham is never cited in the text. The opinions in the text opposite the name "Occham" (along with other names) are not unique to Ockham and in some cases were not held by him. The marginalia are later, as attested to by references to Ockham's Quodlibeta, written after 1320, to "Frater Adam" [Wodeham] (who wrote a decade later than Myronis), and Petrus de Candia (almost a half century later). I am grateful to Katherine Tachau for calling to my attention these marginal references to Ockham in the Mayronis reprint.

150

41. The evidence that Anneliese Maier put forward with regard to Francis of Marchia's knowledge of Ockham is not as certain as one would like. As Maier herself noted, this view of quantity had already been put forward by Peter John Olivi toward the end of the thirteenth century; see A. Maier, *Metaphysische Hintergründe*, 151–75; cf. David Burr, "Ockham, Scotus, and the Censure at Avignon," *Church History* 37 (1968): 144–59, esp. 149–50; David Burr, "Quantity and Eucharistic Presence: The Debate from Olivi through Ockham," *Collectanea Franciscana* 44 (1974): 5–44. Maier, however, was convinced (*Metaphysische Hintergründe*, 202–9) that Marchia referred to Ockham and not Olivi. Her opinion rested chiefly on the grounds that the idea (rejected by Marchia) that God can preserve a substance while annihilating the accidents *absque quocumque motu locali* can be found in Ockham but not Olivi. Although that idea is not found verbatim in Olivi, it does not seem so far removed from his approach. The question is further complicated by the fact that Adam Wodeham, in an immodest passage, claimed that he had proposed this view of quantity in the context of eucharistic theology before Ockham had written about it. Florence, Bibl. Naz., conv. soppr. A. III 508, fol. 140ra: "Quaere prosecutionem in illo tractatu. Et haec argumenta fere omnia fuerant tua antequam Ockham aliquid scriberet de indivisibilibus." Cf. Courtenay, *Adam Wodeham*, p. 64. There is, therefore, more than one possible source from whom Marchia could have drawn this idea of quantity, and we cannot therefore be certain it came from Ockham. In some ways the Olivi source, which is already Parisian, might seem a more direct and likely route.

42. Maier, "Zu einigen Problemen der Ockhamforschung," AM, 195–208; Weisheipl, "Ockham and Some Mertonians," pp. 174–88. The literature on the interrelation of Burley and Ockham is very extensive, since their mutual criticisms touch fundamental problems in fourteenth-century philosophy and science. Thus this issue is treated at various places in the works of Duhem, Michalski, Boehner, Moody, Maier, and others. For an excellent review of the relevant literature and the state of the question as of 1978, see A. Uña Juárez, *La Filosofia del Siglo XIV. Contexto Cultural de Walter Burley* (Escorial, 1978), 385–426.

43. Weisheipl, "Ockham and Some Mertonians," pp. 183–84.

44. P. Doncoeru, "La théorie de la matière et de la forme chez Guillaume d'Occam" *Revue des sciences philosophiques et théologiques* 10 (1921): 21–51; Maier, "Zu einigen Problemen der Ockhamforschung," AM 202; Wiesheipl, "Ockham and Some Mertonians," pp. 180–84.

45. Maier, "Zu einigen Problemen der Ockhamforschung," pp. 198–201, 203–6; Weisheipl, "Ockham and some Mertonians," pp. 178–80.

46. Vat. lat. 1087, fol. 135va:Sed arguitur ulterius pro opinione Okam primo sic: quantitas successiva, quae est motus vel tempus, non est res distincta a mobili cuius est subiective." The position Michael cites and rejects is certainly Ockham's, and it is important to note that it is on a topic in natural philosophy, albeit one related to supposition theory. On Michael de Massa see: D. Trapp, "Augustinian Theology of the 14th Century," *Augustiniana* 6 (1956): 163–75; Trapp, "Notes on some Manuscripts of the Augustinian Michael de Massa (d. 1337)," *Augustinianum* 5 (1965): 58–133; L. Hödl, "Studien zum nominalistischen Schöpfungsbergriff in der spätscholastischen Theologie des Michael de Massa O.E.S.A. (d. 1337)," in *Scientia Augustiniana. Festschrift für Adolar Zumkeller OSA*, ed. C. P. Mayer and W. Eckermann (Würzburg, 1975), pp. 234–56.

47. The quotations from Massa amassed by Hödl, in which Ockham's views on quantity, time, motion, duration, and change are equated with errors of the ancients, are entirely convincing. Although it may not have determined Massa's approach, Burley, who was regent master at Paris when Massa read, would have been pleased with this strong attack on Ockham's natural philosophy.

48. In the question "utrum tempus habeat suum esse completum circumscripto omni opere intellectus nostri," Michael cites six ancient opinions on tome, taken from Avicenna's *Physica* (i.e., *Sufficientia*, 2, ch. 10: *de tempore*, in *Opera Philosophica* (Venice, 1508: reprint

151

Louvain, 1961, fol. 33ʳᵇ). Avicenna's "Alii vero posuerunt tempus ipsum caelum" is repeated by Michael (Vat. lat. 1087, fol. 88ᵛᵃ) as "Sed sexto dixerant aliqui quod tempus est ipsummet caelum, et in sententiam istorum incidunt Okanistae. Sed omnes tales opiniones dico quantum ad illos quae sunt penitus contra omnem iudicium quae habent probabilitatem, sicut sunt opiniones dicentes quod tempus idem est quod motus. Non est opus plus dicere, quia satis dictum est in quaestionibus praecedentibus."

49. It is certainly true that all of Ockham's nonpolitical writings *could* have been available in Paris by 1325, but whether all of them in fact *were*, as is sometimes suggested, is unknown.
Francis de Mayronis, *Quodl.* 1, q. 3, on whether God is able to accept as worthy of eternal life a man existing *in puris naturalibus* without grace, says, "Circa istam questionem, quia de facto versatur coram Christi vicario summo pontifice, ideo reducendum est ad memoriam illud quod dicit salvator noster eius predecessori Matth. 16o: 'quodcumque solveris super terram, erit solutum' etc. . . . . et ideo ad determinandum exspectandum est eius iudicium."
Va. lat. 901, fol. 7ʳᵃ, cited from J. Koch, "Neue Aktenstücke zu dem gegen Wilhelm Ockham in Avignon geführten Prozess," *Recherches de Theologie ancienne et medievale* 7 (1935): 350–80; 8 (1936): 79–93, 168–97; reprinted in *Kleine Schriften* (Rome, 1973), 2: 312.

50. It is common in scholastic commentaries for an author to cite the opinion of someone else (often identified in the margin) under the phrase "aliqui dicunt," or to introduce a counterargument of his own creation with the words "tu dicis." Similarly, school labels do not necessarily refer to specific persons but may only be a personification of one or more ideas derived from an author. Cf. J. Pinborg, *Die Entwicklung der Sprachtheorie im Mittelalter* (Münster, i.W., 1967), p. 142; N. W. Gilbert, "Ockham, Wyclif, and the 'via moderna'," in *Antiqui und Moderni*, Miscellanea Mediaevalia, 9 (Berlin, 1974): 85–125.

51. A similar expression or interest in Ockham's thought in the fourteenth century can be seen not only in the numerous manuscripts of Ockham's works but in the abbreviations that seek to express the essence of Ockham's thought in reduced form. Both varieties can be found in Parisian manuscripts, but few can be dated before 1350. For a description of some of these resumes see Leon Baudry, "Remarques sur trois manuscrits occamistes," *Archives d'histoire doctrinale et litteraire du moyen âge* (1946): 169–74.

52. Lombardi's *Sentences* commentary has received little study. Cf. Martin Grabmann, *Mittelalterliches Geistesleben* (Müchen, 1926), 1:318, 330; (Müchen, 1936), 2:457; (Müchen, 1956), 3:372, 385; J. Koch, *Kleine Schriften*, 2:135–48; *Durandus de Sancto Porciano, O.P.* (Münster I.W., 1927), pp. 314–40.

53. Petrus de Aquila, *Quaestiones in 4 libros sententiarum* (Speyer, 1480; reprint Frankfurt, 1967), Lib. I, dist. xxiii, q. 2. Peter is also of interest because, in contrast to his near contemporary Thomas of Strasbourg, he keeps alive the interest in logic, physics, and mathematics reflected in the *Sentences* commentaries of Marchia, Mayronis, Massa, and Odonis. Most of the attention Peter has received has been on his Scotism, and yet his commentary also contains discussions of the infinite, velocity and motion, the continuum, time, space, the vacuum, *incipit/desinit*, and the intention and remission of forms. His discussions of the issues, however, seem based on the older Parisian sources, not the newer English works. He is, therefore, proof of continuing theological interest in problems of logic and natural philosophy that would eventually seize greedily upon the newer developments in English thought. On Peter of Aquila, see: A. Teetaert, "Scotellus di Tonnaparte," *Diction-naire de theologie catholique* 14.2 (1941): 1730–33; A. Chiappini, "Fra Pietro dell' Aquila 'Scotello' O. Min., celebre scolastico del Trecento (+1361)," *Miscellanea Franciscana* 61 (1961): 283–310.

54. On Thomas of Strasbourg, see B. Lindner, *Die Erkenntnislehre des Thomas von Strass-burg* (Münster I.W., 1930); J. L. Shannon, *Good Works and Predestination according to Thomas of Strassburg* (Westminster, Md., 1940); D. Trapp, "Augustinian Theology," 175–82.

55. Among the many scholars who considered Buridan to be a close disciple of Ockham,

E. A. Moody was the most prominent and specific in his arguments. See especially his "Ockham, Buridan and Autrecourt," *Franciscan Studies* 7 (1947): 113–46. This view has been modified considerably in recent years. In particular, see M. E. Reina, "Giovanni Buridano: Tractatus de Suppositionibus," *Revista critica di Storia della Filosofia* 12 (1957): 175–208, 323–52; M. E. Reine, *Il Problema del linguaggio in Buridano* (Vicenza, 1959); T. K. Scott, "John Buridan on the Objects of Demonstrative Science," *Speculum* 40 (1965): 654–73; R. Paque, *Das Pariser Nominalistenstatut* (Berlin, 1970); T. K. Scott, Nicholas of Autrecourt, Buridan, and Ockhamism," *Journal of the History of Philosophy* 9 (1971): 15–41; and *The Logic of John Buridan*, Opuscula Graecolatina, 9 (Copenhagen, 1976). On other aspects of his thought in relation to Ockham, see M. Grignaschi, "Un commentaire nominaliste de la *Politique* d'Aristotle: Jean Buridan," *Anciens Pays et Assemblees d'Etats* 19 (1960): 123–42; J. J. Walsh, "Nominalism and the *Ethics*: Some Remarks about Buridan's Commentary," *Journal of the History of Philosophy* 4 (1966): 1–13.

56. Maier, *Metaphysische Hintergründe*, pp. 199–200, 209–18.

57. On the process against Ockham, see above, note 12. On Olivi, see David Burr, *The Persecution of Peter Olivi*. American Philosophical Society, n.s. 66.5 (Philadelphia, 1976).

58. For the process against Eckhart, see *Chartularium Universitatis Parisiensis*, ed. H. Denifle and E. Chatelain (Paris, 1891), 2:322, n. 888, hereafter cited as CUP; A. Daniels *Eine Lateinishce Rechtfertigungsschrift des Meister Eckhart* (Münster i.W., 1923); F. Pelster, "Ein Gutachten aus dem Eckhart-Prozess in Avignon," Beiträge Gesch. Phil. M.A., Suppl. 3.2 (Münster i.W., 1935), 1,099–1,124; W. Bange, *Meister Eckharts Lehre vom göttlichen und geschöpflichen Sein* (Limburg, 1937); H. Hof, *Scintilla animae* (Lund and Bonn, 1952); K. G. Kertz, "Meister Eckhart's teaching on the Birth of the Divine Word in the Soul," *Traditio* 15 (1959): 327–63; J. Koch, *Kleine Schriften*, 1:309–44; 2:381–86.

59. CUP 2:320–21, n. 886; 2:414–42, nn. 970–87.

60. CUP, 2:430–43. Cf. T. Kaeppeli, *Le Proces contre Th. Waleys*, O.P. (Rome, 1936).

61. CUP, 2:107ff, n. 642.

62. The drop in English arts students at Paris between 1330 and 1335 is striking, but perhaps even more remarkable is that throughout the early stages of the Hundred Years War a few still came to Paris for their philosophical education. See *Auctarium Chartularii Universitatis Parisiensis*, ed. H. Denifle and E. Chatelain, vol. 1, *Liber Procuratorum nationis Anglicanae* (Paris, 1894). A small trickle of students seems also to have occurred in theology. Because of the animosity between England and Scotland, a healthy flow of Scottish students both in arts and theology attended Paris in the 1330s and 1340s. Many of these students probably shared the intellectual world of John Duns Scotus, William of Alnwick, and Walter Chatton (all from the border region of England and Scotland), but some, such as John de Rathe, a secular theological bachelor from Scotland and a *socius* of Gregory of Rimini, apparently favored Ockham's opinions in epistemology and natural philosophy.

63. CUP, 2:485–86, n. 1023. For contrasting opinions on the meaning of this document, see E. A. Moody, "Ockham, Buridan, and Nicholas of Autrecourt: The Parisian Statutes of 1339 and 1340," *Franciscan Studies* 7 (1947): 113–46; R. Paque, *Das Pariser Nominalistenstatut* (Berlin, 1970); T. K. Scott, "Nicholas of Autrecourt, Buridan, and Ockhamism," *Journal of the History of Philosophy* 9 (1971): 15–41. On the broader dimensions of the importation of English thought into Paris, see N. W. Gilbert, "Richard de Bury and the 'Quires of Yesterday's Sophisms'," in *Philosophy and Humanism. Renaissance Essays in Honor of Paul Oskar Kristeller*, ed. E. P. Mahoney (Leiden, 1976), pp. 229–57.

64. CUP, 2:505, n. 1041. For the literature and problems concerning this document, see William J. Courtenay, "John of Mirecourt and Gregory of Rimini on Whether God Can Undo the Past," *Récherches de Theologie ancienne et médiévale* 39 (1972): 224–56; 40 (1973): 147–74.

65. *CUP*, 2:505–7, n. 1042, for contrasting opinions on this document, see Moody and Paque above, note 63.

66. The date of Rimini's commentary—of crucial importance for the introduction of the newer English thought into Parisian theology—has been a matter of dispute. Before 1955 it was usually placed in 1344. Subsequently, in a series of articles, Damasus Trapp asserted that Gregory began his lectures on book two of the *Sentences* on 17 May 1342. Most recently Venicio Marcolino has established a firm chronology. Gregory read at Paris in the Academic year 1343–44, and the *textus ordinairius* of his commentary was prepared and circulated between 1346 and 1348. The date of his *lectura* is confirmed by his statement that he read in the same year as Francis de Treviso, whom we know to have been *sententiarius* in 1343–44 (*CUP*, 2:526; n. 1059, 2:538, n. 1071). The *terminus post quem* for the *textus ordinarius* is set by Gregory's reference to the "vespers" (a major disputation at the time of inception as master) of Francis de Treviso, which took place in December of 1345 (*CUP*, 2:592, n. 1127; Steph. de Salaniaco and Bernard Guidonis, *De quatuor in quibus Deus Praedicatorum Ordinem insignivit*, ed. Th. Kaeppeli [Rome, 1949], p. 142). The *terminum ante quem* for book two is set by the fact that Francis de Treviso took a copy with him to Italy in 1346. The *terminus ante quem* for the entire commentary rests on the fact that Peter Ceffons had at his disposal in 1348–50 a copy of Gregory's *textus ordinarius* still extant (Troyes 151). See V. Marcolino, "Zur Pariser Lehrtätigkeit Gregors von Rimini," to appear in *Gregor von Rimini. Werk und Wirken*, ed. H. A. Oberman

67. One finds extensive English sources (post 1325) cited in Alphonsus Vargas of Toledo, John of Mirecourt (who incorporates large sections of these English authors in his commentary), Hugolino of Orvieto, Peter Ceffons, and almost every Parisian commentary from 1360 on. The sole exception in the 1340s is the commentary of Paul of Perugia, O. Carm., who cites only Ockham, of the more recent English sources. On Vargas see D. Trapp, "Augustinian Theology of the 14th Century," *Augustiniana* 6 (1956): 213–22. On Mirecourt see C. Michalski, *Wpływ Oksfordu na filozofja Jana z Mirecourt* (Cracow, 1921); G. Ouy, "Un commentateur des 'Sentences' au XIV^c siecle, Jean de Mirecourt, (Unpublished thesis, Ecole des Chartes, Paris, 1946), abstracted in *Ecole Nationale des Chartes. Positions des Theses soutenues par les eleves de la promotion de 1946 pour obtenir le diplome d'archiviste paleographe* (Paris, 1946: 117–22; G. Tessier, "John de Mirecourt," in *Histoire litteraire de la France* 40 (1974): 1–52; W. J. Courtenay, "Jean of Mirecourt and Gregory of Rimini on Whether God can Undo the Past"; J. Murdoch, "*Subtilitates Anglicanae* in Fourteenth-Century Paris: John of Mirecourt and Peter Ceffons," in *Machaut's World* (New York, 1978), pp. 51–86; Courtenay, *Adam Wodeham*, pp. 131–33. On Hugolino's English sources see A. Zumkeller, *Hugolin von Orvieto und seine theologische Erkenntnislehre*, Cassiciacum, 9.2 (Würzburg, 1941), pp. 255–62; D. Trapp, "Augustinian Theology," 222–23. Peter Ceffons's use of recent English authors has not been extensively examined, although it is as rich and diverse as Rimini's, if not more so; see D. Trapp, "Peter Ceffons of Clairvaux," *Recherches de Theologie ancienne et medievale* 24 (1957): 101–54; Courtenay, *Adam Wodeham*, pp. 135–37; Murdoch, "*Subtilitates Anglicanae*."

68. *The Philobiblon of Richard de Bury*, ed. E. C. Thomas (London, 1888), pp. 211-12; passage revised slightly by Murdoch, "*Subtilitates Anglicanae*," p. 51: "Alas! by the same disease which we are deploring, we see that the Palladium of Paris has suffered in these sad times of ours, wherein the zeal of that noble university, whose rays once shed light into every corner of the world, has grown lukewarm, nay, is all but frozen. There the pen of every scribe is now at rest, the generation of books no longer occurs, and there is none who begins to assume the role of new author. They wrap up their doctrines in unskilled discourse, and are losing propriety of all logic, except that our English subtleties, which they denounce in public, are the subject of their furtive vigils." Cf. N. W. Gilbert, "Richard de Bury and the 'Quires of Yesterday's Sophisms'," in *Philosophy and Humanism. Renaissance Essays in Honor of Paul Oskar Kristeller*, ed. E. P. Mahoney (New York, 1976), pp. 229–57.

69. *CUP*, 2:505, n. 1041. All six scholars cited to Avignon were theologians, five of them bachelors and one student. Despite the fact that one of the censured statements in the arts statute of 1340 (*CUP*, 2:n. 1042) "quod Socrates et Plato, vel Deus et creatura nichil sunt," can be found in Autrecourt, that censure must be directed at someone (perhaps repeating Autrecourt) teaching in the arts faculty. The arts masters had no authority whatsoever to censure opinions of theologians.

70. As of November 1340, Autrecourt was already a licentiate in theology, which means that he was a *baccalarius formatus* and had read the *Sentences* in 1338–39 or earlier. He could not possibly have been reading in 1340, as Denifle suggested. Since Autrecourt was also a bachelor in canon law (thus pursuing two degrees), he must have completed his regency in arts well before 1330.

71. *CUP*, 2: 485–86, n. 1023.

72. *CUP*, 2: 505-7, n. 1042.

73. Ockham was aware as much as anyone that, as the statute said, "in scientiis utimur terminis pro rebus quas portare non possumus ad disputationes." Moreover, much of Ockham's logic was motivated by a desire to clear up ambiguities in speech and to reveal the intended truth of a proposition that is, *de virtute sermonis*, false. If, as he says, while standing in my neighbor's garden, I make the statement: "That plant grows in my garden," the statement is false *de virtute sermonis* (since this particular plant is in my neighbor's garden) but true in the sense intended (since a plant of the same species does grow in my garden). Cf. *Summa logicae*, pt. 1, ch. 70 (St. Bonaventure, 1974), pp. 209–10; cf. also F. Inciarte, "Die Suppositionstheorie und die Anfänge der extentionalen Semantik," *Antiqui und Moderni*, Miscellanea Mediaevalia, 9 (Berlin, 1974): 126–41.

74. *CUP*, 2:505. Cf. *Archiv für Literatur und Kirchengeschichte* 5 (1889): p. 261.

75.Most sections of the statute have to do with the failure to distinguish between the true and false senses of an authoritative proposition. The only place where the authors of the statute may stand in opposition to Ockham is on the issue of the object of knowledge. The sixth section of the statute states that knowledge is *de rebus*. The exact wording is: "Ideo scientiam habemus de rebus, licet mediantibus terminis vel orationibus." If by that is meant that our knowledge is ultimately derived from the particulars encountered and known through intuitive cognition, then Ockham, the empiricist, would certainly have agreed. If however, by *scientia* is meant the generalized concepts that comprise scientific knowledge in the strict sense, then the object of knowledge is, for Ockham, the proposition, not some *res extra*.

76. Although Constantine Michalski distorted our picture of the fourteenth century by approaching it through the issues of skepticism and cricitism, he was right in viewing the developments at Paris in the 1340s in terms of the introduction of English thought, not just the importation of nominalism or Ockhamism.

77. *Analecta Franciscana* 2 (1887): 177; 3 (1897): 638.

78. The Italian students known to have been at Oxford in this period are listed in A. B. Emden, *A Biographical Register of the University of Oxford to A.D. 1500*, 3 vols. (Oxford, 1957–59); cf. W. A. Hinnebusch, "Foreign Dominican Students and Professors at the Oxford Blackfriars," in *Oxford Studies Presented to Daniel Callus*, n.s. 16 (Oxford, 1964), pp. 101–34. For London, see C. L. Kingford, *The Grey Friars of London* (Aberdeen, 1915); the Norwich *studium* in this period was described by V. Doucet, "Le Studium Franciscain de Norwich en 1337 d'apres le ms Chigi B.V. 66 de la Bibliotheque Vaticane," *Archivum Franciscanum Historicum* 46 (1953): 85–98. English masters also went to Italy. Thomas Waleys was lector at the Dominican convent in Bologna in 1326–27; see B. Smalley, "Thomas Waleys, O.P.," *Archivum Ordinis Praedicatorum* 24 (1954): 51–52.

79. On the Italian mendicant libraries see K. W. Humphyres', *The Book Provisions of the*

Mediaeval Friars, 1215-1400 (Amsterdam, 1964); K. W. Humphreys, *The Liberty of the Franciscans of the Convent of St. Antony, Padua at the Beginning of the Fifteenth Century* (Amsterdam, 1966).

80. *Le Scuole degli Ordini Mendicanti (secoli XIII-XIV)*. Convegni del Centro di Studi sulla Spiritualita Medievale, XVII (Todi, 1978), especially the contributions by Mariano d'Alatri (pp. 49-72), Jacques Verger (pp. 173-203), and Alfonso Maieru (pp. 305-52).

81. A. Maieru, "Lo *Speculum puerorum sive terminus est in quem* di Riccardo Billingham," in *A Giuseppe Ermini* (Spoleto, 1970), pp. 297-99.

82. Among the Parisian libraries of the fourteenth century, those of the Augustinians (many manuscripts of which survive today in the collection of the Bibliotheque Mazarine) and the Cistercians (much of which survives at Troyes) were particularly extensive and eventually rich in English sources. Moreover, the College St. Bernard had direct contact with England, since among those called to Avignon in 1340 was an English Cistercian. On the Clairvaux Library (much of it from the College St. Bernard at Paris) see the recent catalogue: A. Vernet, *La bibliotheque de l'abbaye de Clairvaux du XIIe au XVIIIe siecle*, vol. 1: *Catalogues et repertoires* (Paris, 1979).

83. For Burley, see Rimini, *Sent.* 1, dist. 17, q. 2, a. 3 (Venice, 1522; reprint St. Bonaventure, 1955), fols. 96 O-Q, 98 A-D; *Sent.* 1, dist. 17, q. 4, a. 2, fol. 107 L-P; *Sent.* 2, dist. 2, q. 1, a. 1, fol. 28 E-L. References to Ockham are extensive; see *Sent.* 1, fols. 1 D, 2 C, 8J, 13 J, 17 L, 23 E, 23 M, 24 D-H, 26 L, 35 M, 45 Q, 53 N, 55 G, 57 F, 64 N, 75 G, 78 M, 79 J, 81 K, 82 F, 82 Q, 119 A, 120 A, 126 N, 130 H, 135 P-Q, 138 Q, 150 E, 152 K, 165 E, 169 J, 180 O; *Sent.* 2, fols. 19 N, 24 H, 41 E, 44 G, 59 G, 70 J, 72 A, 85 H, 87 A, 92 G, 97 N.

84. Citations from Kilvington's *Sophismata* can be found in Rimini, *Sent.* 1, fol. 94 O-P; *Sent.* 2, fol. 36 G. Heytesbury's *Sophismata* is cited in Rimini, *Sent.* 1, fol. 4 K.

85. For Chatton, see Rimini, *Sent.* 1, fols, 53 L, 101 Q, 102 N. On Fitzralph, see Rimini, *Sent.* 1, fols. 165 E, 166 D, 167 E; *Sent.* 2, fols, 12 F, 35 N, 36 D, 36 Q, 40 L, 41 H, 44 H, 45 E, 50 E, 51 P, 85 P, 111 Q.

86. Rimini, *Sent.* 1, 3 M, 13 J, 25 H, 29 O, 31 C, 36 G, 102 G, 116 B, 166 D; *Sent.* 2, fols. 34 B, 36 P, 55 P, 56 J, 66 B, 80 D, 88 B, 92 G, 97 E, 97 O, 113 A, 113 J.

87. Rimini, *Sent.* 2, fols. 105 K, 125 N. Rimini's citations of the *Summa de cause Dei* can no longer with certainty be placed before 1344 (the traditional "publication" date of Bradwardine's work), both because Rimini added references as late as 1346 and because other evidence for an earlier dissemination of *De causa Dei* is now lacking. See above, note 66.

88. For Kilvington, see Rimini, *Sent.* 1, fols. 115 K, 139 A; for Buckingham, see Rimini, *Sent* 1, 163 O; for Halifax, see Rimini, *Sent.* 1, 26 L; and for Monachus Niger, see Rimini, *Sent.* 1, fols. 149 P, 171 D; *Sent.* 2, fol. 43 F. It is not certain if all of these newer English authors were read firsthand by Gregory. Many of his citations to Ockham, Chatton, Fitzralph, and Kilvington can also be found in Wodeham. It should be kept in mind that these are only the places where marginal references identify those opinions Gregory is discussing. His actual indebtedness to the English sources is far greater.

89. Specifically Reading, Rodington, Holcot, and Rosetus among those who eventually become frequently cited. There are also minor figures like Adam of Ely, John Stukele, and Alexander Langeley.

90. In particular, see D. Trapp, "Augustinian Theology of the 14th Century," *Augustiniana* 6 (1956): 182-213; and more extreme: G. Leff, *Gregory of Rimini* (Manchester, 1961); J. Worek, "Augustinismo y Aristotelismo tomista en la doctrina gnoseologica de Gregorio Ariminense," *La Ciudad de Dios* 177 (1964): 435-68, 635-82; Worek, "El Amor de Dios en la Actividad Moral Cristiana segun Gregorio de Rimini," *Revista Agustiniana de Espiritualidad* 8 (1967): 339-62; 9 (1968): 255-312; 10 (1969): 109-53, 431-89; Paque, *Das Pariser Nominalistenstatut*; for a more nuanced view, albeit one that separates "Augustinian Nominalism" from

Ockham, see M. Schulze, "Gregor von Rimini, Lectura super Secundum: Themen und Probleme," in Gregory of Rimini, *Lectura supre Primum et Secundum Sententiarum*, ed. D. Trapp (Berlin and New York, 1979), 4:xli–lxi.

91. D. Trapp, "Augustinian Theology," p. 181: "Thomas of Strassburg marks the turning point in Augustinian Modern theology. I call him the 'last Augustinian of Aegidius' and Gregory the 'first Augustinian of Augustine.' . . . What is so new in Gregory is the fact that he is the best Augustine scholar of the Middle Ages from the milieu which created the Milleloquium."

92. The language here, as in the earlier part of the paper, is derived from J. Murdoch, "From Social into Intellectual Factors: an Aspect of the Unitary Character of Late Medieval Learning," in *The Cultural Context of Medieval Learning* (Dordrecht and Boston, 1975), pp. 271–348.

93. Some of this becomes immediately obvious in glancing at the alphabetical indices that precede books 1 and 2 in the 1522 edition. This type of approach is particularly evident in the first distinction of book 1 (*frui-uti* question), distinction 17 (on grace), and distinction 42–44 (on infinite divine power), the opening distinctions of book 2 (creation, angelology, and Rimini's natural philosophy), and distinctions 30–34 (on original sin).

94. For example, in the prologue, book 1, distinction 3 (on *notitia intuitiva, abstractiva*), and in book 2, distinctions 7–10 (on angelic knowledge).

95. For example, book 1, distinction I (*fruitio* and *delectatio*), distinction 17 (on grace), distinction 28 (on relation), and distinctions 38–44 (on foreknowledge, future contingents, predestination, and divine omnipotence).

96. Distinctions 5–16 of Book 1.

97. The prologue and distinctions 2 and 42–44 of book 1.

98. Rimini, *Sent.* 1, dist. 28, q. 2, a. 1 (132 H): "Ex quibus evidenter patebit quod nulla relatio est entitas ab omni absolute entitate et ab omnibus entitatibus absolutis distincta." (135 H-I): "Nulla relatio est entitas ab omni et omnibus entitatibus absolutis distincta, sed quaelibet (si est entitas) est aliqua entitas absoluta." His position is in direct opposition to that of Scotus and Burley (135 I). For Rimini's modification to Ockham on relation, see *Sent.* 1, dist. 28, q. 1, a. 2 (130 H): "Et hoc modo quidam alius doctor (Ockham) procedit, concedens quidem et bene quod vere absque operatione animae aliquid est simile et aliquid pater et causa, et sic de aliis. Nihilominus tamen nulla res extra quae non est signum est ad aliquid vel relatio." It is on this last point that Gregory differs.

99. Rimini, *Sent.* 2, dist. 1, q. 4; in edition by Trapp, *Lectura super Primum et Secundum Sententiarum* (Berlin and New York, 1979), 4:128: "Nullus motus est alique talis res a permanentibus distincta, ut fingit opinio (i.e., Burley, against whom Gregory is arguing). Secunda, quod nec 'mutatum esse' est aliqua res talis, qualem ponit. Tertia, quod nec mutatio est res a permanente distincta ut dicit." Cf. Rimini, *Sent.* 1, dist. 42–44, q. 3, a. 1 (169 J).

100. Rimini, *Sent.* 2, dist. 2, q. 1; in Trapp, *Lectura*, 4:238–39: "Prima est quod tempus non est aliqua res non permanens, sic divisibilis et successiva, ut dicit opinio (of Burley). Secunda . . . tempus non est res distincta formaliter inhaerens motui, ut dicit opinio. Tertia, quod instans non est 'indivisibile non durans'."

101. Since Rimini does not have a commentary on book 4 of the *Sentences*, where the category of quantity is usually examined, one has to draw upon what he says of quantity elsewhere. See Rimini, *Sent.* 2, dist. 12, q. 2, a. 1.

102. James A. Weisheipl, "Developments in the Arts Curriculum at Oxford in the Early Fourteenth Century," *Mediaeval Studies* 28 (1966): 161; cf. Weisheipl, "Ockham and Some Mertonians," *Mediaeval Studies* 30 (1968): 164–86.

103. J. Würsdörfer, *Erkennen und Wissen bei Gregor von Rimini* (Münster i.W., 1917).

104. Rimini, *Sent.* 2, dist. 7, q. 2, a. 1–2.

105. H. Elie, *Le complexe significabile* (Paris, 1936), pp. 13–16.

106. Ibid., 17–40.

107. A. Maier, "Das Problem der 'species sensibiles in medio' und die neue Naturphilosophie des 14. Jahrhunderts," *Freiburger Zeitschrift für Philosophie und Theologie* 10 (1963): 3–32; in *Ausgehendes Mittelalter* (Rome, 1967), 2:419–51.

108. Gregory's *socii*, Francis de Treviso and John Rathe of Scotland, seem to have followed Ockham on this point.

109. See Ann Brinkley, "Robert Holcot: Toward an Empirical Theory of Knowledge" (Ph.D. diss., Harvard, 1972).

110. See the forthcoming article by Katherine Tachau, "The Problem of *species in medio* at Oxford in the Generation after Ockham," in *Medieval Studies.*

111. In particular, see E. A. Moody, "A Quodlibetal Question of Robert Holcot O.P. on the Problem of the Objects of Knowledge and Belief," *Speculum* 39 (1964): 53–74; H. Schepers, "Holkot contra dicta Crathorn," *Philosophisches Jahrbuch* 77 (1970): 320–54; 79 (1972): 106–36; G. Gál, "Adam of Wodeham's Question on the 'Complexe Significabile' as the Immediate Object of Scientific Knowledge," *Franciscan Studies* 37 (1977): 66–102.

112. G. Gál, "Adam of Wodeham's Question on the 'Complexe Significabile' as the Immediate Object of Knowledge," *Franciscan Studies* 37 (1977): 66–102.

113. Ockham's doctrine was essentially a variation on Scotus's teaching. The habit of grace was not absolutely necessary for meritorious action and salvation but only relatively necessary within the system God has ordained and upholds. *De potentia absoluta* God could reject good works done in a state of grace or accept a sinner without the habit of grace. *De potentia ordinata* God has decided only to reward with grace those who do their best and only to accept as meritorious of eternal life good actions done in a state of grace.

114. The relevant texts have been edited by Girard Etzkorn, "Walter Chatton and the Controversy on the Absolute Necessity of Grace," *Franciscan Studies* 37 (1977): 32–65.

115. Hoffmann, *Die erste Kritik des Ockhamismus; Die Schriften des Ockhamismus; Die Schriften des Oxforder Kanzlers Iohannes Lutterell*; Etzkorn, "Walter Chatton." For further bibliography, see above, note 7.

116. Wodeham, *Lectura Oxon.,* 1, d. 1, q. 10, a. 1 (Vat. lat. 955, fol. 67^v; Paris, Univ. 193, fol. 50ra; Paris, Max. 915, fols. 41va–41vb).

117. Paris, B.N. lat. 15 880 (the earlier text), Vat. lat. 1111, fol. 32^r, Milan, Ambrosiana E 55 inf., fol. 47^v, and Paris, B.N. lat. 14 514, fol. 295^v (the later text).

118. J.-F. Genest, "Le 'De futuris contingentibus' de Thomas Bradwardine" unpublished thesis, Mémoire pour le Diplome de l'Ecole pratique des hautes études [5e section] Paris, 1975), pp. xxi–xxii, xvii–xxviii, 96–114.

119. Ibid.

120. See Courtenay, *Adam Wodeham,* pp. 101–5, for the relevant texts.

121. Gregory only cites Bradwardine's *Summa de causa Dei,* not his early treatises.

122. Rimini, *Sent.* 2, dist. 26–28, q. 1.

123. C. Michalski, *Wplyw Oksfordu na filozofja Jana z Mirecourt* (Krakow, 1921); G. Ouy, "Un commentateur des 'Sentences' au XIVe siècle, Jean de Mirecourt" (unpublished thesis, Ecole des Chartes, Paris, 1946), abstracted in *Ecole Nationale des Chartes. Positions des These soutenues par les élèves de la promotion de 1946 pour obtenir le diplome d'archiviste paleographe* (Paris, 1946), pp. 117–22; G. Teissier, "Jean de Mirecourt," in *Histoire litteraire de la France* 40 (1974): 1–52; W. J. Courtenay, "Jean of Mirecourt and Gregory of Rimini on Whether God Can Undo the Past," *Recherches de Theologie ancienne et medievale* 39 (1972): 224–56, 40

(1973): 147–74; J. Murdoch, "*Subtilitates Anglicanae* in Fourteenth-Century Paris: John of Mirecourt and Peter Ceffons," in *Machaut's World* (New York, 1978), pp. 51–86; Courtenay, *Adam Wodeham*, pp. 131-33.

124. D. Trapp, "Augustinian Theology of the 14th Century," *Augustiniana* 6 (1956): 213–22.

125. On Hugolino's English sources, see A. Zumkeller, *Hugolin von Orvieto und seine theologische Erkenntnislehre*, Cassiciacum, 9.2 (Würzburg, 1941), pp. 255–62; D. Trapp, "Augustinian Theology," 222–23. On Ceffons, see D. Trapp, "Peter Ceffons of Clairvaux," *Recherches de Theologie ancienne et medievale* 24 (1957): 101–54; Courtenay, *Adam Wodeham*, pp. 135–37; J. Murdoch, "*Subtilitates Anglicanae*."

126. See J. Coleman, "Jean de Ripa. O.F.M. and the Oxford Calculators," *Mediaeval Studies* 37 (1975): 130–89.

127. For a fuller discussion of the issues and literature on this question, see my "John of Mirecourt and Gregory of Rimini."

128. In this respect the method of analysis in the theological faculty at Oxford (and eventually at Paris) paralleled that of the arts faculty. Many of the propositions and statements that were debated in the schools and that seem so outrageous to modern "pious ears" were nothing more nor less than arguments that appear logically valid but are known to be false, or arguments that on one level are true and on another level false, e.g., "*Deus deceptor est*," "*Deus possit dicere falsum, mentiri, fallere*," "*Deus peccatum causat*," "*Deu potest facere quod mundum numquam fuisse*," or "*Socrates et Plato, vel Deus et creatura nihil est*." This is not only another example of the interpenetration of philosophy and theology in this period but a warning that we should not hastily conclude that such statements reveal impious, skeptical, or frivolous motives or that the theologians who used them did not take theology seriously.

129. The view that Gregory was responsible for the condemnation of Mirecourt was developed by D. Trapp, "Augustinian Theology," pp. 188–89; "Peter Ceffons of Clairvaux," pp. 147–54. For the evidence against that opinion, see my "John of Mirecourt and Gregory of Rimini," pp. 154–65. V. Marcolino has subsequently established that Gregory left Paris in the summer of 1346 and was teaching at Padua in 1347.

130. Ceffons describes those responsible for the condemnation of Mirecourt as "three shriveled-up old women," suggesting that they were advanced in years. His description would fit Robert de Bardis, who as head of the theological faculty signed the articles of condemnation, but not Gregory of Rimini, who would not have been much older than 35 in 1347. For more detailed examination of the passage in Ceffons, see D. Trapp, "Peter Ceffons of Clairvaux," and W. J. Courtenay, "John of Mirecourt and Gregory of Rimini."

131. On Paul of Perugia, see B. M. Xiberta, *De scriptoribus scholasticis saeculi xiv ex ordine Carmelitarum* (Louvain, 1931), pp. 285–316. The only fragment of Spinello's Commentary discovered to date is found in Madrid, Univ. 58 (118 Z 16), fols. 107ᵛ–122ᵛ. The *principium* and *collatio* of Astensius of St. Colombe can be found in Grax, Univ. 836, fols. 81ʳ–90ʳ.

132. On Hugolina and Bologna, see F. Ehrle, *I piu antichi statuti della Facolta teologica dell' Universita di bologna* (Bologna, 1932), pp. 60–73. It is probable that Autrecourt drew some of his ideas and language from English sources. For the most important literature on Autrecourt, see above, note 63. Michalski's belief that Bradwardine was among Autrecourt's sources was rejected by subsequent scholars on the grounds that the ideas in question appeared in *De causa Dei* (1344) and thus could not be the source for work done before 1340. Genest's discovery that many of the arguments and positions that appear in *De causa Dei* were known earlier from other writings of Bradwardine reopens that question and makes it likely that Michalski was correct.

133. R. N. Swanson, *Universities, Academics and the Great Schism* (Cambridge, 1979), p.

11; "An intellectual *Drang nach Osten* had first foundered, and by 1378 had all but died out: although universities had been erected at Pecs, Cracow, Vienna, and Prague, only the last remained a flourishing institution in 1378."

134. The most recent treatment of this theme is Swanson, *Universities, Academics, and the Great Schism.*

135. Given the importance of the universities in the high and late Middle Ages, we tend to forget that the cathedral schools in nonuniversity towns, e.g., Chartres, Reims, Cologne, Mainz, Canterbury, York, continued to function in the thirteenth and fourteenth centuries. Eclipsed by more prestigious neighbors, they have not received the study they deserve. Similarly, the schools of collegiate churches and those of the canonical confederations that appeared in the eleventh and twelfth centuries have not claimed the scholarly attention won by the Cistercians or the mendicant orders. No one would deny the intellectual and academic significance of St. Genevieve and St. Victor at Paris, but few would be aware of the importance of the Apostelstift in Cologne, the Marienstift in Erfurt, or the Sandstift in Breslau. We are only now beginning to appreciate the social, economic, and intellectual importance of the canonical and monastic movements of the twelfth century that concentrated their attention on the developing towns rather than rural or isolated areas. In particular, see the recent study by Karl Bosl, *Regularkanoniker (Augustinerchorherren) und Seelsorge in Kirche und Gesellschaft des europäischen 12. Jahrhunderts.* Bayerische Akademie der Wissenschaften, Phil.-Hist. Klasse, Neue Fol. 86 (München, 1979). On the Schottenklöster, see J. Scholle, *Das Erfurter Schottenklöster* (Düsseldorf, 1932); J. Lechner, *800 Jahre Schottenabtei* (Vienna, 1960).

136. Jerzy Kloczowski, 'Europa centro-orientale," in *Le Scuole degli Ordini Mendicanti (secoli XIII–XIV)* (Todi, 1978): 127–49.

137. It was not always necessary to change schools in moving from lower to higher studies. Young boys destined for the secular priesthood might begin their education at a cathedral or collegiate school, and the major *studia* of the religious order often provided training at all levels.

138. A. Schneider, "Die Ordensschulen in Köln als Vorläufer der Universität," in *Festschrift zur Erinnerung an die Gründung der alten Universität Köln im Jahre 1388* (Köln, 1938), pp. 5–12; G. M. Löhr, *Die Kölner Dominikanerschule vom XIV. bis zum XVI Jahrhundert* (Fribourg i Schw., 1946).

139. Kloczowski, *Le Scuole degli Ordini Mendicanti*, pp. 136–40.

140. On Magdeburg, see F. Doelle, "Das Partikularstudium der sächsischen Provinz im Mittelalter," *Franziskanische Studien* 14 (1927): 244–51. On Erfurt, see L. Meier, "Contributions a l'histoire de la theologie a l'universite a Erfurt," *Revue d'histoire ecclesiastique* 50 (1955): 454–79; L. Meier, *Die Barfüsserschule zu Erfurt* (Münster, 1958); G. C. Boyce, "Erfurt Schools and Scholars in the Thirteenth Century," *Speculum* 24 (1949): 1–18; H. Grauert, "Auf dem Wege zur Universität Erfurt," *Historisches Jahrbuch der Görres Gesellschaft* 31 (1910): 249–89; J. Pinborg, *Die Entwicklung der Sprachtheorie im Mittelalter* (Münster, 1967).

141. Kloczowski, *Le Scuole degli Ordini Mendicanti*, pp. 140–49.

142. Ibid., pp. 131–33, 143–45.

143. H. Denifle, *Die Universitäten des Mittelalters* (Berlin, 1885), 1:406–8; but cf. H. Grauert, "Auf dem Wege zur Univ. Erfurt," pp. 238–89; J. Pinborg, *Die Entwicklung*, p. 139; E. Kleineidam, *Universitas studii Erffordensis* (Leipzig, 1964), 1:1–9.

144. On relations between Erfurt and Prague, see A. Lang, *Heinrich Totting von Oyta* (Munster i.W., 1937); Kleineidam, *Universitas studii Erffordensis*, 1:1–9. Interrelations and similarities between Cologne and Erfurt are much harder to document. Historians have tended to treat them separately, associating Cologne with the *via antiqua* and Erfurt with the *via moderna*. The work of Ludger Meier and Ernst Kleineidam, however, has made Erfurt

appear far less nominalistic, and Cologne, even in the fifteenth century, was less one-sided than suspected. Gabriel Biel, perhaps the leading exponent of Ockham's thought in the second half of the fifteenth century, acquired his Ockham manuscripts while studying at Cologne, not at Heidelberg or Erfurt.

145. On Conrad's residence in theology at Bologna, see K. Lauterer, "Konrad von Ebrach S.O. Cist.," *Analecta Sacri Ordinis Cisterciensis* 17 (1961): 151–214; 18 (1962): 60–120; 19 (1963): 3–50. For further ties specifically between Erfurt and Bologna, see Z. Kuksewicz, "Theodoric, recteur d'Erfurt, Averroiste Allemand du XIVᵉ siecle," in *La Filosofia della natura nel medioevo* (Milan, 1966), pp. 652–61; "Commentarium super Libros de Anima by an anonymous Averroist of the 14th C Erfurt," *Studia Mediewistyczne* 17 (1977): 65–122.

146. The full list is now available through the computerized index of A. B. Emden, *A Biographical Register of the University of Oxford to A.D. 1500*, 3 vols. (Oxford, 1957–59), compiled by Trevor Aston and his associates at Corpus Christi College, Oxford. Hussite scholars have long appreciated the importance of the Oxford-Prague connection in the second half of the fourteenth century for the arrival of Wyclif's works and ideas in Bohemia.

147. For the individual biographies, see Emden, *Biographical Register of the University of Oxford*.

148. Cambridge, Gonville and Caius College, Ms. 464/571, fol. 64ʳ. The information is taken from the introduction to the edition of the *Summa Logicae* (St. Bonaventure, 1974).

149. Munich, Bibl. Franzis., Ms. 4° 2; Vatican Library, Chigi E. IV. 99; Venice, Bibl. S. Marco, Ms. lat. Cl. VI, 292; Basel, Bibl. Univ., Ms. F. II. 25; Erfurt, Wiss. Bibl., Cod. Amplon. 0 67.

150. Erfurt, Wiss. Bibl., Cod. Amplon. 0 76. This small student copy, similar in nature to clm 23 530, also contains Bradwardine's Insolubilia, Kilvington's Sophismata, and various works of Burley.

151. Erfurt, Wiss. Bibl., Cod. Amplon. Q 270; Vat. lat. 3065.

152. Erfurt, Wiss. Bibl., Cod. Amplon. F. 135; cf. Weisheipl, "Ockham and some Mertonians," p. 196.

153. Cf. Weisheipl, "Repertorium Mertonense," *Mediaeval Studies* 31 (1969): 215–16.

154. Pinborg, "Die Erfurter Tradition im Sprachdenken des Mittelalters," *Universalismus und Partikularismus im Mittelalter*. Miscellanea Mediaevalia, Bd. 5 (Berlin, 1968), pp. 173–85. Pinborg subsequently became more cautious about Aurifaber's dependence on Ockham; see "A Note on Some Theoretical Concepts of Logic and Grammar," *Revue Internationale de Philosophie* 29 (1975): 286–96.

155. Ibid., pp. 181–82.

156. Ibid., p. 182.

157. Pinborg, "Neues zum Erfurter Schullenben des XIV. Jahrhunderts nach Handschriften der Jagiellonischen Bibliothek zu Krakow," *Bulletin de philosophie medievale* 15 (1973): 148.

158. Pinborg, "Nochmals die Erfurter Schulen im XIV. Jahrhundert," *Cahiers de l'Institut du moyen-age Grec et Latin* 17 (1976): 71–81.

159. Buridan's influence in the German *studia* was eventually felt as well, as was the natural philosophy of John of Jandun. A chronological approach to Buridan's influence in Germany has not, to my knowledge, been done.

160. There are a number of manuscripts at Erfurt, Cracow, Munich, and Prague. For the complete list see H. Schepers, "Holkot contra dicta Crathorn," *Phil. Jahr.* 77 (1970): 331–33.

161. W. J. Courtenay, "Some Notes on Robert of Halifax, O.F.M.," *Franciscan Studies* 33 (1973): 135–42.

162. D. Trapp, "Augustinian Theology of the 14th Century," 203–4; "'Moderns' and 'Modernists' in Ms. Fribourg Cordeliers 26," *Augustinianum* 5 (1965): 241–70; Emden, *A Biographical Register of the University of Oxford*, 3:1564.

163. Courtenay, *Adam Wodeham*, pp. 13, 133, 198–201.

164. Ibid., pp. 133–35, 215–22.

165. A. Lang, *Heinrich Totting von Oyta* (Münster i.W., 1937), pp. 139–43.

166. Courtenay, *Adam Wodeham*, pp. 146–47.

167. L. Meier, *Die Barfüsserschule zu Erfurt* (Münster i.W., 1958); E. Kleineidam, *Universitas studii Erffordensis* (Leipzig, 1964).

UNIVERSITY MIGRATIONS IN THE LATE MIDDLE AGES, WITH PARTICULAR REFERENCE TO THE STAMFORD SECESSION

John M. Fletcher

agisterial works of history have the unfortunate characteristic of frequently imposing constraints upon historians for many generations; their very power and authority may inhibit criticism and allow strongly worded opinions to pass as accepted historical truths. No one working on the history of medieval universities can escape the influence of Rashdall, whose great work still remains the best general introduction to the subject. As were all scholars concerned with the history of universities, Rashdall and his contemporaries were deeply impressed by the establishment of these unique institutions; they devoted much of their research to the problem of the origins of the universities and saw with admiration the manner in which a loose community of teachers and students provided itself with the rudimentary organization that eventually produced the medieval universities. Emphasizing the 'popular,' 'democratic,' almost 'volkisch' origins of the universities, Rashdall was particularly concerned to stress the independence of these early scholarly communities and their freedom of action. He pictured masters and students as members of a European community of scholars beholden to no particular city, prepared to move in search of better conditions or more reputable teachers with a readiness astonishing to the modern academic. From these premises, Rashdall drew the influential conclusion that 'half the universities in Europe owed their origin to migrations of groups of scholars from one center to another.'[1] This paper will examine the validity of Rashdall's view

and attempt to show why migrations of scholars were strictly limited in their influence on new university foundations, especially in the later medieval period.

The romantic or idealistic view of medieval education has rightly emphasized how, in the eleventh, twelfth, and thirteenth centuries, scholars would travel for many miles to sit at the feet of some prominent teacher, how they would follow him if he moved to some distant town, and how they would endure many privations to obtain the benefit of his instruction. John of Salisbury in his *Metalogicon* has described his wanderings in northern France between 1136 and 1147 in search of learning. Students were so devoted to Abelard that they were prepared to follow him to Melun, Corbeil, and Paris, and even accompanied him when he tried to conceal himself like a hermit in the desert.[2] Certainly neither Abelard nor his students had any difficulty beyond the usual hindrances that affected the medieval traveller in moving their informal *schola* from one town to another in search of freedom from persecution.

These halcyon days did not last. There was, of course, a considerable period of time when the universities remained little more than collections of masters, each with his own group of students. The formal organization of this fluid group of teachers and students did not come suddenly; when it was near completion, however, the situation as it existed in the time of Abelard had drastically changed. To a considerable extent, the early ease of movement was no longer possible; with this development, the opportunity for large groups of students and masters to desert one university town for another was much reduced.

The decisive intellectual event that separates the world of Abelard from that of the later thirteenth century is the reception and absorption of the corpus of Aristotelian learning. Abelard died in 1143. It was not until the second half of the twelfth century that such translators as Gerard of Cremona made available to the West a large number of previously unknown or half-known Greek texts. Their work also brought to academic circles in Europe many of the standard Arabic commentaries on these texts. Gerard himself made available the seventy-one works listed in his own catalogue and perhaps a score of others before his death at Toledo in 1187.[3] It was not only in science, logic, and philosophy that scholars suddenly found an abundance of learning available to them. The study of law received a tremendous impetus with the increased attention, especially at Bologna, to the texts of the Roman law. Again, these texts did not in themselves satisfy later academics. By the middle of the thirteenth century, Accursius had codified the commentaries made by a century of lawyers into the celebrated *Glossa Ordinaria*. In medicine the works of Galen and Hippocrates were received together with the extensive commentaries made on them by the Arabs. For the theologians, the *Sentences* of Petrus Lombardus and the *Historia Scholastica* of Petrus Comestor now formed essential reading. Almost all these works were unknown to Abelard and his contemporaries; one hundred years later, lecturers and students were expected to have a deep knowledge of the many recently available works relevant to their particular fields of study.

This multiplication of texts itself considerably impeded the ease of movement of teachers and students. Whereas at an earlier date the lecturer needed access only to the few texts that were known in his own area of interest and could often copy out the more essential of them himself, the master of the early fourteenth century was expected to have studied a considerable number of standard works, a body of material that was ever increasing as scholars added their own commentaries to the fundamental Aristotelian and other texts. At this later date, a master needed the company of other teachers with whom he could exchange ideas and books; he needed to have available scribes who could multiply texts for individual or general use; he would find it advantageous to have near him an expanding library from which he could draw both the books needed for his lectures and the more specialist texts that he might require for his studies.

There was, of course, little possibility of the masters and less of the students being able to purchase the books they needed. The prices of even the most elementary texts were prohibitive to all but the very wealthy: books available in late fourteenth-century

165

Oxford, for example, were valued at 10/ –for a *Textus Metaphysice*, 5/ –for a commentary on the *De Celo et Mundo*, and 53/4 for a collection of the works of Albertus Magnus. Texts used in the higher faculties could be even more highly valued: £5 for the text of the Decretals, £4 for the commentary of Hostiensis, and £5 for a copy of Haymo's notes on the Epistles of St. Paul.[4] At this date, a student could live in Oxford for approximately 7d. per week![5]

This serious problem was not resolved until the development of the printing press eventually allowed the production of large numbers of books which, if not cheap, cost much less than the manuscripts. The medieval universities, however, did make a determined and at least partly successful effort to make available, within their limited resources, more copies of essential textbooks. Ingenious use of the '*pecia*' system, the employment of *pronuntiatores* to read out approved texts to an audience of copies, widespread use of 'summaries' or collections of extracts from important texts at least ensured that each academic center had reasonable access to the necessary written material.[6] By the beginning of the sixteenth century, a small college such as Merton College, Oxford, could supply its company of some twenty Fellows with about five hundred books available for distribution annually as well as give access to the collection of more unusual or valuable texts chained in the library.[7] Many universities housed fine collections of books: Erfurt possessed its Amplonianum, Oxford the collection donated by Humfrey, Duke of Gloucester, Bologna the collection of Albornoz housed in his College of Spain, Paris the great library of the Sorbonne. It must be emphasized, however, that this expansion in the number of books available did not result in the creation of large private student libraries. Books remained far too expensive for all but the most wealthy individuals to think of establishing a large personal collection. For the normal master, access to a good library was the only means by which he could obtain the texts he needed, and increasingly, as academic writers produced their own specialized material different from that, for example, usually found in the great monastic libraries, such texts could best be obtained in an established university.

166

For an individual master to leave such an academic center was now hardly advisable if he wished to retain scholastic influence. Such a movement was only possible if sufficient masters left, retired to the same place, and were able quickly to build up equivalent or near equivalent resources to those that they had left behind. In this way an advancement in learning was accompanied by a reduction of the masters' freedom of movement.

We may also suggest that there has been a tendency to minimize the dependence of masters and students on the availability of suitable accommodation in any chosen town. It is certainly true, as W. A. Pantin has reminded us in his study of the halls and schools of medieval Oxford, that "in the age of Grosseteste or of Duns Scotus it would . . . have been possible for a rather ill-informed or unobservant traveller to ride through Oxford without guessing that there was a university there; he certainly would not have found streets lined with academic palaces."[8] The universities of the twelfth and thirteenth centuries generally possessed few if any specialized buildings; their students and masters for the most part lived, studied, and taught in hired accommodations generally of no different character from the other houses in the town. Any large house of the period possessed a number of small rooms that could be used as bedrooms, and perhaps individual or group study-chambers, and a large room that could be utilized as a common dining room or as a lecture hall. The masters and students of this date were certainly not closely bound to a number of buildings essential to their particular needs that they could not leave without damage to their work.

It would, however, be deceptively easy to argue from this that the medieval masters and students could, without difficulty, transport themselves from one university town to another. Although the same type of accommodation that they utilized existed in all large medieval towns, it did not necessarily follow that it was available for the use of masters and students. Today one of the major problems that confronts any university is the difficulty of providing satisfactory lodgings for its students. How much more difficult would it have been for any medieval town, possessing a much smaller stock of housing, to arrange a short notice accommodation for a large group of students and masters? We have no accurate figures for the populations of either the medieval university towns or the medieval universities. It is reasonable to assume, however, that the corporation of students and masters represented, especially in the smaller academic centers, a very sizeable proportion of the total population of the town during term time. The presence of some hundreds of students in any one typical medieval town must have placed a severe strain on its resources.

In fact, there is ample evidence that a supply of available accommodation was one of the first things that the founders of medieval universities looked for. Many universities were deliberately established in towns whose population was declining or stagnant. Louvain at the close of the fourteenth century had suffered from a migration of part of its working population and had lost much of its prosperity. The establishment of a university there in 1425 was probably an attempt to revive the town's fortunes;[9] the decline of population had released accommodation that could be used by the large number of students now expected in the town. An even more notable attempt to utilize housing left vacant by a decline in prosperity can be found in the events that accompanied the establishment and encouragement of the University of Pisa. After a discouraging start in the fourteenth century, the university was strongly supported by the city of Florence that had in the fifteenth century conquered the republic of Pisa. In 1472 the University of Florence was merged with that of the defeated town. In the resolution that decreed this merger, the signory of Florence points out that the scarcity of accommodation in the city and its consequent expense had acted as a deterrent to students; Pisa had lost much of its prosperity and its richer inhabitants and now consequently had an ample supply of large, empty houses available for a substantial student body.[10] Even in the older, established universities there was concern to maintain the stock of housing available to students and masters. Pantin's statement that at Oxford "the same house might pass from private to academic use and *vice versa*"[11] may describe what could happen, but the university statutes were careful to insist that if any house had at any time been used for student

168

accommodation or as a school, it should remain available to the university unless the owner required it for his own use or wished to lease it out for a period of ten years.[12] If such ancient universities as Oxford had difficulty in maintaining lodgings available for their students and masters, it could be expected that newer foundations would experience more serious trouble unless peculiar circumstances made accommodation readily available.

It would seem, therefore, that, when considering the ease or difficulty with which medieval masters and students could secede from one town to another, we cannot necessarily assume that the question of the availability of suitable accommodation was not an issue. The movement of the academic body from one center to another certainly was not hampered by an over dependence on particular specialist buildings; it was, however, very much dependent on the availability in the projected host town of ample housing that could be leased to masters and students at a reasonable rent. There was no possibility, as today, of providing a completely new campus to cater to the special needs of the university. Accommodation had almost entirely to be drawn from the existing stock of the recipient town. Except where there was a combination of very special circumstances, towns that could offer such advantages to a seceding group of students and masters at any particular time must have been very few in number. Stamford may, in fact, have been a town in such a position. There is evidence that the prosperity of the town was fading before 1300, and that it was not to recover until the late fourteenth century. An influx of students would have probably been welcomed to recompense for a decline in other commercial activity. Stamford was also well endowed with religious foundations having large halls available for academic exercises. There had been considerable building during the thirteenth century, and as trade stagnated some of this property would probably have been available to let as accommodation for scholars.[13] It could be that the readiness of the townsfolk of Stamford to assist the migrating scholars by providing suitable accommodation is one explanation of their reluctance to leave the town and return to Oxford.

In general, however, every existing university had an advantage

169

here over any new foundation, except where the chosen town could offer unusually good terms to its incoming academic population. The older centers had grown slowly from modest beginnings and had come to utilize the housing of the towns in which they were situated only over a long period of time. Also, they were usually strong enough to retain an adequate amount of accommodation for their own use and to insist on a reasonable rent for their members. The interesting story of secessions from the great Italian university of Bologna, which we shall discuss in more detail later, clearly shows what advantages were enjoyed by an ancient foundation in this respect. None of the many secessions from Bologna fatally weakened that university; masters and students were generally content to return to the town even after a considerable time had elapsed. One of the reasons why Bologna was always able to attract back most of its students and masters must have been that it was, until the very close of the medieval period, the only Italian town outside Rome that had experience of regularly providing accommodation for very large numbers of students and masters. Nor was Bologna a major commercial city like Florence, where housing was required for other than academic purposes and was expensive; Bologna had not the reputation of Rome as a city that lived off rather than from visitors. On the contrary, Bologna valued its university as a major contributor to its prosperity. Repeated efforts were made by the town to prevent any transference of the *studium* to other towns; from 1127 until 1312 an oath was regularly required from all doctors intending to teach at Bologna that during the next two years they would lecture only in the town.[14] At Bologna, students and masters knew that they could find housing in a sufficient quantity and at a reasonable price in a town accustomed to cater to one of the largest academic populations in Europe. This in itself must have diminished the chance of any large scale permanent secession from the town.

As the universities developed in the later medieval period they became even more closely identified with the town in which they were situated. Specialized buildings were erected for their masters and students: the University Schools at Cambridge, the Divinity

Schools at Oxford, the Schools at Salamanca, a college with a lecture hall at Erfurt, and similar buildings in most of the universities. In the fourteenth and fifteenth centuries, the generosity of many benefactors provided in most of the university towns colleges for the regent masters or for groups of students. Most of them were small, but some were richly endowed with attractive buildings and considerable libraries: New College at Oxford, Kings College at Cambridge, The Spanish College at Bologna, the Amplonianum at Erfurt, the Colegio Viejo at Salamanca, to name but a few. With the erection of every new building and with the foundation of each new college, the dependence of the masters and students on that particular town increased. To leave behind such an elaborate academic 'plant' except as a temporary gesture of defiance was hardly feasible. The possibility of secession from the universities of the late fifteenth century was, for this reason also, very rarely considered.

We must emphasize too the deliberate efforts made by many founders of universities in the later medieval period to ensure that their foundation should not be able to secede from the town where it was established except with the greatest difficulty. In most later universities, some of the lecturing staff received salaries for their work. These payments were usually made from local civic or ecclesiastical funds especially set aside for this purpose. This is well illustrated by the example of Tübingen, established in 1477. There Graf Eberhard obtained papal permission to associate various ecclesiastical appointments with teaching posts he was about to establish in his new university.[15] In the future, certain lecturers would be automatically presented by him or his successors as patrons to the appropriate clerical positions and would then draw their salaries from this source. It was hardly possible to think of masters in this situation suggesting or supporting a secession from Tübingen! By the close of the fifteenth century, lecturing staff in many universities was supported from local funds in such ways. Even to think of a migration from the source of their income could hardly occur to the masters except under the most serious provocation.

Finally, the general tendency of medieval institutions to create their own privileged position in society and support this by the defence of 'liberties' and monopolies must not be ignored. Once universities were recognized and established, they quickly claimed for themselves, for their students, and especially for their graduates rights that brought social and economic authority and security.[16] Among the most important of these were the right to exclude graduates of unrecognized universities, the requirement that all students about to graduate should do so in their own university, and the claim to a monopoly of activity in certain spheres, such as the provision of higher instruction or the supply of medical treatment. These privileges were designed to protect the economic position of the masters of the university who would lose much of their income if student numbers declined, students graduated elsewhere, or others encroached on prospects of employment. The most serious challenge to the position of the masters would come, of course, from the foundation of a nearby rival university, offering tuition in the same subjects, and claiming similar privileges. It is not surprising that institutions, which, in their early years, had challenged many accepted social conventions, quickly became among the most resolute of medieval corporations in the defense of their privileges. As the number of universities increased rapidly during the fourteenth and fifteenth centuries, few areas in Europe remained without a center of higher education. Indeed, some regions, such as the Rhineland, may have already been granted too many universities so that some of the less well-endowed *studia* may have found difficulty in obtaining adequate students and staff. In such a situation, universities were unwilling to encourage new foundations that could draw students and resources away from themselves. When confronted with local secessions or plans to establish new universities, early foundations such as Paris, Oxford, or Cambridge, and even later centers such as Rostock, reacted angrily. Powerful pressure to prevent such institutions from succeeding was brought to bear on ecclesiastical and secular authorities. Such pressure was an additional factor militating against the success of any secession when there existed a strong university already claiming to cater to local needs.

From this brief general discussion it would appear that we must not exaggerate the ease with which medieval masters and students could organize a successful secession in the fourteenth and fifteenth centuries. There were serious obstacles, both academic and practical, to be overcome before this could be done, and these obstacles increased with the passage of time. At the close of the fifteenth century, the threat of a secession seems to have become an outdated weapon in the university armory. By the time, for example, of the important migration of Oxford scholars to Stamford, the chances of organizing a successful large scale movement from the town seem to have already greatly diminished for some of the reasons we have mentioned above.

It is important also to distinguish between the various activities that are generally covered by the term "secession." In the first place, we have the occasional actions of individuals who desert one university for another town, taking with them their own pupils. This frequently happened, for example, at Bologna where lectures in law in the thirteenth century were enticed to other towns with their students by offers of better remuneration.[17] Secessions of this kind are not of great importance; they occur mainly in the higher faculties where students were somewhat better off than their artist colleagues and therefore able to afford to travel and where there was more dependence on the reputation of one lecturer rather than a group of masters. Only rarely did they have any influence on the founding of new universities, although they did give temporary prestige to certain of the law schools of northern Italy. Such migrations as these belong to that period of time when the universities were developing from collections of individual lecturers into powerful organized corporations with a common policy and a planned course of instruction involving many teachers.

Secondly, there were secessions organized by a considerable part of the university, masters and students. Perhaps the most notable instance of this kind of migration occurred at Prague. In 1409 the king of Bohemia by the decree of Kutná Hora brought to a head the long simmering quarrel between the Czech nation and the other three nations of the university, amongst whom the Germans were predominant. In future, he ordered, the Czech nation "in all councils, courts, examinations, elections and other transactions or proceedings of the university" should have three votes and the other nations one only.[18] The Germans bound themselves to leave Prague rather than accept the royal decree; to break their opposition, Wenceslas banned them from Bohemia. As a body, the German masters and students left Prague to strengthen the existing universities of Germany and to found the great University of Leipzig. In a similar way, the Germans and the Scots were encouraged to leave the University of Paris in the late fourteenth century. For the first, it became intolerable to remain in a city owing allegiance to a Pope not supported by the great majority of Germans, and for the second it proved uncomfortable to study at a university proposing a solution to the Schism, withdrawal of obedience, that was not attractive to the Scots. Such secessions as these are important because they arise from a serious split within the university itself which caused such antagonism that there was no choice for the dissenting groups other than to associate themselves with another existing university, or, if their numbers were sufficient and they were able to find a receptive town, establish a new foundation. We would, however, expect that the possibility of establishing a new university would only occur at a time when a few *studia* existed. The later medieval period saw the erection of universities in areas previously without any *studium*. Such a development not only reduced the opportunity for a secession to found a new university but also increased the temptation for a dissident element to seek refuge in a nearby established center where they would probably receive a welcome from a university expecting social, economic, and academic advantages from the newcomers.

Finally, we have those secessions, probably the most famous, where the whole university leaves its host town in order to put pressure on civic or other authorities. Of this type were the great migrations that distinguished the early, troubled history of the University of Paris. In 1229, for instance, after fighting between students and townsmen, the university complained to the bishop and legate. Finding their protests unsuccessful, the masters bound themselves to leave Paris unless justice was done and proceeded to carry out their threat. It was not until the beginning of 1231 that they returned to the city fortified by papal intervention on their behalf. A series of bulls extended the privileges of the university and sanctioned its use of the secession as a means of self-defense.[19] This is probably the most famous as well as the most successful resort to the use of secession during the medieval period, but in its general character it differs little from its use elsewhere. It is important to note that the purpose of such dispersals was not to destroy either the unity of the university or to remove it permanently from its host city. On the contrary, it was utilized when all other means of preserving the existence of the *studium* seemed to have failed and as an effective means of inducing the local authorities to make concessions to the university. Such secessions were followed by the return of the masters to the city; there was no intention to create a rival *studium* elsewhere. Of course, as we shall observe later, other towns did benefit from such dispersals, but this was incidental to rather than an essential part of the purpose of the secession.

It is reasonably certain to what type of secession we may assign that which we find at Oxford in 1333. Unfortunately, the events that preceded the migration to Stamford are not at all clear.[20] Some accounts speak of a struggle between masters and scholars; others seem to suggest that the origin of the migration lay in yet another battle between the two rival nations, northerners and southerners. Whatever the exact origins of the dispersion, it is quite clear that it very soon fell under the control of an element from the northern nation. In July 1335, the names of those scholars and masters who remained at Stamford and carried out scholastic exercises contrary to the royal prohibition were recorded so that they could be threatened with imprisonment. All the masters and the majority, if not all, of the scholars came from the northern nation.[21] It would seem that a substantial number of masters and students from one sector of the university was making a serious attempt to set up another *studium*.

The Stamford migration must, therefore, be considered as similar to those secessions that provided the most favorable opportunities for the foundation of new universities. Like those at Prague in 1409 and earlier at Paris, the 1333 migration seems to have been organized by a coherent element in the university with a long record of common action. Unfortunately, we cannot say what percentage of the northern masters and scholars left Oxford for Stamford or what proportion of them persisted in remaining there despite the king's hostility. Nor can we measure the extent of the split between the northern and southern nation at Oxford before the secession to judge whether the breach can in any way be compared with those that occurred at Prague and Paris. If we could provide this information, it would be much easier to estimate the chances of such a secession succeeding. It would seem, however, that the Stamford secession, as the migration of part of a united sector that claimed the allegiance of half the university, offered a serious threat to the unique position of both Oxford and Cambridge to which they responded with characteristic energy.

Could the rebellious masters and students in 1333 justify their efforts to create a new *studium*? Could they argue that England was in any way less well endowed with universities than other European countries? It would seem from the evidence that their chances of securing recognition of a further foundation at Stamford were slight. The whole of northern and central Europe had at this time not a single university; the case for allowing England, with its relatively small population, to possess three higher academic centers was not strong. France had, by this date, seven universities: Paris, Montpellier, Orléans, Angers, Toulouse, Avignon, and Cahors. Its population, however, was much greater than that of England. It must also be remembered that one of the most pressing arguments for the toleration of this number of foundations was that the earlier universities could not offer instruction in all faculties. Paris was prohibited from teaching civil law by Honorius III in 1219 and so never achieved any great reputation as a *studium* for lawyers, canon or civil. Montpellier attracted medical students in large numbers: its other faculties were added later and never rivaled the great medical school. Orléans, Angers and Toulouse were essentially law schools. This specialization did not occur in

176

England; both Oxford and Cambridge appear to have had from their beginnings the four medieval faculties. Both could grant degrees in theology, a situation then without parallel on the Continent, where Paris held an uncontested precedence. It could not be argued either that the population of England justified a further foundation or that another university was needed to provide instruction in a faculty not found at Oxford or Cambridge. Indeed, it could be argued that England was liberally endowed in comparison to many areas of Europe.

The Stamford dissidents had, however, one strong point in their favor. Both English universities were situated in the south of England, in the area of highest population density and most flourishing economic activity. Most students from the south had an obvious advantage over their colleagues in the north in that they had usually to travel only a short distance to either Oxford or Cambridge. At this date no university existed in Scotland. It could perhaps have been argued that a foundation in the north of England would attract local students, Scots, perhaps those from northern Wales and Ireland, and some from Scandinavia. Dr. Emden has shown that the boundary between the northern and southern nation at Oxford was drawn at the Nene. Stamford, as he points out, lay to the north of the boundary, in territory that could be claimed as under the influence of the northern nation.[22] We cannot say how far these considerations were actively in the minds of those northerners who taught and studied at Stamford. The embryo *studium* was crushed before we might learn whether it could, in fact, attract students from a wide area of the "north." There is, however, no doubt that the University of Oxford regarded the Stamford schools as a serious threat to its own position, for Oxford, unlike Cambridge, could claim to attract many students from all parts of the British Isles. Its frantic efforts to obtain royal help to destroy the schools and its famous requirement of its future graduates that they would never teach at Stamford are ample evidence that Oxford did not underestimate the possibility of the northerners establishing their own *studium*. It was, of course, in the north, at Durham, that a later attempt was

177

made by Oliver Cromwell to break the monopoly of the two ancient foundations.

We have noted above a number of factors that militated against attempts to establish new universities at this date. It must also be borne in mind that, as a university wove itself into the fabric of medieval society its chances of maintaining its monopoly became stronger. By 1333 Oxford, and to a lesser extent Cambridge, had a long and distinguished history. Graduates of both universities occupied many of the important civil and ecclesiastical positions in the country. Both universities, when their position was threatened, could call upon a mass of influential supporters who could usually be expected to say a word in the right quarter at the right time in favor of their old *alma mater*. In this way Paris also was able to spread its influence throughout France. At any time of trouble in the capital, its agents could be found pressing the university's case at the royal court and before the Pope. The combined prestige of the long established universities of Oxford and Cambridge was used to good effect against the masters and students at Stamford. The Bishop of Lincoln, in whose diocese both Oxford and Stamford lay, was himself a university graduate, although it is doubtful he had studied at Oxford.[23] The Queen had apparently already shown interest in the university; in their letter to her, the masters of Oxford refer to "de grantz biens et honneurs qe vus avez sovent fet a vostre petite Universite de Oxenford."[24] Both were asked to assist the university against the Stamford rebels. To combat this type of opposition, any group of masters and students wishing to establish a new university needed eminent supporters. When the Germans left Paris and Prague, they found strong local patronage from the Palsgrave Rupert I and the Landgraves Frederick and William of Thuringia. There was no local prince of such power in England; once Oxford had won the support of the crown, it was only a matter of time before the *studium* of Stamford was suppressed.

Since we have emphasized the problems experienced by those wishing to establish new universities as break-away movements from older foundations, it would be valuable to consider at greater length Rashdall's statement, noted above, that secessions were responsible for the origin of 'half the universities in Europe.' The most important migrations from Bologna are listed by Rashdall as an appendix, with eight towns to which groups of students and doctors retreated noted as becoming 'permanent *studia generalia*.'[25] With the first of these, Reggio, it is not certain that any secession from Bologna did in fact take place, and the *studium* had disappeared by the beginning of the fourteenth century.[26] The secession to Vicenza, probably from Bologna, in 1204 had even less permanent success: the *studium generale* here ceased to exist probably in 1210.[27] The migration to Arezzo in 1215 produced only a temporary *studium*, occasionally revived for a few years by later secessions from Bologna, but never achieving much continuity. More successful were the migrations to Padua, but even here the university for many years had only a nominal existence waxing and waning as groups of students moved to and from Bologna; in 1260 the university had to make virtually a new start.[28] At Vercelli, Bolognese students had established a university when they moved there via Padua in 1228, but the *studium* seems to have had only an intermittent existence and probably disappeared in the late fourteenth century.[29] The various migrations from Bologna to Siena produced little more than the temporary recognition of a *de facto studium* there.[30] Attempts to encourage students and masters from Bologna to settle in Pisa and Florence were not very successful, and the influence of secessions on the establishment of permanent universities in these towns was not considerable.[31]

It would seem from this short survey that the influence of secessions from Bologna as a factor in the foundation of other Italian universities has perhaps been overemphasized. Very few of these movements resulted in the immediate establishment of new *studia*. At the most, they allowed other towns to claim the status of university centers for a few years and encouraged them to attempt later to obtain papal permission to erect a *studium* there. Usually, the Bolognese masters and students returned to their own town after a short time, leaving behind them little but memories and aspirations. It seems somewhat exaggerated to claim, as Rashdall appears to do, that these migrations from Bologna had a decisive influence on the establishment of permanent *studia* in medieval Italy.

The important migrations from the University of Paris had even less influence on the establishment of new *studia* in France. Although we find Paris students and masters taking shelter at Orléans, Angers, and Toulouse, their presence in these towns seems to have left little permanent mark.[32] Orléans and Angers became great centers for the study of law having little in common with the University of Paris. At Toulouse the return of the exiles to their own *studium* left the new foundation empty, and attempts had to be made later to revive the university. In all these cases the attractions of Paris proved too strong for the migrating masters and students. As soon as their demands were conceded, they were ready to move back to the capital, leaving behind little trace of their presence in their host towns. Nor did the only other major secession from a French university succeed in creating a new foundation. The migration of masters and students from Orléans to Nevers in 1316 was successful in that it forced the town to reach a compromise in its efforts to control the activities of the university. In 1320 the scholars returned to Orléans.[33] The only secessions from Paris that did lead to the foundation of lasting universities were those involving the Germans and the Scots. As we have noted earlier, their refusal to recognize the Avignonese papacy supported by their French colleagues and their rejection of the university's policy towards the Schism led them to establish in their own lands universities where no such difficulties would arise. But in France itself, migrations from Paris had little influence on the spread of universities there.

Secessions in other countries can be quickly discussed. The most important, that of the Germans from the university of Prague, has already been mentioned. In the Empire also, following the interdict that was laid on the city of Rostock in 1437, the university there retired to the neighboring town of Greifswald. With the removal of the interdict and the negotiation of satisfactory terms for the university, Greifswald was deserted by the students and masters on their return to Rostock in 1443. Clearly the establishment of the university at Greifswald for so long had had some influence on the town, for a few years later successful attempts to found a *studium* there were made. But this was only incidentally influenced by the secession from Rostock. In fact, the University of Rostock was one of the strongest opponents of the projected *studium* at Greifswald and managed to delay somewhat its foundation.[34] Another migration from Rostock at Lübeck at the close of the fifteenth century did not establish any *studium* there.[35] In other areas, secessions do not appear to have been very common. Spanish universities, for instance, do not seem to have experienced any such migrations as affected Bologna and Paris so frequently. We shall discuss later why this was so.

Few subjects have aroused more controversy than the origins of both English universities. With Oxford, the debate concerning whether an embryonic university existed before the alleged recall of English scholars from Paris by Henry II in 1167 has attracted supporters of both sides, struggling against the lack of evidence for that period.[36] The problem is complicated by the difficulty of deciding at this date what exactly constituted a *studium*; however, it does seem unlikely that any number of masters returning from Paris would have chosen to settle at Oxford if no educational tradition had been there to attract them. With the origins of the University of Cambridge, we seem now to be on safer ground. Dr. Hackett states firmly that "the age of special pleading has long since passed" and that the University of Cambridge owes its origin to the exodus of scholars from Oxford in 1209.[37] Here is an interesting example of a successful secession; the circumstances are, however, peculiar and informative. The flight from Oxford appears to have been a sudden action taken in panic at the prospect of further executions of students by the civic authorities; students fled to many different towns in England, and also abroad; some remained in Oxford. At this date, there was not the highly organized *studium* of later years that might have retained tighter control of its members' actions. The dispersal also took place in face of royal hostility to the university. King John had no reason to respect any ecclesiastical institution as he struggled against the power of the papacy. It was not until 1213 that the town of Oxford made its peace with the university, and not until 1214 that the Papal Legate settled the dispute with an official Ordinance.[38] These three factors, the unorganized character of the Oxford *studium*, the absence of any royal action against those leaving Oxford, and the uninterrupted continuance of teaching at Cambridge for four or five years, were enough to allow the eventual emergence of a university at Cambridge. This was very rapid; by 1225 a chancellor had been appointed, four years only after the first mention of a chancellor at Oxford.[39] During the first half of the thirteenth century, both Oxford and Cambridge developed their constitution and structure at a very rapid pace. The secession to Cambridge was timely and accompanied by unusually favorable factors. It is highly unlikely that it would have been allowed to succeed fifty years later when the university was already emerging as a privileged, powerful institution claiming independence from the Bishop of Lincoln.

Perhaps the most important impression left by this brief survey of the secessions from medieval universities is that as a factor in encouraging the foundation of the new *studia* after 1250, the secession was of little significance. Very few of the universities that existed in 1500 could trace their origins decisively back to a particular migration of masters and students. Secession could strengthen the schools of a town, it could encourage its inhabitants to seek a university of their own, but only very rarely did it produce a permanent institution that possessed an unbroken existence throughout the middle ages and beyond. Rashdall's opinion that 'half the universities in Europe' have their origins in some secession seems to give a misleading impression of the real situation. When the evidence is examined carefully, it would appear more correct to argue that the chances of any late secession producing a new university of some permanence were, in fact, very slight. When the Stamford migration is considered in its European context, there is little justification for regarding its prospects of stimulating a new foundation as ever very bright.

We have so far considered some of the social, economic, and

academic factors that affected secessions from medieval universities. It is evident, however, that a decisive force in each particular case was the political background against which the secession took place. It was of obvious advantage to a powerful ruler to have a university situated in some town over which he himself could exercise a great measure of control. This was all the more important when the university could exercise an influence beyond the borders of his own country. The University of Paris, for example, through its theologians, had a powerful impact on the whole of the European church. The rulers of France, Austria, Bohemia, and of the various states of the Spanish peninsula were very conscious of the value of a university that more or less depended on their own patronage. For similar reasons they each would be reluctant to encourage the foundation of other *studia* that could both detract form the importance of their own universities and escape from the close control and influence that they could exercise over these foundations. It is probably for this reason that the king of France was not prepared to encourage any rival to the University of Paris in his own dominion. It was only when Paris passed into enemy hands in the fifteenth century that he was ready to assist in the establishment of other arts universities in France; the University of Poitiers was founded in 1431 in Charles's temporary capital. Against the combined opposition of the crown and of the University of Paris, it is difficult to see any secession resulting in the establishment of an arts *studium* outside the capital and so likely to pass beyond the influence of the king. Some attempts were made by the more powerful of the French aristocracy to break the Parisian monopoly; the Duke of Brittany, for instance, tried to induce Parisian masters and students to come to Nantes during the great dispersion of 1229.[40] Until the fifteenth century, however, the combined power of the king and the university, usually supported by the Pope, was strong enough to ensure that, after any migration, masters and students would return to Paris.

The few secessions, therefore, that did result in the creation of new, permanent *studia* occurred in areas where political power was divided and where there was no authority resolutely prepared to maintain the monopoly of the parent university. The most likely places we would expect to find successful secessions were in Italy and Germany; in the first area there was no central authority at all, and in the second the imperial power was greatly weakened in the later medieval period. It was to the advantage of other independent cities in Italy to break the monopoly of Bologna and set up their own universities. Accordingly, strong efforts were made to entice masters and students from the town whenever a secession took place. We have, for instance, a detailed contract drawn up between the city of Vercelli and a group of students who in 1228 had left Bologna. In return for a number of concessions, they agree to come to the town and set up a *studium* there. It was in noone's interest except that of the town of Bologna to prevent the development of rival *studia*. On the contrary, strong rulers in other parts of Italy did their best to weaken the *studium*. Frederick II tried to obtain the closure of Bologna university and the transference of its students to Naples where they would be more closely under his control.[41] In Germany, it suited the policy of local princes to welcome those masters and students migrating from Paris and Prague; no German prince had any interest in maintaining the authority of these two universities and there was no strong enough central direction in the Empire to ensure that the energies so released were harnessed for the benefit of the country as a whole, rather than for the profit of individual provinces.

The interesting example of Spain and Portugal shows how royal authority could effectively prevent not only a successful secession but any secession at all. One of the most noticeable features that distinguishes the universities of the Spanish peninsula from those elsewhere in Europe is the extent to which they remained under royal control. It has frequently been pointed out that whereas in France, England, and Italy universities developed haphazardly, and in Germany they were usually founded in the later medieval period as part of the scramble for power and prestige by local princes, in Spain *studia* were established mainly as part of the kings' policies of ensuring that each constituent part of their kingdoms had one university. When founded they were usually endowed by royal patronage and governed and protected by royal authority. When disputes arose, therefore, they could be settled by direct appeal to the crown or to its representatives. There was no need to resort to a secession to induce the king to intervene on behalf of the university. Since any secession would destroy the pattern of royal foundations, it would clearly not be acceptable to the crown and would not be tolerated. It is interesting to see the response of the University of Coimbra to the same sort of situation that provoked the great migrations from Paris, Bologna, and Oxford. First established at Lisbon in 1290, the university was moved to and from the capital until 1537 when it was finally settled at Coimbra. In Lisbon it had encountered the usual hostility of the townsmen and had found itself unable to function properly. The remedy at Paris would have been an immediate secession followed by a campaign at court and before the Pope against the city. At Lisbon the matter was settled by royal intervention under the guise of a papal bull. The university was transferred to the quieter town of Coimbra, itself a royal residence. In its later movements to and from the capital, it is apparent that the decisive power instigating these changes was that of the crown.[42] In such circumstances the secession as used in other European universities had little relevance.

Bearing in mind our general conclusions concerning the importance of political authority in determining the success or otherwise of secessions, is it possible to assert that the migration to Stamford had any chance of success? There is no need, of course, to assert the reality of royal authority in England; from before the Conquest, the crown had commanded a bureaucracy and a taxation system far in advance of those of the mainland. The smallness of the country as compared with France, for instance, enabled central authority to be asserted in the provinces comparatively quickly. When held by an assertive and competent personality, the authority of the English king was probably greater than that of any other European monarch. Edward III was certainly assertive and, if no profound statesman, was not an incompetent ruler. After his success against Mortimer and his associates, he had no great fear of baronial opposition. His attitude to the Stamford secession was to be decisive. Could he in any way be expected to support the cause of the migrating masters and students?

The time was not opportune for the king to take a great interest in such affairs. From 1332–37 the administrative capital of the kingdom was to all intents and purposes York. Until the outbreak of the war with France, the king's efforts were concentrated in the north. His troops were laying siege to Berwick in 1333, and in the following year a large scale military operation was mounted in the Scottish lowlands in an attempt finally to crush nationalistic opposition. Moreover, with the flight of King David to France, there was a growing danger that the Scottish war would provoke the intervention of France and thereby spark off a large scale European conflict.[43] With such immediate preoccupations and with the prospect of more stormy times ahead, any king would have been reluctant to disturb the *status quo* and cause conflicts that might act as a distraction from more pressing affairs. An attempt to support the Stamford secession would have produced irate objections from both Oxford and Cambridge and consequent appeals for papal intervention. Edward III had no wish to antagonize the pope whose diplomatic support could be useful and to whom he had often expressed his peaceful intentions. There was little reason for the king to allow any internal disagreements to distract him from his Scottish and French policies and every advantage to be gained from maintaining tranquillity and order while preparing for a serious challenge to France.

Nor had the king any private reasons to wish to harm the positions of the universities of Oxford and Cambridge. In 1327 he had already made a gift to Oriel College, Oxford, of a house, la Oriole, from which the college was eventually to take its name.[44] At Cambridge he had given some support to his father's new foundation and in 1332 had set up a commission to examine the royal scholars there and to purge them of unsatisfactory members. These efforts were to culminate in the king's reestablishment of his Cambridge society in 1337.[45] It is interesting to see the king's interest in the University of Cambridge, as the nearer and smaller university, would certainly be more seriously affected than the larger and

more famous University of Oxford. In view of his earlier concern
for both Oxford and Cambridge, there seems little hope that his
support for a new foundation at Stamford could have been
enlisted.

There were also positive reasons for the king to be hostile to a
new foundation at Stamford. Both Oxford and Cambridge had
shown themselves ready in the past generally to cooperate with the
English crown. In turn Oxford, and more recently Cambridge, had
received considerable endowments directly or indirectly from the
king. Both universities were within easy access of London; delegates and messengers could travel from both to the capital or make
the journey the opposite way with little difficulty. A new academic
foundation in Stamford might result in a weakening of royal influence over all universities; Oxford and Cambridge would resent the
rival foundation and the king who made it possible, whereas Stamford itself would not necessarily compensate for this by extending
royal authority in its area. Especially when royal power was weakened, the northern magnates were always a threat to the king's
influence in the north. In such circumstances, would it be possible
for the king to maintain control over a university situated at Stamford and attended mainly by northern students? In times of crisis
the resources of such a university could be quite easily deployed
against the royal interests. It may have seemed to the king and his
advisers that it would be the height of folly to provide an intellectual rallying point for those northern sentiments that could at
some future date be turned against the crown.

In conclusion, it would seem correct to argue that when the
Stamford secession is considered in its wider context, the chances
of England obtaining there its third *studium* were very slight, even
though there were some factors that appeared to favor this. It was,
for one thing, a migration by part of a compact, unified group
dissatisfied with relations with other groups in the parent university, and this type of migration was most successful in establishing
new foundations. It could also be argued that the north of England
needed its own university. Against these favorable factors, however, those that were disadvantageous weighed very heavily. Euro-

pean secessions had only produced new *studia* in a very few circumstances, when the combination of events made the moment unusually favorable. The age and prestige of Oxford and Cambridge, each with its four faculties and each attuned to the reception of large numbers of students, provided an attraction and an influence with which Stamford could not compete. Above all, in 1333 the king could see little gain and much loss from a disturbance of the academic *status quo*. For these reasons, as we have outlined above, we may suggest that both the fears of the contemporary Oxford masters and the favorable opinions of later historians toward the migration have been too strongly expressed. European experience had already shown, and was to show later, that usually more than a secession was needed to establish a new, permanent university.

1. Hastings Rashdall, *The Universities of Europe in the Middle Ages*, 3 vols. (Oxford, 1936), 3:86. Hereafter cited as *Universities of Europe*.

2. Charles H. Haskins, *The Renaissance of the Twelfth Century* (New York, 1958), pp. 372–75.

3. Ibid., p. 378; Rashdall, *Universities*, 1:62–63.

4. See the valuations given in Arthur F. Leach, "Wykeham's Books at New College" in *Collectanea. Third Series.* (Oxford, Oxford Historical Society, 1896).

5. A. B. Emden, *An Oxford Hall in Medieval Times* (Oxford, 1927), p. 195.

6. There is an extensive literature relating to medieval book production. See, for the '*pecia*' system, G. Pollard "The *pecia* system in the Medieval Universities" in M. B. Parkes and A. G. Watson, eds., *Medieval Scribes, Manuscripts and Libraries: Essays Presented to N. R. Ker* (London, 1978). For *pronuntiatores*, see *Monumenta Historica Universitatis Carolo-Ferdinandeae Pragensis*, Prague, 1, pt. 1, 1830: 13. For collections of extracts and summaries, see, for example, Oxford, New College, MS. 289.

7. F. M. Powicke, *The Medieval Books of Merton College* (Oxford, 1931), p. 16.

8. W. A. Pantin, "The Halls and Schools of Medieval Oxford," in *Oxford Studies presented to Daniel Callus* (Oxford, Oxford Historical Society, 1964), p. 32. Hereafter cited as "Halls and Schools."

9. Rashdall, *Universities of Europe*, 2:264.

10. Ibid., pp. 49–50.

11. Pantin, "Halls and Schools," p. 35.

12. S. Gibson, *Statuta Antiqua Universitatis Oxoniensis* (Oxford, 1931), pp. 79–80.

13. The situation at Stamford is clearly shown in the introduction and texts of A. Rogers, *The Medieval Buildings of Stamford* (Nottingham, 1970); J. S. Hartley and A. Rogers, *The Religious Foundations of Medieval Stamford* (Nottingham, 1974).

14. Rashdall, *Universities of Europe*, 1:169.

15. J. Haller, *Die Anfänge der Universität Tübingen, 1477–1537* (Stuttgart, 1927), 1:27.

16. The privileges of the medieval universities are discussed in P. Kibre, *Scholarly Privileges in the Middle Ages* (London, 1961).

17. Rashdall, *Universities of Europe*, 1:168–69.

18. V. Chaloupecký, *The Caroline University of Prague* (Prague, 1948), p. 109.

19. Rashdall, *Universities of Europe*, 1:336–38.

20. I have made no attempt here to review or reopen the early controversies surrounding the events preceding and accompanying the Stamford migration. The details of the secession may be found summarized in A. F. Leach's essay in the *Victoria County History, Lincolnshire,* 2:468–72.

21. A. B. Emden, "Northerners and Southerners in the Organisation of the University to 1509" in *Oxford Studies Presented to Daniel Callus* (Oxford, 1964), pp. 5–6. The sixteen named masters must have represented a considerable part of those of the northern nation at Oxford.

22. Ibid., p. 5.

23. A. B. Emden, *A Biographical Register of the University of Oxford to A.D. 1500*, 3 vols. (Oxford, 1957–59), 3:2157.

24. H. H. Henson, "Letters Relating to Oxford in the 14th Century from Originals in the Public Record Office and British Museum," *Collectanea. First Series* (Oxford, Oxford Historical Society, 1885), p. 8.

25. Rashdall, *Universities of Europe*, 1:589.

26. Ibid., 2:6.

27. Ibid., p. 7.

28. Ibid., p. 15.

29. Ibid., pp. 27–28.

30. Ibid., pp. 31–33.

31. Ibid., pp. 45–48.

32. Ibid.,, pp. 143, 153, 163.

33. Ibid., pp. 148–49.

34. Ibid., p. 270.

35. Ibid., p. 263.

36. The 1936 editors of Rashdall, *Universities of Europe*, 3:ch. 1 add their observations to his text.

37. M. B. Hackett, *The Original Statutes of Cambridge University. The Text and its History* (Cambridge, 1970), p. 43.

38. The events of these years are surveyed in C. E. Mallett, *A History of the University of Oxford* (London, 1924), 1:31–33.

39. Hackett, *Original Statutes of Cambridge University*, p. 48.

40. Rashdall, *Universities of Europe*, 1:336, n. 4.

41. Ibid., 2:23, n. 1.

42. Ibid., pp. 110–11.

43. M. McKisack, *The Fourteenth Century 1307–94* (Oxford, 1959), pp. 117–18.

44. Rashdall, *Universities of Europe*, 3:206.

45. A. B. Cobban, *The King's Hall within the University of Cambridge in the later Middle Ages* (Cambridge, 1969), pp. 13–15.

189

THE UNIVERSITY OF CRACOW
AND THE CONCILIAR MOVEMENT

Paul W. Knoll

edieval universities were always in transition. Their dynamic evolution in the twelfth and thirteenth centuries did not bring them to a point of static congruency with any abstract archetypal ideal. Because they had arisen out of society in response to needs that required new educational solutions, they continued to evolve as that society changed in the late Middle Ages and Renaissance. But although the general outlines of early university history are now reasonably well known and understood, the development of European *studia* in the later period is less clear.[1] As A. B. Cobban has noted recently, "The history of the later medieval universities . . . has yet to be written. It is an area of study which forms an uncertain mosaic wherein broad generalizations co-exist uneasily with the findings of monographic research."[2]

One aspect of the changing university that requires particular attention is the role it played in relation to two of the central institutions of this period, the newly-emergent territorial state and the church during a period of deep crisis. The conciliar movement of the fifteenth century provides an instance in which all three of these institutions were closely involved together; in which, as Antony Black has commented, "the role of universities in the affairs of the Latin Church assumed unprecedented proportions";[3] and in which some of the character of the university on the eve of the Reformation and the early modern era is revealed. This study focuses on the University of Cracow and traces its involvement in the councils. It will allow us to see, on the one hand, the way the *studium* there came to serve as a spokesman for national and state interests with regard to the Teutonic Order; and, on the other hand, the way it helped define some of the issues that determined how effectively the church would resolve its crisis.

The University of Cracow, which had originally been founded on the model of Bologna by King Casimir the Great in 1364, did not prosper in its early years. It had to be resurrected a generation later by King Władysław Jagiełło, a Lithuanian-born convert to Christianity.[4] Jagiełło (as he is known in Polish historiography) intended that his new institution, which was modeled upon Paris, would be a means by which the standard of civilization in Polish society would be raised to equal that of surrounding countries. The university was to have as its arena not only the city of Cracow, but all of the lands and provinces in the whole of the kingdom. In short, as the king phrased it in his document of foundation in 1400, the university was intended to play an important role in the national life of Poland.[5] This role was clearly revealed in the university's involvement in the Council of Constance.[6]

Although cursory treatments of this council are usually limited to a description of the three major items for which Constance has been called (ending the Schism, extirpating heresy, and reforming the church in head and members), there were a number of other problems of European-wide import which were also of concern to the assembly. Emperor Sigismund outlined them in an address before a general convocation on 13 July 1415. They included union between the eastern and western churches, peace between France and England, a crusade against the Turks, and the conflict between the Teutonic Order and Poland.[7] With this last item, the issue that had convulsed northeastern Europe for several generations was brought officially before the representatives of Christendom.

The Teutonic Order had been a problem for Poland ever since the early thirteenth century.[8] Under circumstances that have occasioned much subsequent polemical literature, the Knights had established in Prussia a territorially based *Ordensstaat* that pursued a two-fold policy of conversion by force and of territorial aggrandizement.[9] The first was directed in the fourteenth century especially against the still-pagan Lithuanians; the second fell most heavily upon some of the lands of the Polish kingdom. When Poland and Lithuania were united in a personal union in 1385/1386, and when the Lithuanians were converted upon the marriage of their grand duke (the aforementioned Jagieƚƚo) to the Polish ruler, the Order had to determine whether it would give up its policy of conquest and crusade. It chose not to do so. Instead, it charged that the conversion was only superficial and a political sham; further, it assumed that the Poles deserved punishment for accepting a pagan ruler and for allying with pagans.[10] The polemical seeds sowed in the years after 1385 germinated in the following generation and bore bitter harvest in a war from 1409–11. Despite a convincing Polish victory over the Knights at Grunwald (Tannenberg) in 1410, this military conflict had not resolved the outstanding issues between the parties. King Jagieƚƚo resolved to take the diplomatic issue to any forum that would further Polish interests.

Thus when the invitations to attend the Council of Constance came to the king, the Polish church, and the University of Cracow in the fall of 1414, there was no question that a Polish delegation would be sent.[11] Jagieƚƚo's policy was to rely upon the learned faculty of his new *studium* to present the issue of the Order to the council. The Poles at Constance aimed at discrediting the Knights before the assembled delegates of Christendom, of obtaining the dissolution of the Order, and of portraying themselves and their king as both the true defenders of Christendom and as the new missionaries through whom the spread of the Christian faith was being accomplished. The instrument of this diplomatic *Realpolitik* was political philosophy formulated by the faculty of the university and forcefully expressed by its rector.

The Polish delegation to Constance included, among others, Archbishop Nicholas Trąba of Gniezno, Bishop-elect Andrew Ƚaskarz of Poznán, rector Paul Vladimiri of the university, Peter Wolfram, licenciate *in decretis* and a faculty member at Cracow, and some members of the laity.[12] Three of these individuals deserve special identification. Andrew had studied in Prague, earning both an M.A. and Bachelor of Laws degree. Then he went to Padua, where he studied under Francis Zabarella, being promoted to Doctor of Canon Law in 1405. During his years in Italy, he came under the influence of the humanistic movement and became a close friend of Pier Paolo Vergerio. After his return to Poland, his ecclesiastical rise was rapid, and he often served as a royal representative in dealings with the Knights. At Constance, he was particularly active in the committee on matters of the faith, and one recent scholar has suggested that Láskarz was the anonymous *doctor Polonus* who raised an isolated voice in support of John Hus in the proceedings that led to his condemnation.[13] It was also Andrew who was chosen by the council to be one of the several who delivered addresses on 6 April 1415 giving full expression to the principle of conciliarism. He was later a member of the commission appointed to study the issues raised by John Falkenberg's *Satira*. Though not a member of the university faculty, he was nevertheless a learned representative who pursued Polish policy at the council.[14]

Peter Wolfram of Lwów was a recently appointed member of the faculty of the university. He had spent time in Rome early in the century, then matriculated at Prague in 1408. He did not remain long enough to earn a degree, for the next year Jagiełło appointed him his court chaplain. Shortly thereafter he returned to Italy where he eventually gained a licenciate in Canon Law at Bologna in October 1413. By the fall of 1414 he was lecturing in the law faculty at Cracow and serving as royal diplomat. At Constance he participated in several commissions and tried, with limited success, to act as an early-day Boswell by keeping notes about the activities of the participants. While on a mission to Poland in 1416, he drafted the letters that Jagiełło and the university sent to the council. His earlier stays in Italy apparently brought him into contact with humanistic currents, for these letters and his other writings are replete with classical allusions and citations. Although his commission to the council came from the Bishop of Cracow, for whom he acted as procurator, Peter's association with the university and his legal skills contributed effectively to the Polish effort there.[15]

Paul Vladimiri was the leading member of the delegation. Born in the early 1370s in the region of Dobrzyń, which adjoined the territory of the Teutonic Order and was often attacked by them, he began his university studies in Prague, earning an M.A. in 1393 and Bachelor of Laws in 1396.[16] His ecclesiastical career progressed until he became a canon in Płock, but in 1403 he left for Italy to pursue canon law further. At Padua he studied under Zabarella and Peter de Ancarano, receiving the licenciate in Canon Law in 1408. Before returning to Poland, he on at least one occasion represented Jagiełło in Rome in the matter of the Knights. In 1411 the Bishop of Cracow appointed him curator of the cathedral, and the pope issued a special dispensation for him to take a doctoral degree in canon law at Cracow. His promotion came in late 1411 or early 1412. Henceforth his career was closely associated with royal policy and the university. He acted as Jagiełło's agent on several occasions, taught in the law faculty, and in 1414 was elected rector of the *studium*. His reelection for the following academic year, despite his absence in Constance, was a symbol of the school's confidence in him and its support of royal policy.[17] After the council he continued to be involved in political affairs. In 1432 he was in Padua, from where he wrote to Bishop Oleśnicki of Cracow about the ways of settling the conflict between Poland and the Order. He died in the Polish royal capital late in 1435 or early the following year.[18]

At Constance, the confrontation between Poland and the Order was elevated into a fundamental debate on policy and legal theory by the writings of Paul Vladimiri. During the winter of 1415/1416, he prepared materials that were later transformed into a series of treatises on the theoretical powers of both emperor and pope. He studied the question of whether the privileges both powers had granted to the Teutonic Order had any legal validity in either the church or natural law. In addition he analyzed whether it had been lawful for the Order to attack pagans simply because they were pagans and whether it was just for the Knights to wage war against converted pagans under the pretext that they might lapse from Christianity. In this endeavor, Paul was supported not only by general discussions that had taken place at the University of Cracow before his departure but also by detailed suggestions from the faculty there on the issues that he was to present to the council.[19] In addition, he kept his constituency in Cracow informed on the proceedings at Constance and his actions.[20] He did not speak therefore as an isolated private individual, but as the representative of an official opinion of the faculty.

Early in the summer of 1416 Paul distributed two works.[21] The first, entitled *Saevientibus* from it opening word, was given to the German nation, of which the Poles were a part along with the rest of northern and central Europe.[22] It contained an introduction, a section of eleven points treating the power of the pope with respect to infidels, a second section of equal length dealing with the power of the emperor in the same context, and a concluding section that argued against the opinion of Hostiensis, who held that since the coming of Christ all pagan states had ceased to be legitimate, and therefore a war against unbelievers was always a just war. Shortly thereafter, Paul distributed the second work, entitled *Opinio Ostiensis*, to all the nations.[23] It contained a short statement of the position of Hostiensis, a longer rebuttal, and fifty-two articles or *conclusiones*, which summarized his previous treatises. In tightly structured arguments, Paul asked whether the documents upon which the Order based its activity were valid. Even if they were not forged (though he and the other Polish representatives clearly considered them to be), this was to him an independent issue from the more crucial, theoretical question of whether, and in what degree, imperial and papal power extended to the lands of the unbeliever. He argued in a precise conciliar sense that papal power was limited by divine and natural law. It was nevertheless superior to imperial power, for unlike the pope the emperor did not have the right to dispose of the lands of unbelievers. Thus imperial grants in pagan lands were invalid, and Paul dismissed the privileges that supposedly had allowed the Order to spread the faith by force and by war. He went on to argue that non-Christians possessed their lands by natural law, and that it was not legal, even for the pope, to command that they be converted by force or that their lands be taken from them without proper justification.

The effects of these treatises had scarcely been absorbed when Paul again took the offensive. Later that summer he distributed two more works. The first, *Ad aperiendam*, repeated much from his earlier treatises, but went further.[24] It charged that the Order had failed to respond adequately to his accusations, and since it no longer fulfilled its tasks, it had fallen into heresy and should be dissolved. The second work was a series of systematic points of accusation, both historical and theoretical, against the Order. It summed up his previous works in a devastating recapitulation (in its final redaction) of 156 articles.[25] In this same summer, the faculty of the University of Cracow sent a long letter to the council, expressing its approval of the decree *Haec sancta* and of the condemnation of Wyclyf, Hus, and Jerome of Prague. This letter emphasized the faculty's full support of the Polish delegates.[26]

The effect of Paul's treatises upon the Knights was considerable. Their diplomacy had earlier been focused upon specific minimal goals in negotiation, and their propaganda had been characterized by narrow political aims, with little reference to theoretical legal formulations. Confronted by the learned and reasoned attacks by Paul Vladimiri, the Order was forced to change its tactics. In a report to the Grand Master on 28 June 1416, the general procurator wrote that he had given monies to some doctors to prepare answers in kind.[27] These were not long in coming. One was prepared by the Bamberg canonist John Urbach (or Auerbach, called Frebach in Polish historiography) and appeared near the end of 1416 or early in 1417.[28] It consisted of eighteen conclusions with accompanying justifying statements. Paul responded to its distribution with a treatise of his own, *Quoniam error*, which is divided into a dogmatic and a polemical section.[29] The first discussed the legality and reliability of the privileges of the Order, the question of whether the Knights may be said to possess true dominion over their lands, and the problem of whether they actually constitute a religious order that can be approved by the church. The second

196

section answered in detail each of the points raised in the Urbach paper.

A second treatise, more an attack upon the Poles than a defense of the Order, appeared late in 1416. Written by the Dominican John Falkenberg in one form as early as 1412, it had been presented to the Grand Master at that time for approval, but had been ignored since it did not fit the style of the Knights' propaganda. Four years later, however, the needs of the order had changed, and in a revised version it was distributed to the council.[30] Known as the *Satira*, it was the work of an individual who had spent time in his Order's monastery in Cracow and had earlier been involved in polemics against professors from Cracow and Polish political and ecclesiastical policy in general. Falkenberg's love for the Poles was nonexistent, his learning was abundant, and his pen had soaked for years in the purest vitrol. The *Satira* accused the King of Poland ("Jaghel") of being an idol and the Poles of worshiping him[31]; they and he were despised by God as heretics and shameless pagan dogs; the best service to be rendered Christendom would be to kill Poles and their king, for they were heathen, and heaven's purposes were served by any who kill Poles; Poland and its king were a plague besetting the church; and so forth. All this invective was tricked out with biblical and canonical apparatus, giving it the appearance of respectability. But it went too far and brought to a climax the confrontation of Poland and the Order at the council.

Paul immediately wrote a short response, *Iste tractatus*, but it was the Polish delegation as a whole that tried to bring about a condemnation of the *Satira* and have Falkenberg accused of heresy.[32] They were successful in persuading the council to appoint a commission, which included Cardinals Zabarella, Orsini, and D'Ailly, to investigate the matter. By the end of the council, this group was prepared to condemn the author and his work. Despite continued agitation by the Poles, however, nothing was decided. The new pope, Martin V, ruled that only that which was formally on the agenda of the council could be acted upon and approved. Since this issue had not yet been officially presented, there was nothing that could be done. He did promise, however, to investigate the matter further. Subsequently, this immediate issue was resolved to Poland's satisfaction.[33]

Poland won no specific territorial or boundary concessions in negotiations at Constance; neither did it attain its optimum goal of the dissolution of its longtime foe. It did, however, achieve the considerable victory of demonstrating to the leadership of Europe the justness of its cause. In this process, Paul Vladimiri was an effective spokesman for the national concerns that King Władysław Jagiełło pursued. But Paul was not simply a royal representative; he was also known as a learned member of the Cracow faculty and as the university's rector. His presence and activity at Constance symbolized the extent to which the *studium* was as much a part of the *regnum Poloniae* as it was an institution of late medieval *Christianitas*.

Even though the university and its faculty had been an instrument of royal and national policy at Constance, it was to be different at Basel. The faculty were committed to a conciliarist approach to healing the ills that afflicted the larger church. Because the king and the Polish church generally supported Eugenius, or at least maintained a position of official neutrality between pope and council, the university consistently found itself either in advance of royal opinion or in opposition to it. For example, the faculty urged from the beginning that a Polish delegation be sent to the council; but it was not until Eugenius grudgingly allowed his legates to be incorporated at Basel in 1433 that Jagiełło and Bishop Zbigniew Oleśnicki of Cracow (the *de facto* leader of the Polish church) decided it was appropriate to send representatives.[24] Even after this, the professors were far more fervent in their support for Basel and conciliarism than the king or the Polish church. This involvement and the implications of the failure of the program to which they were committed reveal as much about the nature of this late medieval university as does its activity on behalf of the monarch and national policy at Constance.

The first Polish participants to attend the Council of Basel arrived in 1433. They included Dersław of Borzynów, professor of

198

canon law and rector of the university in 1431, who was a royal representative; Thomas Strzempiński, *doctor decretorum* and rector in 1432 and 1433, representing the Archbishop of Gniezno; and Nicholas Kozłowski, a noted preacher and later dean of the theology faculty, who was Oleśnicki's delegate. These were followed in 1434 by Bishop Stanisław Ciołek of Poznań, Nicholas Lasocki, sometime professor at Cracow (both of these individuals were actively involved in the humanistic movement), and Professor Lutek of Brześć, who eventually became Bishop of Cracow. The involvement of faculty members in the affairs of the council was reflected in the fact that in 1433 Professor Nicholas Tempelfeld in Cracow requested prayers for the whole congregation at Basel and "the doctors and masters of our kingdom who are working there for the common good."[35]

One of the Poles at Basel, Dersław of Borzynow, was sufficiently active that he even became a public personality. Aeneas Sylvius Piccolomini, who described him as "pleasant and learned in conversation," has left us a humorous anecdote about him. (It may or may not be true, for Aeneas had no love for the Poles and was talented enough to embellish, if not even manufacture, a good caricature.) Aeneas tells us that Dersław was a member of the conclave that eventually elected Felix V. The Polish professor tried on one occasion to slip more than the single kind of meat allowed into the conclave. When his fat duck was confiscated by the chamberlain, he objected. He was told that the same restrictions applied to all, even the president of the council, Cardinal Louis of France. Dersław objected: "What, are you comparing me with the Cardinal, a Frenchman, austere and without a stomach? . . . As ill luck would have it I have been put beside him, and the transparent screen reveals to me all that he does. Up to now I have never seen him drinking or eating. . . . I am a Pole, he is a Frenchman. My stomach is hot, his is cold. Hunger is health for him, death for me. . . . Let the French fast and the Poles eat."[36] Behind this story lies the reality that Dersław was both of sufficient importance at Basel and aggressively enough committed to the program of the council that he was a participant in the act of creating a new schism.

When the council took this step against the pope, however, the necessity of finding support within Europe for its position became of paramount concern. It hoped to win monarchs, national churches, and the universities to the side of Felix. Thus, for example, in May 1440, the newly elected conciliar pope sent a legate to the new Polish king to ask for Polish adherence (Jagiełło had died in 1434). King Władysław III, nicknamed Warneńczyk, promised only to discuss the issue at a forthcoming Diet. The legate then went to Cracow where he was given a letter from the rector of the university, John of Dobra, to transmit to the council. Its contents are no longer extant, but its tenor may be judged from the address: *Sanctissimo domino nostro Felici in summum pontificem sacrosanctae generalis synodi Basiliensis auctoritate electo.*[37] Coming in the wake of the ambiguous royal response, these events buoyed the legate, and he returned to Basel with an optimistic report of his progress. Prior to his return, news reached the council of the meeting of the Diet, at which it had been decided to maintain the existing neutral position. Despite this setback, the council decided on 21 September 1440 to send another embassy to Poland.

Three members were chosen: Marco Bonfili, a Spanish theologian, Dersław of Borzynów, and Stanisław Sobniowski, the last two being the only Poles remaining at the council, since other representatives had gradually returned home in previous years. By mid-November, the Basel delegation was in Cracow, where they were to remain for several months. Their arrival was the occasion for two welcoming speeches in the chief university building, the *Collegium maius*, which revealed the deep commitment of the university faculty to the council. Both were given by John of Ludzisko, who, after earning an M.A. at Cracow in 1422, had spent additional years of study in Italy.[38] There he earned a doctor's degree in medicine at Padua in 1433. He had only recently returned to Cracow, where he was teaching in both arts and medicine.[39]

The first of his speeches, presented in the name of the university, praised the efforts of the council to reform the church and discussed the problems that cried out for attention. His tone is dark and pessimistic, conjuring up the image of a wrathful God and His threatened punishment if these abuses were not removed. It is instructive that John's concern was essentially directed to moral issues and the question of the quality of spiritual life, rather than to problems of institutional structure and governance. He concluded by affirming the importance of the council, which, he said, had been legitimated by the Holy Spirit. He also praised the new pope. Through the speech runs a profound concern for the well-being and health of Christendom and a deep commitment to the conciliar movement.[40] After the jeremiad came the soothing charm of the muses: eloquence, *humanitas*, and the new culture of the Renaissance also supported reform and the cause of the council. John's second speech, presented in the name of the city of Cracow, revealed the rhetorical prowess and humanistic interests he had developed in Italy. His address was a threefold glorification of the delegation that had come to Cracow, of the council itself, and of Felix. As in the former speech, there was here an emphasis upon the importance of reform, but there was also a stress upon the ideals of humanism. There were numerous citations from antique authors and many allusions to Greek and Roman history that John used to illustrate his themes of praise, reform, and eloquence. In concluding, he commended adhesion to Felix as a desirable goal.[41]

During the winter of 1440/1441, the university discussed the question of whether to declare its allegiance to the council and to Felix. Eventually it was decided to do so, and individual members of the faculty were invited to submit treatises for review, one of which would be chosen to express the university's position. As the result of a complex organizational procedure, five such works were eventually prepared.[42] One was presented by Benedict Hesse, a professor of theology;[43] a second, by Lawrence of Racibórz, also a theologian.[44] A third work came from the pen of John Elgot, a canon lawyer;[45] the fourth was written by the theologian James of Paradyż.[46] None of these four was completely acceptable to the faculty (though Benedict's treatise was eventually taken to Basel and presented as a second Cracovian statement). As a result, Thomas Strzempiński, canonist, theologian, many-time rector and eventual Bishop of Cracow (d. 1460), was delegated to prepare a conflation of these that would express official university opinion.[47]

Let us summarize briefly each of these expressions of Cracovian conciliar thought.[48]

Benedict discussed a single proposition: whether it was necessary to obey the council and the pope whom it had elected. He answered decisively in the affirmative, even making this a principle of belief. He asserted the superiority of the council within the church and the legality of the elevation of Felix. In theory one must, according to Benedict, obey both the council and the pope; in practice, if they conflict, he enjoins obedience to the council. His position is comparable to the more extreme sections of a similar treatise that the University of Erfurt had prepared.[49] Lawrence's conciliar treatise, which he called an *Opusculum*, was cast in the classic form of a scholastic argument. He put forth nine *conclusiones*, examined the arguments *pro et contra*, then summed up with a resolution. His position that the authority of both the church and of Peter was derived directly from Christ was not dissimilar to the early conciliarist Pierre D'Ailly, and Lawrence accepted the legality of the council of Basel and the election of Felix. Since it was obvious to him that the council could not always be in session, he attributed to the pope and the college of cardinals the power to exercise authority for the church. But the fundamental principle of this treatise was that when in session the council takes precedence, being *maius et dignius in auctoritate et potestate*.[50]

Elgot's treatise consisted of two separate sections. In the first, he presented a general discussion of the nature of the church, distinguishing between the material and the spiritual aspects. The latter he divided into the unfaithful and the faithful, whom he described as being either particular (i.e., individual administrative units) or universal: the church of the predestined, the church militant, and finally the representative church. This last classification brought him to his second section, which consisted of six detailed theses. Their thrust was a moderate one. With Lawrence, he saw the Church, whose power was derived directly from God, as being represented in both the council and the "Roman church," i.e., the pope and the cardinals. When a council was not in session, they were equivalent to it in power and authority; when it was in session, it was superior to them. On the specific issues of time, he was explicit: the council in Basel was truly a general council, Eugenius illegally attempted to dissolve it, his deposition and the election of Felix was justified and legal and all the faithful ought, under threat of loss of salvation, to obey him as the pope.[51]

James chose to present his views in 1440/1441 in a symbolic twelve propositions, and much of his argument turned on the position of the pope. He rejected any attribution to him of *plena potestas*, viewing him instead as the principle member of the church, but drawing his power and authority only indirectly from Christ. His position was not *caput ecclesiae* or that of *vicarius Christi*, but rather that of a minister or instrument of the whole. Above all, he had in no way been given infallible powers by Christ, for the pope was *peccabilis*, *fallibilis*, and *obliquabilis*. James, along with Hesse, interpreted the incident of the keys in Matthew as a symbolic act in which Christ gave authority to the church, with Peter as its servant. The true church was represented only in a general council, which may not be dissolved by a pope. The acts of such a council, such as the deposition of Eugenius and the election of Felix, were legitimated by the Holy Spirit. Of all the formal conciliar documents to emerge from Cracow, this one is the most imaginative and creative.[52]

In contrast, Strzempiński's treatise is less striking. His work is most properly regarded as a compilation, but it was successful, if not particularly original. In seven conclusions he discussed the unity and the infallibility of the church as a whole. Although he designed Christ as the true head of the church, he attributed to the pope the position of chief minister and vicar of Christ. As for the council, it represented the whole church and derived its authority directly from Christ. He regarded its power as superior to that of the pope. In particular, it was incumbent upon all Christians to obey the decrees of a general council, a status he explicitly accorded to Basel. Finally, he recognized its suspension and deposition of Eugenius and the legitimacy of the election of Felix.[53] When completed, this work was approved by the faculty, dedicated to Bishop Oleśnicki, the chancellor of the university, and sent with

Bonfil to Basel. Despite, or perhaps because of, its derivative nature, this treatise may be seen as both characteristic and representative of conciliar thought in the fifteenth century.

In seeking the support of the king and the Polish church, the ambassadors of the council had less success. Only belatedly, and temporarily, was Oleśnicki won to support of Basel, but the monarchy never abandoned its neutrality.[54] Eventually, of course, the cause of Basel was lost throughout Europe. With the accession of Nicholas V as Eugenius' successor in 1447, monarchs, churches, and universities throughout Europe began to return to the Roman obedience. On 6 July 1447 King Casimir the Jagiellonian of Poland (Władysław's successor) and Oleśnicki formally declared their support of Nicholas.[55] Not only was Poland firmly in the papal camp, support for Basel was everywhere disappearing.

Only the University of Cracow now stood in opposition to Polish national and ecclesiastical policy. In 1448 the issue came to a head. Nicholas sent a legate to Poland, with (among other responsibilities) the commission to obtain the submission of the *studium*. When he arrived in June, he was warmly greeted by all in the city — except the faculty, who ostentatiously ignored his presence.[56] This act created a great scandal and brought them much criticism, as they themselves recognized.[57] The legate complained to the king, and in response Casimir summoned the faculty before him, demanding repeatedly that they abandon Basel and recognize Nicholas. They remained obdurate. Then the legate informed the university that it alone of all the *studia* of Europe remained opposed to Rome; all the others had submitted.

The faculty could not believe this. One can sense their agony as they sought, fearing the worst, to determine the truth of this statement. There is almost a plaintive note as they asked for information and guidance from their fellow academics. On 16 July they wrote to Paris, eleven days later to Vienna, Leipzig, Erfurt, and Cologne, telling of their plight and seeking to determine both the status of the movement and a basis for their own policy.[58] They also sent a deputation to Basel to learn first hand the fate of the council.

Later that summer the returns from the canvas began to trickle in. Vienna responded on 12 August and counseled submission;[59] the remnants of Basel, who had fled to Lausanne, informed Cracow on 26 August of their own desperate negotiations with Rome;[60] the faculty at Cologne indicated its own resignation in the face of the inevitable in two letters on 19 September (though their beadle in a separate message vowed to continue the flight and exhorted Cracow to stand firm);[61] and Leipzig wrote on 26 September to add its voice to the majority for the recognition of Nicholas.[62] Only Erfurt remained loyal for the time being to Felix, and its letter of 3 October did little to resolve the problem which confronted Cracow.[63] Finally Paris spoke. The source of the conciliar movement's origins six decades before praised the contribution of the Polish university and applauded its service to the church. But in its letter of 3 October (which reached Poland after that from Erfurt), it tactfully suggested that it was hard "to swim against the current" and that Cracow should follow its own lead and abandon Basel.[64]

The climax had come; the resolution followed. After having assured himself of a cardinal's hat and a satisfactory pension, Felix resigned on 7 April 1449. The bedraggled survivors of what had once been the proud assemblage of Christendom dismissed for the last time in Lausanne on 25 April. Not until 3 July did the University of Cracow, as the last supporter of the council and Felix, submit. Only then, in an act of some ambiguity, did it recognize Nicholas. It sent its declaration to a representative in Rome to deliver to the pope. In it, there was an acceptance of Nicholas; there was no explicit renunciation of the conciliar theory that had been refined and defended by the faculty during the decades of Cracow's engagement in the councils.[65]

Several features of the foregoing discussion should be emphasized here by way of conclusion. With regard to the life of the University of Cracow itself, it should be noted that over the period of the three councils, a fledgling institution that timidly deferred to royal wishes at the time of Pisa was transformed into a vigorous one that could either, in the case of Constance, aggressively support national interests or, with regard to Basel, oppose the king by

pursuing ecclesiastical policies and supporting theological formulations not consonant with royal wishes. It is often suggested that
many late medieval universities came increasingly under the control of the political jurisdiction in which they were located.[66] This
generalization, at least in this form, will not hold for Cracow in
this period. Although there can be no doubt that it did effectively
serve a variety of the concerns of its society, it was by no means a
simple tool of national and local needs. The relationship between
studium and society in the late Middle Ages is therefore far more
complex than such simple formulations would suggest and deserves
closer attention than it has hitherto received.[67] Cracow is an interesting case to examine, for despite the explicit designs of its founder
in 1400 and the increasingly important role the university played
in the life of the nation, relations between the monarchy and the
school were not too close in the last half of the century.[68] In
general, whenever there was an attempt to limit its independent
sphere of action, the school successfully resisted it well into the
sixteenth century.[69]

Another important point in this context has been suggested by
A. C. Black in a discussion of some implications of the failure of
the conciliar movement. Paraphrasing John of Segovia by saying
that "the papacy triumphed not through doctrine but through
worldly means,"[70] Black concludes that the conciliar period saw a
"divorce between the rulers of the Church and their most highly
qualified advisors" which was "fatal for the medieval Church. Not
only were reforms bypassed, but the papacy emerged from the
struggle intellectually tarnished."[71] After the mid-fifteenth century,
the universities of Europe, which before had been so important in
shaping European thought and civilization, were to be largely
ignored by the Church. It was not until a new religious thrust
emerged in the sixteenth century that the *studia* were again to be
influential in the definition and dissemination of religious culture.
By then, however, their impact was largely limited to Protestant
Europe. Elements of these developments can be found in embryo
at Cracow in the period of this study. The thrust of its theology
was not speculative and theoretical. As reflected in the thought of

James of Paradyż and the other writers we have discussed, it was oriented toward practical questions and immediate issues of reform. When its goals were frustrated, it had no other contribution to make, and it is not surprising that the intellectual vitality of the theological faculty at Cracow should have been impaired. The greatest accomplishments of the Cracow professoriate came in the period of the three councils.[72]

The University of Cracow was a school engaged in the national life, but it was not one whose dimensions—whether academic, institutional, or intellectual—were limited to a narrow, controlled definition of that life. Cracow was also a vital part of one of the most significant moments in the life of the late medieval church. In neither case was it an institution that, modeled upon the earlier archetypal *studia*, was simply a petrified remnant of an earlier ideal. It was, along with the other universities of this period, a vibrant force and a dynamic manifestation of a phenomenon that was constantly in transition.

1. Literature on this topic to 1960 is reviewed by Sven Stelling-Michaud, "L'histoire des universités au moyen âge et à la renaissance au cours des vingt-cinq dernières années," in *International Congress of Historical Science, Rapports* 1 (Stockholm, 1960): 97–143. More recent materials are discussed by Jacques Paquet, "Aspects de l'université médiévale," in Jacques Paquet and Josef IJsewijn, eds., *Les universités à la fin du moyen âge* (Louvain, 1978), pp. 3–25.

2. A. B. Cobban, *The Medieval Universities, Their Development and Organization* (London, 1975), p. 117.

3. Antony Black, "The Universities and the Council of Basle: Collegium and Concilium," in Paquet and IJsewijn, *Les universités*, p. 511. On a related point, see Peter McKeon, "Concilium generale and studium generale," *Church History* 35 (1966): 24–34.

4. The early history of the university and the refoundation of 1400 are discussed by Jan Dąbrowski, "Czasy Kazimierza Wielkiego," and Zofia Kozłwska-Budkowa, "Odnowienie Jagiellońskie Uniwersytetu Krakowskiego," both in Kazimierz Lepzy, ed., *Dzieje Uniwersytetu Jagiellońskiego w latach 1364–1764* (Cracow, 1964), pp. 15–36 and 37–43, respectively. In English, see Paul W. Knoll, "Casimir the Great and the University of Cracow," *Jahrbücher für Geschichte Osteuropas* 16 (1968): 232–49.

5. "Profecto ad hoc summi dispositione praesidii plurimarum terrarum obtinuimus principatum et regni Poloniae recepimus dyadema, ut ipsum regnum claritate doctarem personarum illustremus . . . ipsumque caeteris regionibus coaequare . . . eiusdem Studii generalis . . . ad decus nostrae sacrae Coronae Poloniae instaurandum decrevimus, incrementa felicia ampliare frequentius affectantes et longinquarum incolas regionum ad eius allicere desiderantes accessum" (*Codex diplomaticus Universitatis Studii Generalis Cracoviensis*, edited

by Zegota Pauli and Franciszek Piekosiński, 5 vols. (Cracow, 1870–1900), 1:26, n. 16 [hereafter cited CDUC]).

6. Cracow's involvement with the Council at Pisa was minimal. The university responded favorably in support of the council, but never sent a delegation. The unwillingness of the school to participate more actively is explained by royal support of the Roman line. The professors wished to avoid any conflict between them and the king at this early point in the history of the *studium*. On this point, see Władyław Abraham, "Udział Polski w soborze pizańskim 1409," *Rozprawy Akademii Umiejętności: wydział historyczno-filozoficzny* 47 (1905): 135, nn. 1 and 151–53.

7. Heinrich Finke et al., eds., *Acta concilii Constanciensis*, 4 vols. (Münster, 1896–1928), 2:413.

8. *Ordo militum hospitalis S. Mariae Theutonicorum Hierosolymitani* called *Der Deutsche Orden* in German historiography and *Krzyżacy* (Knights of the Cross, because of the symbol on their tunics) in Polish historiography. In this study I use the terms Teutonic Order, Order, Teutonic Knights, and Knights interchangeably.

9. One end of the spectrum is discussed by Erich Caspar, *Hermann von Salza und die Gründung des Deutschordensstaats in Preussen* (Tübingen, 1924); the other is reflected in Ludwik Ehrlich, ed., *Paweł Włodkowic, Pisma wybrana: Works of Paul Wladimiri, A Selection*, 3 vols. (Warsaw, 1966–69), 1: xiv–xx, hereafter cited as *Pisma wybrana*; and in Stanislaus F. Belch, *Paulus Vladimiri and His Doctrine Concerning International Law and Politics*, 2 vols., (The Hague, 1965), 1:101–3, hereafter cited as *Paulus Vladimiri*. On the more general question of Polish relations with the Order in the fourteenth and fifteenth centuries, see my *Rise of the Polish Monarchy, Piast Poland in East Central Europe 1320–1370* (Chicago, 1972), pp. 2ff., 49–58; Hartmut Boockmann, *Johannes Falkenberg, der Deutsche Orden und die polnische Politik* (Göttigen, 1975), pp. 53–82 especially for a description of Teutonic Order propaganda from 1386 to 1409.

10. See Boockmann, *Johannes Falkenberg*, pp. 54–57, nn. 14, 26, and 27.

11. The invitation to the king was delivered in conjunction with the arrangement of a truce with the Knights; *Kodeks dyplomatyczny Litwy*, . . . ed. E. Raczyński (Wrocław, 1845), 7:189. The invitation to the Polish church came independently; Augustin Theiner, ed., *Vetera Monumenta Poloniae et Lithuaniae*, 4 vols. (Rome, 1860–1864), 2:9. The invitation has not survived, but was undoubtedly similar to that sent other *studia*.

12. *Codex epistolaris saec. XV*, ed. A. Sokołowski, J. Szujski, and A. Lewicki, 3 vols. (Cracow, 1876–94), 2:no. 56. Other Polish representatives came to Constance, but, as in the case of the visit of Professor Andrew Kokorzyński in 1417 described by Joannes Długosz, *Historiae Polonicae*, in *Opera Omnia*, ed. A. Przeździecki, 5 vols. (Cracow, 1873–78), 4:205, they were pursuing private issues incidental to the work of the council.

13. See the comment of F. M. Bartos in *Festschrift für Hermann Heimpel* (Göttingen, 1971), 2:670. This represents a change in his earlier view that Paul Vladimiri was the one who had supported Hus; see "Z publicistiky velikého schismatu a Koncilu basilejského," *Vestnik Ceské Akademie Ved a Umeni* 53 (1944):19f., and "Speculum aureum i jego przypuszczalny autor: Paweł z Brudzewa,"*Reformacja w Polsce* 11 (1948–52):39.

14. An older biographical notice is contained in *Polski Słownik Biograficzny* (Cracow [later Wrocław], 1935ff.), 1:103–6.

15. On Peter, see Kazimierz Morawski, *Historya Uniwersytetu Jagiellońskiego, Średnie wieki i Odrodzenie*, 2 vols. (Cracow, 1900), 1:173f., hereafter cited as *Historya UJ*; and Krystyna Pieradzka, "Uniwersytet Krakowski w służbie państwa i wobec soborów w Konstancji i Bazylei," in Lepszy, *Dzieje Uniwersytetu*, p. 98.

16. Jan Fijałek, "Ostatnie słowo Pawła Włodkowica o zakonie krzyżackim,"*Przeglad Kos-*

cielny 1 (1902): 92–93, has accurately, if poetically, described Dobrzyń as a land "soaked in blood and tears as a result of constant attacks and violence by the Knights."

17. That Paul was a royal, not a university, delegate at Constance is reflected by his statement that he was "rector protunc universitatis studii . . . cum aliis dominis pro ambassiatore missus." *De annatis*, in *Starodawne Prawa Polskiego Pomniki*, ed. Michał Bobrzyński, et al., 12 vols. (Cracow and Warsaw, 1856–1921), 5:304. He was also listed as "ambassiator regis Poloniae" in some of the records of the council; see Belch, *Paulus Vladimiri*, 1:132, n. 94, and Ludwik Ehrlich, *Paweł Włodkowic i Stanisław za Skarbmierza* (Warsaw, 1954), p. 50. When Paul was promoted to doctor at Cracow, his teacher, Stanislaw of Skalbmierza, justified this in part by arguing, "et experiencia negociorum secularium facit in pericia magis latum . . . Ideo, reverende magister, cum Deus debit vobis os et sapientiam . . . magis pro profectu Rei publice, suadeo ut accipiatis insignia doctoralia, quibus estis dignus." Cited by Kozłowska-Budkowa, "Uniwersytet Jagiellonski w dobie Grunwaldu," *Prace Historyczny* 8 (1961): 66, n. 36.

18. In addition to the biographical details in Fijałek, "Ostatnie słowo," see the biographical sections in Ehrlich, *Pisma wybrana*, 1: xi–xiv; in Belch, *Paulus Vladimiri*, 1: 115–55; and Kurt Forstreuter, "Aus den letzen Jahren des Paulus Wladimiri," *Zeitschrift für Ostforschung* 19 (1970): 467–78. Recent bibliography dealing with Paul and his works is reviewed by Jacek Wiesiołowski, "Prace i projekty Pawła Włodkowica – Konstancja, zima 1415/1416 roku," *Roxzniki Historyczne* 35 (1969): 93–95; and by Jan W. Woś, "Paulus Wladimiri aus Brudzeń – Vorläufer oder Fortsetzer," *Zeitschrift für Ostforschung* 25 (1976): 438–61.

19. On the eve and in the aftermath of the battle of Grunwald (Tannenberg) in 1410, there was much discussion about the nature of the just war and the use of pagans in a Christian army at the university. The most tangible result of this was the treatise by Stanislaw of Skalbmierz *De bellis justis*. For discussion and edition, see Ludwik Ehrlich, *Polski wyklad prawa wojny XV wieku* (Warsaw, 1955). The discussions about the content of the Polish delegation's presentation at Constance are reviewed by Pieradzka, "Dwie polskie relacje kronikarskie o soborze w Konstancji," *Mediaevalia, w 50 rocznice pracy naukowej Jana Dabrowskiego* (Warsaw, 1960), p. 215.

20. See the comments in Paul's letter of 22 January 1416 to Jagiello, printed in Wiesiolowski, "Prace i projekty," pp. 118–20: "eadem universitas suum ministerium ad hoc realiter prestitit, licet per me cuius rector eram anno preterito et nunc prestat ministrando dictis negociis bonum principium atque causam, que divina gratis operate videtur posita in fundamento solido, cui non potuerit resistere omnis adversarii vestri hostesque dicti Regni."

21. The treatise *Saevientibus* is undated; the *Opinio Ostiensis* is dated in many manuscripts 6 July 1415, and in it Paul refers to the first work as having been given to the German nation the day before: "in tractatu supradicto et tradito Germanice Nacioni A.D. Millessimo CCCCXV die quinta mensis Julij." On this straightforward basis, it has been nearly universal to place these two treatises in early July 1415. Recently Boockmann, *Johannes Falkenberg*, pp. 225–28, particularly n. 179, has convincingly argued that the appearance of these works belongs to late spring or early summer 1416. I have followed his dating in the text. Even if the traditional dating is correct, this does not essentially change the narrative of events as given above.

22. Text in Ehrlich, *Pisma wybrana*, 1: 2–98; and Belch, *Paulus Vladimiri*, 2:792–844.

23. Ehrlick, *Pisma wybrana*, 1: 113–37; and Belch, *Paulus Vladimiri*, 2:864–84.

24. Ehrlick, *Pisma wybrana*, 1: 144–259 and 2:2–16f. It is apparent from Paul's letter of 22 January 1416 to Jagiello (Wiesiolowski, "Prace i projekty," p. 118f.) that he had essentially finished *Ad aperiendam* at that time, for he gives a summary of its structure and contents.

25. Belch, *Paulus Vladimiri*, 2:n. 6. That these also were essentially complete by early 1416

is clear from the letter referred to above: "Pro cuius heresis exterminacione efficaci . . . feci CLVI articulos et plures adhuc intendo facere. . . ." Wiesiolowski, "Pracy i projekty," p. 120.

26. *CDUC*, 1: 110–13, n. 58: "Nostram praeterea Cracoviensem, quae in sua novitate sicut novellae olivarum in campo fidei audacter militans fructificat, velitis paternis complecti visceribus, ipsamque cum suis suppositis in agendis suo tempore gratiosius habere commendatam" (p. 113). This was drafted and carried by Peter Wolfram.

27. *Die Berichte der Generalprokuratoren des Deutschen Ordens an der Kurie*, edited by Kurt Forstreuter and Hans Koeppen, 3 vols. (Gottingen, 1960–71), 2:n. 164: "Ich habe etlichen doctoribus gelt gegeben, redliche entwert doruff zu schreiben."

28. Belch, *Paulus Vladimiri*, 2:1,116–80. On the person of Urbach, see Boockman, "Aus den Handakten des Kanonisten Johannes Urbach. Die Satira des Johannes Falkenberg und andere Funde zur Geschichte des Konstanzer Konzils," *Deutsches Archiv* 28 (1972): 497–532.

29. Ehrlich, *Pisma wybrana*, 2:216–398.

30. The history of this treatise is discussed by Boockmann, *Johannes Falkenberg*, pp. 37–49; and "Jan Falkenberg i jego obrona Zakonu Krzyżackiego," *Zapiski Historyczne* 41 (1976): 669–83.

31. Assumed until recently to have been lost, two versions were independently discovered in Leipzig by Zofia Włodek and in Zeil in Hartmut Boockmann. It has now been twice edited; by the former scholar in "La Satire de Jean Falkenberg, Texte inédit avec introduction," *Mediaevalia Philosophica Polonorum* 18 (1973), and by the latter, in *Johannes Falkenberg*, pp. 312–53.

32. Ehrlich, *Pisma wybrana*, 2:182–209; Belch, *Paulus Vladimiri*, 2:n. 7.

33. The record of the last session of the council, in which the Poles failed to obtain condemnation of the *Satira*, is printed in H. von der Hardt, ed., *Magnum oecumenicum Constantiense concilium*, 6 vols. (Frankfurt and Leipzig, 1697–1700), 4:1548ff. See also Długosz, *Historia Polonicae*, 4:211. The affair of Falkenberg had a strange denouement. After further negotiations an agreement was reached. On 17 January 1424 a Polish delegation led by Andrew Łaskarz and Paul Vladimiri met in Rome with Martin V and Falkenberg. The Dominican formally abjured his satire on the Polish king and his subject and the Poles agreed to drop all demands for further action. *Cod. epist.*, 2:n. 134.

34. The tortuous course of early Polish policy to the council is traced by Ludwik Grosse, *Stosunki Polski z soborem Bazyleiskim* (Warsaw, 1885), pp. 23–42; and Teofil Zegarski, *Polen und das Basler Konzil* (Poznan, 1910), pp. 11–29.

35. His sermon was delivered upon the death of John de Saccis of Pavia, the reformer of the medical faculty at Cracow, and is partially printed by Morawski, *Historya UJ*, 1: 238.

36. Aeneas Sylvius Piccolominus, *De gestis concilii Basiliensis Commentariorum, Libri II*, ed. and trans. Denys Hay and W. K. Smith (Oxford, 1967), pp. 214, 234–36.

37. See Jan Fijałek, *Mistrz Jakb z Paradyża i Uniwersytet Krakowski w okresie soboru bazlejskiego* (Cracow, 1900), 1: 169f.

38. Until recently, the first of these speeches had been attributed to James of Paradyz by all scholars who wrote on this topic. J. Stanisław Bojarski ("Jan z Ludziska i przypisywane mu mowy uniwersyteckie," *Studia Mediewistyczne* 14 (1973): 62–77) has discussed this address within the context of John of Ludzisko's other speeches and shown that both were given by him.

39. For John's biography, see Bojarski, "Jan z Ludziska," *Materialy i Studia Zakladu Historii Filozofii Starozytnej i Sredniowiecznej*, Series A: *Materialy do historii filozofii sredniowiecznej w Polsce* 9 (1967): 3–24; and J. Stanislaw Bojarski, "Jan z Ludziska i przpisywane mu mowy uniwersyteckie," *Studia Mediewistyczne* 14 (1973): 11–38.

40. The text of the speech is printed by Fijałek, *Mistrz Jakób*, 1: 210–25.

41. Text in *Johannis de Ludzisko Orationes*, J. Stanisław Bojarski (Wrocław, 1971), pp. 79–88.

42. Fijałek, *Mistrz Jakób*, 1: 228–95, was the first to untangle the threads of conciliar creation at Cracow in this period. He made effective use of the testimony at Basel of Bonfili as reported by John of Segovia in *Monumenta conciliorum generalium seculi XV. Concilium Basiliense. Scriptores*, 4 vols. (Vienna [and Basel], 1857–1935), 3:956f. All earlier works are hopelessly confused; later works depend upon Fijałek.

43. His biography is treated by Fijałak, *Studya do dziejów Uniwersytetu Krakowskiego i jego wydziału teologicznego w XV w.* (Cracow, 1898), pp. 143–51. See also *Pol. Słow. Biog.*, 9:485–86.

44. For biographical details, see *Filozofia w Polsce: Słownik pisarzy* (Wrocław, 1971), p. 417.

45. See *Pol. Słow. Biog.*, 6:227f.; and Fijałek, *Mistrz Jakób*, 1:272–81.

46. The best study of his life, despite its antiquated elements, remains Fijałek, *Mistrz Jakób*, 1: 44–153, 2:1–115. The range of his works is discussed by L. Meier, "Die Werke des Erfurters Jakob von Jüterbog in Ihrere handschriftlichen Uberlieferung," *Beiträge zur Geschichte der philosophie und Theologie des Mittelalters* 37, no. 5 (1955).

47. His biography in *Filozofia w Polsce: Słownik*, p. 402.

48. There is no satisfactory modern edition and study of the Cracovian treatises. I hope to prepare such a work that will include the writings of other fifteenth-century east central European masters regarding the church.

49. His treatise is discussed in Fijałek, *Mistrz Jakób*, 1: 325–31, 413f., and printed in *Mon. conc. gen.*, 3:pt. ii, 535ff. The Erfurt position is discussed, with reference to older literature, by Joachim W. Stieber, *Pope Eugenius IV, The Council of Basel and The Secular and Ecclesiastical Authorities in the Empire* (Leiden, 1978), pp. 73–81.

50. Lawrence's treatise is discussed by Fijałek, *Mistrz Jakób*, 1: 295–300; there is no modern edition.

51. The last sentence contains, slightly condensed, the essence of his six conclusions. For a fuller discussion, see Fijałek, *Mistrz Jakób*, 1:300–310.

52. His treatise is discussed, in conjunction with that by Strzempiński by Fijałek, *Mistrz Jakób*, 1:311–49, and partially edited, 1:349–80. There is no complete modern edition.

53. For an analysis of the individual Cracovian sources which he drew upon in this compilation, see Fijałek, *Mistrz Jakób*, 1: 345–47. The treatise is printed in Caesar Bulaeus, *Historia Universitatis Parisiensis Carolo Magno ad nostra tempora*, 6 vols. (Paris, 1665–1673), 5:479–517.

54. John Elgot carried Oleśnicki's declaration on behalf of Felix to Basel in 1442, addressing the pope as "vero et unico summo pontifici." *Cod. epist.*, 2:no. 282.

55. Casimir's letter to Nicholas in *Cod. epist.*, 2:no. 18; Oleśnicki's graceful return to papal obedience in *Cod. epist.*, 1: pt. ii, no. 16.

56. His visit is described by Długosz, *Historia Polonicae*, 5:50.

57. *CDUC*, 2:75, no. 136: "magno cum scandalo populi, cum magna etiam infamia nominis nostri."

58. *CDUC*, 2:73, no. 136 to Paris; 2:78, no. 138 to others.

59. *CDUC*, 2:80, no. 139.

60. *CDUC*, 2:81, no. 140.

61. *CDUC*, 2:86–87, nos. 142 and 143 for the university; 2:89, no. 144 for the beadle.

62. *CDUC*, 2:93, no. 145.

63. *CDUC*, 2:95, no. 146.

64. *CDUC*, 2:96, no. 147.

65. *CDUC*, 2:118, no. 160.

66. See, for example, the discussion of the late fifteenth-century University of Paris in Hastings Rashdall, *The Universities of Europe in the Middle Ages*, ed. F. M. Powicke and A. B. Emden, 3 vols. (Oxford, 1936), 1:580ff.; and the comments of Cobban, *Medieval Universities*, p. 118f.

67. Some interesting contributions in this regard are contained in the volume of studies presented upon the 550th anniversary of the founding of Louvain; see Pacquet and IJsewijn, *Les universités*, pp. 497–630. There are also some suggestive comments in the study by Laetitia Boehm, "Libertas Scholastica und Negotium Scholare: Entstehung and Sozialprestige des Akademischen Standes im Mittelalter," in *Universitaät und Gelehrtenstand 1400–1800* (Limburg an der Lahn, 1970), pp. 15–61.

68. These included such disparate elements as the reform of the Polish church, the attack upon Hussite influence, the emergence of national identity as reflected in language, administration, education, and even patriotism, in addition to the defense of national interests in dealings with the Teutonic Knights.

69. See, for this, Henryk Barycz, *Historja Uniwersytetu Jagiellońskiego w epoce humanizmu* (Cracow, 1935), pp. 337–46.

70. *Mon. conc. gen.*, 3:949.

71. Black, "Universities and the Council of Basle," p. 523.

72. Some general characteristics of the contributions of the theologians at Cracow in this period are provided by Marian Rechowicz, "Po założeniu Wydziału Teologicznego w Krakowie," in *Dzieje Teologii Katolickiej w Polsce*, vol. 1: *Średniowiecze*, ed. Marian Rechowicz (Lublin, 1974), p. 109.

THE CAREERS OF OXFORD STUDENTS
IN THE LATER MIDDLE AGES

Guy Fitch Lytle

hat was the fundamental purpose of universities in late medieval English society? Why did a variety of people and organizations endow them with property or provide money toward their support? Why did those in positions of authority grant them extensive privileges and protection? Why did parents suffer economic hardship and young men endure physical and mental rigors for an Oxford education during this period?

The answers are simple. Universities existed primarily to train youths for careers in the church and state. That training produced the necessary qualified personnel to staff royal, noble, and ecclesiastical administrations, to serve the sundry needs of the church, and to ply the emerging professions in an increasingly complex society. A university degree that led to such employment and promotion also offered a promising avenue of social mobility and a chance to create or to augment personal and familial fortunes great or small. A further question then comes to the fore: how well, and in what ways, did Oxford and its students conform to this ideal?

Of course universities had other social functions in addition to their obvious intellectual roles. They were appropriate institutions for the charitable requirements of a late feudal, Christian society. Students, masters, and servants constituted an important economic market. Some universities (especially prominent theological faculties) claimed and exercised rights to prescribe or to proscribe particular ideas for society at large. But despite the importance of these activities, the basic point remains: the careers of its graduates demonstrate to a great extent the social role, attraction, and influence of a university.

Much useful information has been gathered about the social and geographical origins of students and about the intellectual history and legal status of universities as institutions. But for a full understanding even of these topics, some attention to careers is necessary. We cannot measure the impact of a university education on social mobility if we have not traced the former student's employment and status in his society as an adult. Even more importantly, we cannot seriously begin to fathom the mentalities of various types of university men until we recognize that the bulk of their writings occurred after they had departed their cloisters of learning and, for the most part, represented practical response to the demands and experiences of their careers.

Yet not enough has been done to analyze these careers. As Trevor Aston pointed out recently, the "careers of individual alumni of the medieval University of Oxford have been studied a good deal. But they have all been more or less famous . . . men, and the generality of members, has hardly been studied at all."[1] Despite good accounts of university graduates' careers in specific regional settings or in particular types of occupation, especially in England, no comprehensive analysis of the vocations of the general run of students from any medieval or Renaissance university exists. Common assumptions still hold that northern universities, at least before those social and educational transformations associated with the Renaissance or the Tudor and Stuart eras, were training grounds for future ecclesiastics.[2] So they were. But did all students in late medieval universities become priests? If not, what employment did they seek and find? Was a university degree a requirement for promotion or important positions?

Trevor Aston has identified and frequently illuminated many important concerns of the social historians of late medieval Oxford. Basing his account on the computerized index of Dr. Emden's biographical dictionary, which admittedly records only a minority of Oxford's students, and, due to the nature of the sources, is "emphatically . . . not . . . a random sample," Mr. Aston

214

is able to tell us much about the composition of the student body. Then he turns to the question of the lives of students after leaving Oxford:

> What then of the career opportunities of Oxford's alumni? These may be roughly divided into ecclesiastical preferment, royal, episcopal, noble and papal service or administration, and lastly practice as a notary public. In regard to ecclesiastical preferment, in which of course large numbers of Oxford's alumni shared to some extent, we may reasonably concentrate our attention on the highest only: on episcopal and decanal appointments in the secular church and on headships of houses among the regulars. . . . What I have almost entirely omitted . . . [includes] preferment to parochial cures, to cathedral chapters below the rank of dean and the like. . . .[3]

I have no significant argument to raise here against either the general conclusions or the limited but substantive findings Mr. Aston reports. However, on our way to a more complete study of the careers of Oxford men and their place in late medieval English society as a whole, I believe that we must address some further questions. First, we need to supplement the data compiled by Dr. Emden by seeking out manuscripts and printed sources that eluded his search; second, we must consider much more carefully the parish clergy, laymen, and dropouts, who together comprised the overwhelming quantitative majority of Oxford's alumni. Such analysis is clearly important to a complete account of any university, but in a period when literacy was still a rare attribute, any higher education at all would have endowed the Oxford student with an eye in the kingdom of the blind. The power of Oxford in the hierarchical society of late medieval England may have been due to the success of that minority of graduates who reached high office; but, for the historian who is equally concerned both with what it meant to be a university man in the late Middle Ages and with the total relationship between a university education and the institutions, mentalities, and social relationships that surrounded it, the ambitions and fates of that majority of students with less talent, less luck or fewer connections remain an important problem. We must painstakingly reconstruct what it meant to be a university student in late medieval England.

The following remarks and their style of presentation seek to do just this in two ways. First, preliminary descriptive statistics focus attention on some rather dark areas in our understanding of Oxford career-patterns; second, following these tables are the stories of a fairly large number of individual alumni. As with any portraitist's sketchbook, one may feel that there are too many studies of disembodied hands, noses, or limbs, or that the range of sitters is too limited. But even though the examples are largely and intentionally drawn from one dominant and representative college,[4] the collective impression is generally correct, and the various traits already visible here reflect clearly some of the complexities of the relationship between university education and English society during a transitional period for both.

The profusion of details also has another objective. Historians must try to be aware of all of the types of sources, however obscure or intractable, that may yield light, however diffuse or refracted, on their subjects. Here, as elsewhere, attention is directed to the whole spectrum of possible data.[5] But, despite the strictures of Professor Elton and others, historians must also be sensitive to the importance and meanings of gaps and silence in the testimony. Although negative evidence is never a comfortable resting point, it can goad complacency and encourage us to seek corroboration in new and unusual quarters. Now to Oxford.

In the charter of foundation and in his introduction to the statutes, William of Wykeham, a late fourteenth-century Bishop of Winchester, clearly set out his motives and ambition for his "New College." He wished to cure, so far as he could, "the general disease of the clerical army, which we have observed to be grievously wounded due to the fewness of the clergy, arising from pestilence, wars, and other miseries of the world." He thus hoped to reverse the decline in the number of students attending the university that had long produced "men of great learning, fruitful to the church of God and to the king and realm."[7] Although he recognized the value of learning *per se*, Wykeham, like other founders, made it abundantly clear that he considered the primary function of the college and the university to be the training of an intellectual and administrative elite to serve the needs of both church and state.

216

The only opposition to this ideal was voiced by that strand of ecclesiastical reformist thought from Grosseteste to Colet that condemned the practice of allowing or requiring clerics to serve two masters. But throughout the later Middle Ages, that position was repeatedly refuted both in theoretical treatises penned by academics and churchmen and in the actual careers pursued by university graduates.[8] The integration of church and state was a fundamental characteristic of late medieval English life.

Oxford graduates with degrees in arts, law, theology, and medicine certainly achieved considerable success as bureaucrats, diplomats, and grandees of the church hierarchy. But although members of this group of graduates were of great importance both to the nation itself and as models and patrons for subsequent generations of students, they comprised only a relatively small elite within any particular cohort of university matriculants. Thus some attempt must be made to survey the careers of *all* of those men who attended Oxford during this period.

In fact, the majority of students *did* enter the church. But my research so far suggests that many of the students who came to Oxford remained there for a few months, several years, or even longer only to leave (usually without a degree) to follow some essentially lay career. Some became common lawyers, schoolmasters, or physicians, but the majority of these "dropouts" seem to have become landholders, immediately or by a subsequent inheritance, or to have served as manorial officials on the estates of magnates or bishops, or to have engaged in various activities and employment outside the academic and ecclesiastical world altogether, and—unfortunately—often beyond our ken. Perhaps the career patterns of the sixteenth century and later were already beginning by or even before 1400.[9]

The available evidence is, for a social historian, highly unsatisfactory. It is scattered and diffuse, usually nonserial, and often incommensurable. Some Oxford student found his way—by talent (or lack of it), by training, connections, or accidents—into almost every conceivable job in the church and the state, or in urban or rural society. Thus, again, the proliferation of details in this paper is necessary both to demonstrate the sources we must use to answer our main questions and to provide some sense of the texture and overall reality of the lives lived by educated men after they left university.

It is relatively easy to discover those graduates who became priests and held vicarages, rectories, or some higher positions in the church, since copious and systematic ecclesiastical records have survived. Official accounts that enable us to trace those who held important positions in the late medieval government have also endured. Members of religious orders, especially monks in the greater houses, have left a number of traces. But no equivalent documentation exists for occasional or unemployed clergymen, for many of the lower ranks of the civil service, or for almost any student who pursued a lay career. Furthermore, since matriculation and class lists are lacking, many students (especially those who withdrew before taking a degree) left no record at all of even having attended the university. The pattern for one college (New College), for which at least the names of the members are known, must therefore provide whatever fragile backbone this body of late medieval data can rely on.

But first, the figures for the second half of the fifteenth century for that large group of students who were not in colleges and yet whose careers have been traced do tell us some things. In table 1, the overwhelming preponderance of masters of arts and theologians in the ranks of the secular clergy is what one would expect. Although it is also known that over 25 percent of those with law degrees actually practiced in various church and secular courts, one may suspect that a majority of the 308 lawyers who appear only as parish or cathedral clerics would also have had their services engaged from time to time by local clients. But the intriguing aspect of the figures in this table lies rather with what we do not know. What happened to the more than 20 percent of lawyers, the 50 percent of those designated merely as *magistri*, and the 75 percent of students with only a B.A. or less, who simply vanish from view? Lists of ecclesiastical ordinations are by no means complete (although the gaps are fairly few by this time), nor are they inevita-

TABLE 1

CAREERS: SECULAR STUDENTS, NONCOLLEGIANS, 1451–1500

Career	No degree/ B.A.	M.A.	Magister*	Law	Theology	Medicine	Totals
	No career						
Died young	17	3	***	1	***	***	21
	Ecclesiastical Careers						
Secular clergy	78	251	109	308	47	4	797
Church administrator/ lawyer	5	3	11	75	2	***	96
Civil servant, church administrator	1	5	4	32	6	***	48
Education	3	6	12	***	2	***	23
University (Oxford)	1	5	3	5	2	***	16
Entered religious order	1	***	1	3	2	**	7
Ordained to major orders†	63	20	12	32	2	1	130
Subtotal	153	290	152	455	63	5	1,117
	Lay Careers						
Lawyers/government officials	10‡	***	1	27	***	2	40
Landholder	1	1	***	***	***	***	2
Lay schoolmaster	4	***	6	***	***	***	10
Physician	***	***	***	***	***	3	3
Other	1	***	1	***	***	***	2
Subtotal	16	1	8	27	0	5	57
	Unknown						
Not known to have been ordained	455	86	187	102	11§	4	845
Total							2,040

SOURCE: *BRUO*, with my own additional research

*The majority of these students were probably M.A.s, but some undoubtedly were lawyers.

†Also includes student-chaplains within the university.

‡Fifty percent of these were simply public notaries and college proctors.

§Eight of the eleven received testimonial letters from the university, but there is no evidence that they ever got jobs.

bly accurate or clear; but it seems quite unlikely that all traces of such a high number of university-trained men would be lost due to the sloppiness either of registrars or of church procedures.[10] No doubt a far larger number died before they could effectively begin a career than is indicated by the few known deaths listed here, but no visitation of plague or epidemic in the late fifteenth century could account for all these missing careers. It does not seem far-fetched, especially in light of the examples given below, to suggest that many, perhaps most, of these students either sought lay careers or had them thrust upon them by external conditions.

There are very few indications in these statistics or elsewhere that students who gained endowed places in colleges originally intended to follow lay careers. Yet the statutes of most of the colleges provide one important source that recognized at least the possibility that this might happen. Even though some colleges (e.g., Balliol and Queens) required fellows to seek ordination, other colleges seem to have anticipated a more secular-minded student body. Wykeham's statutes for New College reflect this attitude: if a scholar or fellow

> shall enter into a religious order, or shall bind himself to the service of any person, or if he marry a wife, or withdraw from college with the intent of deserting his study, which we will have to be understood as the case by the very fact that any of them has absented himself from the said college for more than two months in one year, except for reasons of bodily illness or the management of college business . . . or unless for other true and reasonable grounds to be intimated to the warden and others . . . or if he hath acquired a patrimony, inheritance, or secular fee, or yearly pensions to the value of one hundred shillings sterling, then we enact, by the authority of our present statute, that he be removed from the said college and deprived of its commons and benefits within six months and that thenceforth he be taken for no fellow. . . . But if any one of the fellows or scholars aforesaid shall obtain an ecclesiastical benefice with cure, or without cure, the fruits, returns, and proceeds of which exceed the annual value of 10 marks sterling,

he was to resign his fellowship within one year.[11] Wykeham and other fourteenth- and fifteenth-century founders were not advocating that their students should marry or become household officers in the retinues of kings or noblemen, and certainly they had made every effort to ensure that their recruits were well-motivated. But they seem to have recognized the fact that many Oxford men, especially undergraduates, either would be tempted by, and avail themselves of, job opportunities outside the church or would be forced into lay jobs by economic, familial, or other circumstances.

Table 2 lists the reasons, where known, why New College men resigned their fellowships. The number who died while still at Oxford reminds us of the hazardous condition of life and health even after the major outbreaks of plague had ceased. Of those whose careers are known, the overwhelming majority became beneficed clerics, who, for the most part, remained rectors or vicars throughout their lives. Winchester College, the preparatory school for New College, employed 80 former students. Another 70 left to serve as administrators in the households of kings, queens, aristo-crats, and bishops, and 20 more graduates began to practice in ecclesiastical courts immediately upon leaving the university. Only a few fellows directly mentioned marriage or inheritance as their

TABLE 2

INDICATIONS OF EARLY CAREERS OF OXFORD STUDENTS:
REASONS FOR GIVING UP NEW COLLEGE FELLOWSHIPS, 1386-1547

Died at university	254*
Burnt as Lollard/Protestant	2
Expelled	5
Beneficed (church living worth 10 marks or more)	312
Appointed at Winchester College	80
Entered religious order	13
Church lawyer/administrator	20
Household service (royal, lay, Episcopal)	70
Inherited estates (worth £5 or more per annum)	3
Married	9
Common lawyer	22†
Lay schoolmaster	40†
Unknown ("having lost the desire to study")	533

SOURCE: Ms. Register of Fellows, Warden Sewell, comp., VCH, Oxon., iii, 158.
*One hundred twenty-four were still undergraduates.
†Most of these occur in the early sixteenth century.

TABLE 3

CAREERS: NEW COLLEGE, ca. 1380–1520

Career	ca. 1380–1450					1451–ca. 1520					Totals
	No degree	Arts	Law	Theology	Medicine	No degree	Arts	Law	Theology	Medicine	
Died young	57	17	14	***	***	44	18	9	***	***	159
No Career											
Ecclesiastical Careers											
Secular clergy	23	39	39	38	1	16	73	60	25	1	315
Eccles. admin.	***	***	20	2	1	1	4	18	3	1	50
Royal and eccles. admin.	***	2	6	3	***	***	***	9	2	***	22
Religious orders	1	3	1	***	***	***	***	1	***	***	6
Academic educational	6	21	8	12	1	4	15	6	8	***	81
Ordained to major orders	11	10	11	–	***	2	9	5	1	***	49
Lay Careers											
Law/gov't. admin.	9	1	5	***	***	3	***	***	***	***	18
Landholding	6	***	1	***	***	6	***	***	***	***	13
Lay schoolmaster	***	***	–	***	***	1	***	1	***	***	2
Other service	9	4	3	***	1	5	***	2	***	2	26
Unknown											
No record of ordination	100	30	32	***	***	117	16	17	***	***	312

SOURCE: BRUO, with my own additional research.

reason for leaving, but over 500 students dropped out either without giving an excuse or by simply reporting that they had "lost the desire to study." It is the size of the last group that calls for further analysis and quite possibly a revision of generally accepted ideas about how university men earned their livelihoods and the roles they played in late medieval society.

Not all New College men remained in the careers that they began when they went down from Oxford, so table 3 gives the principal occupations of these students, divided according to their faculty. Wykeham's own priorities—the church and its administration, royal service, and education—were well-served by the graduates of his college. One suspects that he could have felt that his largess had not been wasted, since the qualitative contributions of New College men to the church, to the state, and to learning were even more important than these figures can suggest.[12] Nonetheless, since the primary duty of the universities as institutions was to train successive generations of clerks for the various administrative and pastoral tasks of the church, scholarly attention has focused on these careers. This is not surprising, since even at New College, about two-thirds of all matriculants lived and worked as clerics after they left Oxford. But what about those who did not proceed in the church beyond that first tonsure that was usually required of all beginning university scholars? At New College, 35 percent of those who matriculated and physically survived their stay in Oxford never appeared in the extensive ecclesiastical ordination and presentation records for the century and a half prior to the Reformation. Perhaps some of these young scholars drifted into the ranks of the underemployed chantry priests and overworked curates whose idleness or overeager search for positions was presenting growing problems both for the church and for society. But it seems equally likely that many of these students might eventually be discovered (as some of their classmates already have been) in the court rolls and other records of manors and guilds of the countryside and towns of southern England. Do the surviving records support this hypothesis?[13]

It is often hard, and perhaps misleading, to distinguish university students who lapsed into purely secular careers from their Oxford classmates and later colleagues who filled identical positions and performed the same secular functions, but who were nominally clerics and received payment in the form of benefices. The overlapping and the ambiguity of lay and religious roles were characteristic of late medieval England.[14] Still, some genuine laymen can be identified, especially, among the sons of noblemen who inherited their fathers' lands, status, and political position, among those graduates (from whatever social origin) who held high offices in the government, and among the New College "dropouts."

While several dozen upper-class youths made careers in the church and frequently became bishops (e.g., the Grays and Courtenays), a few prefigured their Tudor descendants in pursuing lay careers. John Tiptoft resided in University College between 1440 and late 1443. In the last year his father died, and John succeeded to his estates and honors as Lord Tiptoft and Powys. In 1446 he inherited his mother's property, and in 1449 he was married for the first of three times (to the widow of the Duke of Warwick) and was created Earl of Worcester.[15] He served the state almost continually until the 1470s as a royal commissioner, diplomat, justice, king's councillor, constable of the Tower, constable of England, and treasurer, except for the period of 1458-61 when he combined a pilgrimage to the Holy Land with a fairly serious "grand tour" of the major universities and centers of humanism in Italy. Tiptoft himself became a passable scholar, and he was even more significant in English cultural history as a book collector and patron of learning.[16] At a less exalted level, Thomas Fiennes, Lord Dacre, studied arts at Oxford for two years and at Cambridge for at least one year during the late 1480s, then briefly enrolled at Gray's Inn. About 1492 he married the daughter of Sir Humphrey Bourgchier and served for a year as constable of Calais. For forty years after 1493, he seems to have lived quietly at Hurstmonceaux, Sussex.[17] But the number of noblemen attending university in the fifteenth century was, if not completely negligible, still quite small; and most of them continued to become prominent clerics, even when they inherited considerable property from their families and served the state as high-level administrators, ambassadors, and royal councillors (e.g., Peter Courtenay, John Stafford).[18]

Throughout the later Middle Ages, royal service was by far the most certain avenue of advancement for graduates from all social classes into the ranks of the "lords spiritual" and to other ecclesiastical and secular rewards. Oxford never had a college, like King's Hall, Cambridge, explicitly founded to provide clerks for the kings' service, but Wykeham and other patrons certainly saw public affairs as a valid and honorable vocation for university graduates. Since the aristocracy did not have a complete monopoly on political offices, nonnoble graduates could legitimately aspire to some of these positions. In the second half of the fifteenth century, just over 5 percent of the known Oxford noncollegiate students held some position (other than royal chaplain) in the government. Of this group, forty-eight were clerks and received ecclesiastical benefices and about thirty-five got salaries or fees from secular sources. Collegians, with the exceptions of members of New College and All Souls, were much less likely to serve the king in any capacity other than chaplain, probably because few of them were trained in civil law. The figures for New College men were quite similar to the noncollegians (cf. tables 1 and 3).

Although these statistics show that only a lucky few among Oxford's students could anticipate notable careers in government, it is as yet impossible to determine with any precision the proportion of civil servants in each government department who had received at least some university education. In the fifteenth century, clerks could be found sitting on the council (usually as bishops), presiding as judges with special jurisdictions (usually in cases involving the admiralty and chivalry, where their training in Roman law was relevant), and handling the increasing amounts of paperwork filtering through the various secretariats.[19] Perhaps the most important administrative development in this period was the emergence of the king's secretary as a major government official. The holders of this position were almost all graduates, usually with degrees in law, and two were New College men: Thomas Bekynton and Richard Andrew. A number of other known graduates found positions as assistants to these top administrators.[20]

Service either in the royal household itself or as special envoys abroad continued to be another frequent area for the employment of graduates, most of whom were clerics even as late as the early sixteenth century. Between the accession of Richard II and the death of Henry VII, 122 Oxford secular students (excluding New College) joined the royal household as king's clerks (8 were probably laymen, since they received no ecclesiastical preferment). Although some graduate royal clerks appear in several of the following categories, it is perhaps useful to record that 45 (1 layman) are known to have served in important policy-making or bureaucratic offices; 43 (3 laymen) sat as judges of one sort or another; 82 (4 laymen) were sent as envoys to other governments abroad and more than 20 (1 layman) argued cases before the Roman curia.[21] Administrators trained in Oxford's law schools accomplished important reforms in the late medieval English bureaucracy (Bishop Stapledon significantly improved the organization of the Exchequer in the 1320s; Thomas Bekynton raised the literary quality in the Chancery during the early fifteenth century). Very few embassies failed to include at least one *magister* among the ambassadors and several others in the entourage.[22] Much work remains to be done on the transition from the medieval to the Tudor bureaucracy before the quantitative and qualitative relationships between the crown, the church, the universities, and public administration become clear. But there can be no doubt that in the fifteenth century the universities were important training grounds for civil servants and that the number of laymen, strictly speaking, among this group of graduates was still small.

Since it is not the purpose here to give a detailed account of the careers and activities of king's clerks, perhaps a couple of examples will suffice to show the range of functions just one graduate might be called on to perform. Richard Martyn (B.Cn.L., 1449) started out as a chaplain in John Tiptoft's household and moved on to the royal household by 1471. During the 1470s he served in the following offices: chancellor of the earldom of March; tutor and councillor for Edward, prince of Wales; master in the chancery; royal chaplain; ambassador to treat with the Scots, the Burgundians, and Spanish, and the French on matters of peace, ransom, and royal marriage; king's councillor; and chancellor of Ireland. Only judgeships eluded him, and that was probably due to his lack of a higher degree in civil law. Martyn was rewarded with numerous benefices and prebends, and he ended his life as bishop of St. David's.[23] A less exalted and less political function for graduates in the royal household was recorded in the famous cookbook of the court of Richard II, *The Forme of Curry*. The manuscript was compiled by the king's master cook with the "assent and advisement of masters of physic and of philosophy" who dwelled in the household.[24]

Among the late medieval university men active in government who were laymen in the more strict sense, lawyers and MPs were the most common. Neither of the two most famous Oxford undergraduates who achieved political prominence under the early Tudors bothered to take a degree. Both Edmund Dudley and Thomas More studied briefly at Oxford before going on to one of the inns of court and then to careers as lawyers, judges, MPs, undersheriffs, members of the king's council, and high state officials. Both married twice, and both died on the Tower scaffold.[25] But there were other less renowned examples, mostly from the late fifteenth century:

1) Henry Tyngilden, an undergraduate at Magdalen in the 1490s and probably the son and grandson of Surrey MPs, was a JP for the county between 1514 and 1520.[26]

2) Robert Caxtone, B.C.L., was an attorney for Lincoln College, St. Fridewide's abbey, and the university itself during the 1480s. From 1483 on he was JP for Oxford, and in 1491 he was elected MP for Oxford borough.[27]

3) Robert Rydon, B.C.L., was in the service of Archbishop Bourgchier before 1482 when he was appointed to the office of "king's promoter of all causes civil and criminal or concerning crimes of lese majesty before the king's judges of the constableship

and admiralty." Rydon was vice-admiral of England for twenty-five years and clerk of Henry VII's council for seventeen years; he was sent on numerous embassies and was JP for Kent in 1501 and 1506. He was married and made provisions in his will for his son to attend Oxford.[28]

4) John Batmanson (Oxford B.C.L.; Cambridge LL.D., 1493) married, was ambassador to Scotland (1509–), and legal advisor on the probate of the will of Lady Margaret Beaufort.[29]

5) Nicholas Trappe, B.C.L., and a freeman of Wells, married, served as mayor of Wells (1497, 1501, 1502), and was elected MP for that city in 1504. Trappe died in 1510, and his will contained a sizeable bequest of lands to New College where a relative of his had studied earlier.[30]

Several New College men, in addition to those great ecclesiastical lawyer-bishops mentioned earlier, were recruited into state service in various capacities:

1) Ralph Greenhurst (New College, 1389–1401; D.C.L.) was married and acted as an envoy to Brittany, Aragon, Burgundy, France, and Genoa between 1411 and 1413.[31]

2) Richard Sturgeon (1399–1405; "civilista") was a chancery clerk for thirty-five years (1415–49).[32]

3) Richard Wallopp (1414–15; no degree) inherited land in Hampshire and was an MP, JP, commissioner, and tax collector for that county until the 1440s.[33]

4) Bartholomew Bolney (1422–23; Lincoln's Inn) was married and began his career as steward for Battle Abbey; he served as JP and commissioner of array for Sussex between 1444 and 1476; and he also presided as a justice of gaol delivery (1456), commissioner of *oyer* and *terminer* (1465, 1470), and commissioner *de waliis et fossatis* in Sussex (1462, 1465, 1474).[34]

5) John Newport (1472–76; Lincoln's Inn) was a sergeant-at-law and was married. The son and nephew of prominent MPs and royal officials, he was appointed to commissions of the peace for ten southern and western counties, and he also held the position of sheriff of Salop.[35]

6) John Kyngesmyll (1474–79; Middle Temple) sergeant-at-law,

king's sergeant, and counsel for several colleges, was named to the commissions of the peace for several counties between 1493 and 1509, tried cases in the Court of Requests, and was a justice of assize (1503) and of the common pleas (1504–9). Like most of the others, he was married. [36]

Still other New College laymen apparently entered the king's service, but no details of their activities or positions have survived.

The careers of these Oxford men reflect one aspect of an important change in English public administration during the fourteenth and fifteenth centuries. As Joseph Strayer has described it, "Few new departments were created. . . . The expansion came rather in the amount of service required from unpaid local notables, especially through the establishment of the office of Justice of the Peace. By the end of the fourteenth century these justices, country gentry and urban oligarchs, were responsible for the enforcement of statutes and administrative orders at the local level, for the arrest of lawbreakers, and for the trial of minor offences."[37] The "Renaissance" connection between the universities and some of the gentry was already at least partially a reality.

The social ambiguity of this transitional period can be illustrated by three cases. Roger Huswyfe matriculated at New College in 1400 but left after two years to enter the legal profession. Later he declined nomination to be a sergeant-at-law, since he had decided to take holy orders. After his ordination to the priesthood, he resumed residence at Oxford in order to study theology (B.Th., 1437). No further record of Huswyfe appears in any ecclesiastical registers, and since he was mentioned in several royal documents as a feoffee in land transactions between 1448 and 1461, perhaps he practiced law after all.[38] Thomas Kent probably studied at Oxford before going to Pavia where he became a doctor of both laws by 1442. He held two London rectories until 1443–44, but married by 1448. Kent was clerk of the council and secondary in the privy seal office from 1444 until the late 1460s, served as underconstable of England, and was an envoy to Burgundy, Prussia, Scotland, Spain, France, and Brittany in the 1450s and 1460s. He owned several manors, which he left to his second wife in

1469.[39] During the first decade of the next century, James Whitstones (Oxford, Cambridge, and Bologna, 1480s–90s; D.Cn.L) was simultaneously vicar general and chancellor of the bishop of Lincoln, president of Lady Margaret Beaufort's council, and JP for Leicestershire. Throughout the same period, he held twelve rectories, vicarages, and prebends.[40] Fifty years later, such career patterns would be very unlikely.

It was common in the fourteenth century for Duchy of Lancaster administrators—stewards, receivers, chancellors, attorneys general—to be churchmen, even monks, and a number of them were Oxford men. But by the reign of Henry IV, it had become the exception for a cleric to hold office in the Duchy, and they had been replaced by common lawyers, knights, and other literate laymen.[41] It is impossible as yet to say how many of the latter group had any university training. In any case, examinations of the members of other magnate, episcopal, and monastic households yield a number of Oxford graduates performing secular jobs.

Every great lord had his own council to advise him on legal, financial, and other matters. According to A. E. Levett, "a group of permanent trained experts would form a very important— perhaps the most important—section of the council. These were men trained in the law, sometimes in the law of England, sometimes *utrius jurisperiti*, sometimes themselves foreign, trained in one of the great continental law schools.[42] Although the role of Roman law here has been recently discounted,[43] a statute of the realm under Edward IV said that "no person of what estate, degree, or condition that he be . . . (shall) give any such livery or badge, or retain any person other than his menial servant, officer, or man learned in the one law or the other."[44] Magnates retained university men as administrators, advisors, physicians, and chaplains just as the kings did. Humphrey, Duke of Gloucester, employed at least four New College graduates as chancellors and secretaries, possibly including the M. John Russell (apparently a layman) who wrote the well-known description of life in an aristocratic household, *The Book of Nurture*.[45] Richard Beauchamp, Earl of Warwick, made John Baysham (an Oxford B.Cn.L.) his supervisor and receiver-general in the 1420s. The exacting nature of these offices can be shown from Baysham's itinerary of 1420–21. In February he set out from his rectory at Olney, Bucks., to travel to Kirtling, Cambs., to arrange for the repair of the manor house, and then to London. During the same month, he also supervised the felling of timber in Worcestershire and the enclosure of some demesne land in Buckinghamshire and made another trip to London. In the summer he made inspection tours of all the earl's manors in the counties of Warwick, Worcester, and Northampton, visited Coventry to renegotiate his lord's debts and borrow money from the mayor, dealt with a dispute concerning the tenants at Elmley Castle, arranged for the repair of the millpond at Potterspury, and supervised the enclosure and emparking of land at Claverdon. He also drew up his own yearly accounts, consulted with the steward of the earl's lordship of Bernard Castle, and visited London on business several times. During the following summer, he had to cross the channel to discuss various matters with the Earl of Troyes. As a reward for his services, Baysham received several church livings in the gift of the Beauchamps.[46] This case is atypical only in the degree of its documentation.

Spiritual lords brought rather more university men into their households. Several Oxford men were among those whom Archbishop Neville appointed to manage his York estates: William Potman (All Souls, 1447–66; D.C.L.) was overseer of all his temporary possessions and later became archdeacon of the East Riding; M. Edmund Chaderton resided in the household and among other functions acted as surveyor of the estate at Hexham (he too became an archdeacon, as well as a canon of several cathedrals); on the other hand, William Appulby (Balliol, 1460s; M.A.) never advanced to a rectory, despite serving Neville as warden of Scrooby manor. The first two were also employed by the king.[47] About 15 percent of the stewards, auditors, receivers, and treasurers of the Archbishops of Canterbury from 1300 until the early sixteenth century were *magistri*, mostly trained at Oxford.[48] William Porte (New College, 1418–23), although only a B.A., was steward of Cardinal Beaufort's household and owned property in Hampshire and Dorset. He was married twice.[49] The use of secular clerk-lawyers by the religious orders can perhaps best be illustrated by a case in the 1480s in which William Brecknock, inspector general of Cluniac houses in England, attempted to visit Bermondsey Abbey to correct physical ruin and spiritual abuses there. When the abbot refused to receive him, he decided to "make further process according to the law." Brecknock entered the nave of the abbey church, and there found "the said John Marlowe, abbot, with one M. John Cooke, doctor of law (an Oxford D.C.L., king's councillor, ambassador, and archdeacon of Lincoln), of one confederacy which had gathered the multitude of lay people (who) notoriously and with force took your said beseecher, pulled him from his doctors, notaries, and others of his learned counsel . . . intending to murder him."[50] The routine activities of lawyers on the behalf of monasteries was no doubt usually much less exciting than this episode.[51] These graduates formed an efficient administrative class spread thinly across England. Many were also prominent canon lawyers and diocesan officials, and most of them remained at least nominally clerics.

Another "career" that according to the statutes forced the resignation of a college fellowship—"taking a wife"—was undoubtedly a lay pursuit, even though clerkly dalliance was a popular literary theme in the Middle Ages, and more than a few Oxford graduates had to be reprimanded for incontinence.[52] A number of the royal bureaucrats mentioned above were married, and one may suspect that, among the undergraduates who left Oxford without a degree, there were many men like Chaucer's jolly Jankin. As the wife of Bath described him:

> My fifth husband, God his soul bless!
> Which that I took for love, and no riches,
> He sometimes was a clerk of Oxenford
> And had left school, and went at home to board.[53]

A rather different marriage relationship than that envisioned by the wife of Bath can be observed in the correspondence between William Swan (B.C.L. by 1406), a lawyer for various English interests at the peripatetic papal curia, and his wife, Joan, who was, at least rhetorically, subservient.[54] John Walingford (B.Cn.L., 1452), and later B.U.J), was married and lived in Oxford where he was employed by Exeter, Merton, and Oseney Abbey.[55] M. Henry Trewonwell studied at Oxford in the 1440s and 1450s and was appointed warden of the free chapel at Wighton, Norfolk, by the crown in 1451. After 1459 he was the registrar of the consistory court of Canterbury and a notary public by papal authority, and he was granted a papal indulgence to continue after his marriage in 1462.[56] These latter examples show that well-educated men, not just dropouts, could marry and still pursue the careers they were trained for, even in canon law, although the number that did so was probably small.

The virtually complete absence of personal letters deprives us of further examples as well as a sense of human emotions on these matters, but wills do provide some evidence. In 1410, Denys Lapham, a married clerk, left "to Thomas my son £100 silver and all my books, vis. (my) *corpus juris civilis* and all my canon law books . . . (including) my small decretal . . . if he wishes to become a clerk and student in civil or canon law or a student in an English university." But throughout the will Denys assumed that Thomas, too, would have male heirs.[57] William Lynch (Oriel, 1477–?; M.A.) was a physician to the royal family between ca. 1490 and 1513. At his death Lynch bequeathed, among other items, £20 each to a son and daughter and the residue to his wife. She was the executor and was given explicit power to alter any aspects of the will.[58] In a somewhat different case, Elizabeth Wallop, widow of Richard Wallop, Esq., left 40s. per annum to her nephew Giles in 1505 for his exhibition at New College for six years if he was neither promoted to a benefice during that time nor married. Giles studied at New College from 1508 to 1512, but then resigned to get married, though he still took his B.A. two years later.[59] Perhaps it was the possibility of marriage, along with the lure of wealth, that attracted more young men to the emerging legal and medical professions during this period.

But if the professions probably account for only a minority of

Oxford students who did not go into the church, it is no surprise that far fewer can be found in the records of urban crafts and guilds. At the end of the fourteenth century, a London mercer's son who had studied at Oxford for more than ten years returned home to be apprenticed in his father's company; and M. Adelard Bate made provision in 1515 for his nephew to be educated at Oxford and then to be "bound prentice with some honest mercer for 5 or 6 years."[60] Thomas Feroure was a scholar at Oxford in the first half of the fifteenth century, but he later became a yeoman mason and perhaps master mason of the works at Calais.[61] Nicholas Lancaster, D.C.L., served as an alderman of the city of York around 1500.[62] But a university education *per se* in no way prepared youths for lives as merchants or artisans, and so there were few reasons to invest time, effort, or money in acquiring formal learning if such a career was one's goal.

Details of the activities of the great majority of Oxford-trained laymen will probably remain largely undiscovered. There is no trace of most of these students at all after Oxford, but evidence from certain formularies gives some insight into their possible fates and fortunes. One undergraduate, having discovered his inability to learn at this level, asked to be allowed to join the army or to engage in some other more congenial occupation. In another letter, a father promised the delights of manual labor to a son who had complained that studying was too hard and that he wished for more worldly and profitable work. A third youth was told that if he left school he would have to go into business like his brothers.[63] Many others found at least occasional employment in one of the increasing number of secular and ecclesiastical jobs that required an acquaintance with Latin, but not holy orders (References to *literati* appeared increasingly in the witness lists in bishop's registers, charters, deeds, and other sources; they also served as proctors.). Some inherited property and perhaps used a rudimentary knowledge of legal procedures to secure and advance their holdings.

Inheriting property often altered students' career choices. If they came into property while still enrolled, most colleges had statutes requiring them to leave. Although the prospect of inheriting property after leaving university did not effectively bar students from pursuing ecclesiastical careers, New College men with sizeable legacies in fact did find occupations outside the church. Most of the New College men who served the state (e.g., Newport and Kyngesmill cited above) did so from the firm base of a sizeable patrimony in land.[64] Others came into estates of varying sizes. John Browne (New College, 1444–48; a "civilista" and then a student at the inns of court) received the manors of Melburn and Melreth, Cambs., and Verthall and 'Whitcolne,' Essex, from his father, a lawyer, in 1454. By his death in 1467, he had also inherited the manor of Rookwood Hall alias Brownes in Roothing Abbess, Essex. In 1487 the family was styled armiger.[65] Philip Morant entered New College in the same year that John Browne did and studied civil law until 1449. About that time, his father, the bailiff of Andover, died; and a note on the deed of a contemporary property transaction suggests that Philip took possession.[66] Richard Wyard (New College, 1464–d.1478) was rather unlucky. He earned his B.C.L. by 1474 and then apparently inherited the family manor of Wyard's in Alton, Hants. Although he had not yet resigned his fellowship, he was listed as the owner at the head of the 1477 manorial rental, but he died the following year, and the manor passed to his brother.[67] In 1447, M. Walter King resigned the place he had occupied at New College for sixteen years, ostensibly to accept promotion to a benefice. His institution has not been confirmed in any source, however, and it was probably no coincidence that in 1447 his father died and bequeathed the residue of all he owned to Walter and his mother.[68] Similar examples can be drawn from other Oxford colleges (e.g., Hugh Massingbred of Magdalen) and from Cambridge.[69]

Sometimes the evidence is more tantalizing than revealing, as in the case of the New College manor of Writtle, Essex. Thomas Heveningham (New College, 1438–42; then to the inns of court) married, lived, and died in Writtle. According to a manuscript copy of the inscription on his granddaughter's memorial brass, her first husband was Thomas Bardfield (New College, 1471–79;

B.C.L.), but nothing is known about his career.[70] The college register says that Stephen Coope departed from New College in 1492,
after only one year of study, *per decessum* (but the *de* has been
erased).[71] In a Writtle deed of 1495, Stephen Coope's name
appeared in the middle of a group of twelve laymen and one clerk
who were receiving a messuage and ten acres of land from five
other laymen. He would have been twenty-three at the time, and
thus old enough to be involved in village activities, but the entry
could also possibly refer to his father or a kinsman, if any of the
Coopes shared the same Christian name.[72] Most of the college
manors offer possible identifications like this example from Writtle,
but little can be discovered about the lives of the men involved or
the value, if any, that they derived from their stay at Oxford.[73]
Again, if nothing else, these data show that the universities were
not exclusively the training grounds for ecclesiastical careers.

The line between clerks and laymen was blurred further by the
agricultural activities of parish vicars who farmed either the glebe
lands or personal land holdings. The former subject has been studied quite well by Ault; and wills, inquisitions *post mortem*, manorial
accounts, and other records describe the busy participation of
magistri in land transactions as owners, buyers, sellers, leasers, feof-
fees, estate managers, and the like.[74] Graduates could also be found
holding manorial courts, compiling accounts, and doing other
things that failed to distinguish them from laymen.[75] Some feelings
of anticlericalism may well have been stirred up by these practices
or by cases like that of Nicholas Dolfyn, yeoman of Plumsted,
Kent, in 1500. When he was indicted for the theft of a bull and
four cows, he pleaded "benefit of clergy," since before his marriage
he had been a Dominican friar at Oxford in subdeacon's orders.[76]
In 1467, Richard Hannes of Stratford-upon-Avon was referred to
as "yeoman, *alias* late of Oxford, 'scoler' *alias* fishmonger, *alias*
wool-buyer" in a general royal pardon.[77]

A remark by Pope Urban V, a notable if self-interested patron of
universities in the later fourteenth century, helps to summarize the
account thus far of the complex relationships between higher education, lay status, worldly occupations, and the church: "I hope

that the Church of God may abound in learned men. I admit that all those that I am educating and maintaining will not be ecclesiastics. Many will become monks or secular priests, but others will remain in the world and bring up families. What of that? Whatever may be the status they embrace, even if they were to take up manual labor, it would be useful to them to have spent some time in study."[78] In the fifteenth-century foundation statutes of Sevenoaks school, the master had to have his B.A. and be competent in the science of grammar, but "by no means be in holy orders" (although the majority of schoolmasters were probably still clerics at this time).[79] In 1473 Margaret Paston told the family's chaplain that she hoped that her son Walter, who was then going up to Oxford, would "do well, learn well, and be of good rule and disposition . . . (but would not) be too hasty in taking (holy) orders that should bind him, till that he be 24 years of age or more, though he be counselled to the contrary, for often haste rueth . . . I will love him better to be a good secular man than to be an unworthy priest.[80] Such sentiments were clearly a prelude to the changing relationship between the church and society that would occur during and after the Reformation. Oxford as an institution was generally a conservative force in that period, but perhaps its contribution to the spread of effective lay literacy above the elementary level was greater than has been allowed. In a negative sense, the graduate clerk who gained advancement through his success as a civil servant rather than as a man of God increasingly provoked the ire of reformers both within and outside the church. The university was caught in the middle, and it would consequently undergo some fundamental changes during the Tudor century.

But after these claims have been made for the likelihood that a fairly large number of university students either wanted, or were forced, to follow some sort of lay career, the church certainly remained the goal and achievement of a majority of Oxford's matriculants. If we exclude those who died at university, some 55.3 percent of noncollegiate Oxonians definitely entered the church in the second half of the fifteenth century and 58.5 percent of New College men did so (tables 1 and 3). The details of these students' careers and the contributions they made are as multifarious as those essentially secular activities already examined. But since the existence of a number of good monographs and guides to the sources for the late medieval English church makes a brief survey here somewhat redundant, it is possible to conclude by considering several aspects of the relationship of a university education to promotion and reward within the church.[81]

The triumph of rich, worldly, administrative clerks over their poor, learned, and pious brethren in the hunt for church preferment was a constant theme in satirical, complaint, and sermon literature from the twelfth until at least the seventeenth century.[82] We need not doubt the genuine anguish expressed in the dual lament that worthy clerks got too few livings and that the ones they did receive were scandalously impoverished; but the social historian must go further. Were the complaints equally valid for every generation? Did they not often reflect the disappointments of heightened expectations despite real improvements of the graduates' lot? The answers to these and similar questions mattered to contemporaries, as they must to us. Given the intense practicality that governed the lives and ambitions of parents and students alike during the late Middle Ages, if scholars were unable to find suitable jobs and adequate rewards when they completed their education, the universities would face precipitous decline. Such a development it was thought, would result in a decrease in "virtue and cunning," and insubordination and wickedness would quickly spread to destroy the realm.[83] Bishop Wykeham and many others certainly believed that Oxford (and England) was suffering just such a crisis in the second half of the fourteenth century. Was that opinion true? The evidence is somewhat inconclusive. As I have argued elsewhere, shifting patronage patterns may have produced genuine problems for university graduates seeking ecclesiastical positions.[84] Recent analyses, however, have raised some questions about the nature and extent of this "crisis."[85] More research will be necessary to resolve this issue conclusively.[86] Meanwhile, a bit of additional research on the dioceses of Winchester and Hereford (table 4) and some very preliminary samples from Exeter and York

TABLE 4

Parish Church Livings Presented to University Graduates

Diocese	Date	Magistri (Percentage)	All probable university students (Percentage)
Hereford[1]	1283–1299	5.5	11.5
	1300–1324	5.4	17.5
	1325–1349	3.8	14.9
	1350–1374	8.2	17.9
	1375–1399	5.7	10.0
	1400–1424	3.3	10.7
	1425–1429	7.6	10.0
	1450–1474	15.4	18.0
	1475–1492	18.0	20.4
	1503–1524	27.5	29.7
	1429–1439	25.3	26.2
Winchester[2]	1305–1316	10.8	
	1385–1400	7.1	
	1447–1456	23.9	
	1492–1501	30.6	
	1531–1541	34.0	

SOURCES: 1Compiled from all the surviving bishops' registers. I acknowledge the substantial help of Dr. Joel Lipkin, who computerized the data in the registers and produced tentative figures for all university students as a research project in my Folger Institute seminar. The *magistri* calculations are mine. 2Compiled from the printed registers of Bishops Woodlock, Wykeham, and Gardiner; and the Hants. Rec. Office Ms. registers of Bishops Wayneflete and Langton. (This table gives additional and corrected data to that presented in my article "Patronage Patterns and Oxford Colleges," pp. 124–25.)

NOTE: These figures, as well as those in my "Patronage Patterns and Oxford Colleges," are only meant as preliminary indications, and final versions must await the full quantitative analysis of bishop's registers now in progress.

show some variations from region to region in the fourteenth century, but provide little support for the alternative view that things were getting significantly better before the second quarter of the fifteenth century. Only a comprehensive quantitative analysis of the late medieval preferment patterns of parochial, collegiate, and cathedral clergy will provide us with the needed information.[87]

The question of bishops is much clearer, and here, fortunately, there is general agreement among scholars. There was a steady increase in the percentage of graduates elevated to the episcopacy.

239

In an early fifteenth-century sermon, Bishop Hallum of Salisbury (Oxford, D.Cn.L.) said that a man should be promoted to the highest ecclesiastical offices if he were the best candidate, even if he were illiterate, because nowhere do we read of the apostles attending school.[88] But of the 129 men raised to English bishoprics between 1377 and 1509, at least 114 (88.4 percent) attended some university, and only 15 (11.6 percent) left no such evidence (including six religious). This almost 90 percent compares favorably with 50 percent under Henry III and 70 percent under Edward III.[89]

Did a student's choice of faculty or college, or the quality of his academic work, make any difference to his future success in the competition of high ecclesiastical positions? Table 5 shows that lawyers taken all together commanded an increasing majority of bishoprics (especially D.C.L.s), but doctors of theology were still the most frequently promoted single category of graduates among the bishops. Lawyers were also the largest beneficiaries of appointments to prebends, but not by the margin one might have expected (table 6). Among the appointments to places at the cathedrals of Bath and Wells and Lincoln, predominance belonged to civil lawyers who had the best road to promotion (table 7). Although it is not clear that membership in a college *per se* was a notable advantage to promotion, since roughly 25 percent of known fifteenth-century noncollegians with ecclesiastical careers rose above the level of the parish clergy while about 23 percent of New College students did so, colleges could offer special patronage advantages.[90] Finally, it is rare to find any overt mention of a man's intelligence or learning as a reason for his presentation to a living, although it must be presumed that the outstanding lawyers in the royal service who became bishops often rose because of their skill and training. When Bishop Kellawe of Durham collated M. James de Aviso to a prebend in Norton in the early fourteenth century, he gave as his reason "*virtutum studiis quibus vigilanter insistis*"; and the king's council did recognize the qualities of "blood, virtue, and cunning" when it recommended George Neville, M.A. and chancellor of the University of Oxford, for the next vacant bishopric.[91] But service in the administration of the state and the church far outdistanced scholarship as a qualification for advancement.

240

TABLE 5

ACADEMIC DEGREES OF BISHOPS

Reign	Degree	
	Theology	Law
Henry III	15	1
Edward II	10	9
1377–1509	48	55
1377–1509:		
No known degree	15	
Attended university, but no known degree	3	
B.A.	1	
M.A.	4	
Magister	2	
B.Cn.L.	1	
D.Cn.L.	14	
B.C.L.	2	
D.C.L.	23	
B.U.J.	2	
D.U.J.	13	
Sch.Th.	4	
B.Th.	7	
D.Th.	37	
B.M.	1	
D.M.	1	

Late Medieval Cross-sections:
   1415–7 theologians, 7 lawyers, 2 *magistri*, 4 with no degree, 1 unknown
   1483–9 theologians, 9 lawyers, 3 M.A.s
   1509–5 theologians, 11 lawyers, 1 physician, 4 with no degree

SOURCES: *BRUO*, iii, 1613; T. Aston, G. D. Duncan, T. A. R. Evans, "Medieval Alumni of the University of Cambridge," *Past and Present* 86 (1980).

TABLE 6

Higher Ecclesiastical Promotion of Oxford Graduates in the Late Middle Ages (CA.1380–CA. 1520)

	Noncollegians		Collegians (excluding New College)		New College				
	Lawyers	All other graduates	Lawyers	All other graduates	B.A. or less	M.A. or Magister	Lawyer	Theologian	Physician
Prebend in collegiate church*	53	59	11	60	1	7	15	9	***
Cathedral canon and prebendary	156	78	10	84	3	10	25	14	1
Cathedral dignitary (Deans, Chancellors)	58	22	5	31	***	***	13	8	1
Archdeacon	83	21	13	17	0	0	0	0	0
Bishop/Archbishop	40	19	5	20	***	***	7	3	1

SOURCE: BRUO

* Excluding ecclesiastical fellows of Winchester College or Eton College.

TABLE 7

Academic Degrees of Cathedral Canons: 1450–1530

Degree/Faculty	Bath and Wells		Lincoln	
	Number	Percentage	Number	Percentage
*Magister**	27	14.0	43	22.8
M.A.	18	9.3	10	5.3
Law	63	32.6	74	39.2
Civil law	33	17.1	43	22.8
Canon law	13	6.7	24	12.7
Both laws	17	8.8	7	3.7
Theology	27	14.0	31	16.4
Medicine	8	4.1	6	3.2
Music	3	1.6	***	***
Graduates	146	75.6	164	86.8
No degree	47†	24.4	25	13.2
Total	193	100.0	189	100.0

SOURCE: J. LeNeve, *Fasti Ecclesiae Anglicanae, 1300–1541*, (London, 1962–67). Figures for Bath and Wells samples are from *Fasti Ecclesiae Anglicanae*, vol. 8, ed. B. Jones; figures for Lincoln are from *Fasti Ecclesiae Anglicanae*, vol. 1, ed. H. P. F. King, with addition and corrections by Dr. A. B. Emden and myself.

NOTE: Figures include all graduates, not just those from Oxford.

* Includes some B.A.s who are styled *magister* in the bishops' registers; most of the men in this category were probably M.A.s.
† Five of the forty-seven were monks, but apparently not graduates.

Although promotion to places in the upper reaches of the church hierarchy gives the best measure of success, the question must also be asked whether an education assured graduates a certain level of monetary reward in late medieval England? How did they compare in this regard to clerks who did not attend universities? Although there was a continuous debate during the Middle Ages about whether a man should charge fees for teaching, the canonists were united in agreeing that a cleric was entitled to a standard of living appropriate to his "quality" or to his "nobility and learning."[92] But in an exchange between a humanist and a gentleman, when the latter "heard us praise learning, he became wild, overwhelmed with an uncontrollable rage, and burst out

'. . . To hell with your stupid studies. Scholars are a bunch of beggars. Even Erasmus is a pauper, and I hear he's the smartest of them all. . . . I'd rather see my son hanged than be a student.' "[93] The most characteristic feature associated with the scholar's estate in medieval literature was his poverty. Sometimes this was seen as a virtue, but more often it was the cause of complaint and cynicism. Sharp contrasts were also drawn between the lack of worldly rewards for the philosopher (or arts student) and the more visible success of those with legal or medical degrees. In the fourteenth century, Richard de Bury had complained that beside the few scholars who were laborious and lifelong soldiers of wisdom, there stood those who offered only "the fuming must of their youthful intellect to philosophy and reserved the clearer wine for the money-making business of life"; such complaints would echo far into the early modern era and beyond.[94]

Masters themselves were quite naturally concerned about such matters. Thomas Ruthall (D.Cn.L. by 1499) wrote a book on the state of the realm that he intended to give to Henry VII, but by mistake, and to his great embarrassment, he presented to the king instead an identically bound volume in which he had compiled an inventory of all his owned property and sources of revenue.[95] About the same time, Caxton drew a sharp distinction between the relative advancement of two Oxford M.A.s and he also called into question the usual gauge of success:

> There were dwelling in Oxford 2 priests, both Masters of Arts, of whom the one was quick and could put himself forth, and that the other was a good simple priest. And so it happened that the Master that was pert and quick, was soon promoted to a benefice or two, and afterwards to prebends, and for to be Dean of a great prince's chapel; supposing that his fellow, the simple priest, should never have been promoted, but be always at most a parish priest. So, after a long time, that this worshipful man, this Dean, came riding into a good parish, with 10 or 12 horses, like a prelate; and came into the church and found there this good simple man, at one time his fellow, who came and welcomed him lowly. And the other said, "Good morrow, Master John," and took him slightly by the hand, and asked him where he dwelled. And the good man said, "In this parish." "How," said he, "are you here; a soul [i.e., chantry] priest or a parish priest?" "Nay sir," said he "for lack of a better, though I bet not able nor worthy, I

am parson and curate of this parish." And then the other removed his bonnet and said, "I pray you, what is this benefice worth a year? "Forsooth," said the good simple man, "I know not, for I never make accounts thereof." "And you know not what it is worth?" "No, forsooth," said he, "but I know well what it shall be worth to me." "Why, what shall it be worth?" "Forsooth, if I do my true diligence in the cure of my parish in preaching and teaching, I shall have Heaven therefore; and if there be souls that have been lost by my default, I shall be punished therefore; and hereof I am sure." And with that word the rich Dean was abashed, and thought he should do better, and take more heed to his cures and benefices, than he had done. This was a good answer of a good priest and an honest [one].[96]

Taking graduates as a whole, they seem to have done rather better than the literature of the time suggested. In Durham diocese, *magistri* held 26 percent of the richer livings (i.e., all rectories, deaneries, and prebends) but only 14.5 percent of vicarages.[97] Other figures (table 8) clearly show that members of New College received benefices worth far more than the national average; and preliminary results yield a similar picture for graduates in southern and western dioceses. More work must be done before the truth of the common attacks by M.A.s and theologians on the greed of

TABLE 8

INCOME: VALUE OF BENEFICES

Value	English benefices*		Welsh benefices†		New College benefices‡	
	Number	Percentage	Number	Percentage	Number	Percentage
Under £5		10	192	24	19§	11.2
£ 5–£10		50	366	46	36	21.3
£10–£15		19	{ 184	{ 24	31	18.3
£15–£20		8			21	12.5
Over £20		13	53	6	62	36.7
Total churches	397		795		169	

* Compiled from the *Valor Ecclesiasticus*, vol. 3, by P. Heath and *Medieval Clerical Accounts* (York, 1964), p. 24, n. 102.
† G. Williams, *The Welsh Church from Conquest to Reformation* (Cardiff, 1962), p. 283.
‡ New College, names A–C (excluding bishops). Values were based on the *Valor Ecclesiasticus*. Other aspects of the New College figures are: seventeen (27.4%) of the sixty-two wealthy benefices were worth more than £35 (M. William Blake was provost of St. Elizabeth's College, Winchester, at £112 14s. 4 1/2d. p.a.; M. Thomas Brente was vicar of Halifax, Yorkshire, at £84 13s. 6d. p.a.); twenty-two (40%) of those livings worth £10 or less were held jointly with other benefices; sixteen (51.6%) of them worth £10–£15 were held jointly with other benefices.
§ The majority were cathedral canonries held in plurality.

lawyers and physicians can be determined, but pluralism provides one guide to the comparative wealth of different types of graduates. The popes had set a scale for the total value of benefices that graduates could accumulate and, at least in theory, doctors of theology or of either law are equal and in the highest class. But a survey taken in the Canterbury province (excluding London) in 1366 discovered 80 lawyers, 45 M.A.s (or magistri), 10 theologians, 4 physicians, and 1 graduate with degrees in both medicine and law among the 140 graduate pluralists. Recent work on the early Tudor period has found little change in this situation.[98]

Much more remains to be learned about the issues that have been raised here, and many other themes wait to be explored. In some ways the subject is too large and the details too rich to be treated solely in the mode attempted here. But if there is now a general consensus about the overall role of university men in the church and state in the fifteenth and early sixteenth century, historians must still be very careful to include all the important questions, to search out all the relevant evidence, and to view affairs through the self-interested, but often perceptive, eyes of contemporary participants before we admire too easily our collective portrait. (The fourteenth century, on the other hand, remains an unsolved problem.) This whole subject is rather like a large ball of yarn that consists not of one unbroken thread but of many strands of different length, quality, and hue. For several years now, a number of scholars have been trying to weave those strands into a variegated cloak. Although the slightest pressure may split the quite fragile seams that join one historian's work to that of another, the current aura of intensive research and healthy debate should produce an acceptable garment before it is too far out of fashion.

To the people of the later Middle Ages, the university man might be a "wise clerk" or a "cunning man" who settled arguments and solved problems in the village and who was sometimes awesome and sometimes merely useful as he practiced divination and cast horoscopes.[99] Some people might possibly have applied to former students the contemporary proverb that "of all treasure, cunning is the flower."[100] Poets and preachers, frequently graduates themselves, might expose the corrupt, foolish, presumptuous, or long-winded *magister* to the bite of their sly, populist wit or the wrath of their righteous indignation.[101] A few people might fret, with little justification, about the immorality or unruliness of medieval students.[102] But for most people, a university alumnus was a figure of authority: the lawyer, doctor, priest, teacher, administrator, and expert. As such he stood in a crucial place in his society: he linked the various halls of power to the town and village, learned culture with popular culture. He might be an oppressive adversary or a useful and necessary facilitator. He commanded power and respect not as intellectual *per se*, but rather as the possessor of certain skills or as the holder of an office that he had been trained or certified to perform during his years at the university. If this is right, then Andrew Borde for once missed the mark when he reported a jest of John Scoggin, M.A.:

> A Master of Art is not worth a fart
> Except he be in schools;
> A Bachelor of Law is not worth a straw
> Except he be among fools[103]

The university man might be the local boy who made good or the son of a neighbor come home to serve as the parish vicar or the bailiff of the manor. He was one of the village and yet different. The historian of late medieval students must make sense of these dichotomies.

For the historiographical context of this article, including citations to a considerable secondary literature which need not be duplicated here, see my "Patronage Patterns and Oxford Colleges, ca. 1300–ca. 1530," in L. Stone, ed., *The University in Society* (Princeton, 1974), pp. i., 111–49; T. Aston, "Oxford's Medieval Alumni," *Past and Present* 74 (1977): 3–40; and T. Aston, G. D. Duncan, and T. A. R. Evans, "The Medieval Alumni of the University of Cambridge," *P & P* 86 (1980): 9–86, which was kindly shown to me by the authors, but after this paper was completed (1978). Reference throughout is, of course, also made to the late A. B. Emden's *A Biographical Register of the University of Oxford to 1500*, 3 vols. (Oxford, 1957–59), hereafter cited as *BRUO*, and *A Biographical Register of the University of Oxford A.D. 1501 to 1540* (Oxford, 1974), hereafter cited as *BRUO, 1501-40*. I have used the standard abbreviations for historical periodicals, English public records, and academic degrees (e.g., B.C.L.= Bachelor of Civil [Roman] Law; B.Cn.L= Bachelor of Canon

Law; D.U.J.=Doctor of Both [canon and civil] Laws; M. =Master or *Magister*; D.Th. =- Doctor of Theology).

Research for this article and for related studies has been aided by support from the Penrose Fund of the American Philosophical Society, the University Research Institute at the University of Texas at Austin, the Folger Shakespeare Library, and the American Council of Learned Societies – to all of whom I am very grateful.

I would like to thank James Kittelson, Pamela Transue, and Joseph H. Lynch of the Ohio State University for a forum and for useful criticism, and my colleagues in the History of the University of Oxford project (especially the editors Trevor Aston, Jeremy Catto, and James McConica, and my fellow "social historians," Sir Richard Southern and Jean Dunbabin) for advice and criticism of my work.

1. Trevor Aston, "Oxford's Medieval Alumni," *Past and Present* 74 (1977):3. Recent supplements to the classical works of Rashdall and d'Irsay are A. B. Cobban, *The Medieval Universities* (London, 1975) and J. Verger, *Les universités au moyen âge* (Paris, 1973). See also the valuable collection of essays and references in J. IJsewijn and J. Paquet, eds., *The Universities in the Late Middle Ages/Les universités à la fin du moyen âge* (Louvain, 1978); and J. Paquet, "Recherches sur l'universitaire 'pauvre' au moyen âge," *Revue belge de philologie et d'histoire* 56 (1978): 301–53. I am currently revising and expanding my 1976 Princeton thesis into a volume provisionally entitled *University Scholars and English Society in the Later Middle Ages*, to be published in 1984. For other aspects of the roles of universities and graduates in late medieval society, see my "Universities as Religious Authorites in the Later Middle Ages and Reformation," in G. F. Lytle, ed., *Reform and Authority in the Medieval and Reformation Church* (Washington, 1981), esp. the note on p. 97.

2. H. Kearney, *Scholars and Gentlemen* (London, 1970), p. 15, expresses an enlightened version of this view.

3. Aston, "Oxford's Medieval Alumni," pp. 5, 27, 34-35.

4. I have argued the case for New College (founded 1379) as the model for late medieval Oxford in all of my articles and in my forthcoming book. For some insights into that college as an institution, see J. Buxton and P. Williams, eds., *New College Oxford 1379-1979* (Oxford, 1979) and Roger Custance, ed., *Winchester College* (Oxford, 1982).

5. See especially my "The Social Origins of Oxford Students in the late Middle Ages: New College, c. 1380-1510," in Ijsewijn and Paquet, *Universities in the Late Middle Ages*, pp. 426-54.

6. It is also commonly assumed that, because of the destruction and diffusion of ecclesiastical and other sources on the Continent, no comparable analysis of the careers of late medieval European students will be possible. Perhaps this is true. If so, then the English pattern may take on an even greater significance in our understanding of universities *in toto*, and thus we must be as complete in our research as possible. But I also want to demonstrate to my colleagues the wide variety of sources we all must plough before we have to abandon hopes for a more fruitful harvest. Another approach is to study masters, of whatever university, as they operated in a particular locale. Several such studies of English dioceses are now in progress; but for the moment, see Christine Renardy, *Le monde des maîtres universitaires du diocèse de Liège, 1140-1350* (Paris, 1979).

7. *Statutes of the Colleges* (Oxford, 1853), vol. i; New College, vol. ii; =Stat. Coll.

8. I examined this debate in a lecture, "Thomas More's Dilemma and English Public Schools" (Folger Shakespeare Library, 1975) which will appear in a different form in my essays on Winchester College (see note 5) and in my books (see note 2).

9. For the most recent account of the relations of the Tudor university to its society, see V. Morgan, "Approaches to the History of the English Universities in the Sixteenth and Seventeenth Centuries," in G. Klingenstein et al., eds., *Bildung, Politik und Gesselschaft* (Wien, 1978), pp. 136-64. (I owe this reference to Mordechai Feingold and R. J. W. Evans.)

For bibliography on prominent medieval English university graduates, see the notes to the Aston articles listed in n. 1.

10. See, for example, H. S. Bennet, "Medieval Ordination Lists in English Episcopal Records," in *Studies presented to Sir Hilary Jenkinson* (London, 1957), pp. 20–34; the best recent work on the sources for late medieval English ecclesiastical personnel is that of Joel Arthur Lipkin; see especially his "Pluralism in Pre-Reformation England: a quantitative analysis of ecclesiastical incumbency, c. 1490–1539" Ph.D. diss., Catholic University of America, 1979).

11. *Stat. Coll*, vol. i. (New College), pp. 64–65; cf. ibid., (Balliol) pp. 17–18; (Merton) pp. 6, 11, 27; (Oriel) 9; (Queen's) 15 (but also see 20); (All Souls) 66–67; (Lincoln) 13–14.

12. The careers followed by alumni of the monastic colleges or mendicant *studia* cannot be treated in the same fashion, since both their vows and the orders of their superiors determined and limited their pursuits. Monks and friars were trained primarily to act as teachers and preachers, usually in their own houses, but the educated religious were also called on to lead their orders and communities and to act as administrators of monastic properties. From the reign of Richard II through that of Henry VII, at least 135 Oxford monk-scholars became abbots or priors (12 were later elevated to bishoprics), more than 20 served parish livings, and 4 were royal chaplains. Among their more secular pursuits, 64 monks functioned as lawyers and administrators in ecclesiastical matters within their order, and 11 also acted in other cases; 12 monks were selected to go on embassies to various princes abroad. (See especially, Barbara Harvey, "The Monks of Westminster and the University of Oxford," in F. R. H. DuBoulay et al., eds., *The Reign of Richard II* [London, 1971]; R. B. Dobson, *Durham Priory, 1400-1450* [Cambridge, 1973]; and, of course, D. Knowles, *The Religious Orders in England*, 3 vols. [Cambridge, 1948–59]). The works of Little, Hinnebusch, and others (A. G. Little, *The Grey Friars in Oxford* [Oxford, 1891]; W. A. Hinnebusch, *The Early English Friars Preachers* [Rome, 1951]; F. Roth, *The English Austin Friars, 1249-1538*, 2 vols. [New York, 1966]), have described the very important role played by Oxford-trained friars in the institutional and intellectual life of their several orders, and thus further details are unnecessary here. But it should be noted that 24 Oxford-trained mendicants became bishops during this period, and at least 25 acted as parish priests. Proportionally fewer friars were found among lawyers and administrators (about 35), 8 were chaplains to the king or queen, and 6 ambassadors were either Franciscans or Dominicans. Most of the religious scholars seem to have been content to practice their established rules and live outwardly unremarkable lives in their houses.

13. For a very preliminary analysis, see my "A University Mentality in the later Middle Ages: the pragmatism, humanism, and orthodoxie [sic] of New College, Oxford," in *Genese et Dubuts du Grand Schisme d'Occident* (Colloques Internationaux du Centre National de la Recherche Scientifique, no. 586: Avignon, 1978) (Paris, 1980). pp. 201–30. This paper was originally written in 1976 and was printed without a chance to make additions or corrections at the proof stage; a revised version appears in Custance, *Winchester College*, ch. 5, and a much more comprehensive treatment will comprise the final section of my *University Scholars and English Society*.

Since this paper was originally drafted and delivered, several studies have appeared that provide important insights into questions of lay literacy in the later Middle Ages and the relationship between worldly learning and ambition and the universities. See especially M. T. Clancy, *From Memory to Written Record* (London, 1979); A. Murray, *Reason and Society in the Middle Ages* (Oxford, 1978); J. K. Hyde, "Some Uses of Literacy in Venice and Florence in the 13th and 14th Centuries," *TRHS* (5) 29 (1979): 109–28; J. Verger, "Remarques sur l'enseignement des arts dans les universités du Midi à la fin du moyen âge," *Annales du Midi* 91 (1979): 355–81; and L. G. Duggan, "The Unresponsiveness of the Late Medieval Church: a reconsideration," *Sixteenth Century Journal* 9 (1978): 3–26.

14. The Henrician Reformation, perhaps ironically, and the subsequent developments of

political humanism and religious piety separated and realigned these roles. (For one attempt to look anew at the question of lay vs. clerical religious roles, see my "Religion and the Lay Patron in Reformation England," in G. F. Lytle and S. Orgel, eds., *Patronage in the Age of the Renaissance* [Princeton, 1981]). It may well be true, however, that, as in the case of the ostensibly higher social status of sixteenth century students, later developments in part simply recongized, officially and symbolically, social changes that had begun much earlier. (See the extensive debate between Lawrence Stone, Joan Simon, David Cressy et al. in the pages of *Past and Present* [1,964ff.]; Elizabeth Russell, "The Influx of Commoners into the University of Oxford before 1581," *E.H.R.* 92 [1977]: 721–45; my "The Social Origins of Oxford Students in the Late Middle Ages," [n. 5]; and J. McConica, "Scholars and Commoners in Renaissance Oxford," in Stone, *University in Society*, 1:151–81).

15. R. J. Mitchell, *John Tiptoft* (London, 1938), p. 18 passim.

16. R. Weiss, *Humanism in England in the Fifteenth Century*, rev. ed. (Oxford, 1967), ch. 7.

17. *BRUO*, 2:683.

18. Ibid., 1:499–500; 3:1,750–52; E. F. Jacob, "Archbishop John Stafford," *TRHS* (5) 12 (1962): 1–24.

19. For a beginning, although much research remains to be done, see F. Pegues, " 'Clericus' in Legal Administration of 13th Century England," *E.H.R.* 71 (1956): 526–29; G. P. Cuttino, "King's Clerks and the Community of the Realm," *Speculum* 29 (1954): 395–409; A. L. Brown, "The King's Councillors in 15th Century England," *TRHS* (5) 19 (1969): 95–118; J. L. Kirby, "Councils and Councillors of Henry IV, 1399–1413," *TRHS* (5) 14 (1964): 35–65; J. R. Lander, "Council, Administration and Councillors, 1461 to 1485," *BIHR* 32 (1959): 138–80; J. Otway-Ruthven, *The King's Secretary and the Signet Office in the XV Century* (Cambridge, 1939); A. L. Brown, "The Privy Seal Clerks in the Early 15th Century," in *The Study of Medieval Records*, ed. D. A. Bullough and R. L. Storey (Oxford, 1971), pp. 260–81. I had been unable to consult a number of recent articles and English theses in this field when I originally wrote this section. For numerous further citations, see my *University Scholars and English Society*.

20. In addition to the works cited in the previous note, see A. Judd, *The Life of Thomas Bekynton* (Chichester, 1961) and important current work by Griffith, Richardson, and Pronay.

21. Calculated from the public records as recorded in *BRUO*; for diplomats, see especially J. Ferguson, *English Diplomacy* (Oxford, 1972), ch. 8.

22. In addition to notes 20–22, J. R. Strayer, *On the Medieval Origins of the Modern State* (Princeton, 1970), 72, passim.

23. *BRUO*, 2:1,236–37.

24. *Forme of Curry, a roll of ancient English Cookery, compiled about A.D. 1390, by the master-cooks of King Richard II*, ed. by an antiquary [S. Pegge], (London, 1780), prologue.

25. For quick reference to the basic facts and the massive literature, see *BRUO*, 1:597–98; 2:1,305–8.

26. J. C. Wedgwood, *History of Parliament: Biographies of the Members of the Commons House, 1439–1509* (London, 1936), pp. 857–58 (Wedgwood); *L.P.F.D. Henry VIII*, i., (ii), 1545; iii., (i), 396.

27. Wedgwood, *History of Parliament*, pp. 166–67.

28. *C.P.R. 1476–85*, 343, 392, *1485–94*, 180, 350, 475, 645; *1494–1509*, 115, 145, 246, 290, 461, 506; *L.P.F.D. Henry VIII*, i. (i) 65, 260, 668; PRO, PCC wills, old ref. 2 Fetiplace.

29. *BRUO*, 1:131–32.

30. Ibid. 3:1,890; Wedgewood, *History of Parliament*, p. 865; PRO, PCC wills, 34 Bennett.

31. *BRUO,* 2:816.

32. *C.P.R. 1413–16,* 297; *1446–52,* 309; *C.C.R. 1447–54,* 130.

33. *Victoria County History* (hereafter cited as *VCH*), *Hampshire* (hereafter cited as *Hants.*), iv.528; *C.C.R. 1435–41,* 81; *Cal. Fine Rolls 1445–52,* 37.

34. *C.P.R. 1441–6,* 400, 479; *1467–77,* 196, 199, 351, 463, 633; Eleanor Searle, *Lordship and Community* (Toronto, 1974), p. 428 and ch. 4; *BRUO,*1:215; M. Clough, ed., *The Book of Bartholomew Bolney* (Lewes, 1964).

35. *VCH, Hants.* 3:259–67; *BRUO,* 3:1,357.

36. Wedgwood, *History of Parliament,* p. 516; *BRUO,* 2:1,074.

37. Strayer, *On the Medieval Origins,* 73.

38. *BRUO* 2:990.

39. Ibid., 2:1,037–38.

40. Ibid., 3:2,039; *C.P.R. 1494–1509,* 646; *L.P.F.D. Henry VIII,* i, (i), 220.

41. R. Somerville, *History of the Duchy of Lancaster* (London, 1953), pp. 190, 263, and a list of officers.

42. A. E. Levett, *Studies in Manorial History* (Oxford, 1938), p. 26.

43. See the excellent recent work by Carole Rawcliffe, *The Staffords, Earl of Stafford and Dukes of Buckingham 1394–1521* (Cambridge, 1978), chs. 3–9; Carole Rawcliffe, "Baronial Councils in the Later Middle Ages," in C. Ross, ed., *Patronage, Pedigree and Power in Later Medieval England* (Gloucester, 1979), pp. 87–108.

44. *Statutes of the Realm* (London, 1810–22), 2:426–29; cf. 113–14, 240–41.

45. See *BRUO,* 1:157–59 (Bekynton); 3:1,831 (Swanwich), 1,608–10 (Russell), 1,933–34 (Upton); F. J. Furnivall, ed., *The Babees Book* (London, 1868), pp. 115–228.

46. C. Ross, *The Estates and Finances of Richard Beauchamp, Earl of Warwick* (Warwick, 1956), 8ff.

47. York, Borthwick Inst., Reg. Neville, ii., fo. 18v; i., fo. 41, 45v; *BRUO,* 3:1,506–7; *C.P.R. 1483–86,* pp. 449, 453, 498, 509–10, 542.

48. Calculated from F. R. H. Du Boulay, *The Lordship of Canterbury* (London, 1966), appendix B; for the most recent work on Canterbury, see C. Harper-Bill, "The *Familia,* Administrators and Patronage of Archbishop John Morton," *J. Rel. Hist.* 10 (1979): 236–52.

49. *BRUO,* 3:1,501–2. Much other work on episcopal households by R. Haines, M. Aston, and others will be analyzed in the introduction to my *A Bishop's Household in the Late Middle Ages* (to appear shortly).

50. PRO, C1/47/58.

51. For example, Knowles, *Religious Orders,* 1:271, n.2.

52. See, for example, C. and K. Sisam, eds., *Oxford Book of Medieval English Verse* (Oxford, 1970), pp. 129–31.

53. F. N. Robinson, ed., *The Works of Geoffrey Chaucer* (Boston, 1957), p. 81.

54. E. F. Jacob, *Essays in Later Medieval History* (Manchester, 1968), 70f., 77–78.

55. *BRUO,* 3:1,962–63.

56. Ibid., 3:1,904.

57. London, Guildhall, Commissary Court of London Wills, 9171/2, fo. 278.

58. PRO, PCC wills, 34 Holder.

59. J. Challoner-Smith, "Wills preserved in the Probate Registry, Winchester," *Papers & Proc. Hants Field Club & Archaeol. Soc.* 10 (1927): 54; *BRUO, 1501–40,* p. 603.

60. PRO, PCC wills, 9 Fetiplace; I consider this problem in a forthcoming study of late medieval and Renaissance, and Reformation adolescents.

61. PRO, E 315/330, fo. 49; J. H. Harvey, *English Medieval Architects* (London, 1954), pp. 105-6.

62. York, Cathedral, Reg. of Wills (1493-1543), fo. 29; *BRUO*, 2:1,089.

63. C. H. Haskins, *Studies in Medieval Culture* (N. Y., 1958), p. 20ff.

64. Lytle, "Social Origins of Oxford Students" Wedgwood, *History of Parliament*, pp. 516-17, 630-31; *VCH, Berks.* 3:237.

65. London, Guildhall, Comm. Ct. of London Wills, 9171/5, fo. 124v; PRO, C 140/28; *VCH, Essex*, 4:192, 199; New College Archives, 9757, fo. 8v-9, hereafter cited as NCA.

66. Winchester College Muniments, 2378, hereafter cited as WCM. See also WCM 2379, 2486a-2491, 2511.

67. WCM, 2030; see also WCM, 2036, 14599.

68. London, Guildhall, Comm. Ct. of London Wills, 9171/4, fo. 216v.

69. *BRUO*, 2:1,241.

70. J. H. Upton, *History of Writtle Church* (Guildford, 1930), pp. 106-9; New College, Warden Sewell's Register, 42; *BRUO*, 2:914; 1:107, 243 (Emden did not realize that the last two entries refer to the same man).

71. NCA, 9746, p. 499.

72. I. Jeayes, "Deeds from a Parish Chest," *Trans. Essex Archaeol. Soc.*, n.s., 19 (1927-30): 45, n. 28.

73. For example, William Smyth of Heyford, Oxon.: *BRUO*, 3:1,722; NCA, 9745, fo. 237v-8.

74. W. O. Ault, "The Village Church and the Village Community in Medieval England," *Speculum* 45 (1970): 197-215; Merton Coll. Rec., 3100; PRO, PCC wills, F.2. Porch; *VCH, Berks.*, 4:238ff.; *Cal. Inq. Post Mortem*, 14:167-72; J. H. Lumby, ed., *A Calendar of the Norris Deeds* (Manchester, 1939), pp. 16-19, 103, 108-17, 134.

75. For example, in Worcestershire, see A. F. Leach, ed., *Documents Illustrating Early Education in Worcester* (London, 1913), pp. 932ff.; T. Nash, *Collection for the History of Worcestershire* (London, 1781), 2:225; and also the examples of "lay" activities cited earlier.

76. *BRUO*, 1;584.

77. *C.P.R. 1467-77*, 42.

78. Ludwig von Pastor, *The History of the Popes* (N.Y., 1969 ed.), 1:56.

79. A. F. Leach, ed., *Educational Charters and Documents* (Cambridge, 1911), pp. 424-25.

80. J. Gairdner, ed., *Paston Letters* (London, 1872-5), no. 716.

81. Among many, see especially M. Bowker, *The Secular Clergy in the Diocese of Lincoln 1495-1520* (Cambridge, 1968); P. Heath, *The English Parish Clergy on the Eve of the Reformation* (London, 1969); K. Edwards, *The English Secular Cathedral in the Middle Ages*, 2d ed. (Manchester, 1967); Lipkin, "Pluralism in Pre-Reformation England."

82. For citations and analyses of this literature, see J. A. Yunck, *The Lineage of Lady Meed* (South Bend, 1963), pp. 143ff., 296ff.; H. Maynard-Smith, *Pre-Reformation England* (London, 1963), p. 54 and n.; J. W. Blench, *Preaching in England in the late Fifteenth and Sixteenth Centuries* (Oxford, 1964), pp. 326ff.; the various works of G. Owst; and Lytle, "Patronage Patterns and Oxford Colleges."

83. H. Anstey, ed., *Epistolae Academicae Oxon.* (Oxford, 1898), 2:359ff; H. Wharton, *Anglia Sacra* (London, 1961), 2:367; E. Dudley, *The Tree of Commonwealth*, ed. D. M. Brodie (Cambridge, 1948), pp. 63-64.

84. Lytle, "Patronage Patterns and Oxford Colleges," passim.

85. Aston, Duncan, Evans, "Medieval Alumni of the University of Cambridge,"; W. J.

Courtenay, "The Effect of the Black Death on English Higher Education," *Speculum* 55 (1980):696–714, doubts the claim that Oxford declined significantly in size in the second half of the fourteenth century; R. L. Storey in private communications and in his chapter in the New College history (see note 5) has different views on the role of college advowsons in patronage. I am grateful to all of these critics for interesting points, even those I cannot ultimately accept.

86. See my *University Scholars and English Society* for my own reassessment of the problem and for citations of further research and debate.

87. Joel A. Lipkin has already completed the computerization of all the bishop's registers of institutions for the late fifteenth and early sixteenth centuries; I have begun working on the previous one hundred and fifty years. See Margaret Bowker, *The Henrician Reformation* (Cambridge, 1981).

88. Oxford, Jesus College, MS. XII, fo. 205v.

89. M. Gibbs and J. Lang, *Bishops and Reform, 1217–1272* (Oxford, 1932); J. R. H. Highfield, "The English Hierarchy in the Reign of Edward III," *TRHS* 6 (1956):115–38; the 1377–1509 figures are my own research.

90. Lytle, "Patronage Patterns and Oxford Colleges."

91. *Proc. and Ord. Privy Council*, pp. vi., 168; see also, L. R. Betcherman, "The Making of Bishops in the Lancastrian Period," *Speculum* 41 (1966): 397–419.

92. G. Post, "Masters' Salaries and Student Fees in the Medieval Universities," *Speculum* 7 (1932):181–98; G. Post, K. Giocarinis, and R. Kay, "The Medieval Heritage of a Humanistic Ideal," *Traditio* 11 (1955):195–234; B. Tierney, *Medieval Poor Law* (Berkeley, 1959), p. 147, n. 28.

93. R. Pace, *De Fructu qui ex Doctrina Percipitur*, ed. F. Manley and R. S. Sylvester (New York., 1967), pp. 22–23.

94. *Philobiblon*, ed. M. Maclagan (Oxford, 1960), pp. 100–101; see also J. Mann, *Chaucer and the Literature of Estates Satire* (Cambridge, 1973), p. 79ff.; and note 83 above.

95. *BRUO*, 3:1,613.

96. W. Caxton, *Aesop: Life and Fables* (Westminster, 1484), Sig. s. 6ʳ–6ᵛ. The best modern accounts of Caxton's own additions to his sources are N. F. Blake, *Caxton's Own Prose* (London, 1973) and, for Aesop especially, R. T. Lenaghan, *Caxton's Aesop* (Cambridge, Mass., 1967).

97. R. Donaldson, "Patronage and the Church: a study in the social structure of the secular clergy in the diocese of Durham (1311–1540)," (Ph.D. diss., U. of Edinburgh, 1955), pp. i., 343–45.

98. See C. J. Godfrey, "Pluralists in the Province of Canterbury in 1366," *J. Eccl. H.* 11 (1960):23–40; and the work of J. A. Lipkin.

99. K. Thomas, *Religion and the Decline of Magic* (New York, 1971), chs. 2 and 8.

100. F. J. Furnivall, ed., *Queen Elizabeth's Academy* (London, 1898), pp. 68–70.

101. For example, Robinson, ed., *Works of Geoffrey Chaucer*, p. 101; Blench, *Preaching in England*, passim; Owst, various works, passim.

102. A. B. Cobban, "Medieval Student Power," *P & P* 53 (1971): 28–66; for England, see my *University Scholars and English Society* (see note 1).

103. *The First and Best Parts of Scoggins Jests* (London, 1626), Sig. 1.

UNIVERSITY STUDIES AND THE CLERGY
IN PRE-REFORMATION GERMANY

James H. Overfield

 spectacular expansion of educational opportunities occurred in Germany during the one hundred and fifty years before the onset of the Protestant Reformation. Throughout the Empire, countless towns and cities established local schools or expanded existing ones. The appearance of printed books lowered the cost of reading and made available to the German public hundreds of titles that had been inaccessible or exorbitantly expensive. The most striking development, however, was the wave of university foundations from the late fourteenth to early sixteenth century. Before the establishment of the University of Vienna in 1377, no university existed in the German-speaking area of the Empire. Individuals seeking advanced academic training had to travel to Prague, Bologna, Paris, or another foreign university city. By 1508 this situation had been radically altered. In that year the foundation of the University of Frankfurt-an-der-Oder brought the number of German universities to thirteen. In the decade before the Reformation, these institutions annually were attended by an estimated six thousand students.[1]

In what ways, if any, did these new opportunities for university training affect educational levels within the pre-Reformation Catholic clergy? How many university students later entered careers in the Church? How many clergymen studied at the universities? Were there any discernible patterns of change in the decades directly preceding the Reformation era? For Reformation scholars

254

these are questions of obvious interest and importance. If it could be shown that clerical educational standards were stagnant or declining before the Reformation, it would be justifiable to conclude that the meager performance of poorly trained priests was a significant factor in stimulating the anticlericalism that drove so many Germans into the arms of Lutheranism. The subject is of equal significance to students of German university history. Even before the onset of the Reformation, the German universities had entered a period of momentous change marked both by increased state control and the abandonment of traditional scholasticism for a curriculum that reflected the ideals of Renaissance humanism. Understanding of these changes would be clarified if one could show they were preceded or accompanied by shifts in the clerical orientation of the students.

If, however, such questions are interesting and important, answers have been elusive and difficult. Sixty years ago a German scholar, Herman Lauer, commented, "A great darkness lies over the educational situation of the clergy at the end of the Middle Ages."[2] Today, despite deep, ongoing, scholarly interest in the pre-Reformation era, the subject continues to be discussed in terms that are vague, overly general, and based on highly fragmentary evidence. This study seeks to enhance our understanding of the clergy's educational status by evaluating previous work on the subject, discussing relevant methodological problems, and presenting new data on clerical matriculations at the pre-Reformation German universities. Finally, on the basis of our current knowledge, it offers some speculative ideas about the impact of universities on the late medieval Church in Germany. It suggests that despite the pious hopes of university founders and patrons, the institutions they established created new tensions and frustrations that weakened rather than strengthened the Church as it entered the tumultuous era of the Reformation.

Previous evaluations of the clergy's educational status have been based almost exclusively on literary sources. This in turn explains why most historians have assumed that educational standards

remained abysmally low and perhaps were falling as the Reformation approached. For it is an indisputable fact that in late medieval
Germany denunciations of the clergy's educational deficiencies
were commonplace. The unknown author of the *Reformatio Sigismundi*, the well-known reformist treatise of the 1430s, succinctly
voiced a complaint later repeated by countless critics of the
Church: "We all know what pain and harm have been occasioned
by the practice of beneficing unlearned and unqualified priests.
Such men cannot preach the gospel, nor can they administer the
sacraments. We call such men 'blind guides.' Follow them and you
fall into a ditch." He demanded that any clergyman appointed to a
parish church should hold at minimum a Bachelor of Arts degree.[3]
Several decades later, an Osnabrück friar, Johann Schippower,
scornfully commented that German priests had the education of
donkeys, understood almost nothing of holy scripture, "could neither write nor speak Latin and indeed had hardly learned how
recite the Lord's Prayer in German."[4] Such a dim view was also
reflected throughout the pamphlet *Institutio vitae sacerdotalis*, first
published in 1485 by the abbot of Sponheim, Johann Trithemius:
unlettered men are raised to the priesthood; bishops are indifferent; study of the scripture is unknown; knowledge of Latin is
pathetically low.[5] Some critics even sought to quantify the clergy's
shortcomings. Felix Faber, the Dominican chronicler, stated that
in 1490 out of one thousand priests in the diocese of Ulm not one
had a university degree;[6] Jacob Wimpheling, the Alsatian humanist, described a situation in Strassburg that was only marginally
better: there the priesthood in the 1490s included one Bachelor of
Theology and three Bachelors of Arts.[7] Even prestigious members
of the hierarchy conceded that priestly educational levels were
deplorably low. Uriel of Gemmingen, the archbishop of Mainz
from 1508 to 1514, admitted in a letter circulated among the Mainz
clergy in 1512 that "In our diocese can be found large numbers of
clergy, among them some with the cure of souls which we must
painfully admit are largely uneducated and ignorant; are incapable
either through word or example to inspire their flocks to the path
of eternal life; indeed are completely incompetent to explain the
sacraments and teach the word of God."[8]

Although such pronouncements are important gauges of public opinion on the eve of the Reformation, it cannot be assumed that they accurately reflect the true level of learning among German clergymen. Many of the harshest critics of the late medieval church had backgrounds that undoubtedly prejudiced their views. Faber, Trithemius, and Schippower, for example, were all regular clerics, whose feuds with the secular clergy were becoming more frequent and acrimonious as the Reformation approached. The author of the *Reformatio*, Wimpheling, Trithemius, and even Archbishop Uriel were reformers of varying degrees of commitment, and they too must have been tempted to exaggerate the abuses they sought to publicize and correct.

Wimpheling is the best example of the dangers inherent in utilizing literary sources. For as the contentious humanist moved from controversy to controversy, his rhetoric about clerical learning showed remarkable contrasts. As an academically trained priest who felt his own career had been stymied because of simony and nepotism, much that he wrote scathingly censured church leaders for their failure to reward educational achievement.[9] But as a secular priest who embroiled himself in several feuds with the regulars, he was also capable of buoyant enthusiasm when describing scholarly accomplishments of the secular clergy. In 1506 he wrote: "God is my witness, in the six Rhenish bishoprics, I know countless persons among the secular clergy who are morally pure and well-endowed with broad learning suitable for the cure of souls. I am also familiar both in cathedrals and parish churches not with just a few, but many distinguished prelates, canons and vicars, all men of most blameless reputation, complete piety, generosity and humility."[10]

Furthermore, some reformers, although convinced that many aspects of the Church were deplorable and alarming, were indifferent to the "abuses" resulting from the clergy's supposedly deficient training. Synodal records from the Diocese of Speyer, for example, show that pre-Reformation bishops continually denounced the prevalence of drunkenness, gambling, swearing, and concubinage among their priests. But not once is concern expressed about educational shortcomings.[11]

Less frequently than literary sources, university matriculation records have also been used as a source to measure the clergy's educational interests and attainments. These documents are accessible, since with the exception of the University of Mainz, whose early records have been largely destroyed, the *matricula* of every German university founded before the Reformation has been published. The other great advantage of such records is that they provide continuous data from the late fourteenth century down to the Reformation and, in some cases, beyond.

Like literary sources, however, university matriculation rolls must be used with care. In theory they contain the name of every individual who presented himself to the rector, swore to uphold the university's statutes, paid certain fees and, having had his name recorded, could officially begin his studies. The rector, for his part, was required not only to list the student's name, place of origin and the amount of payment but also to note nobles, paupers, and members of the clergy. Seemingly, therefore, matriculation records provide precise data on both overall enrollment patterns and the social and professional background of at least three important groups within the student population. Regrettably, this is not the case. On the one hand, they include the names of many nonstudents, for at most universities anyone who had any business with the university was expected to enroll. Thus along with students one finds the names of professors, servants, apothecaries, tutors, merchants, surgeons, and even medical instrument makers. On the other hand some students, in the hope of escaping required payments or university discipline, never matriculated. Although the number of these nonregistered students is impossible to determine, the frequent attempts by university authorities to deal with this problem suggests it was not insubstantial.[12] Further difficulties and frustrations confront researchers who seek information on the social and professional background of students. New rectors were chosen twice a year, at the beginning of each semester. Although most seem to have conscientiously identified nobles, paupers, and clergy, some were notably careless. Thus all statistics based on matriculation records must be viewed as fairly accurate, but not precise, approximations of enrollment patterns.

258

As a basis for evaluating the importance of universities in training pre-Reformation clergymen, matriculation records can be used in three ways. First, postuniversity careers of matriculated students can be traced to establish the number who entered church careers. Second, given a list of clergymen from a particular diocese, monastery, or collegiate church, matriculation rolls can be examined to determine how many had attended universities. Third, since rectors generally identified clergymen in the matriculation records, statistics can be generated from the matriculation rolls themselves to measure changes over time in the number of clerical matriculants.

Historians have, on a limited basis, utilized all three approaches. The single attempt to compile biographical data on all matriculants at a single university over an extended period is Werner Kuhn's recent study, *Die Studenten der Universität Tübingen zwischen 1477 and 1534. Ihr Studium und ihre spätere Lebensstellung.*[13] Of the approximately 5,800 matriculants at the University of Tübingen between 1477 and 1534, he was able to find information on the later careers of 1,604 (just short of 28 percent). He found that 1,095 entered church careers (68 percent of those students about whom information was known or 19 percent of all matriculants); of these, 457 had been clerics at the time of matriculation, and Kuhn assumed, perhaps erroneously, that they all continued as churchmen after they left the university.[14] Other categories were as follows: law and government service, 314; scholars or academics, 110; medicine, 33; military, 13; notaries and advocates, 13; printers and bookbinders, 13; others, 13.[15]

If the percentage of students about whom Kuhn found information made up a random sample of the whole, his findings would be significant indeed. They would suggest that an overwhelming majority of Tübingen students later pursued church careers. This seems, however, not to have been the case. Of all professional groups in the late medieval and early Reformation period, clergymen were most likely to have left some historical record. Furthermore, the nature of Kuhn's sources dictated his conclusion that an overwhelming majority of Tübingen students went on to church careers. In particular he relied mainly on ordination registers from the diocese of Constance and on a series of Württemberg visitation records from the late 1530s. The latter provided a nearly complete list of all beneficed clergy in the territory at the time. Naturally many of the clergymen listed in these documents were found to have matriculated at Tübingen, which was just to the north of Constance and the only university in Württemberg. It is possible that if Kuhn had found data about all 5,800 matriculants, the number of clergy would not have been substantially higher.[16]

Several scholars have published studies in which they began with lists of clergymen and then investigated matriculation records to determine how many had enrolled at universities. Results have been inconclusive. Martin Brecht, for one, found that of the 200 Catholic priests who later became Lutheran ministers in the Duchy of Württemberg, 121 (60.5 percent) had matriculated at a university, most frequently the University of Tübingen.[17] But other scholars have achieved substantially lower results. Friedrich Wilhelm Oediger, for example, could verify university enrollment for only 19.8 percent of the 365 clergymen in the west German archdiaconate of Xanten around 1500.[18] Most writers have found the number of matriculation in their samples to have been around 40 percent.[19]

Such studies obviously expose the exaggerations of a man like Felix Faber, who claimed that in the 1490s the priesthood in Ulm included not a single university man. They also hold the greatest promise for establishing the true educational level of the pre-Reformation clergy. At present, however, they are too few in number to draw meaningful conclusions.[20] Further work is needed, especially for the years before the late fifteenth and early sixteenth centuries.

Only one scholar, Horst Rudolph Abe, has compiled and interpreted statistics on matriculating students at a German university who were already clergymen at the time of enrollment. He found that at the University of Erfurt clergymen were substantially represented among matriculants during the institution's first two decades, but thereafter their numbers steadily declined until by the early sixteenth century they made up only a small and insignificant group within the university's student population.[21] With a similar approach, this study offers statistics on clerical matriculations at twelve of the thirteen universities established in Germany before the Reformation.[22]

In table 1, which presents data on clerical enrollment patterns to 1520, matriculating clergymen have been divided into three categories. The first group includes members of the regular clergy, whose specific orders were sometimes mentioned, but in many cases were identified only by the Latin word *professus*, *religiosus*, *frater*, or *monachus*. For this reason no attempt has been made to classify the regulars according to order. The second category, canons, is comprised of secular clergy who held benefices in cathedral or collegiate chapters. They were normally designated by the term *canonicus*, but rectors did occasionally list the specific office or title the individual held within his chapter. Thus a canon might have been designated as *prepositus*, *decanus*, *archidiaconus*, *scholasticus*, *cantor*, or *custos*.

The third category includes the remainder of the secular clergy. This large and heterogeneous group has for the sake of convenience been designated the parish clergy, although it is self-evident that almost every cleric who matriculated at a university was a nonresident.[23] Individuals in this group were listed with one of the following titles: *rector*, *pastor*, *parochus*, *plebanus*, *curatus*, *vicarius*, *capellanus*, *altarista*, *sacerdos*, *presbyter*. Since the generally accepted meaning of these titles often changed during the medieval period and varied from region to region, it is difficult to determine exactly what function or role a rector had in mind when he identified a matriculant as a *parochus* rather than a *curatus*, or a *capellanus* rather than an *altarista*. According to Ludwig Pfleger, who has thoroughly examined this problem of terminology, the following usages seem to have been most common in fifteenth-century Germany.[24] *Rector* and *pastor* referred to a nonresident holder of a benefice from a parish church. *Parochus*, *plebanus*, *curatus*, and *vicarius* were, on the other hand, all used to describe priests with cure of souls. *Capellanus* denoted in some cases a priest who assisted a parish priest; in others it was used interchangeably with the term *altarista*, which referred to a priest whose sole function was to perform commemorative masses and who had no involvement with parishioners. Two terms, *sacerdos* and *presbyter*, identified an individual as an ordained priest, but implied nothing about his duties or functions.

Students designated in the matriculation records as *clerici* have not been included in table 1. Several factors determined this decision. The term *clericus*, first of all, does not appear in the records of all German universities. Numerous students were designated *clerici* in matriculation rolls of Cologne, Heidelberg, Greifswald, and Freiburg-im-Breisgau; but at Vienna, Erfurt, Wittenberg, Ingolstadt, Tübingen, Rostock, and Frankfurt-an-der-Oder, the term was used infrequently, and at Leipzig, not at all. Furthermore, even at universities where the term was common, its use often fluctuated wildly from one semester to the next. At the University of Greifswald, for example, in the summer semester of 1486, fifty-two out of fifty-seven enrolling students (91.2 percent) were designated as *clerici*; in the following semester, however, with a new rector, only one of fifty-seven matriculants was identified as a *clericus*. Similar, if less extreme inconsistencies could be cited in the records of other institutions and thus make statistical compilations rather meaningless.

An added consideration (and perplexity) is that in the matriculation records of several universities, the term *clerici* had all but disappeared by the end of the fifteenth century. At the University of Heidelberg, for example, *clerici* made up between 25 percent and 30 percent of all matriculants between 1401 and 1450; but from 1451 to 1500 they made up less than 10 percent, and between 1501 and 1520 fewer than ten *clerici* were listed out of the more than 2,900 students who enrolled. A similar trend is apparent at the University of Cologne, where until the 1470s the number of matriculating *clerici* normally averaged 20 percent, and in some five-year periods, for example between 1426 and 1430, reached levels as high as 45 percent. But after the 1470s students designated as *clerici* became rarities. With the exception of the years between

1511 and 1515, when sixty-three out of 1,662 matriculants (4 percent) were identified as *clerici*, their number never exceeded 1 percent in any other five-year period. In fact, between 1501 and 1510, only two *clerici* appear, and between 1516 and 1520, only one.

The most important reason for excluding *clerici* from the statistical tables is that they simply were not clergymen in any meaningful sense. The term was generally applied to individuals in minor orders and most typically referred to those who had taken the first tonsure. Such a step did not mean the abandonment of the lay world. Although first tonsure did imply clerical status, it was not regarded as an order or sacrament, but merely as a sign of pious intention. Canon law prescribed no age limits for receiving first tonsure, and it seems to have been conferred most commonly on many young boys who displayed early signs of piety or interest in their local church. The Cologne matriculation book records, for example, that Symonde de Oudorp, *clericus*, enrolled in 1409 at the age of eight.[25] Ecclesiastical demands and restrictions were minimal: celibacy was not required, secular careers could be pursued, and the clerkly state could be abandoned without difficulty or shame. Only when an individual entered the subdiaconate did a man assume responsibilities that separated him from the lay world. Some *clerici* in matriculation records undoubtedly went on to become ordained priests, but to determine their number accurately presents enormous problems, perhaps insurmountable for the researcher.[26]

Three patterns emerge among the institutions included in table 1. Vienna, Heidelberg, Cologne, Erfurt, and Tübingen show a high incidence of clerical matriculations during their early years and thereafter a steady decline. Cologne and Heidelberg experienced the heaviest enrollment of churchmen, a fact attributable to the greater number of ecclesiastical principalities and religious establishments in western Germany than in the more sparsely populated areas to the east. A second pattern is evident for Ingolstadt and Freiburg-im-Breisgau, where clerical enrollments never reached the same high percentages as at Cologne and Heidelberg but remained moderately high (just under 10 percent at Freiburg, and around 4.4 percent at Ingolstadt) from the universities' foundings to 1520. Greifswald might also be included in this second group, although the pattern of clerical matriculations was decidedly more erratic than at Freiburg or Ingolstadt. A third group includes Leipzig, Rostock, Wittenberg, and Frankfurt-an-der-Oder, where clerical enrollments were steady but at a substantially lower level than at the other institutions.

Combined totals for all twelve universities are presented in table 2. The percentage of clerical enrollments was highest between 1396 and 1405, then declined for the next three and a half decades and never exceeded 5 percent after 1441. In absolute terms, between 1386 and 1450 (approximately 394 vs. 350), clerical enrollments failed to keep pace with total matriculations, and as a result, clergymen comprised a smaller and smaller fraction of all matriculating students.[27]

As shown in table 3, the most striking trend within the clergy itself was the changing ratio between regular and secular matriculants. Between 1386 and 1450, an average of approximately 124 canons and 128 parish clergy enrolled during each five-year period; but from 1451 to 1520, the average numbers slumped to approximately 79 canons and 87 parish clergy. In contrast, an average enrollment of 98 regulars from 1386 to 1450 had risen to 228 per five-year period from 1451 to 1520. As a result, whereas between 1377 and 1400 seculars made up 86.7 percent of enrolling clergy, between 1501 and 1520 they comprised only 35.9 percent.

Pre-Reformation matriculation records offer only scanty information about the intended area of study of enrolling students. In fact the University of Cologne was the only institution where rectors generally recorded this information.[28] Table 4 summarizes faculty enrollments of all matriculants at Cologne from 1388 to 1520. It shows, not surprisingly, that of the four faculties, the faculty of arts was always the most heavily enrolled; it also shows that the percentage of matriculants who intended to pursue arts course studies increased dramatically from the late fourteenth to early sixteenth century. Enrollments in the advanced faculties, on the other hand, all steadily declined. The most substantial decrease was in the number of students who intended to study theology.

Table 5 shows, however, that clergymen at Cologne did not reflect the pattern of the general student population. Although the percentage of clergy studying arts increased between 1389 and 1520, law, in particular for regulars, was always the most heavily enrolled faculty. In the years between 1490 and 1520, almost 50 percent of all clergy about whom we have information intended to pursue legal studies. Meanwhile, interest in theology waned, most markedly among the seculars. In the university's early years, canons and parish clergy comprised better than two-thirds of all clergy who matriculated as theology students. Between 1491 and 1520 they made up only 15 percent.

What insights do these statistics offer into the condition of the pre-Reformation Catholic church in Germany? They suggest, first of all, despite the oft-repeated assertion that the late Middle Ages was a period of general deterioration for the religious orders, that university studies were in fact assuming greater prominence for the regulars as the Reformation approached. Two factors may help explain this trend. First, whereas many regulars previously had received philosophical or theological training in *studia* operated by the orders themselves, many of these institutions were abandoned in the fifteenth century as universities spread throughout the Empire. In 1503, for example, the general chapter of the Cistercians decided that houses in southern Germany should send all their scholars to the University of Heidelberg and abandon their own cloister schools.[29] As a result, the number of Cistercians who matriculated at Heidelberg increased dramatically; in fact between 1505 and 1515, out of the ninety-one regulars who matriculated, fifty-one were members of that order. Furthermore, in the view of some scholars, educational attainment in the late 1400s had increasingly become both a source of prestige and a prerequisite for advancement within the religious orders. Having examined the careers and educational attainments of monks in fifteenth-century Heilsbronn, D. Hermann Jordan concluded that "in the second

265

half of the fifteenth century it appears as if university studies and promotion became a requirement for the office or title of abbot."[30] Paul Nyhus has noted in a recent study a similar trend among the south German Franciscans on the eve of the Reformation. He argues that the friars' interest in learning "increased markedly" around 1500 and points out that from 1483 until the onset of the Reformation only doctors of theology held the office of provincial. He has written, "Increasingly they defined their ministry to society in terms of teaching and writing. . . . By the turn of the century intellectual prowess earned prestige in the order. The chronicles provide glowing accounts of disputations on philosophical and theological topics before packed audiences at provincial capitals."[31]

If, as the Reformation approached, professional advancement for regulars was increasingly tied to academic achievement, the opposite seems to have been true for secular clergymen. Ever since the time of the conciliar movement reformers had sought to guarantee academically trained priests a larger share of benefices. German representatives at the Council of Constance considered it particularly important to have university graduates in the hierarchy. After some months of negotiation and debate, the German Concordat of 1418 required that one-sixth of all canonicates and prebends in cathedral and collegiate churches were to be reserved for individuals who at minimum held the Master of Arts degree and had completed five years toward an advanced degree in theology or law. The Concordat further stipulated that parish churches with two thousand or more communicants should be reserved for priests with degrees in theology or law.[32] The provisions of the German Concordat remained a dead letter. Instead, the fifteenth century saw increasing numbers of rich benefices in cathedral chapters and episcopal sees reserved with papal approval for younger sons of noble families.[33] In the cathedral chapters of Cologne, Trier, Strassburg, Speyer, and many others, commoners could not legally become canons. Erasmus ironically remarked that Christ himself would have been denied a place in the Strassburg cathedral chapter because he lacked noble blood.[34] Other lucrative livings that were legally open to commoners were often filled on the basis of family ties and connections. The life of Thomas Wolf, Jr., a member of a wealthy Strassburg family, provides an example of the formidable barriers faced by a university-trained cleric who lacked influential relatives, friends, or patrons. At the age of seven, Wolf was named to a canonicate at St. Thomas Church in Strassburg, where his uncle, Thomas Wolf, Sr., was already a canon and where his great-uncle, Johann Hell, had held such a position before his death. By the time he began to study law at Bologna at the age of seventeen, he had also become a canon at St. Peter's in Strassburg. On completing his legal training, he steadily continued to collect livings until his death in 1509.[35] With justification Geyler von Kaisersberg denounced a church ruled by "ignorant, uneducated pleasure-seekers whose only claim to office was their noble birth and family connections."[36]

The aristocratic monopoly on lucrative livings in the Church was the most likely cause for the gradual fall in the number of matriculants among the secular clergy. A young noble or patrician whose family status assured him a place in a cathedral chapter and who in some cases may have received a canonicate at the age of seven or eight had little incentive to pursue serious university training. Furthermore, nonnoble clerics would be less likely to endure the physical and financial hardships of university studies once they realized that academic achievement would have little impact on professional advancement. Thus in a church where birth and connections were increasingly decisive factors in the competition for benefices and where the professional prospects for the university-trained were diminishing, Jacob Wimpheling must have expressed the frustration of many when he wrote in 1515, "Able, learned and virtuous priests who might raise the moral and professional level of the clergy abandon their studies because they see no prospect for advancement."[37]

It is interesting to speculate to what extent the professional frustrations of the university-trained clerics turned them against the Church they had originally hoped to serve and later drove them into the Protestant camp. It has been suggested that similar frustrations meaningfully contributed to the alienation and bitterness of intellectuals in both early seventeenth century England and pre-Revolutionary France. Mark H. Curtis, in his article "The Alienated Intellectuals of Early Stuart England," has argued that Oxford and Cambridge, after several decades of spectacular growth during the reign of Elizabeth, were by the early seventeenth century producing more graduates than Stuart society could effectively absorb.[38] By training too many graduates for too few jobs, the universities helped create, "an insoluble group of alienated intellectuals who individually and collectively became troublemakers in a period of growing discontent under the Stuart regime.[39] Robert K. Darnton, in his article, "Social Tensions and the Intelligentsia in Pre-Revolutionary France," has described a somewhat similar phenomenon in Paris in the decade before the Revolution.[40] Hundreds of would-be Voltaires flocked to the city, where they found neither the patronage nor the publishing outlets to enable them to fulfill their literary ambitions. Forced to write for the popular press or produce sensational fiction suitable for the vulgar reading tastes of the lower class, they flooded France with a body of scurrilous writing against crown and aristocracy, whom they blamed for thwarting their careers as writers. Did the conjunction of burgeoning university enrollments and contracting professional opportunities create similar tensions in the pre-Reformation German Church? If so, such tensions may help explain why the Church was subjected to more hostile and sustained criticism before the Reformation and why it was abandoned without remorse or hesitation by so many priests once the Reformation began.

In any case the university movement failed to loosen the aristocracy's grip on important positions in the hierarchy of the Church. It also appears that the university movement failed in any significant way to provide better preparation for young men destined for careers as parish priests. In fact, once their more sensational exaggerations are discounted, contemporary critics of the priesthood's educational deficiencies were close to the truth: despite the many new opportunities for learning, the parish ministry continued to be dominated by priests who were marginally trained and theologically naive.

In addition to the data derived from matriculation records, several other types of evidence point to this conclusion. We know, for example, that education standards for ordination in the fifteenth century remained minimal. An ability to pronounce and understand the literal meaning of the words of the mass and an acquaintance with the Church's most basic rites and doctrines continued to be the sole qualifications prescribed by most canonists. Even if rigorously enforced, such requirements necessitated neither university training nor for that matter any formal schooling.[41]

Furthermore, even when it can be demonstrated that a priest had once matriculated at a university, it does not mean that his university experience better prepared him for his calling to the parish ministry. Most matriculants—70 percent or more at most institutions—received no degree whatsoever. In other words most students remained at the university less than the one and a half or two years normally required for the Bachelor of Arts degree. Only 4 percent of all matriculants received their Master of Arts.[42] Attainment of advanced degrees was rarer still. Only 1.6 percent of all Tübingen matriculants between 1477 and 1534 received any degree in theology;[43] only twenty-three theological degrees were awarded at Ingolstadt between 1486 and 1505;[44] and at Leipzig, where in 1502 a student complained that "theology grows like grass in winter,"[45] only five doctorates in theology were awarded in the sixty-seven years between 1472 and 1539.[46] Since many theology students were members of religious orders and since most graduates remained in academic life or else entered government service, this left only a handful of priests with theological training to serve the church through preacherships or at the parish level.

Even for degree recipients, it is questionable how much their university experience helped prepare them for a priestly vocation. The arts course curriculum scrupulously avoided religious subjects and by the fifteenth century was largely a matter of mastering Aristotelian logic and its many medieval commentators. Rhetoric and literary studies were neglected altogether. Required lectures on ethics and metaphysics, which might have enriched a person involved in pastoral work, were often left untaught since professors found it difficult to say anything on these subjects without

269

embroiling themselves in potentially controversial theological issues. Late scholastic logic was a powerful and sophisticated analytical tool the mastery of which must have provided teacher and student with both intellectual challenge and satisfaction. Nonetheless, it is difficult to imagine how a knowledge of supposition theory, *modus significandi*, and syncategorematic particles would be of much use to a parish priest.[47]

Even theological studies were of marginal utility for the parish clergy, whose training had never been the principal mission of theological faculties. Instead, their role was to produce men who had mastered a body of highly technical and speculative theological knowledge; these men in turn were to serve as sources of authority within the Church and as teachers to communicate this knowledge to future generations. Thus theological training involved analysis and commentary on a number of theological issues raised in Peter Lombard's *Sentences* and criticism of previous scholastic writers. The methods of logic and dialectic learned in the arts course were the theologian's main analytical tools. The Bible, however, was not ignored. Bachelors and Doctors of Theology at every German university were required by statute to regularly lecture on the scriptures. But the lectures by the bachelors were brief, cursory, and superficial, and those of the doctors tended to be lengthy, rambling, and pedantic. Two examples from the University of Ingolstadt illustrate this point. Georg Eisenhart, a Bachelor of Theology, covered *Isaiah*, a book with sixty-six chapters, in the two and a half weeks between 21 October and 6 November 1481. On the other hand Georg Zingel, a Doctor of Theology, took four years to lecture on the twelve chapters of *Ecclesiastes* and seventeen years to lecture on the thirteen chapters of *Hebrews*.[48] Neither approach was likely to produce the kind of Biblical knowledge that a parish priest might effectively use in preaching or teaching.[49]

Unquestionably, the strongest indicator of deficient priestly training in the late medieval Church is provided by the fundamental changes in clerical preparation instituted by both Protestants and Catholics after the onset of the Reformation. The Lutherans took the lead. Confiscated Catholic properties were converted into seminaries or "monastery schools" whose sole purpose was to train suitable young men for the ministry.[50] After three or four years in such a school, formal theological training at a university usually followed. But this theological training differed markedly from that of the pre-Reformation era. Reforms inspired by Luther and Melanchthon at Wittenberg during the 1520s and early 30s later became standard at all Lutheran universities. The length of the theology course was shortened; the great scholastic *doctores* and their fine-spun commentaries were abandoned; Luther's writings, Melanchthon's *Loci communes*, and especially the Bible became the principal texts. The faculty's mission was broadened to include the preparation of competent ministers in addition to the training of academic theologians. Finally, as princely and city governments consolidated and centralized the administration of the Lutheran state churches, strict enforcement of ordination requirements and regular pastoral visitations became routine.[51]

Change came later within the Catholic church. Only in 1563 did the council of Trent adopt its famous decree calling for the establishment of diocesan seminaries for the training of priests. These new institutions were vocational schools designed to provide practical, not purely theological training. The Council dictated that students shall "study grammar, singing, ecclesiastical computation, and other useful arts, shall be instructed in Sacred Scripture, ecclesiastical books, the homilies of the saints, the manner of administering the sacraments, especially those things that seem adapted to the hearing of confessions and the rites and ceremonies."[52] After completing work at the seminary, students were encouraged to further their theological training at the university level. By the 1560s Catholic theology faculties, moribund or worse for at least three decades, were being revitalized by the Jesuits. At the same time, the Jesuits instituted comprehensive changes in the goals and methods of theological instruction that reflected the practical spirit of Ignatius. The theology course at Ingolstadt, Vienna, Cologne, Freiburg, and elsewhere came to be shortened, standardized, and simplified. The scholastic passion for disputation and controversy gave way to the acceptance of Aquinas as the preeminent theological authority. The study of scriptures received greater emphasis, as did aspects of theology relevant to pastoral care. The training of capable and dedicated men who could confidently and effectively preach, teach, and administer to the spiritual needs of the laity became a primary goal of Catholic theological education.[53]

Despite the obstacles and disappointments that accompany any new enterprise, it seems indisputable that the efforts to upgrade clerical education were generally successful. Whether Protestant or Catholic, clergymen around 1600 were entering their vocation with theological and practical preparation immeasurably superior to that of their clerical predecessors a century before. In fact, the very success of the effort created new and unprecedented difficulties. It was now being suggested that the sophisticated learning of some clergymen hindered their attempts to reach and influence the common mass of believers. In 1607 a Protestant official in the Rhineland expressed concern that the "courtly and ornate" language of the clergy had become incomprehensible to their less cultured listeners. As a result the people avoided church and resisted their minister's message because they resented his superior erudition.[55] This at least was one problem that the pre-Reformation Church had never had to confront.

1. The best source of information on enrollment patterns in the German universities remains Franz Eulenburg, *Die Frequenz der deutschen Universitäten*, Sächsische Akademie der Wissenschaften, Philologische-Historische Klasse, *Abhandlung* 54 (Leipzig, 1904). The figure of six thousand students is an educated guess. We know from matriculation records that just short of three thousand students began university studies per year. Disagreement exists, but most experts feel a typical student remained at a university for approximately two years.

2. Herman Lauer, "Die theologische Bildung des Klerus der Diözese Konstanz in der Zeit der Glaubenserneurerung," *Freiburger diözesan-Archiv*, N. F., 20 (1919): 120.

3. "The Reformation of Emperor Sigismund," in Gerald Strauss, ed., *Manifestations of Discontent in Germany before the Reformation* (Bloomington, Indiana, 1971), p. 12.

4. Cited in Alois Schröer, *Die Kirche in Westfalen vor der Reformation* (Münster, 1967), p. 202.

5. *Institutio vitae sacerdotalis* (Augsburg, 1500?), 16 leaves, no pagination.

6. Franz Falk, "Klerikales Proletariat am Ausgange des Mittelalters," *Historisch-politische Blätter* 112 (1893): 550; same figures cited in Willy Andreas, *Deutschland vor der Reformation* (Stuttgart, 1932), p. 103. The original quote may be found in *Felicis Fabri Monachi Ulmensis Historiae Suevorum, Libri II*, M. Goldast, ed. (Frankfurt/ Main, 1605), pp. 67, 68.

7. Cited in Ludwig Pfleger, "Untersuchungen zur Geschichte des Pfarrei-Instituts im Elsass," *Archiv für Elsässische Kirchengeschichte* 7 (1933): 79.

8. Fritz Hermann, *Die evangelische Bewegung zu Mainz im Reformationszeitalter* (Mainz, 1907); also cited in Andreas, *Deutschland vor der Reformation*, p. 105.

9. See in particular his *Apologia pro republica christiana* (Pforzheim, 1505).

10. The passage is taken from Wimpheling's *De Vita et miraculis Joannis Gersonis* (Strassburg, 1505); discussed in Joseph Knepper, *Jakob Wimpheling* (Freiburg-im-Breisgau, 1902), pp. 197, 198.

11. Benno Eichholz, *Bemühungen um die Reform des Speyerer Klerus besonders unter Bischof Ludwig von Helmstedt* (Münster, 1968). See also Pfleger, "Untersuchungen zur Geschichte des Pfarrei-Instituts im Elsass," pp. 70–71. Criticisms of low educational levels were also rare in the lists of grievances drawn up by cities and presented to the emperor at various times before and shortly after the Reformation. See Anton Störmann, *Die Städtischen Gravamina gegen den Klerus am Ausgange des Mittelalters und in der Reformationszeit* (Munster, 1916).

12. At Heidelberg in 1428 the university senate warned professors to exclude nonregistered students from academic exercises. But 140 years later, despite frequent renewals of its plea, the university was still attempting to deal with what was apparently a perennial problem. In 1568 the Palatine Elector decreed that any townsperson feeding or providing housing for nonmatriculated students would be punished. See Gustav Toepke, ed., *Die Matrikel der Universität Heidelberg von 1386 bis 1662*, 3 vols. (Heidelberg, 1884–86), 1:xx-xxii. By comparing graduation lists with matriculation records, Andre van Belle has recently estimated that at the University of Louvain (f. 1425) between 1483 and 1500 just under 25 percent of all students never matriculated; between 1429 and 1447, however, only 6 percent were nonmatriculants; see his "La Faculté des Arts de Louvain: Quelques Aspects de son Organization au XVe Siècle," *Les universités à la fin du Moyen Age*, ed. Jacques Paquet and Jozef IJsewijn (Louvain, 1978), pp. 46, 47.

13. *Göppinger akademische Beiträge*. Nr. 37, 38 (Göppingen, 1971).

14. See below for a discussion of the term *clericus*.

15. The only other attempt at mass biography of matriculants at a German university was made by Gottfried Kliesch in his study of Silesian students at the University of Frankfurt-an-der-Oder between 1506 and 1604. Of the 599 Silesian matriculants, he was able to find later career information on 260 (43 percent), of which 108 had become clergymen. *Der Einfluss der Universität Frankfurt (Oder) an die schlesische Bildungsgeschichte* (Würzburg, 1961), p. 47.

16. Some of these methodological problems are discussed more fully in Karl Konrad Finke, "Review of Kuhn, *Die Studenten der Universität Tübingen zwischen 1477 und 1534*," *Schwäbische Heimat* (23 January 1972), 4:258, 259. Kuhn's study points up if not the impossibility, at least the great difficulty in utilizing prosopographical methods much before 1600 when record-keeping became much more thorough and complete. See the discussion by Lawrence Stone, "Prosopography," *Historical Studies Today*, ed. Felix Gilbert and Stephen Graubard (New York, 1972), pp. 107–40.

17. "Herkunft und Ausbildung der protestantischen Geistlichen des Herzogtums Württemberg im 16. Jahrhundert," *Zeitschrift für Kirchengeschichte* 80 (1969): 167–69. On the education of the Württemberg clergy, see also, Julius Rauscher, "Die ersten reformatorischen Visitationen und der Zustand der württembergische Kirche am Ende des Mittelalters," *Blätter für württembergische Kirchengeschichte*, N. F., 24 (1925): 1–22.

18. "Niederrheinische Pfarrkirchen um 1500. Bemerkungen zu einem Erkundungsbuch des Archidiakonates Xanten," *Annalen des Historische Vereins für den Niederrhein* 135 (1939): 35.

19. Of 289 newly ordained priests in the diocese of Eichstätt between 1493 and 1577, 127 (43.9 percent) were found in matriculation rolls; Johann Gätz, "Die Primizianten des Bistums Eichstätt aus den Jahren 1493–1577," *Reformationsgeschichtliche Studien und Texte* 63 (Mün-

ster i.W., 1934). Of the 305 clergy named in the visitation report on church conditions in the Margraviate of Brandenburg in 1528, 140 (45.9 percent) had enrolled at least in one university; Georg Lenckner, "Die Universitätsbildung der in 1528 vom Markgrafen von Brandenburg visitierten Geistlichen," *Zeitschrift für bayerische Kirchengeschichte* (1933), 8:46–61. In the Diocese of Chur, between 1500 and 1520, 156 (41 percent) were filled by individuals who had attended a university. Oscar Vasella, *Untersuchungen über die Bildungsverhältnisse im Bistum Chur mit besonderer Berucksichtigung des Klerus* (Chur, 1932), pp. 95ff. See also by Vasella, "Uber das Problem der Klerusbildung im 16. Jahrhundert," *Mitteilungen des Instituts für Osterreichische Geschichtsforschung* (1950), 58:441–56. Of 86 clergy in the area of St. Gallen around 1500, 34 were university matriculants; Paul Staerkle, "Beiträge Zur spätmittelalterlichen Bildungsgeschichte St. Gallens," *Mitteilungen zur Vaterländischen Geschichte herausgeben vom Historischen Verein des Kantons St. Gallen* 40 (1939: 136.

20. Several studies have appeared describing university studies for members of specific orders. The Dominicans have been explored most thoroughly as the result of Gabriel Löhr's work: "Die Dominikaner an den ostdeutschen Universitäten Wittenberg, Frankfurt-Oder, Rostock und Griefswald," *Archivum Fratrum Predicatorum* 22 (1952): 294–316; "Die Dominikaner an den Universitäten Erfurt und Mainz," *Archivum Fratrum Predicatorum* 23 (1953): 236–74; "Die Dominikaner an der Universität Heidelberg," *Archivum Fratrum* 21 (1951): 272–93.

21. Horst Rudolph Abe, "Die soziale Gliederung der Erfurter Studentenschaft im Mittelalter (1392–1521), Teil I–Der Anteil der Deistlichkeit an der Erfurter Studentenschaft im Mittelalter," *Beiträge zur Geschichte der Universität Erfurt* 8 (1961): 5–38.

22. The following matriculation records have been utilized: Gustav Toepke, ed., *Die Matrikel der Universität Heidelberg von 1386 bis 1662*, 3 vols. (Heidelberg, 1884–86); Franz Gall, ed., *Die Matrikel der Universität Wien*, 3 vols. (Vienna, 1954–70); Hermann Keussen, ed., *Die Matrikel der Universität Köln, 1389–1559*, 3 vols. (Bonn, 1892–1931); Georg Erler, ed., *Die Matrikel der Universität Leipzig*, 3 vols. (Leipzig, 1895–1902); Adolf Hofmeister, ed., *Die Matrikel der Universität Rostock*, 5 vols. (Rostock, 1889–1912); J. C. Hermann Wiessenborn, ed., *Acten der Erfurter Universität*, pt. 1 (Halle, 1881); Hermann Meyer, ed., *Die Matrikel der Universität Freiburg-im-Breisgau, 1460–1656* (Freiburg-im-Breisgau, 1907); Gotz Freiherr von Polnitz, ed., *Die Matrikel der Ludwigs-Maximilians Universität* (Munich, 1937); Ernst Friedländer, ed., *Ältere Universitäts Matrikeln, Universität Frankfurt-an-der-Oder* (Berlin, 1878); Heinrich Hermelink, ed., *Die Matrikeln der Universität Tübingen*, 3 vols. (Stuttgart, 1906); C. E. Förstemann, *Album Academiae Vitebergensis* 1 (Leipzig, 1841); Ernst Friedländer, ed.,*Ältere Universitäts Matrikeln, Universität Griefswald* (Berlin, 1893).

23. This group also included many pluralists. When one individual held a benefice from a parish church and a canonicate from a cathedral or collegiate church, he has been included among the canons.

24. Pfleger, "Untersuchungen zur Geschichte des Pfarrei-Instituts im Elsass," *Archiv für Elsässische Kirchengeschichte* (1933), 7:3–40; see also, Heinrich Schaefer, *Pfarrkirche und Stift im deutschen Mittelalter* (Stuttgart, 1903), pp. 43–78; Schröer, *Die Kirche in Westfalen vor der Reformation*, pp. 169–71.

25. Keussen, *Die Matrikel der Universität Köln*, 1:xxi.

26. The loss or inaccessibility of ordination records from the late middle Ages is the main stumbling block to such a project. Furthermore, it is often difficult to trace individuals through a series of documents because of the inconsistent use of names. Matriculation records often did not mention a student's family name but only his given name and birthplace. An added problem is that students often listed the nearest large town as their birthplace if they deemed their own village too unknown or obscure. Frank Baron has recently cited two such examples: Nicholas von Cues (Cusanus), who referred to himself as Nicholas Trevirensis (of Trier) while in Italy, and Conrad Celtis, who matriculated at

Heidelberg as one from Würzburg even though his home town was Wyttfield, a small village near the larger town. When he received his master's degree, however, he used his actual home town. If he had not become a famous humanist, few historians would be able to catch the fact that the Conradus Celtis de Epipoli of the matriculation record was the same person as Conradus Bickel de Wyttfeld who received the Bachelor of Arts. See Baron's article, "The Historical Doctor Faustus at the University of Heidelberg" in *Les universités à la fin du moyen âge*, ed. Jacques Paquet and Jozef IJsewijn (Louvain, 1978), pp. 386, 387.

27. German clergymen continued to study at foreign universities in the pre-Reformation period. But if the situation at the University of Bologna was typical, foreign study patterns reflected the situation in Germany, namely that in the late medieval period clerical matriculations increased slightly, but at a slower rate than lay enrollments. From 1351 to 1450 clergymen comprised approximately 35 percent of all who enrolled as members of the German nation at Bologna. But from 1451 to 1520, the percentage dropped to approximately 18 percent, largely because average yearly enrollments for that period were better than twice as high as they had been in the preceding century. Throughout the period, cathedral canons were the most heavily represented clerical group. These figures are derived from Ernst Friedländer and Carlo Malagola, eds., *Acta Nationis Germanicae Universitatis Bononiensis* (Berlin, 1887).

28. Such information is also given in the Ingolstadt *matricula*, but only for later in the sixteenth century.

29. Albert Braun, *Der Klerus des Bistums Konstanz im Ausgang des Mittelalters*, *Vorreformationsgeschichtliche Forschungen* 14 (Munster: 1938), p. 91.

30. D. Hermann Jordan, *Reformation und gelehrte Bildung in der Markgrafschaft Ansbach-Bayreuth* (Leipzig, 1917), p. 25.

31. *The Franciscans in South Germany, 1400-1530, Reform and Revolution*, in *Transactions of the American Philosophical Society*, vol. 65, part 8 (Philadelphia, 1975), pp. 16-21.

32. The relevant passages of the German Concordat are printed in Joannes D. Mansi, *Sacrorum Conciliorum Nova et Amplissima Collectio* 27 (Paris, 1903), col. 1190; see also Alexander C. Flick, *The Decline of the Medieval Church* (New York, 1930), 2:120.

33. Joseph Lortz has written that "Perhaps the deepest cause" of the unspirituality in the pre-Reformation German church "lay in the monopoly which, for the most part, the German nobility possessed of appointment in high prelatic posts" (*The Reformation in Germany*, trans. Ronald Walls [London, 1968], 1:94).

34. Cited in Miriam Chrisman, *Strassburg and the Reform* (New Haven, Conn. 1967), p. 32. For a fuller discussion of the extent of aristocratic domination, see Lortz, *The Reformation in Germany*, pp. 92-97; Schröer, *Die Kirche in Westfalen vor der Reformation*, pp. 100-104.

35. On Wolf and other similar cases, see Francis Rapp, "Die Elsassischen Humanisten und die geistliche Gesellschaft," *Die Humanisten in ihrer politischen und sozialen Umwelt*. *Mitteilungen der Kommission für Humanismusforschung*, eds. Otto Herding and Robert Stupperich (Boppard, 1973), 3:101-3.

36. Cited in Johannes Janssen, *Geschichte des deutschen Volkes* (Freiburg-im-Breisgau, 1913), 1:733.

37. Included in Wimpheling's *Responsa et replice ad Eneam Silvium* (Strassburg, 1915), translated in Strauss, *Manifestations of Discontent in Germany*, p. 44.

38. Published in *Crisis in Europe, 1560-1660*, ed. Trevor Aston (London, 1965), pp. 309-31.

39. Ibid., p. 331.

40. *Past and Present* no. 51 (Summer 1971): 81-115.

41. On ordination requirements, see Oediger, *Über die Bildung der Geistlichen im späten Mittelalter* (Cologne, 1953), *Studien und Texte zur Geistesgeschichte des Mittelalters*, 2:80-97;

Hubert Jedin and John Dolan, eds., *The Handbook of Church History*, 5 vols., trans. Anselm Briggs (London, 1970), 4:574–77.

42. Georg Kaufmann, *Die Geschichte der deutschen Universitäten*, 2 vols. (Stuttgart, 1888, 1896), 2:305, cites the following percentages for several pre-Reformation universities: Leipzig: 30 percent of all matriculants received the Bachelor of Arts, only 4 percent the Master of Arts; Basel: Bachelor of Arts, 24 percent; Master of Arts, 4 percent; Freiburg-im-Breisgau: Bachelor of Arts, 24 percent; Master of Arts, 4 percent; Erfurt: Bachelor of Arts, 29 percent; Master of Arts, 4 percent; Greifswald: Bachelor of Arts, 15.6 percent; Master of Arts, 4 percent.

43. Werner Kuhn, *Die Studenten der Universität Tübingen zwischen 1477 und 1534. Ihr Studium und ihre spätere Lebensstellung. Göppinger akademische Beiträge.* Nv. 37, 38 (Goppingen, 1971), pp. 60–65.

44. Winifred Kausch, *Die Geschichte der theologischen Fakultat Ingolstadt im 15. und 16. Jahrhundert. 1472–1605* (Berlin, 1977), pp. 124, 125.

45. This was one of several complaints about the Leipzig theological faculty included in reform proposals from faculty and students submitted to the government of Duke George of Saxony before an intended statute revision. Another student claimed lectures were held so irregularly a student needed "the years of Methuselah" to complete his degree requirements. The opinions have been published in Walter Friedensburg, ed., *Die Universitat Leipzig in Vergangenheit und Gegenwart* (Leipzig, 1898).

46. Theodor Brieger, *Die theologischen Promotionen auf der Universitat Leipzig, 1428–1539* (Leipzig, 1890), pp. 1ff.

47. For an excellent discussion of the late scholastic arts curriculum, see Walter J. Ong, *Ramus, Method and the Decay of Dialogue* (Cambridge, Mass.: 1959), esp. pp. 52–91, 131–44.

48. Kausch, *Die Geschichte der theologischen Fakultät Ingolstadt*, pp. 75, 76. There are other examples. Henry of Langenstein (d. 1397), a prominent theologian and conciliarist who had taught at the University of Paris, took thirteen years to complete four chapters of *Genesis*; and according to Aeneas Sylvius (to be sure no friend of scholasticism), Thomas Hasselbach, whom he encountered at Vienna in the 1450s, had been lecturing on Isaiah for twenty-two years and had failed to complete the first chapter. On Langenstein, see Gerhard Ritter, *Die Heidelberger Universität* (Heidelberg, 1936), p. 214; on Hasselbach, see Aeneas Sylvius Piccolomini, *Ausgewählte Texte*, ed. Berthe Widmer (Basel, 1960), p. 279.

49. There were of course exceptions to the rather undistinguished performance of the theology faculties at the German universities before the Reformation. Heiko Oberman, for example, sees in the career of Gabriel Beil, the Tübingen theologian, "not the barren wastelands of sterile debates, but a richness of deep pastoral and searching theological concern." See Oberman's *The Harvest of Medieval Theology* (Cambridge, Mass., 1963), p. 5. See also Oberman's *Werden und Wertung der Reformation* (Tubingen, 1977).

50. Gerald Strauss, *Luther's House of Learning. Indoctrination of the Young in the German Reformation* (Baltimore, 1978), pp. 16, 17.

51. Recruitment, training, and ordination of the Protestant clergy in the Rhineland has been closely analyzed in Bernard Vogler, *Le Clergé protestant rhenan au siècle de la réforme* (Paris, 1977).

52. Hans J. Schroeder, ed. and trans., *Canons and Decrees of the Council of Trent* (St. Louis, 1941), p. 176.

53. Kausch, *Die Geschichte der theologischen Fakultät Ingolstädt*, pp. 120–21.

54. This point has been recently discussed in Strauss, *Luther's House of Learning*, esp. pp. 300–309.

55. Vogler, *Le Clergé protestant rhenan au siècle de la réforme*, p. 125.

TABLE 1

Clerical Matriculations at Twelve German Universities to 1520

University of Vienna*

Years	Total enrolled	Regulars		Canons		Parish clergy		Secular		Clergy	
		Number	%	Number	%	Number	%	Number	%	Number	%
1376-1380†	572	3	0.5	18	3.1	32	5.6	50	8.7	53	9.3
1381-1385	684	3	0.4	30	4.4	51	7.5	81	11.8	84	12.3
1386-1390	868	13	1.5	43	5.0	76	8.8	119	13.7	132	15.2
1391-1395	671	9	1.3	18	2.7	16	2.4	34	5.1	43	6.4
1396-1400	758	15	2.0	16	2.1	27	3.6	43	5.7	58	7.7
1401-1405	813	12	1.4	29	3.6	21	2.6	50	6.2	62	7.6
1406-1410	847	1	0.1	12	1.4	7	0.8	19	2.2	20	2.4
1411-1415	2,047	27	1.3	49	2.4	32	1.6	81	4.0	108	5.3
1416-1420	1,310	21	1.6	28	2.1	19	1.5	47	3.6	68	5.2
1421-1425	1,627	14	0.9	23	1.4	16	1.0	39	2.4	53	3.3
1426-1430	1,413	15	1.1	30	2.1	21	1.5	51	3.6	66	4.7
1431-1435	1,173	35	3.0	20	1.7	12	1.0	32	2.7	67	5.7
1436-1440	2,127	43	2.0	22	1.0	13	0.6	35	1.6	78	3.7
1441-1445	1,896	33	1.2	16	0.8	10	0.5	26	1.4	59	3.1
1446-1450	2,731	41	1.5	26	1.1	6	0.2	32	1.1	73	2.7
1451-1455	3,003	31	1.0	11	0.4	6	0.2	17	0.6	48	1.6
1456-1460	2,322	39	1.7	19	0.8	4	0.2	23	1.0	62	2.7
1461-1465	1,281	32	2.5	2	0.2	8	0.6	10	0.8	42	3.3
1466-1470	2,091	30	1.4	9	0.4	8	0.4	17	0.8	47	2.2
1471-1475	2,113	28	1.3	6	0.3	2	0.1	8	0.4	36	1.7

TABLE 1

CLERICAL MATRICULATIONS AT TWELVE GERMAN UNIVERSITIES TO 1520, CONTINUED

Years	Total enrolled	Regulars		Canons		Parish clergy		Secular		Clergy	
		Number	%	Number	%	Number	%	Number	%	Number	%
		University of Vienna,* continued									
1476-1480	1,653	35	2.1	9	0.5	4	0.2	13	0.8	48	3.0
1481-1485	440	12	2.7	2	0.5	3	0.7	5	1.1	17	3.9
1486-1490	1,333	16	1.2	14	1.1	4	0.3	18	1.4	34	2.6
1491-1495	1,674	16	1.0	5	0.3	2	0.1	7	0.4	23	1.4
1496-1500	2,817	38	1.3	8	0.3	7	0.2	15	0.5	53	1.9
1501-1505	2,616	31	1.2	12	0.5	11	0.4	23	0.9	54	2.1
1506-1510	2,218	26	1.2	3	0.1	8	0.4	11	0.5	37	1.7
1511-1515	2,778	64	2.3	7	0.3	11	0.4	18	0.6	82	3.0
1516-1520	3,157	39	1.2	7	0.2	3	0.1	10	0.3	49	1.6
		University of Heidelberg (founded 1386)									
1386-1390	1,274	22	1.7	88	6.9	91	7.1	179	14.0	201	15.8
1391-1395	358	8	2.2	30	8.4	20	5.6	50	14.0	58	16.2
1396-1400	595	20	3.4	46	7.7	47	7.9	93	15.6	113	19.0
1401-1405	528	16	3.0	61	11.6	66	12.5	127	24.1	143	27.1
1406-1410	431	19	4.4	26	6.0	28	6.5	54	12.5	73	16.9
1411-1415	480	17	3.5	22	4.6	18	3.8	40	8.3	56	11.7
1416-1420	727	27	3.7	41	5.6	27	3.7	68	9.4	95	13.1
1421-1425	614	41	6.7	33	5.4	19	3.1	52	8.5	93	15.2

1426-1430	561	26	4.6	27	4.8	14	2.5	41	7.3	67	11.9
1431-1435	864	39	4.5	22	2.5	20	2.3	42	4.9	81	9.4
1436-1440	724	33	4.6	22	3.0	13	1.8	35	4.8	78	10.8
1441-1445	610	40	6.6	24	3.9	13	2.1	37	6.1	77	12.6
1446-1450	619	24	3.9	23	3.7	8	1.3	31	5.0	65	10.5
1451-1455	664	30	4.5	26	3.9	13	2.0	39	5.9	69	10.4
1456-1460	624	40	6.4	20	3.2	8	1.2	28	4.5	68	10.9
1461-1465	483	23	4.8	9	1.9	6	1.2	15	3.1	38	7.9
1466-1470	525	25	4.8	5	1.0	15	2.9	20	3.8	45	8.6
1471-1475	553	27	4.9	11	2.0	5	0.9	16	2.9	43	7.8
1476-1480	493	45	9.1	9	1.8	7	1.4	16	3.2	61	12.4
1481-1485	604	41	6.8	6	1.0	0	–	6	1.0	47	7.8
1486-1490	549	41	7.5	9	1.6	5	0.9	14	2.6	55	10.0
1491-1495	673	48	7.1	9	1.3	4	0.6	13	1.9	61	9.1
1496-1500	725	33	4.6	7	1.0	2	0.3	9	1.2	42	5.8
1501-1505	646	8	1.2	5	0.8	3	0.5	8	1.2	16	2.5
1506-1510	751	45	6.0	4	0.5	3	0.4	7	0.9	52	6.9
1511-1515	847	65	7.7	1	0.1	6	0.7	7	0.8	72	8.5
1516-1520	709	42	5.9	10	1.4	2	0.3	12	1.7	54	7.6

University of Cologne (founded 1388)

1386-1390	842	6	0.7	38	4.5	8	1.0	46	5.5	52	6.2
1391-1395	352	11	3.1	20	5.7	12	3.4	32	9.1	43	12.2
1396-1400	362	18	5.0	46	12.7	40	11.0	86	23.8	104	28.7
1401-1405	360	13	3.6	47	13.1	52	14.4	99	27.5	112	31.1
1406-1410	464	19	4.1	38	8.2	73	15.7	111	23.9	130	28.0
1411-1415	509	12	2.4	28	5.5	45	8.8	73	14.3	85	16.7
1416-1420	652	19	2.9	24	3.7	38	5.8	62	9.5	81	12.4

TABLE 1

CLERICAL MATRICULATIONS AT TWELVE GERMAN UNIVERSITIES TO 1520, CONTINUED

University of Cologne, continued

Years	Total enrolled	Regulars		Canons		Parish clergy		Secular		Clergy	
		Number	%	Number	%	Number	%	Number	%	Number	%
1421-1425	1,132	40	3.5	55	4.9	74	6.5	129	11.4	169	14.9
1426-1430	900	42	4.7	33	3.7	54	6.0	87	9.7	129	14.3
1431-1435	911	31	3.4	19	2.1	43	4.7	62	6.8	93	10.2
1436-1440	1,048	37	3.5	26	2.5	34	3.2	60	5.7	97	9.3
1441-1445	1,138	34	3.0	28	2.5	42	3.7	70	6.2	104	9.1
1446-1450	840	18	2.1	30	3.6	34	4.0	64	7.6	82	9.8
1451-1455	1,004	23	2.3	25	2.5	40	4.0	65	6.5	85	8.5
1456-1460	1,189	17	1.4	25	2.1	38	3.2	63	5.3	80	6.7
1461-1465	1,348	22	1.6	26	2.0	31	2.3	57	4.2	79	5.9
1466-1470	1,403	26	1.9	23	1.6	45	3.2	68	4.8	94	6.7
1471-1475	1,277	27	2.1	12	0.9	25	2.0	37	2.9	64	5.0
1476-1480	1,753	19	1.1	12	0.7	31	1.8	43	2.5	62	3.5
1481-1485	1,874	16	0.9	7	0.4	18	1.0	25	1.3	41	2.2
1486-1490	2,154	17	0.8	6	0.3	22	1.0	28	1.3	45	2.1
1491-1495	2,020	16	0.8	9	0.4	27	1.3	36	1.8	52	2.6
1496-1500	2,260	15	0.7	13	0.6	28	1.2	41	1.8	56	2.5
1501-1505	1,681	13	0.8	4	0.2	12	0.7	16	1.0	29	1.7
1506-1510	1,588	17	1.1	8	0.5	12	0.8	20	1.3	37	2.3
1511-1515	1,662	22	1.3	12	0.7	44	2.6	56	2.4	78	4.7
1516-1520	1,340	26	1.9	8	0.6	19	1.4	27	2.0	53	4.0

University of Erfurt (founded 1392)

1391-1395	770	16	2.1	54	7.0	67	8.7	121	15.7	137	17.8
1396-1400	993	28	2.8	38	3.8	47	4.7	85	8.6	113	11.4
1401-1405	1,130	31	2.7	27	2.4	46	4.1	73	6.5	104	9.2
1406-1410	1,352	21	1.6	27	2.0	60	4.4	87	6.4	108	8.0
1411-1415	865	20	2.3	10	1.2	13	1.5	23	2.7	43	5.0
1416-1420	958	11	1.1	18	1.9	9	0.9	27	2.8	38	4.0
1421-1425	1,127	13	1.2	19	1.7	18	1.6	37	3.3	50	4.4
1426-1430	990	17	1.7	16	1.6	15	1.5	31	3.1	48	4.8
1431-1435	895	34	3.8	12	1.3	15	1.7	27	3.0	61	6.8
1436-1440	1,107	31	2.8	9	0.8	13	1.2	24	2.2	54	4.9
1441-1445	1,544	23	1.5	30	1.9	13	0.8	43	2.8	66	4.3
1446-1450	1,077	18	1.7	13	1.2	8	0.7	21	1.9	39	3.6
1451-1455	2,033	29	1.4	28	1.4	9	0.4	37	1.8	66	3.2
1456-1460	2,096	40	1.9	18	0.9	7	0.3	25	1.2	65	3.1
1461-1465	2,022	43	2.1	10	0.5	9	0.4	19	0.9	62	3.1
1466-1470	1,970	24	1.2	9	0.5	5	0.3	14	0.7	38	1.9
1471-1475	1,350	23	1.7	7	0.5	8	0.6	15	1.1	38	2.8
1476-1480	1,388	9	0.6	9	0.6	6	0.4	15	1.1	24	1.7
1481-1485	1,789	32	1.8	4	0.2	2	0.1	6	0.3	38	2.1
1486-1490	1,647	47	2.9	19	1.2	6	0.4	25	1.5	72	4.4
1491-1495	1,522	28	1.8	6	0.4	14	0.9	20	1.3	48	3.2
1496-1500	1,550	26	1.7	5	0.3	5	0.3	10	0.6	36	2.3
1501-1505	1,414	24	1.7	10	0.7	7	0.5	17	1.2	41	2.9
1506-1510	1,362	25	1.8	12	0.9	6	0.4	18	1.3	43	3.2
1511-1515	1,434	24	1.7	12	0.8	12	0.8	24	1.7	48	3.3
1516-1520	1,539	42	2.7	14	0.9	6	0.4	20	1.3	62	4.0

TABLE 1

CLERICAL MATRICULATIONS AT TWELVE GERMAN UNIVERSITIES TO 1520, CONTINUED

University of Leipzig (founded 1409)

Years	Total enrolled	Regulars		Canons		Parish clergy		Secular		Clergy	
		Number	%	Number	%	Number	%	Number	%	Number	%
1406-1410	617	6	1.0	1	0.2	6	1.0	7	1.1	13	2.1
1411-1415	813	8	1.0	8	1.0	15	1.8	23	2.8	31	3.8
1416-1420	1,081	9	0.8	16	1.5	15	1.4	31	2.9	40	3.7
1421-1425	1,401	11	0.8	23	1.6	15	1.1	38	2.7	49	3.5
1426-1430	939	12	1.3	8	0.9	8	0.9	16	1.7	28	3.0
1431-1435	875	13	1.5	11	1.3	16	1.8	27	3.1	40	4.6
1436-1440	890	16	1.8	3	0.3	11	1.2	14	1.6	30	3.4
1441-1445	1,442	15	1.0	5	0.3	5	0.3	10	0.7	25	1.7
1446-1450	1,027	11	1.1	1	0.1	6	0.6	7	0.7	18	1.8
1451-1455	1,769	23	1.3	8	0.5	4	0.2	12	0.7	35	2.0
1456-1460	1,805	18	1.0	3	0.2	4	0.2	7	0.4	25	1.4
1461-1465	2,007	36	1.8	2	0.1	1	–	7	0.5	39	1.9
1466-1470	1,642	11	0.7	8	0.5	5	0.3	13	0.8	24	1.5
1471-1475	1,352	26	1.9	0	–	0	–	0	–	26	1.9
1476-1480	1,468	38	2.6	0	–	12	0.8	12	0.8	50	3.4
1481-1485	1,845	53	2.9	1	–	2	0.1	3	0.2	56	3.0
1486-1490	2,172	40	1.8	2	0.9	0	–	2	0.1	42	1.9
1491-1495	1,974	37	1.9	0	–	3	0.2	3	0.2	40	2.0
1496-1500	1,706	38	2.2	3	1.8	0	–	3	0.2	41	2.4
1501-1505	2,117	42	2.0	0	–	1	0.5	1	0.5	43	2.0

1506-1510	2,272	72	3.2	0	–	8	0.4	8	0.4	80	3.5
1511-1515	2,339	71	3.0	2	0.1	1	–	3	0.1	74	3.2
1516-1520	1,772	54	3.0	1	0.1	1	0.1	2	0.1	56	3.2

University of Rostock (founded 1419)

1416-1420	487	1	0.2	2	0.4	4	0.8	6	1.2	7	1.4
1421-1425	760	11	1.4	8	1.1	9	1.2	17	2.2	28	3.7
1426-1430	679	2	0.3	1	0.1	3	0.4	4	0.6	6	0.9
1431-1435	798	13	1.6	7	0.9	2	0.3	9	1.1	22	2.8
1436-1440	405	10	2.5	1	0.2	5	1.2	6	1.5	16	4.0
1441-1445	822	10	1.2	1	0.1	7	0.9	8	1.0	18	2.2
1446-1450	700	17	2.4	1	0.2	0	–	1	0.2	18	2.6
1451-1455	736	10	1.4	2	0.3	2	0.3	4	0.5	14	1.9
1456-1460	735	14	1.9	4	0.5	1	0.1	5	0.7	19	2.6
1461-1465	646	7	1.1	0	–	1	0.2	1	0.2	8	1.2
1466-1470	818	11	1.3	2	0.2	6	0.7	8	1.0	19	2.3
1471-1475	973	7	0.7	3	0.3	2	0.2	5	0.5	12	1.2
1476-1480	926	7	0.8	2	0.2	1	0.1	3	0.3	10	1.1
1481-1485	835	12	1.4	0	–	3	0.4	3	0.4	15	1.8
1486-1490	319	5	1.6	0	–	0	–	0	–	5	1.6
1491-1495	879	10	1.1	1	0.1	2	0.2	3	0.3	13	1.5
1496-1500	888	6	0.7	0	–	1	0.1	1	0.1	7	0.8
1501-1505	941	6	0.6	0	–	2	0.2	2	0.2	8	0.9
1506-1510	1,031	12	1.2	2	0.2	10	1.0	12	1.2	24	2.3
1511-1515	1,044	13	1.2	2	0.2	3	0.3	5	0.5	18	1.7
1516-1520	791	5	0.6	1	0.1	3	0.4	4	0.5	9	1.1

TABLE 1

Clerical Matriculations at Twelve German Universities to 1520, continued

Years	Total enrolled	Regulars		Canons		Parish clergy		Secular		Clergy	
		Number	%	Number	%	Number	%	Number	%	Number	%

University of Greifswald (founded 1456)

Years	Total enrolled	Regulars Number	%	Canons Number	%	Parish clergy Number	%	Secular Number	%	Clergy Number	%
1456-1460	528	12	2.3	13	2.5	17	3.2	30	5.7	42	8.0
1461-1465	205	12	5.9	2	1.0	8	3.9	10	4.9	22	10.7
1466-1470	199	16	8.0	5	2.5	5	2.5	10	5.0	26	13.1
1471-1475	207	12	5.8	5	2.4	6	2.9	11	5.3	23	11.1
1476-1480	204	6	2.9	1	0.5	3	1.5	4	2.0	10	4.9
1481-1485	215	7	3.3	–	–	–	–	–	–	7	3.3
1486-1490	366	14	3.8	6	1.6	7	1.9	13	3.6	27	7.4
1491-1495	217	–	–	1	0.5	3	1.4	4	1.8	4	1.8
1496-1500	295	5	1.7	2	0.7	12	4.1	14	4.7	19	6.4
1501-1505	229	2	0.9	2	0.9	3	1.3	5	2.2	7	3.1
1506-1510	178	2	1.1	1	0.6	5	2.8	6	3.4	8	4.5
1511-1515	210	11	5.2	1	0.5	4	2.0	5	2.4	16	7.6
1516-1520	196	8	4.1	1	0.5	3	1.5	4	2.0	12	6.1

Freiburg-im-Breisgau (founded 1460)

Years	Total enrolled	Regulars Number	%	Canons Number	%	Parish clergy Number	%	Secular Number	%	Clergy Number	%
1456-1460	215	5	2.3	4	1.9	51	23.7	55	25.6	60	27.9
1461-1465	456	12	2.6	10	2.2	21	4.6	31	6.8	43	9.4
1466-1470	234	17	7.3	6	2.6	8	3.4	14	6.0	31	13.2
1471-1475	247	11	4.4	9	3.6	6	2.2	15	6.1	26	10.5

1476-1480	200	10	5.0	6	3.0	4	2.0	10	5.0	20	10.0
1481-1485	234	14	6.0	3	1.3	8	3.4	11	4.7	25	10.7
1486-1490	344	18	5.2	3	0.9	10	2.9	13	3.8	31	9.0
1491-1495	456	18	3.9	11	2.4	11	2.4	22	4.8	40	8.8
1496-1500	382	15	3.9	8	2.1	12	3.1	20	5.2	35	9.2
1501-1505	568	15	2.6	9	1.6	12	2.1	21	3.7	36	6.3
1506-1510	597	21	3.5	8	1.3	5	0.8	13	2.2	34	5.7
1511-1515	578	35	6.0	14	2.4	22	3.8	36	6.2	71	12.3
1516-1520	468	21	4.5	16	3.4	10	2.1	26	5.6	47	10.0

University of Ingolstadt (founded 1472)

1471-1475	1,511	21	1.4	25	1.7	29	1.9	54	3.6	75	5.0
1476-1480	926	18	1.9	16	1.7	11	1.2	27	2.9	45	4.9
1481-1485	1,257	17	1.4	25	2.0	8	0.6	33	2.6	50	4.0
1486-1490	1,231	23	1.9	22	1.8	10	0.8	32	2.6	55	4.5
1491-1495	885	9	1.0	19	2.1	5	0.6	24	2.7	33	3.7
1496-1500	829	16	1.9	17	2.1	11	1.3	28	3.5	44	5.3
1501-1505	491	2	0.4	12	2.4	3	0.6	15	3.1	18	3.7
1506-1510	832	8	1.0	21	2.5	6	0.7	27	3.2	35	4.2
1511-1515	1,061	9	0.8	28	2.6	12	1.1	40	3.8	49	4.6
1516-1520	1,207	12	1.0	28	2.3	8	0.7	36	3.0	48	4.0

University of Tubingen (founded 1477)

1476-1480	625	13	2.1	11	1.8	38	6.1	49	7.8	63	10.1
1481-1485	552	33	6.0	11	2.0	10	1.8	21	3.8	64	11.6
1486-1490	464	15	3.2	8	1.7	2	0.4	10	2.2	25	5.4
1491-1495	497	12	2.4	3	0.6	3	0.6	6	1.2	18	3.6
1496-1500	429	28	6.5	1	0.2	1	0.2	2	0.5	30	7.0
1501-1505	444	8	1.8	0	—	1	0.2	1	0.2	9	2.0

TABLE 1

CLERICAL MATRICULATIONS AT TWELVE GERMAN UNIVERSITIES TO 1520, CONTINUED

Years	Total enrolled	Regulars		Canons		Parish clergy		Secular		Clergy	
		Number	%	Number	%	Number	%	Number	%	Number	%
University of Tubingen (founded 1477)											
1506-1510	625	19	3.0	5	0.8	2	0.3	7	1.1	26	4.2
1511-1515	604	16	2.6	10	1.7	2	0.3	12	2.0	28	4.6
1516-1520	458	2	0.4	5	1.1	1	0.2	6	1.3	8	1.7
University of Wittenberg (founded 1502)											
1501-1505	1,121	57	5.1	8	0.7	12	1.1	20	1.8	85	7.6
1506-1510	965	55	5.7	13	1.3	29	3.0	42	4.4	97	10.1
1511-1515	1,158	50	4.3	6	0.5	10	0.9	16	1.4	66	5.7
1516-1520	1,714	60	3.5	5	0.3	2	0.1	7	0.4	67	3.9
University of Frankfurt-am-Oder (founded 1506)											
1506-1510	1,454	10	0.7	8	0.6	3	0.2	11	0.8	21	1.4
1511-1515	736	17	2.3	2	0.3	0	–	2	0.3	19	2.6
1516-1520	781	16	2.0	0	–	4	0.5	4	0.5	20	2.6

* Although Vienna received its charter in 1365, the matriculation book begins in 1377. The first entry includes the names of 291 students who had matriculated before 24 June 1377.

† With a few exceptions, each five-year period includes ten semesters, beginning with summer semester of the first year and ending with the winter semester of the second. At most universities, the summer semester began in March or April, the winter semester in November or December.

TABLE 2

Clerical Matriculations at Twelve German Universities: Composite

Years	Total enrolled	Regulars		Canons		Parish clergy		Secular		Clergy	
		Number	%	Number	%	Number	%	Number	%	Number	%
1376-1380	572	3	0.5	18	3.1	32	5.6	50	8.7	53	9.3
1381-1385	684	3	0.4	30	4.4	51	7.5	81	11.8	84	12.3
1386-1390	2,984	41	1.4	169	5.7	175	5.9	344	11.5	385	12.9
1391-1395	2,151	44	2.0	122	5.7	115	5.3	237	11.0	281	13.1
1396-1400	2,708	81	3.0	146	5.4	173	6.4	319	11.8	400	14.8
1401-1405	2,831	72	2.5	164	5.8	206	7.3	370	13.1	442	15.6
1406-1410	3,711	66	1.8	109	2.9	174	4.7	283	7.6	349	9.4
1411-1415	4,714	85	1.8	117	2.5	123	2.6	240	5.1	329	7.0
1416-1420	5,215	78	1.5	129	2.5	112	2.1	241	4.6	319	6.1
1421-1425	6,661	121	1.8	164	2.5	151	2.3	315	4.7	436	6.5
1426-1430	5,482	114	2.1	115	2.1	115	2.1	230	4.2	344	6.3
1431-1435	5,516	165	3.0	91	1.6	94	1.7	185	3.4	350	6.3
1436-1440	6,301	170	2.7	83	1.3	89	1.4	172	2.7	342	5.4
1441-1445	7,452	155	2.1	104	1.4	90	1.2	194	2.6	349	4.7
1446-1450	6,994	129	1.8	94	1.3	62	0.9	156	2.2	285	4.1
1451-1455	9,209	146	1.6	100	1.1	74	0.8	174	1.9	320	3.5
1456-1460	9,444	185	2.0	106	1.1	130	1.4	236	2.5	421	4.6
1461-1465	8,448	187	2.2	61	0.7	85	1.0	146	1.7	333	3.9
1466-1470	8,882	160	1.8	67	0.8	97	1.1	164	1.8	324	3.6
1471-1475	9,583	182	1.9	78	0.8	83	0.9	161	1.7	343	3.6
1476-1480	9,636	200	2.1	75	0.8	117	1.2	192	2.0	392	4.1
1481-1485	9,645	237	2.4	59	0.6	54	0.6	113	1.2	350	3.6

TABLE 2

CLERICAL MATRICULATIONS AT TWELVE GERMAN UNIVERSITIES: COMPOSITE, CONTINUED

Years	Total enrolled	Regulars		Canons		Parish clergy		Secular		Clergy	
		Number	%	Number	%	Number	%	Number	%	Number	%
1486-1490	10,579	236	2.2	89	0.8	66	0.6	155	1.5	391	3.7
1491-1495	10,797	194	1.8	64	0.6	73	0.7	137	1.3	331	3.1
1496-1500	11,881	220	1.9	64	0.5	79	0.7	143	1.2	363	3.1
1501-1505	12,268	207	1.7	62	0.5	67	0.5	129	1.0	336	2.7
1506-1510	13,878	312	2.2	85	0.6	97	0.7	182	1.3	494	3.6
1511-1515	14,451	397	2.7	97	0.7	127	0.9	224	1.6	621	4.3
1516-1520	14,132	327	2.3	91	0.6	62	0.4	153	1.1	480	3.4

TABLE 3

Clerical Matriculations at Twelve German Universities: Seculars vs. Regulars

Years	Total clergy	Regulars		Canons		Parish clergy		Seculars	
		Number	%	Number	%	Number	%	Number	%
1376-1400	1,203	172	14.3	485	40.3	546	45.4	1,031	85.7
1401-1425	1,871	422	22.6	683	36.5	766	40.9	1,449	77.4
1426-1450	1,521	584	38.4	487	32.0	450	29.7	937	61.6
1451-1475	1,741	860	49.4	412	24.7	469	26.9	881	50.6
1476-1500	1,827	1,087	59.5	351	19.2	389	21.3	740	42.7
1501-1520	1,931	1,243	64.3	335	17.3	353	18.3	688	35.6

TABLE 4

CLERICAL MATRICULATIONS AT TWELVE GERMAN UNIVERSITIES OF COLOGNE, 1389-1520: ALL STUDENTS

Years	Total enrolled	No data		Arts		Theology		Law		Medicine	
		Number	%	Number	%	Number	%	Number	%	Number	%
1389-1430	5,573	1,687	30.3	2,425	43.5 (62.4)	417	7.5 (10.7)	985	17.7 (25.3)	59	1.1 (1.5)
1431-1460	6,131	847	13.8	4,083	66.6 (77.3)	261	4.3 (4.9)	899	14.7 (17.0)	41	0.7 (0.8)
1461-1490	9,809	441	4.5	8,201	83.6 (87.5)	126	1.3 (1.5)	1,022	10.4 (10.9)	19	0.2 (0.2)
1491-1520	10,552	205	1.9	8,978	85.1 (86.8)	89	0.8 (0.9)	1,263	12.0 (12.2)	17	0.2 (0.2)

NOTE: Percentages in parentheses are based only on the number of students about whom information was given.

TABLE 5

Faculty Enrollment at the University of Cologne: Clergy

Years	Total enrolled	No data		Arts		Theology		Law	
		Number	%	Number	%	Number	%	Number	%
Canons									
1389-1430	329	118	35.9	50	15.2 (23.7)	40	12.2 (19.0)	121	36.8 (57.3)
1431-1460	153	40	26.1	32	20.9 (28.3)	18	11.8 (15.9)	63	41.2 (55.8)
1461-1490	85	21	24.7	16	18.8 (25.0)	8	9.4 (12.5)	40	47.1 (62.5)
1491-1520	52	3	5.8	15	28.8 (30.6)	3	5.8 (6.1)	31	59.6 (63.6)
Parish Clergy									
1389-1430	396	123	31.1	30	7.6 (10.1)	104	26.3 (38.1)	139	35.1 (50.1)
1431-1460	231	21	9.1	41	17.7 (19.5)	61	26.4 (29.0)	108	46.8 (51.4)
1461-1490	171	19	11.1	35	20.5 (23.0)	19	11.1 (12.5)	98	57.3 (64.5)
1491-1520	143	11	7.7	29	20.3 (22.0)	6	4.2 (4.5)	97	67.8 (73.5)

TABLE 5

FACULTY ENROLLMENT AT THE UNIVERSITY OF COLOGNE: CLERGY, CONTINUED

Years	Total enrolled	No data		Arts		Theology		Law	
		Number	%	Number	%	Number	%	Number	%
All Clergy									
1389-1430	892	291	32.6	91	10.2 (15.1)	212	23.8 (35.3)	298	33.4 (49.6)
1431-1460	543	85	15.7	85	15.7 (18.6)	169	31.1 (36.9)	204	37.6 (44.5)
1461-1490	383	59	15.4	71	18.5 (21.9)	83	21.7 (25.6)	170	44.4 (52.5)
1491-1520	305	23	7.6	73	23.9 (25.9)	60	19.7 (21.3)	149	48.9 (52.8)
Regulars									
1389-1430	167	50	29.4	11	6.6 (9.4)	68	40.7 (58.1)	38	22.8 (32.5)
1431-1460	149	24	16.1	12	8.1 (9.6)	90	60.4 (72.0)	33	22.1 (26.4)
1461-1490	127	19	15.0	20	15.7 (18.5)	56	45.0 (51.9)	32	25.2 (29.6)
1491-1520	110	9	8.2	29	26.4 (28.7)	51	46.4 (50.5)	21	19.1 (20.8)

NOTE: Percentages in parentheses are based only on the number of students about whom information was given.

TWO ATTITUDES
TO HEBREW STUDIES:
ERASMUS AND RABELAIS

M. A. Screech

niversities rarely exist in a vacuum. Renaissance universities were no ivory towers. Clashes within the University of Paris, for example, or between gown and regal power made the Quartier Latin look at times like an armed camp. It can almost be said to be one of the minor battlefields of history. Francis I did not arrest Béda, exile him, haul him back, exile him again for good, and then invite Melanchthon to debate the faith with "selected theologians" of Paris, without disturbances – especially since he "selected" his theologians by casting some in jail. Such policies were not arrived at without pressure from influential humanists; when implemented, they were not always quietly accepted. When Francis I forced the University of Paris to approve of the Henrican divorce, his troops were out in force.

The history of universities cannot be restricted to matters of syllabus, organization, social origins of students, scholarly aspirations, or the eventual destinations of graduates, vital though they may be. Political power and public opinion mattered. Governments were aware that opinion could be manipulated. When, for example, Béda, exiled while still syndic of the Sorbonne, was recalled late in 1533, Francis I was advised to have epigrams written against him and circulated throughout the kingdom. At another level, Erasmus could take on Béda and, indeed, the whole theological faculty of Paris – and win. According to Erasmus, Béda would have made a good court fool, 'so seriously ridiculous' as he was. For Francis I, Erasmus was a man to be courted—to be invited to Paris as a *lecteur royal*, an honor he declined.[1]

What Erasmus thought about Hebrew is of vital concern. Through his writings he influenced scholar, layman, and literate prince. Rabelais's importance was of a different kind. His comic and satirical genius was put to the service of many causes, and he was in the household of powerful patrons. These included the du Bellay clan: Jean (Bishop of Paris); Guillaume, the "Seigneur de Langey"; and René, to whom was entrusted the task of keeping up pressure for reform in the University of Paris.

Erasmus was unambiguously in favor of the study of Hebrew. He saw it as less absolutely essential than Greek, but Greek was not in itself enough: "I exhort all theologians again and again . . . to undertake the task of Greek learning, and Hebrew too, if possible."[2] In theory there was nothing new in this. Pope Clement V's Constitution of 1311 had recommended the study of Hebrew in the universities, though results were disappointing. Nevertheless, Hebrew had acquired firm papal approval. Canon law supported it too. The *Decreta* of Gratian are quite firm about this: each language has its own idioms, which appear absurd when turned literally into another; Scripture must be understood in accordance with the idiom of the original language.[3] The authority cited in the glosses for this was St. Jerome. Moreover, canon law authorized that direct approaches be made to practicing Jews when there were disagreements among Christians about traditional Jewish matters such as fasting: "We are obliged therefore to have recourse to the Hebrews and to seek true knowledge from the fountain rather than from rivulets."[4]

The glossators supported this by reference to civil law. Canon law, although unsympathetic to Jewry, forbade compulsory conversion. *Part 1, Distinctio 45, caput 3, Qui sincera intentione* of the *Decreta* forbade the molesting of Jews, permitted customary rites and ceremonies and ordered that conversions should be made by kindness; to do otherwise was to serve selfish personal ends, not God's. The same point was made in the following *capita 4, Licet plerumque*, and 5, *De Judaeis*. Saracens who oppressed Christians could be rightly fought; Jews did not oppress Christians and were not to be treated as Saracens could rightly be.[5] That many were prepared to serve other ends but God's we all know. Erasmus, however, seems to have been quite at ease within the letter of canon law, yet he is increasingly presented as extremely anti-Semitic. This is the case in Professor Guido Kisch's essay, *Erasmus' Stellung zu Juden und Judentum.*[6] Professor Kisch's work is balanced and scholarly, but it leaves out some important aspects, relying perhaps too much on the correspondence and omitting some evidence that shows Erasmus in a less stark attitude.

More disturbing is an article published in the distinguished *Proceedings of the Sixth World Congress of Jewish Studies* (Volume 2, 1975). There Erasmus is termed the first anti-Semite (p. 87), compared to Hitler (p. 91), and credited with anticipating the Final Solution. Here the documentation is so patchy that it is impossible to reply to it. The point about the Final Solution, with all its terrible implications, is made not with a reference to any work of Erasmus, but to a section of Luther's *Table Talk* which appears in no way to be germane.[7]

When such views, born of suffering beyond measure, are being read into Erasmus, one must make one's points with care and with completeness, with scholarly detachment and yet with compassion, basing one's case not only on what Erasmus wrote but, so far as one can, on all of what he wrote. Erasmus's attitude toward what he conceived as Judaism and as Judaizing tendencies within Christianity is cold enough in all conscience without distorting it. There is a potential of hate within the gospel of love. Erasmus did not hate easily, but his conception of the *philosophia Christi* owed much to the Apostle to the Gentiles. Paul's opposition to Jewish legalism underlies much of what Erasmus wrote about the Jews and their religion.

It is important to get Erasmus's attitude toward the Jews as a race as clear as possible. This is not simply a question of justice toward an influential and attractive writer. If Erasmus had detested Jews as a race in a way anticipating twentieth century bestiality, it would have been serious indeed. Hebrew had largely to be learned from

Jews. In the universities it was partly taught by converts from Judaism. If Erasmus had considered all such scholars as mere *marranos* or *semijudaei*, then his influence was such that he might have set back the study of Hebrew for at least a generation.

But he did not.

Erasmus wanted Hebrew to be studied not primarily to convert Jews and certainly not so as to reach the works of Jewish exegetes or mystics. He wanted the Old Testament to be established on a sure textual foundation. The Hebrew original, the *Veritas Hebraica*, contained teachings that foreshadowed Christ, his Church, and the *philosophia Christi*. As he grew older, he attached more and more importance to the Old Testament. It is already important in the *Enchiridion Militis Christiani*: It grew more so as the years advanced.[8]

Erasmus never doubted that those who seek the basic meaning of the Old Testament must either know Hebrew or follow those who do. He can be cited many times about this. His *Annotationes in Novum Testamentum* make this clear from the outset. Erasmus's own knowledge of Hebrew remained very limited indeed, but he knew where to turn for help. He relied heavily upon his friends the Amerbachs and then on J. Cellarius or Robert Wakefield who became professor of Hebrew at Louvain. In the annotations to the New Testament he often cites *Capnio noster*—Reuchlin, that is—a point sometimes overlooked by those who claim that he was cold toward him.[9] What Erasmus admired in Reuchlin was not his cabalistic studies—Reuchlin's version of the cabala, like Pico's before him, meant little that was pleasant to him, with one major exception that will be explored later. What Erasmus admired in Reuchlin was his mastery of the three tongues, Hebrew, Greek, and Classical Latin, that put him in the category of St. Jerome. The "Apotheosis of Reuchlin," added to the *Colloquies* in 1529, must rank as one of the most generous praises one great man has ever made of another.

As time went on, an increasingly important source of knowledge of Hebrew for Erasmus was St. Jerome, or else St. Augustine and the early fathers generally. This was at one with the basic assumptions of his theology, which led him to jump over much – but by no means all – of what had been written in the Latin middle ages, seeking his version of the *philosophia Christi* in the New Testament as understood by Origen, Jerome, and the scholars of the earlier Church. Erasmus was so sharp a critic of Thomas Aquinas or Nicolas of Lyra for relying on ill-informed intermediaries that his own reliance on Greek- or Latin-speaking fathers for knowledge of Hebrew is quite extraordinary.[10] This reliance on early Christian sources often led him far astray. But even a casual reading of the *Annotationes in Novum Testamentum* shows that he could be critical of the conclusions of St. Jerome himself, in the light of better scholarship. He did on at least one occasion consult an erudite Jew: he could profitably have done so much more often.[11]

Erasmus did claim some slight knowledge of specifically Jewish exegesis, but he showed scant sympathy for it. He borrowed a few ideas from Rabbi Solomon. He did not, he says, wish to reject Hebrew commentators entirely, especially the ancient ones. Yet he did not think too much attention should be given to them either: their commentaries were full of "smoke" – empty promises – and of stupid fables. Moreover, they were motivated by a desire to prove Christianity wrong as well as by hatred of Christ.[12] Did Erasmus really know enough to say this, or was he following a fairly current Christian line? He wrote like one who knew his Jewish writings almost exclusively from hostile sources. The general attitude of even Christian cabalists toward their Jewish mentors was not infrequently unsympathetic, even harsh. (The aims of the Christian cabala included the conversion of Jews by means of methods and authorities they could understand.)

How Erasmus, who was so open in so many ways, could be so blinded about Jewish scholarship is, I think, in part recoverable. He identified the unconverted Jews of his own day and, indeed, since Paul, with those qualities of legalism that Paul condemned; these defects were precisely those he so constantly attacked within the Church. He did not see the main danger to the Church in neopaganism but in neo-Judaism. He did not mean by that Jews as such, nor those Christians who were attracted to Jewish learning:

he meant those who brought legalism into the Church—a church that ought to be marked by faith and Christian liberty, subordinated to the spirit of love. Neo-Judaism in this sense is the major butt of the comedy in the *Praise of Folly*. When laughter had evaporated, it remained the major butt of his harsh comments in the *enarrationes* on the Psalms. In this particular sense, he "saw Jews everywhere"—not least in the monasteries and in the chairs of scholastic professors of theology.

Erasmus made no fundamental distinction between Jewish and monkish religions: both were concerned with "shadows," with legalism, with a Christ-rejecting confidence in works or ceremonial. For Erasmus, all opponents of the revealed light of the *philosophia Christi* were either primarily neopagans or else neo-Judaizers masquerading as Christians. He constantly worked variations of St. Paul's condemnation of Jews for requiring a sign or of Greeks for seeking wisdom (1 Corinthians 1:22). For Erasmus both the Hebrew Scriptures and the pagan philosophers had to be "spiritualized" before they could be compatible with Christianity. In themselves they were "carnal" opponents to it at worst; but at best, they were shadowy preparations for it, and even, at times, inspired anticipations of it.[13]

Erasmus found it easy to accommodate aspects of Greek philosophy to the *philosophia Christi*: it had largely been done for him by the fathers he admired. But, like those same fathers, he could only accommodate the Old Testament to it by departing radically from any meanings that an unconverted Jew could possibly find in it. Erasmus passionately accepted the Church's view that the Old Testament contained shadows of all the truths of the New, that shadows or sparks of Christ and his religion are to be found there.[14] The prophets speak of Christ, and Christ often speaks directly through their mouths; the Mosaic Law is the shadow of which the New Testament is the real substance; the historical events in Kings, say, or Chronicles are, under special Providence, anticipations of events and persons of the new dispensation.[15]

This is not a personal or idiosyncratic view. It was that of the early Church and of a continuing tradition within the medieval and Renaissance Church. Erasmus supported it unambiguously. For those who hold such theories, Hebrew and the Hebrew Scriptures are vital adjuncts to Christianity. But they are not an end in themselves. Without allegory or figurative exegesis, one is left with the shadows. And to remain content with them is to reject revealed reality and so to be self-condemned.

These concepts derive from the New Testament itself, in which Christ is made to claim that "all things must needs be fulfilled which are written in the law of Moses, and the prophets, and the psalms, concerning me": then, Luke tells us, Christ "opened their mind, that they might understand the Scriptures."[16] Paul reinforces this system of exegesis.[17] Allegory is the Christian key to the Hebrew Scriptures.

That this tradition flourished in Renaissance universities amongst the Christian humanists owes something, but not everything, to Erasmus. It was a standard tradition from the earliest times.[18] A convenient way to grasp the importance of this exegetical theory is to read Erasmus's massive paraphrase of Luke 24:44–45. In it, the figurative Old Testament testimonies to Christ and his Church are interpreted by Erasmus writing not as a philologist but as a prophet whose privilege was to unveil the *arcana Scripturae*. One can then see why Erasmus could not have conceived of Hebrew in a Christian university being studied and taught other than by Christians. Converted Jews would be ideal. (Erasmus honored sincere and learned Jewish converts.)

This method of exegesis, especially when guided principally by Origen, Jerome, or the fathers generally, completely excludes anything specifically Jewish, except insofar as Jewish scholarship might contribute something toward the elucidation of the shadowy literal aspects of the Old Testament. Not to pass from shadow to light was to remain willfully benighted. Even modern Jewish allegory or spirituality was assumed to be literal or carnal, since it rejected Christ. In this sense Erasmus and indeed the Church in general was unsympathetic or hostile to Judaism. Even in its pre-Christian glory, nothing was to be learned from Judaism except in relation to Christian verities.

Toward the cabala, Christian or Jewish, Erasmus retained a deep reserve tinged with suspicion. It is best to see this in the light of his quiet rejection of the *prisca theologia*, which had been an integral part of the restoration of Platonism in fifteenth century Italy. From the start, under the influence of Gemisthus Pletho, Platonism and *prisca theologia* were one; from the start Hermes Trismegistus was seen as a contemporary of Moses. His inspired doctrines may be found in Platonism, in Pythagorean symbols, in Indian Gymnosophists. Such studies welcomed good magic – Ficino was a Christian magus. As Pico and Agrippa conceived of it, the cabala formed part of this semisecret mystical tradition, which supplemented the mainstream of the Christian revelation.[19]

Ficino may have taught Erasmus much. But Erasmus rejected all this mystical tradition, with its Orphic hymns and its magic rings, its sympathetic, demonic, and spiritual magic. He declined to accept that the cabala enshrined inspired Pythagorean truths. This suspicion toward what he saw going on in Italy helps to explain his lack of sympathy for Reuchlin's more authentic cabala. Reuchlin had a real but limited knowledge of authentic Jewish cabalism, mainly drawn, it seems, from the *Gate of Light* of Joseph ben Abraham Gikatilia (ca. 1247–1305).[20]

The quarrels that burst out when a converted Jew, Pfefferkorn, together with the Dominicans, led a concerted attack on Hebrew learning, condemning Reuchlin and seeking to destroy all Jewish books apart from the Old Testament, are too well known to be rehearsed here. Less widely understood is Erasmus's attitude to the Christian cabala. He is often said to be uniformly hostile despite the very courteous reception he gave to the clear *exposé* of a chastened version of the Christian cabala, stripped of Pico's and Agrippa's fantasies, addressed to him by Paul Ricci, a learned Jewish convert with whom he remained on warm and friendly terms.[21] And the evidence of the *Annotationes in Novum Testamentum* shows how the spreading knowledge of Hebrew was leading Erasmus fundamentally to rethink problems of scriptural exegesis. What Erasmus could not accept was that the cabala had apostolic authority behind it – a contention that would, of course, have made it a potential rival to scripture.

Partisans of certain cabalistic movements among Christians wished to make St. Paul himself into a cabalist. Had not Paul asked Timothy to send him his cloak and "the books, especially the parchments"?[22] In his *Annotationes* Erasmus, with a mixture of irony and indignation, rejects the claim that these are allusions to cabalistic books. In the *De Ratione concionandi* he makes the rejection both wider and clearer: "Paul did indeed ask for books to be sent to him, especially ones written on parchment. I do not think they were books of Plato, of Pythagoras or cabbalistic or Talmudistic ones, but books of the Old Testament."[23] The importance of the inclusion of Pythagoras here is that Reuchlin believed that the secret teachings of Pythagoras had been preserved by the cabala. Similarly important is all omission to such matters in the *Adages*, even when explaining "*Pythagorean Symbols.*"

Any allusion in Erasmus to Pythagoras and his doctrines may contain implied judgments on the cabala. When in the *Enchiridion* he condemned Christian exegetes who were content with Aristotle and who rejected the "Platonists and the Pythagoreans," he was at very least ambiguous.[24] Such remarks can be taken as somewhat favoring the cabala—provided, that is, its connections with Pythagoras could be proven. That was where Erasmus was most skeptical.

Yet however totally Erasmus thrust aside much of the Cabbala according to Pico, Agrippa, or Reuchlin, he kept an open mind about one central teaching of the Christian cabalists. It concerns the most important claim advanced by Reuchlin in his dialogue *De Verbo mirifico* first published in Basel in 1494 and often reprinted. To understand this is to realize how shattering an impact Hebrew was having on intelligent men. It merits a digression.

The New Testament was widely held to be infallible in all its detail when properly understood. Erasmus shook this belief. The impact on readers of what he wrote in his annotated edition of the Greek New Testament, the first ever, was all the greater for its judgment concerning the opening chapters of the first Gospel. St. Matthew, we are told, probably wrote in Hebrew; this is a view held by St. Jerome. Erasmus drew the conclusion that the Greek version, being a translation, cannot accurately represent the origi-

301

nal in all its nuances. Therefore, there may be a lost *Veritas Hebraica* for the first book of the New Testament. By asserting this Erasmus boldly proclaimed the possibility of errors in one of the four Gospels. A Hebrew text known only in Greek translation cannot be relied upon for detail.

The loss of this version is particularly regrettable, since without it Erasmus cannot decide whether one of the most important assertions of the Christian cabalists is true or not. The point at issue concerns the original Hebrew name of Jesus and its mystical connections with the ineffable name of God, the holy and unutterable tetragrammaton. Some Christian cabalists believed that Christ's deity was hidden mystically in his Hebrew name. Jesus the Christ's name was not, they said, written with the same characters as that of other people called Jesus, such as Jesus son of Nave.[25] Erasmus discusses this in his annotation on Matthew 1:11–12: *Jesus, he who is called Christ.* "Some learned men," he noted, assert that the name of *Jesus* was written in Hebrew with the same characters as were used for the ineffable name of God; within this tetragrammaton was inserted the penultimate letter of the Hebrew alphabet, Šin. Erasmus wished that this could be taught, supported by solid arguments, since it was both "plausible and pleasing to Christian ears." Unfortunately only the Hebrew original of Matthew could decide the matter. And he did not have it.[26]

The point at issue is an important one in an age where the mystical power of names was increasingly accepted as a reality, largely under influences deriving eventually from Plato. The name of God (written in Hebrew, of course, without vowels) is the tetragrammaton *Yhvh*. Reuchlin turned Jesus' name into the pentagrammaton *Yhsvh*; in this way the Hebrew name of the Son was held to be embraced within the ineffable holy name of God the Father.[27]

To Thomas Wolsey Erasmus had written *Caballa et Talmud, quicquid hoc est, meo animo nunquam arrisit.* But that was not his last word: in his letter to Paul Ricci he played several times on this phrase; there were aspects of the cabala that Ricci's clear exposition helped him to appreciate.[28] One of the aspects that Erasmus would like to have believed was the central doctrine that Christ's name

302

mysteriously reveals his fellowship with the Father. When Erasmus expanded his annotation to Matthew 1:11–12 so as to include this very favorable judgment on the aims of the Christian cabalists, he was lending his authority both to the study of Hebrew by Christian scholars and also to a sympathetic attitude towards the aspirations of the Christian cabalists as represented by Reuchlin and Ricci.

No follower of Erasmus who read his *Annotationes* need ever have rejected the Christian cabala out of hand, however skeptical he might have been about, say, Agrippa's version of it. Erasmus was firmly convinced that names have mystical meanings concealed in their etymologies. (This Cratylic belief was acted upon by Jerome, Augustine, and many others.) Could the Savior's name be the supreme example of such hidden meanings? If so, it gave to Hebrew a very special dignity. On this central point, Matthew's gospel as Erasmus had it was inadequate. Only the rediscovery of the *Veritas Hebraica* of Matthew could give him the required assurance. For that reason alone, Erasmus deeply regretted the loss of the original Hebrew version.[29] But Erasmus is not consistent about this.

Matthew's gospel may be a translation. This need not, of itself, undermine the total inerrancy of Holy Writ. The Holy Ghost may be held to have guided translators infallibly just as he guided the original authors. Erasmus never used that argument – dismissing, indeed, the legend that the Septuagint was *the* example of miraculously inspired accuracy. Doubtless he saw that to do otherwise was to play into the hands of those who wanted to make an inerrant Vulgate normative even above the Hebrew or Greek *Veritates*.

For students of the *Annotationes in Novum Testamentum*, the dilemma is posed virtually from the outset. And Hebrew is again the moving cause. It concerns the reply given to the Magi by the priests and scribes of the people: the Magi asked where the Christ was to be born,

And they said unto him, in Bethlehem of Judaea: for thus it
is written by the Prophet:
  And thou Bethlehem, in the land of Judah,
Art in no wise least among the princes of Judah,[30]

For out of thee shall come forth a governor
Which shall be shepherd of my people Israel.[31]

The answer given by the priests and scribes does not stand up to
scrutiny. The priests and the scribes do not quote scripture cor-
rectly. Erasmus, in an important annotation, first discussed
Jerome's ingeniously anti-Jewish suggestion that this loose quotation from Micah 5:2 was incorrect because the priests and scribes
were casual about their scriptures, and forgetful. Erasmus could
not accept this. The New Testament never described them that
way; they were condemned not for slackness or ignorance but for
ambition and avarice, so that "seeing, they could not see." Moreover, there were other cases where the New Testament authors
cited the Old Testament wrongly—wrongly when judged either
from the *Veritas Hebraica* or the Septuagint. The conclusion that
Erasmus drew from this was not that the New Testament was just
like any other work of literature—he never held such a view—but
that it was, for hidden purposes unknown to man, not inerrant in
detail:

> The heavenly Spirit directed all this mystery of our salvation by arcane
> counsels and by reasons hidden from the human mind. It is not within our
> power—nor is it in accord with Christian modesty—to prescribe how he
> should regulate his own business.
>   Christ alone is called the truth. He alone is exempt from all error.

The Holy Ghost presumably inspired Cyprian or Jerome, and they
are not infallible. So, too, with reservations, for Holy Writ:

> The highest authority is owed to the apostles and evangelists; but perhaps
> Christ, for a reason hidden from us, wished something human to remain in
> them too, perceiving that this too leads to the restoring of the human race.

Augustine believed Peter to have erred, even after receiving the
Spirit; Paul and Barnabas quarrelled; one of them had to have
been wrong. If a scholar were to believe that the slightest error
invalidated scriptural authority, then he would have to face the

problem of which text he was claiming infallibility for: probably no manuscript used by the Catholic Church was so correct as not to admit of emendation . . . Erasmus claimed to have Jerome's support for much of what he was saying, but if one rejects St. Jerome's explanation of how the priests and scribes came to quote Micah wrongly, "then I prefer to believe the text to be corrupt, either among the Hebrews or among ourselves; or else, if something has been changed, then it has been changed for the better by God's counsel; or else, finally, that the Scripture is indeed incorrupt but that our weakness cannot comprehend the mystery."[32] This discussion does not allow one to take refuge in the interpretations of an infallible Church. The Church is no guarantee against textual error; philology is needed there too, as Erasmus tirelessly insisted: "For how many centuries has Psalm 41 (2) been sung in Churches as, "So yearns my soul for God, the living fountain" (ad Deum fontem vivum)." Yet fontem vivum is a scribal corruption of fortem vivum, as the Veritas Hebraica and the Septuagint show.[33] To appreciate the force of this point, one needs to recall that this psalm, Quemadmodum—"Like as the hart desireth the water-brooks"—is particularly associated with the crucified Christ.

Philology is vital; Catholic tradition important. But the ultimate authority for Erasmus was Christ the living truth. His spirit could inspire the prophetic exegete. Erasmus believed he was inspired in this way. To overlook this is to falsify his most basic assumptions. The Holy Ghost requires men to make the scholarly effort to learn Greek, Hebrew, and so on, but he works through private inspirations no less vital for being secret.[34]

Philology by itself is not enough, but it cannot be dispensed with. And a knowledge of Hebrew is vital for deciding major questions of Christian doctrine. Erasmus, for example, had a bitter quarrel with Faber (Lefèvre d'Etaples) over the sense of Hebrews 2:7: ἠλάττωσας αυτον βραχύ τι παρ' ἀγγέλους which means—what? That Christ, on the authority of Psalm 8, Domine Dominus noster (4–6), was foretold as Messiah, being made "a little"—or is it "for a while?"—lower than "the angels"—or is it, "than God?" Once more this is no obscure passage of Scripture: it forms a pericope for the

305

mass of Christmas day. Faber, noting the Hebrew original, wished the text to be taken as meaning that Christ was made a little lower than God. Everything depends upon what is meant in Hebrew by the word *elohim*, since David sang prophetically of Christ, so far as Christians are concerned: "For thou hast made him little (?) lower than *elohim*." Erasmus detested Faber's doctrine, not least because he himself held a fully kenotic doctrine of the incarnation. In the *Annotationes* Erasmus defended his interpretation with fifty-seven reasons. Several derive from Hebrew erudition.[35] The forty-second consists in the direct evidence of a learned Spanish Jew whom he had consulted on the matter: "A certain Spanish Jew, a man in my opinion uncommonly versed in his literature, says that the difference between *Eloim* and *Malachim* is that angels, too, are called *Eloim* whenever it is a question of their dignity, standing in the presence of God; when it is a question of their function—that is, when they are sent somewhere—they are called *Malachim*."[36] We are dealing, says Erasmus, with a *collatio*, a similitude, of dignity; the Chaldaean paraphrase supports this contention by using *Malachim*, not *Eloim*; this in turn supports the Septuagint and hence the accepted reading of Hebrews 2:7.[37]

By raising such fundamental issues, Erasmus made the study of Hebrew basic to the study of the new Testament and its theology. This particular issue was to remain disputed within the universities. The Revised Version still has the same hesitations; it still all revolves around what was meant by *elohim*.[38]

For Erasmus the philologist's task was a primary one: the prophetic exegete who built upon this foundation was greater, but the higher needed the lower. And one could be both, as he was. The Old Testament was the work of the Holy Ghost, albeit working through fallible men and fallible copyists. To deny the validity of allegorical exegesis was flatly heretical; no compromise was possible with such "carnalness."[39] The allegorical truths were such that the original authors or actors may have had no notion of them.[40]

The philological meaning of the Old Testament text was the starting point of all sound allegorizing—hence the vital role of Hebrew philology. But to remain there, to reject the Christian allegories, was Judaism; yet to reject the literal sense was to subvert the whole of Scripture.[41] These spiritual allegories, without which Christian exegesis of the Old Testament did not exist, were not a matter of private fancy although there was room for ingenuity and a large area of tolerance. Some, like Origen, could go too far; but in essence they were the work of the Holy Spirit. That was what made them important. The full weight of Erasmus's authority supported the centrality of the mystical sense of the Old Testament. The New Testament had its flesh and its spirit, but in another sense.

Again, critics are sometimes confused over this. According to Erasmus, the pagan poets could and should be allegorized. But you could not allegorize Livy as you could—and must—allegorize Kings or Judges.[42] Erasmus's conception of the historical events unrolled in the Old Testament was, *sensu stricto*, an "amazing" one, one fundamental to traditional Christian exegesis that he tirelessly championed: the life of David, or even of some minor Old Testament princeling or prophet, was not so narrated as to be open to spiritual allegory; it was, under special divine providence, actually lived in such a way as to be open to such allegories. It was not a question of an account of David's life, for example, being arranged by a biographer so as to prefigure Christ: his life, even at times in its smallest detail, was potentially a hidden prefiguration of Christ, his Church, and his doctrines. It was God's plan that this should be. That is what made the Old Testament absolutely unique.[43] To remain at the historical level was to do nothing of fundamental value.[44]

The Old Testament may well seem ugly, with its wars, its adulteries, its apparent immoralities. That is because it is like the *Silenus of Alcibiades*. Alcibiades likened Socrates to the fat and ugly Silenus, the devotee of Bacchus: he was externally ugly, but within he was the repository of divinely revealed truth. *Mutatis mutandis*, Christ, and the Old Testament are both like that, only more so.[45]

In some of his comments, Erasmus can be quoted as placing less value on the Old Testament: he would rather lose all the books of the Jews than to disturb Christian peace on their account; he could wish that Christians did not so often give the Old Testament precedence over the New. Those remarks must be read in context. To take them as his considered opinion is absurd. From his earlier works to his latest, the Old Testament, mystically understood, plays a vital role.

Erasmus saw the Old Testament in a traditionally Christian way. First it was, as for Paul, the "schoolmaster to bring us to Christ" (Galatians 3, 24). It was still a prime vehicle for bringing Jews to Christ. It could not play this role in the conversion of the Gentiles, as Paul's example shows: Gentiles do not acknowledge its authority. This use of the Old Testament to convert the Jews was, in Erasmus's time, restricted, since, he says, Jews were not numerous and Christians had little contact with them.[46] The second use was therefore more important. The Old Testament strengthened Christians in their faith. Within it were all the shadows, the *umbrae*, of the truth as made manifest in Christ and his Church. Erasmus constantly referred to the *umbrae* of the Old Testament, "shadows" that derive their substance from the realities that project them. It is in this sense that he paraphrased John 4:22, "Salvation is from the Jews."

> And therefore the beginning of salvation set forth from the Jews, who, through the prophets, hold the promises of the coming Messiah and who, through the Law, hold the figures and shadows of Evangelical piety.[47]

Here Erasmus was following an unbroken tradition. Examples to show this could be multiplied almost at will: Jerome writing to Augustine says, as a matter quite obvious and needing no elaboration: "For the grace of the Law which has passed away we have received the lasting grace of the Gospel and instead of the shadows and images of the Old Testament, truth has been established through Jesus Christ."[48] Augustine in *De Doctrina Christiana* alludes to the *imaginaria* that the Jews celebrated *per umbram*. Centuries later, exegetes were saying the same thing. The mainspring from which these allegories flowed was the interpretative genius of the early fathers. Erasmus produced editions of some of them—his *Jerome* was famous—and translations of others; most influential of all is perhaps his translation of some works of Origen. This meant that patristic allegorical exegesis was encouraged in the universities by the very accessibility and excellence of Erasmus's work as editor and translator.

Because Jews refuse to accept the Christian "realities" that are said to have projected their *umbrae* on to the Old Testament, such patristic statements often contain implied or explicit condemnations of Jewish "stubbornness." That is the case in the quotation just made from Jerome. When Erasmus did the same, he was certainly not being in any way original or unfaithful to tradition. His originality lay elsewhere. This doctrine of the shadows and the verities, of the carnal and the spiritual, of the literal and the figurative, was in accord with Platonic philosophy and presumably derived from it in very early Christian times. Erasmus realized this and wedded it firmly not only to Paul's contrast between the flesh and the spirit but also to a Platonic concern with spiritual realities; only lesser men could be madly happy with the mere shadows of reality.

Erasmus saw this in terms of Plato's myth of the cave in the *Republic*. According to this myth, mankind resembles permanent dwellers within a cave, deluded into taking for realities the shadows projected on the walls of their cave by real spiritual objects outside their ken. Then, one day, a lover of truth ventures out of the cave; he discovers the spiritual realities that project the shadows; he returns and tells his fellow men the good news that what they take for realities are but fleeting shadows. They refuse to believe him and cast him out.

In the *Praise of Folly*, this myth plays an important role, being used to distinguish between the good insanity of the Christian Fool and the insanity of the mass of carnal men. The majority who dwell in the cave take their transient *umbrae* for eternal realities and so think that the true Christian is insane. This majority includes monks, scholastic theologians, slack, immoral, or time-serving Christians, as well as Christian legalists and those who are Jews—not by race but by religion. That they are truly insane the Christian Fool knows for certain. That is what is meant by one of Erasmus's most dismissive sayings about practicing Jews: the Christian scholar perceives the spiritual truths that throw their shadows on to the Old Testament; those Jews who not only reject the realities but mistake mere shadows for them, *insaniant in speluncis suis*, "remain mad within their caves."[49]

Erasmus's laughter was not an indulgent warm one. His wit was a way of writing people off. Individuals or groups were dismissed as mad jokes. He never seemed to have realized how wounding his laughter at monks, scholastic theologians, or practicing Jews must have been to those who were on the receiving end. Most of us find Erasmus's witty dismissal of error in the *Praise of Folly* or the *Colloquies* thoroughly enjoyable. But it can be cruel. Many monks, after all, not only "judaized," but deeply believed that they were right to do so.

Erasmus had enough knowledge of monasticism, say, or of Christians who through hyperscrupulousness distorted Christ's religion of grace, liberty, and love into a trust in ceremonial works of penance or what he saw as the equivalents of the ever-broader phylacteries that Christ condemned.[50] But he knew next to nothing about Jewish spirituality and took next to no steps to find out about it. He assumed that the whole Jewish tradition since Philo of Alexandria, whom he honored, had little or nothing to offer, save carnal reflections on shadows taken for realities. The beliefs of practicing Jews were to be laughed at in the same way as those of monks and other carnal Christians. So far as the Jews were concerned, Erasmus was at one with such of his favorite authors as Jerome and Augustine, though he was less coldly hostile to Jewry than Augustine frequently was.

What Erasmus did value—and value highly—were the mystical truths that he believed to be hidden within Hebrew names and to be sought in their Hebrew etymology. This belief was as deeply imbedded in patristic theology as it was in the Renaissance.

The strengths and weaknesses of Erasmus's prophetic exegesis can best be judged from his psalm commentaries, the only sustained commentaries on the Old Testament writings that he undertook. Psalm 33 (34), *Benedicam Domino*, is a case in point. Erasmus bases his spiritual interpretation on the alleged etymologies of two proper names: *Achis*, which he takes to mean *Quomodo est?* ("How can this be?"), and *Ahimelech*, interpreted as "My Father and King." Since his Hebrew was inadequate, he relied for his etymologies on Augustines's sermons on this psalm and on the relevant parts of Jerome's *Appendix Breviarum*.[51] Again, in the *enarratio* of Psalm 83 (84), *Quam dilecta*, he saw vital allusions to Christ within three proper names: *David*, taken to mean "Strong in hand," *Asaph*, "gathering together," and *Korah*, "Calvary." Again he relied on St. Jerome.[52] In his exploitation of these "etymologies," Erasmus went beyond his sources. I think that there is no doubt that, although his knowledge came from Jerome, Augustine, and the early Latins, he was emulating Origen.

Erasmus can make these ideas quite arresting. Augustine uses *Achis-Quomodo est?* in an entirely anti-Jewish way. His examples all stress Jewish incredulity. Erasmus includes within his list of Jews who replied with a *Quomodo* the Virgin Mary.[53] Erasmus does not reject Jews: he rejects Judaism. He does not, in the spirit of Christian anti-semitism, play up the deicidal responsibilities of an entire people. At the Crucifixion the mob shouted, "His blood be upon us and upon our children." Erasmus paraphrased this in these terms: "But Christ, more merciful to them than they were to themselves, rejects nobody from pardon, provided that they repent. Many indeed later worshipped the Cross of Christ who, in that crowd, yelled *Tolle, tolle, crucifige*."[54] Nevertheless, he saw the Jewish faithful of his own times as being no different from Achis. In face of the Christian's claim to have superseded their carnal law, their reply is still *Quomodo lex abrogata est?*[55] Erasmus can write harshly of such Jews. Not infrequently his language is Scriptural. Such enemies sharpen their teeth against the Christian; they are forced to hide it, but they do it none the less. Heretics, he adds, are no different.[56] One could wish that he had been sensitive to the gulf separating a Hebrew prophet lambasting powerful compatriots for their blindness or hardness of heart and a Christian prophet applying these same texts to a pathetic minority within Christendom. But then, he used the same texts to take on powerful majorities in his own church. He lumped Jews, monks, scholastics together with all those other varieties of carnal men who prefer to walk in darkness without seeing the great light.

But some Jews could and did become followers of the light. He condemned those who scornfully dubbed such converts *marranos*. His use of the term *we* to do so probably suggests a change of heart.[57] There is, he insists, inhumanity "when we use the word *marranos* shamefully" for Jewish converts. They ought to be more honored than Christians by birth. If it is right to blame children for their ancestors, what about us, whose ancestors worshiped sticks and stones?[58] Erasmus's relations with such men could be friendly. He had no qualms about Paul Ricci holding high academic appointments; nothing suggests that the Jewish blood of some of the *lecteurs royaux* at Paris worried him one little bit. When Erasmus condemns practicing Jews as an *hominum genus* dedicated to stubborn error, it can be made to sound totally racist. But it was not; his usage elsewhere makes it plain that he was not necessarily talking of 'race' in a modern sense.[59]

Erasmus's influence was a wide and pervasive one. He lent his authority unequivocally to the study of Hebrew; he was brought to think more kindly of the Christian cabala; he welcomed Jewish converts into the church. For him the study of Hebrew was no disinterested scholarly pursuit. It was a vital concern for Christian scholars. Erasmus strongly supported the study of Hebrew in the Universities, but he would never have dreamed of giving the chairs to unconverted Jews. For him, Hebrew was needed to understand the New Testament and to understand the literal meaning of the Old as well as its spiritual meaning, insofar as it was to be discovered through Hebrew etymologies. But the most important role of the Old Testament was as a subject of meditation for the Christian, who might well be granted the boon of ecstatic amazement, as he glimpsed the Providence of God behind the "shadows" of the Old Testament and the "realities" of the New.

Erasmus had at first taken no pleasure at all in the Talmud and Cabala: *nunquam arrisit*. In this he was in striking contrast with Rabelais, for whom the cabala and Jewish tradition would be a source of smiling comedy. It was also for him a source of mysterious wisdom, but whereas Erasmus could write that, for him, Jewish learning *nunquam arrisit*, Rabelais shows that it pleased him enough to produce in him many different modes of laughter.

No major author has ever expressed his indebtedness to another more generously and more unreservedly than Rabelais in his famous letter to Erasmus of 1532. It was in this same year, probably, that he published *Pantagruel*. This little book was to prove a watershed in the history of European literature. It was presented to the reading public under the guise of a comic legal textbook; the very name of the giant, "Pantagruel," was a linguistic joke, suggesting that the Breton imp *Penthagruel* had a name the etymology of which was to be sought in Greek (*Panta*) and Hagarene (*gruel*). This linguistic joke doubtless arose from Erasmus's condemnation of Agostino Steucho in 1531 for doing much the same thing in all seriousness. In *Pantagruel* Rabelais made a strong plea for studying Greek—"without which it is a disgrace that anyone should call himself learned." Also included in his ideal system of education were Hebrew and Chaldaean. These were to be studied not for their own sake but in order to understand the Old Testament. About the same time as the letter to Erasmus, Rabelais, in a little work, the *Pantagrueline Prognostication* for 1533, drew directly on Erasmus's *Annotationes in Novum Testamentum* to establish his Platonico-Christian syncretism, in which Socrates leads to a great source of truth, St. Matthew.

In *Pantagruel* Rabelais sports knowledgeably with Jewish lore. Pantagruel's ancestor during the Flood was a giant named Hurtaly: he rode astride Noah's Ark just as Og, King of Bashan, the *Hapalit*, did in the story told in the *Pirkei de-rabbi Eliezar*. He assumed that his readers all knew about "Rabbi Kimy," whose *Grammatica* had been published the previous year in the Latin translation of Sebastian Muenster, with notes by Elias Levita. One of his jokes apparently depends on readers knowing that the Hebrew future serves as an imperative in negative commands. An entire episode, that of Thaumaste, is concerned with the search for cabalistic secrets within the tradition of Pico and Agrippa. We are made to laugh at the gullibility of this thaumaturgical English Thomas, but in such a way as to prefer his simpleminded quest for hidden truths to the noisy and ostentatious debates of Sorbonne theologians in the scholastic tradition.[60]

All this created an atmosphere favorable to Hebrew studies and a more than indulgent tolerance even of what Erasmus called "cabbalistic smoke." Later, in the *Quart Livre de Pantagruel* (1552), Rabelais attached great importance to the etymologies of Hebrew names. In the *Tiers Livre* (1546), he dealt sympathetically with Old Testament marriage customs.

But in some ways the most interesting of Rabelais's comments concern important events in the Paris of January 1534. At that time Béda, the syndic of the theological faculty, the Sorbonne, was back in office, recalled from exile for reasons that need not concern us here, but definitely not restored to royal favor. Hardly was he back when he sought a court interdict forbidding the *lecteurs royaulx* from advertising lectures on the Hebrew Old Testament, or, indeed, from giving them without prior approval from the Faculty of Theology of which he was head. The defendents were Pierre Danés, François Vatable, Paul Paradis, and Agathie Guidacier. The case against them was made by the Crown, obliged to act on Béda's initiative.[61]

The defense alleged that it was first a matter of Royal prerogative: the King had appointed those men as experts. To appoint professors of Hebrew implied the right to study the Old Testament: apart from grammars there were no other Hebrew books to read.[62] The counsel for Béda and the Crown did not tear into this extraordinary assertion. He simply stated that it did not follow that the King intended the Old Testament to be studied, since it was not likely that there were no books at all in Hebrew apart from the Old Testament: it was probable that there existed commentaries and histories in Hebrew. He made no mention of the cabala, no mention of the Talmud. It was as though Erasmus's preferences were taken to be cold sober fact.[63] The counsel for Béda made so weak a case that one almost wonders whether it was part of a put-up job to disgrace Béda and safeguard the study of Hebrew under the *lecteurs royaulx* within the University of Paris.

Béda himself showed that what he feared was a continuation of the undermining of the Vulgate, such as had been already attempted "by Erasmus, Faber and others." He made no attack on *marranos*, despite the fact that Paul Paradis was a convert, but did allege that you could not trust the Hebrew texts of scripture since many of them had come from Germany and "many of the Jews who have their books printed are Lutherans." Such scholars may be presumed to have falsified their documents. It was certainly not enough, under these conditions, to say, *Ita habent Hebraea* ("the Hebrew texts read thus").[64]

The accounts of the trial leave us up in the air; but Béda was evidently unsuccessful. Rabelais's comments on this serious clash between the theologians and the Crown appear partly in the comic and satirical book titles added to the expanded *Pantagruel* of 1534, enlarging the amusing catalog of imaginary books held in the library of Saint-Victor's monastery. This list, from 1534 onward, includes the following:

- *Callibistratorium caffardie, actore M. Jacobo Hocstratem hereticometra.*
- *Taraballationes doctorum Coloniensium adversus Reuchlin.*

These comic book titles can loosely be translated as:

- *Concerning the Hypocrisy of Female Genitals, by Magister Jacob Hoochstrat, Measurer of Heretics.*

and

- *The Fuss and Bother of the Doctors of Cologne against Reuchlin.*

These join the *Ars petandi in societate per M. Ortuinum* (*The Art of Farting in Company, by Magister Ortuinus*). It was the doctors of Cologne who had been in the forefront of the attacks on Reuchlin; foremost amongst these was Ortuinus Gratius. These titles, added in 1534 to a book already assuming a certain elementary knowledge of Hebrew, and very definitely in favor of Hebrew studies, scathingly opposed to the Sorbonne and mockingly sneering about Béda, can only have been satirical comment on Béda's attempt to muzzle the *lecteurs royaulx* in Hebrew. Rabelais's patrons, the du Bellays, were at loggerheads with the Sorbonne. Their protégé gleefully made common cause with them.

Rabelais's sympathy for Hebrew studies was probably a continu-

315

ing influence from his Franciscan days. It was the Dominicans who opposed them, not the Franciscans. The Sorbonne had played a leading part in the condemnation of Reuchlin's *Augenspiegel*. Rabelais suggested that in trying to fetter the *lecteurs royaulx* in Hebrew they were up to their old tricks, seeking to replay their battles against Reuchlin. It seems that Rabelais was led by all this to read the *Epistolae obscurorum virorum*, perhaps for the first time.

Before *Gargantua*, the chronicle that followed *Pantagruel*, there is no sign that Rabelais had read this uproarious satire at the expense of Ortuinus Gratius and of others among the Cologne theologians, enemies of humanist erudition in general and of Reuchlin and Hebrew studies in particular. Several of the jokes against the Sorbonne contained in *Gargantua*, especially the confused oration of Janotus de Bragmardo, their public orator, come straight out of the concerns of the *Epistolae obscurorum vivorum*.[65] The actual legal proceedings instituted by Béda against the *lecteurs royaulx* in Hebrew made no allusion at all to Reuchlin, to the cabala, to any other Hebrew studies other than that of the Old Testament. Rabelais deliberately widened the question in order to include them. This was no temporary fit of enthusiasm for a discipline under attack from his enemies. The same concern appeared in the *Tiers Livre de Pantagruel* (1546). At the end of chapter 14, there is a serious allusion to the "Caballistes et Massorethz interpretes des sacres Letres." Their way of distinguishing good and bad spirits is treated with respect. But this is followed, in chapter 15, by several jests linking the grosser monastic traditions to a secret "caballistique institution des anciens non escripte mais baillée de main en main." It is at this point that Panurge, the butt of the humor, links together "Pythagoras, Socrates, Empedocles et nostre maistre Ortuinus."[66] The concerns are those of the *Pantagruel* of 1534. The pure cabala is honored; the "Pythagorean" cabala of Reuchlin, Agrippa, and so on is largely treated as a matter of humor, but its enemies, especially Ortuinus and his supporters, are classed amongst the enemies of Pantagruelism and humanism.

Rabelais, a convinced Erasmian, brought an element of fun and joy into the whole question of Hebrew learning. Hebrew was at times placed in the same scale of honor as Greek. Jewish legends could be a source of indulgent amusement, not of shocked piety. Like Erasmus he could draw upon even "Chaldaean" to make his points: he condemned those false astrologers known as "Chaldaeans" with the Chaldaean reading of Psalm 64(65), where it is "silence," not "hymns of praise," that behooves God in Zion.[67] He did not need to know Chaldaean or Syriac to make this point, but he had to be sympathetic toward the study of them. He was.

There are the odd sneers in Rabelais. He was in favor of taking Hebrew medicine seriously, but he used a term for Jewish doctors, *Talmudistes*, that has pejorative undertones. (In the *Tiers Livre* he applies it to certain canon lawyers). On the other hand, in his marriage propaganda he drew very favorably on Old Testament practice. But, of course, most of the Old Testament laws had been superseded by Christ's. As Pantagruel says, "Nous ne sommes mie Juifz."

But there is a warmth in Rabelais. His comedy is in sharp contrast with Erasmian wit. It can be just as dismissive, but it is remarkably free from fear or hatred. He can write in such a way as to assume that at least an elementary knowledge of Hebrew, even a secondhand knowledge, was part of the intellectual equipment of civilized men. In the *Quart Livre*, Hebrew names abound. We are supposed to know what they mean. We certainly miss a good joke if we fail to spot that the Queen and the Infanta of the island of the Andouilles are both given a priapic name, *Niphleseth*, which derives from that sexual "horror," that *miphletseth*, that figures in 1 Kings 15:13 (and 2 Chronicles 15:16).

One should not exaggerate the amount of Hebrew learning that this joke presupposes. It is at least probable that a few "obscene" words of Hebrew had entered into student slang, even amongst students whose real knowledge of Hebrew was nonexistent. What Rabelais's *Chronicles* do is to remind us of an intellectual climate amongst the *gens sçavans et studieux* in France, a climate that encouraged a deep respect for Hebrew learning within Christian universities, a certain tolerance for the cabala, and a sustained mockery of the opponents of Reuchlin, especially the Cologne

317

theologians and their leader, Ortuinus Gratius. Rabelais's *Chronicles* show that, in such circles in France, there was no fear of the Jews or of Jewish learning.

But it was left to another admirer of Erasmus to make affectionate relationships with Jews into a reality: Celio Calcagnini of Ferrara, a famous scholar living in a town that had welcomed a large Jewish community. Marot wanted to study under him: Rabelais probably knew him—he borrowed a great deal from his *Opera* of 1544. My excuse for citing him here is fourfold: he was an Erasmian and accepted Erasmus's version of the *philosophia Christi*; he was influential in a court much frequented by Frenchmen (including Marot, Rabelais, and Guillaume du Bellay) since his wife, Renée, was of the French Royal family; the text does not seem to be known at all widely; it is a pleasure to do so.

Calcagnini was called upon to give an oration at the graduation of a Jewish doctor called Reuben. He praises Reuben, whom he addresses as *Ruben charissime*, for his remarkable natural endowments. He points out how unjust it would be to deprive him of the outward insignia of such inward excellence; he reminds his listeners that religion is a matter of grace "which ravishes us towards a love of heavenly things and numbers us amongst the dwellers in heaven."

And to Reuben he says: "I hope that you as well will be led from the letter to the [spiritual] sense, and may be called from darkness into light, into the light of that true philosophy which that great interpreter of truth, nay, Truth himself, Christ, made known to the people, and may lead you to that saving medicine of souls which alone can commend us sickly mortals to eternal health and salvation." He confers on Reuben the traditional insignia: a closed book soon to be opened, a ring, a doctor's bonnet. "And finally I greet you with a kiss; there is no greater sign of love than this among your people also." And he ends with a call to avoid contentiousness and a prayer that "we"—Reuben and himself—"may live this life happily and the next life blessedly."[68]

Erasmus accepted no racial divisions within the church, a church that included Jews such as Paul and the Virgin Mary. He believed

318

that "many" had been saved under the Law of Moses—not merely a handful as Augustine believed.[69] But Erasmus's efforts were mainly bent toward purifying the Church of practices that he saw not so much as neo-Pagan as neo-Judaic; Erasmus was less concerned with converting the infidel, whether Jew or Gentile.

To judge from admirers such as Rabelais and Calcagnini, Erasmus's influence was not a cramping one. Everyone gave primacy to Greek, the language of the New Testament. The study of Hebrew within Christian universities was given immense encouragement by Erasmus. That it was important for recovering the basic meaning of the *Veritas Hebraica* was unquestioned by him and by humanists in general. Erasmus also saw Hebrew as vital for the understanding of the New Testament: there is no need to go beyond the first few pages of his *Annotationes in Novem Testamentum* to convince oneself of that. Hebrew was also one of the keys that opened up the *arcana*, the hidden, veiled "secrets" of the Old Testament, enabling them to be understood with a Christian sense. This ability to reconcile the Old Testament with the New by prophetic insight was a valued source of contemplative ecstasy, confirming the faith of the amazed Christian as he glimpsed the majesty of God's plans, foreshadowed in the Old Testament and made manifest in the New. With the aid of Hebrew scholarship, Erasmus showed that neither Holy Writ nor Holy Church were infallible in the ways once taken for granted. By doing so, he unleashed a tiger. Some of the questions that he raised remain unsolved today.

By the end of the sixteenth century, Hebrew was an accepted study in the universities. The position it gained was solid and durable. But it was studied less for its own sake than as a tool of Christian theology. It was taught by Christians to Christians. Such a view of Hebrew studies is in accordance with Erasmus's deepest convictions. For centuries professors of Hebrew were likely to be Christian priests or ministers. No university professor of Hebrew in England was a Jew until University College London was created outside the control of the ecclesiastical establishment.

What Erasmus and Rabelais did, each in their own way, was to welcome Hebrew as an ally of Christian humanism. And both of them saw Hebrew as finding its place within the central studies of Christian universities.

1. For the points raised here, see *Etudes Rabelaisiennes* 11 (1974), "Some Reflections on the Dating of *Gargantua A* and *B*," and 13 (1976), "Some Further Reflections on the Dating of *Gargantua*." (In this present study, LB stands for *Lugduni Batavorum*, i.e., the Leyden edition of Erasmus's *Opera Omnia, ed. J. Leclerc, 1703–06; TLF stands for Textes Litteraires Francais*, the series published by Droz of Geneva.)

2. LB6, **2v°.

3. *Decreta* 1, *distinctio* 38, *caput* 14, *Lecutio divinarum*.

4. *Decreta* 1, *distinctio* 76, *caput* 7, *Jejunium quarti*.

5. *Decreta* 2, *Causa* 23, *questio* 8, *caput* 11, *Dispar nimirum*.

6. Guido Kisch, *Erasmus' Stellung zu Juden und Judentum* (Tubingen, 1969).

7. See H. S. May, 'Erasmus and the Jews—a psychohistoric reevaluation,' in *Proceedings of the Sixth World Congress of Jewish Studies (held at the Hebrew University of Jerusalem 13–19 August, 1973, under the Auspices of the Israel Academy of Sciences and Humanities)* (Jerusalem: World Union of Jewish Studies, 1975), 2:85–93. For a more scholarly view, see W. L. Gundersheimer, 'Erasmus, Humanism and the Christian Cabala,' in *Journal of the Warburg and Courtauld Institutes* 26, 1963, pp. 38–52. Points made in Dr. Gundersheimer's study are not repeated here.

8. These points are further developed in my book *Ecstasy and the Praise of Folly* (London, [1980]). Even the lists of names in the Old Testament genealogies commanded Erasmus's wondering respect; cf. LB5, 868F–870BC.

9. Cf., amongst many examples, LB6, 984E, where the Vulgate reading of Hebrews 1, 12 is corrected against the Greek original interpreted in the light of Reuchlin's interpretation of this text and its allusion to Psalms 102, 26.

10. E.g., LB 6, 572F–573E.

11. Cf. LB5, 240Ab; 401Bff.; 523Dff.; 551C–F; LB6, 56–57; 549–50; 573ff.; 757–60; 814C; 926C; LB9, 630Fff. Many relevant references in Kisch and Gundersheimer.

12. LB5, 202BC.

13. Cf. amongst many examples, LB5, 132AC; 142F; 294E–295A; 313F–314A; 371A–372C (cf. LB2, 773D); 373ff.

14. LB6, 5r°.

15. Cf. 171Fff.; 201Bff. 207C; 294Eff.; 371Aff.

16. Luke 24, 44–45.

17. For example in Corinthians 9, 8ff.

18. Cf. LB5, 201ff.; 312ff.;1043ff. Consult also Henri de Lubac, *Exegèse médiévale* (Paris, 1959), passim; that study is an excellent corrective to anachronistic interpretations of Erasmus's exegetical practice.

19. Consult D. P. Walker, *The Ancient Theology* (London, 1972); also his *Spiritual and Demonic Magic from Ficino to Campanella* (London, 1958), especially chapter 3.

20. Cf. Gundersheimer and the many works mentioned in his study, *Journal of the Warburg and Courtauld Institutes* 26 (1963): 38ff. A most useful introduction to the subject remains

J. L. Blau's *The Christian Interpretation of the Cabala in the Renaissance* (New York, 1944), despite its being in part superseded by later studies.

21. Amongst more recent studies, see G. Vallese, *Erasmo e Reuchlin* (Naples, 1964), and C. S. Meyer, "Erasmus and Reuchlin" in *Moreana* no. 24, 1969, pp. 65–80.

22. 2 Timothy 4, 13.

23. LB5, 798D.

24. LB5, 29. Erasmus is in fact defending the obligation of interpreting the Old Testament as a series of spiritual symbols (amongst, of course, many other things).

25. Ecclesiasticus 46, 1.

26. LB6, 4, n. 12.

27. Blau, *The Christian Interpretation of the Cabala in the Renaissance*, p. 48f.

28. Erasmus's letter to Paul Ricci takes up the expression *nunquam arrisit* and uses it several times: '*Sed in primis arrisit candor ille et perspicuitas*; . . . *Arrisit animus ille gratiis et amicitiae natus*; . . . *Arrisit denique te, hoc est absoluto veroque philosopho, digna moderatio.*' (cf. *Erasmi Epistolae*, ed. P. S. and H. M. Allen, 4, 1160). The letter dates from November 1519; this suggests that Erasmus's more favorable attitude towards the cabala dates from this very contact with Ricci. As recently as 19 October 1519, he repeated, in a letter to Albert of Brandenberg, the very remark he had first made to Wolsey; cf. *Erasmi Epistolae*, 3, 967 ("*mihi sane neque Cabala neque Talmuc unquam arrisit*") and 4, 1033 ("*Cabala et Talmud, quicquid hoc est, meo animo nunquam arrisit*"). By taking up this same phrase in November 1519, Erasmus is drawing attention to his real change of heart about the Christian cabala brought about by Ricci.

29. It cannot be too often emphasized that the *Annotationes* as printed by the Lugduni Batavorum *Opera Omnia* are a composite work, representing only the last stage of Erasmus's annotations. No indication is given of the various stages of the text. It was in 1519 – the year of the letter to Ricci – that Erasmus added the following to his note on *Qui vocatur Christus*: "*Quamquam video doctos aliquot in hac sententia, ut existiment servatoris nostri Iesu nomen nonnihil diversum esse, a ducis Iesu & Iesu sacerdotis vocabulo, quod Hebraeis scribitur [IHVS]. Caeterum nostri Iesu nomen iisdem scribi literis quibus olim effabile dei nomen signabatur, interposita una duntaxat consonant Sin. Quod utinam doceri possit solidis argumentis, quam dictu plausibile est & gratiosum auribus Christianorum. Optarim equidem vel hanc unam ob causam extare evangelium Matthaei verbis & literis Hebraicis scriptum. Quod si esset, nil negocii foret, hanc de nomine Iesu opinionem, vel refellere, vel astruere.*" Writers on Erasmus, Reuchlin, and the Jews generally have all but left the *Annotationes in Novum Testamentum* out of account. That can only fundamentally distort Erasmus's attitudes and Erasmus's thought: the *Annotationes* are arguably the most important work he ever undertook.

30. Neither the Hebrew original nor the Greek Septuagint support Matthew's contention that Bethlehem is "in no wise least"; both make Bethlehem "small" or "unimportant."

31. Matthew 2, 5–6.

32. LB6: 11C–14F.

33. LB5, 1052AB.

34. LB5, 798F.

35. LB6, 989C–E.

36. LB6, 989C.

37. The "certain Spanish Jew" who taught Erasmus the distinction between *elohim* and *malachim* was Matthew Adrianus, a converted physician acquainted with Reuchlin, Pellican, Oecolampadius and the Amorbachs (EE3 n. 686). In 1519 Erasmus expanded his note on Hebrews 2,11; article 42 begins: "*Adrianus Matthaeus, homo mea sentenia non vulgariter*

exercitatus in suis literis." From 1522 his name was replaced by "*Quidam Hebraeus Hispanus*," probably because of the great offense caused by his inaugural lecture as professor of Hebrew at the *Collegium Trilingue* at Louvain (1519). Adrianus resigned, soon quarrelling also with Luther and others.

38. Cf. RV, Hebrews 2, 7 and margin; Psalm 8, 4–6 and margin.

39. LB5, A to C.

40. LB5, 1019C.

41. LB5, 313F f.; 1019C; cf. 470C; 1038Ff.; 1050ff.; 371Aff.

42. LB5, 29DE.

43. LB5, 371ff.

44. LB5, 27D,ff.; especially 29Cf.; 313Fff.; 311Dff. and 371Aff.

45. LB2, 371A–372C; 5, 29A.

46. LB5, 132B.

47. Cf. LB6, *5rᵒ, Preface to *Novum Instrumentum.*

48. PL33, 258, co.. 2, Cap 4, 14.

49. LB5, 523DE.

50. Matthew 23, 5.

51. PL26, 919F.; Pl36, 300f.

52. LB5, to 472AC from the beginning.

53. LB5, 379F; cf. 434E.

54. LB7, 140EG.

55. LB5, 380AB.

56. LB5, 240B f. (Some of these points are further developed in my *Ecstasy and the Praise of Folly,* chapter six, "The Inspired Exegesis of a Christian prophet," [Dackworth, 1980]).

57. Erasmus used both the term *marranos* and *semijudaei* in pejorative senses. This is mentioned by writers on Erasmus and the Jews (e.g. by Kisch, *Erasmus' Stellung zu Juden und Judentum,* p. 6f.), but the more important condemnation of such terms in *De amabili Ecclesiae Concordia* is almost consistently ignored.

58. LB5, 474CD.

59. In a famous phrase Erasmus wrote: "*An quisquam est nostrum qui non satis execretur hoc hominum genus? Si Christianum est odisse Judaeos, hic abunde Christiani sumus omnes*" (*Erasmi Epistolae,* 139–41). This has been taken in a racist sense, ignoring not only Erasmus's irony but also interpreting *hoc hominum genus* to mean the Jews as "a race"; cf. Gundersheimer, "*Erasmus, Humanism and the Human Cabala,*" p. 48. But Erasmus also uses the phrase to mean a kind, or type, of men. And however the phrase is to be interpreted, Erasmus is adamant that Christ excludes *nullum hominum genus* from salvation (LB 6 * 2vᵒ) Confusion can be caused by Erasmus's sustained applications of Christ's and Paul's condemnation of Jewish legalism to the contemporary church, to which, therefore, all these texts can be applied. When, for example, Erasmus glossed Matthew 23, 8, so as to make the word *Rabbi* apply to *Magistri Nostri*—the professors of theology of his day—it was no joke in the context of his *Paraphrases* (LB7, 120, 8).

60. On this and cognate questions see *Rabelais* (London, 1980), where these points are developed.

61. Consult Abel Lefranc, *Histoire du Collège de France* (Paris, 1893), especially p. 142ff.; also *Etudes Rabelaisiennes* 11 (1974), "Some Reflexions on the Dating of *Gargantua* A and B," and 13 (1976), "Some Further Reflexions on the Dating of *Gargantua.*"

62. The text of this legal action is given in Bulaeus, *Historia Universitatis Parisiensis* 6:239-44. On the point raised here, cf. p. 242: "Ne fait riens si on vouloit dire qu'ils peuvent lire & enseigner les langues Grecques & Hebraicques sans lire les Lettres saintes. [. . .]; les autres ne peuvent lire autres livres en Hebreu que la Bible, si n'est quelque Grammaire, *quae tantum continent regulas & observantias illas Grammaticulas,* par la lecture de laquelle seule il est impossible, *docere linguam Hebraicam.* Parquoy, *qui prohibuerit lecturam sacrarum litterarum Bibliae, per consequens & Hebraeas litteras quae alias doceri non possunt.*"

63. Bulaeus, *Historia Universitatis Parisiensis,* 6:243.

64. Bulaeus, 239f.

65. *Gargantua*, TLF, notes to episode of Janotus.

66. TL, TLF, XVI, 86–87.

67. *Pantagrueline Prognostication*, TLF; *Almanach pour l'an 1535.*

68. Full text of this oration in Celio Calcagnini, *Opera aliquot*, 1541, p. 556.

69. LB5, 293–94.

EUROPEAN UNIVERSITIES, 1300–1700:
THE DEVELOPMENT OF RESEARCH,
1969–1981, AND A
SUMMARY BIBLIOGRAPHY

J. M. Fletcher and Julian Deahl

he last few years have seen a steady increase in the number of scholars working on the history of universities in the late medieval and early modern period. Their work has been stimulated by a number of factors.

First, pressure from the International Commission for the History of Universities, energetically led by its president, Professor A. L. Gabriel, has encouraged the production of valuable bibliographies and has sponsored the production of individual and group research projects. At the time of writing, we still await the completion of work on the *Corpus Scholarium Bononiensium 1265–1330* and the final volumes of the analysis of the records of the German National at the University of Orleans, both supported by the Commission. Second, the establishment of a Professorial Chair in the History of Education at the University of Munich and a Readership in the History of European Universities at the University of Aston in Birmingham has encouraged the formation of groups of scholars whose publications have been produced or will be expected in the future. Third, the decision of the University of Oxford to support the official publication of its history has led several scholars to investigate in greater depth the development of the English universities. Fourth, the success of such journals as *Pedagogica Historica* in Belgium and the *History of Education* in Great Britain has assisted the introduction of new

324

reviews such as *Histoire de l'Education* in France and *The History of European Universities: Work in Progress and Publications* followed by *History of Universities* from Great Britain. These periodicals have printed articles and news of publications that have encouraged the cooperation of scholars working in this field. Finally, we have seen the celebration of several important anniversaries by universities established during the period 1300–1700. Many have commemorated their jubilees by the publication of works relating to their history. Especially important are the series produced from Uppsala (founded 1477), Marburg (founded 1527), Tubingen (founded 1477), Wurzburg (founded 1575), and Copenhagen (founded 1475); commemorative volumes from other universities are being prepared. Celebrations of the foundation of Vilnius (1579) have inspired publications in a surprising number of countries.

The publication of so much material on the history of European universities 1300–1700 has rendered our work of producing a short bibliography extremely difficult. Other scholars with no special interest in university history, but with a concern for the intellectual controversies of the fourteenth century, the development of the Renaissance, Reformation and Counterreformation, and the spread of scientific concepts in the seventeenth century, have also produced much work that is of some value to historians of the universities in this period. We have, therefore, attempted to indicate the most important books and articles produced during the past twelve years and to give some attention to works relating to university studies where we believe they have some relevance to this bibliography. We hope to give some idea of the variety of research during the past decade and also to show the particular fields on which scholars have concentrated.

Historians of European universities are now much better equipped with bibliographies than they were twelve years ago. We have noted here the major works, but many individual universities have produced selective bibliographies and guides that we have had no space to record. The work of Marie-Henriette Julien de Pommweol, *Sources de l'Histoire des Universités Françaises au Moyen Age: Université d'Orléans* (Paris, 1978), for example, is the first of what must be a valuable series of specialist publications. Especially important are the two volumes compiled by S. Guenée recording books relating to the history of French universities and Protestant academies founded before the Revolution; volume one (1981) contains a valuable bibliography for the history of the University of Paris. With the establishment of the new annual periodical (recording publications from 1977), *The History of European Universities: Works in Progress and Publications*, a regular bibliography will be available.

Recent years have also seen the republication of many out-of-print standard works. These have not been recorded in our bibliography, but we must draw attention to the existence of considerable numbers of important reprints now available from such firms as Scientia (Germany), Forni (Italy), and Kraus (Switzerland). Several international firms also supply copies in book or microfilm form of unpublished theses relating to the history of universities. Again, we have not had space to record such theses.

Perhaps the shadow of Rashdall's great work *The Universities of Europe in the Middle Ages*, last revised in 1936, still hangs heavily over scholars, for general works published during the past decade are useful but much less substantial than his pioneering study. We are still without a major general study of the history of European universities for the period 1500–1700. The reluctance of any one scholar to attempt the task of creating a synthesis of existing knowledge has led to the production of several collections of essays on general themes by groups of historians, the latest being that gathered under the general title *The Universities in the late Middle Ages* (Louvain, 1978), that entitled continuity and change in early modern universities, published in the inaugural volume of *History of Universities* (1981), and a short selection *University and Reformation* (1981) from The University of Copenhagen symposium.

Similarly, the great age of the publication of major sources seems understandably to have passed. The Oxford Historian Society has now completed publication of the medieval archives of the university. Few new collections of statutes have appeared, and it is probable that here little remains to be added to the work of earlier scholars. There are, however, a number of important projects in progress. Dr. de Ridder-Symoens and her collaborators are publishing the Acta of the German Nation at Orleans; Dr. Fletcher has published two of his projected three volumes of the Registrum Annalium of Merton College, Oxford, and, in collaboration with C. A. Upton, is transcribing the internal records of the college for the Tudor period; scholars at Padua are preparing editions of the various Acta of the university. Professor Gall and his colleagues continue work on the Matricula of the University of Vienna, and Professor Uiblein prepares additional volumes of faculty Acta for publication. We have recorded the production of useful source material from Franeker (Netherlands), Prague, Dole (France), Paris, Mainz, Jena, Parma, Salamanca, Lisbon, and other academic centers. Although it is not here our main concern, we must note that the situation as it concerns many of the major works of philosophers, theologians, and scientists of the period 1300–1700 is not so satisfactory. We still lack modern editions of many of the influential works produced at this time, although, of course, Erasmus has been well served by the work of recent scholars.

Earlier writers were often attracted to the history of universities by the desire to publicize the achievements of one scholar or record the origins of a group of students. This interest continues with the production of biographies of eminent personalities and collections of the names of students from one particular area or country. We have been unable to record all but the most significant of these biographies, but mention must be made of the late Dr. Emden's completion of his biographical register of the University of Oxford to 1540, the magnificent culmination to a lifetime of study of the university's history. This necessary work of identifying, where possible, the origins and careers of students is an indispensable preliminary to any attempt to analyze the social structure of the university. At present this has been or is being done for members of the German Nation at Orleans and for students at Prague, Tübingen, and other universities.

The events of 1968 in Paris, and later at other universities in Europe and North America, naturally focused attention on the

327

political role of the university and the possibility of students influencing its character and curriculum. Indeed, Dr. Cobban entitled his article in *Past and Present* (1971), "Medieval Universities" (1975). This interest, however, seems to have been of short duration, and has left only the series of essays published as *Universities in Politics* (1972) as evidence of the turbulence of the late 1960s. In fact, recent publications seem to mark a return to an earlier tradition with the series of articles from Dr. Swanson and, in 1979, his book *Universities, Academics and the Great Schism*, together with Dr. Bernstein's *Pierre d'Aily and the Blanchard Affair* (1978) and the various essays printed in *Génèse et débutes dû Grand Schisme d'Occident* (1980). There are also signs among younger historians of a revival of interest in the problems of conflict between town and gown during this period. This is perhaps partly stimulated by a desire to apply new methods of sociological enquiry to an old problem.

Classical studies of the history of universities placed great emphasis on the constitutional and administrative provisions made by early communities of scholars or founders. Recent work has examined rather the structure of the constituent parts of the university, its faculties and nations, for example, and has stressed the tension that often existed within this "united" community. There has been some concern to show how far the salaried masters were becoming an elite within the universities with close contacts with other groups of high social status outside. The interaction between this group and academic reformers, especially supporters of the New Learning, is beginning to receive attention, particularly from Professor Boehm in her recent articles. We are now much more aware of the tensions that existed within the universities and that were often reflected in local and national political maneuvers.

The most significant advance during the past years in the study of the character of the universities in this period has been encouraged by the influence of the sociologists and their techniques. The work of Franz Eulenburg in *Die Frequenz der deutschen Universitäten* (1904) was never really continued until recently. During the past few years attempts have been made, especially by Professor Stone and others in *The University and Society* (1975) and by Professor Kagan in *Students and Society in Early Modern Spain* (1974), to throw light on the numbers, age, social origins, and studies of university students; the graph, table, and statistical analysis are now recognized parts of many recent works on the history of universities. Perhaps it is not surprising that some of the conclusions reached by these methods have been challenged, for example in E. Russell's pointedly entitled article "The Influx of Commoners . . . An Optical Illusion" (*English Historical Review*, 1977). Such methods seem at the moment to be used mainly by Anglo-American historians, but European scholars are becoming aware of the value of such studies. Dr. de Ridder-Symoens has recently written of university history 'als Bron voor Sociale Geschiedenis' (*Tijdschrift voor Sociale Geschiedenis*, 1978). Such an interest will mean at least a temporary move away from a close study of statutes, charters, faculty *acta*, and such evidence toward an investigation of the biographies of individual students in an effort to compile meaningful statistics relating to the student population.

This, in turn, will mean a movement away from research into records produced by the university or held by the university toward an attempt to recover details of individuals from records in their communities of origin and from records of their subsequent careers outside the universities. This work is only beginning, but already positive results have been achieved in the preliminary publication of Professor McConica's "The Social Relations of Tudor Oxford" in *Transactions of the Royal Historical Society* (1977) and in the work of Dr. de Ridder-Symoens and her collaborators. On a smaller scale, the investigations of local historians, especially in the Low Countries and Germany, into the careers of students from their localities are of some value in specific cases. Further such projects can be expected in the future.

Such investigations are leading to a deeper inquiry into the question of the standing of the medieval and renaissance students. Stimulated by Dr. Fletcher's paper, *Wealth and Poverty in the Medieval German Universities* (1965), and his publication of the *Liber Taxatorum* (1969), other scholars have begun to investigate the concept of 'paupertas' in early universities. The situation of Scandinavian students, for example, has been studied by Mornet in a paper in *Le Moyen Age* (1978). The position has been excellently summarized in the brilliant and comprehensive paper by Professor Paquet, "Recherches sur l'Universitaire 'Pauvre' " in *Revue Belge de Philologie et d'Histoire* (1978). Similarly, the place of the nobility in universities has recently been more deeply investigated especially as this problem is closely associated with the changing role of the European universities in the sixteenth and seventeenth centuries. Such questions have especially attracted British, American, and German scholars and have already produced important studies by Stone, Müller, and Overfield. Typically, Müller subtitles his work on the university and the nobility, "Eine Soziostrukturelle Studie." The wider implications of such research have been discussed especially by Kearney in his *Scholars and Gentlemen: Universities and Society in Pre-Industrial Britain* (1970), but his views have not found general acceptance, and the criticism of his methods and conclusions made especially by Professor McConica (*English Historical Review*, 1972) must be carefully considered.

In the applications of these new attitudes to the university as a whole, there has been a revival of interest in the methods of supporting both universities and their staffs. The important study of 1929 by Fritz Ernst in his *Wirtschaftliche Ausstattung der Universität Tübingen in ihren ersten Jahrzehnten* came perhaps at the wrong time to encourage further research in this field, but the choice of the topic "The Economic and Material Frame of the Medieval University" for the Proceedings of the International Commission at San Francisco in 1975 has reopened this issue. Professor Gabriel subsequently (1977) edited the papers presented there under the same title. Interest has also been shown in the position of the salaried lecturers, and a number of studies, such as that by Rosen on the professors of the University of Basel (1969), have assisted in the understanding of how these appointments were financed.

A further indication of a growing concern to examine the development of universities from less traditional sources has been the interest shown in financial records. Here the English universities are in a very advantageous position since many of the colleges have detailed accounts of their income and expenditure. Such records have been very revealingly used by Dr. Cobban in his study of The King's Hall, Cambridge, (1969), and we can expect a deeper insight into Tudor Oxford from work now in progress by Fletcher and Upton on the domestic accounts of Merton College. Unfortunately, we do not have any detailed study of the accounts of the manors of the English colleges, so we lack any adequate knowledge of the methods used to control and exploit these estates.

Early historians, especially those writing for a more general readership, showed greater interest in the more lurid details of student life in the universities. This concern has now to some extent been elevated to a more serious attempt to understand the experiences of students using the methodology of sociological investigation. Murder in a university town, for example, has been examined under the heading of "Patterns of Homicide" for medieval Oxford by Hammer in *Past and Present* (1978). A most valuable source of information on student life in early seventeenth-century Spain has been edited by Haley (1977) as *Diario de un Estudiante de Salamanca*. The compiler of this diary was da Sommaia who studied at the university from 1603 to 1607. Another fringe activity of universities has been examined for Uppsala by a study of the academic choir, appropriately entitled "frnre 'chorus musicus' till symfonisk samverkan." Activities at Leyden in the late sixteenth century can now be studied from the substantial volumes issued by Witham under the general heading *De Dagelijkse Zaken van de Leidse Universiteit 1581–96*. This more serious interest in the day-to-day problems of student life can only be welcomed.

The limitations of the classical writers on the history of medieval universities—there is unfortunately no comparable general work on the later universities—have long been acknowledged; the editors of Rashdall's work in 1936, for example, were well aware of the inadequacies of his survey. They pointed out that little attention had been given to the investigation of the character of medieval teaching methods, the details of lectures and disputations, and to the content of the curriculum in the various faculties. Before 1936,

331

and especially after the Second World War, there has been a determined effort to remedy these deficiencies.

Important recent publications that throw light on the conduct of
lectures and academic exercises have appeared from Uppsala and
Prague. The former has issued (1977) *Specimens of the Oldest Lecture
Notes taken in the medieval University of Uppsala* as part of its Acta
Universitatis Upsaliensis, and from Prague we have a study by Kejv
of quodlibetical disputations under the general title of *Kvodlibetni
Disputace na Prazske Universite* (1971). We require many other such
studies before we can claim to have a full understanding of the
teaching activities of universities during this period.

Investigations into the content of the curricula of medieval and
Renaissance universities has developed rapidly during the past fifty
years. The scope of this research has presented us with considerable difficulty. We have attempted to indicate very briefly the lines
of inquiry of the past twelve years, but have not noted works that
appear to be directed to those concerned more with the study of
philosophy, law, theology, and medicine, as such, than with the
interaction of these studies with the university curriculum at this
date. It is never possible to maintain a clear division between the
two spheres, but we have printed here a selection of works that we
hope suggests the recent interests of scholars and their attempts to
remedy the deficiencies noted by earlier commentators on the
great standard works. We would emphasize the importance of the
article material published in eastern Europe, especially in the relevant Polish journals, which has perhaps not received the attention
it deserves.

As the largest faculty in most northern universities, and as the
faculty that then included a number of subjects that today are
considered as specialist areas in their own right, the Faculty of Arts
of the medieval and Renaissance universities has attracted considerable interest in the past twelve years. It is especially gratifying to
see the development of a readiness to study sympathetically the
character of medieval grammatical studies that were so strongly
criticized by Renaissance scholars whose attacks were too readily
accepted as justified by later historians. Building on such earlier

studies as those by Grabmann, recent scholars have given us a fuller understanding of the works of the "modistae" and the so-called "speculative" grammarians. Bursill-Hall has provided us with a translation of, and a commentary on, the most important of the texts used by these grammarians in his edition of the *Grammatica Speculativa* of Thomas of Erfurt (1972) Such an approach to grammar had, of course, a close connection with the study of linguistic logic, and this has been examined in a number of specialist articles that space has not allowed us to record. After such studies, we are now much better able to understand the reaction of humanistic supporters to these studies which, of course, they regarded as a corruption of the grammatical works they wished to see used.

The study of both grammar and rhetoric as university subjects appears to have assumed less importance in the sixteenth and seventeenth centuries, probably following the foundation of advanced grammar schools and other centers of Renaissance studies. The fate of the Master of Grammar at Cambridge has been traced by Bartlett (1977) in a peculiarly subtitled paper: "The Decline and Abolition of the Master of Grammar: An Early Victory of Humanism at the University of Cambridge." Medieval rhetoric has attracted valuable studies by Murphy (1971), Miller (1974), and others. Scholars, such as Jardine, have discussed the development of the study of dialectic in the Renaissance and post-Renaissance period with considerable interest in the interaction of new concepts of rhetoric and older approaches to Aristotelian logic.

The great history by Prantl (1855–70) remains unrivaled still as an introduction to the study of logic in the medieval period, but its comprehensiveness is matched by its bias against the very works it investigates. During the twentieth century, we have gradually become aware of the diversity of much of the medieval logical tradition, although we are still without good editions of many major texts and proper research into many areas, especially of fifteenth-century logic. However, the situation has been greatly improved by the publications of the past decade, but many of these are in thesis form or printed as short articles or editions of texts of too slight a nature to be included in this bibliography. We must, however, draw attention to the publications of L. M. de Rijk, of Polish scholars, of Spade, of Ashworth, and of Maieru, whose study *Terminologia Logica della tarda Scholastica* is a major contribution to our understanding of new movements in late medieval logic. When the work of Julian Deahl, who is in the process of analyzing the study of logic in the early fifteenth century, is added to the already published material, we shall be in a better position to evaluate the medieval legacy in logic. This is becoming all the more desirable as scholars working on the Renaissance period, such as McConica, Jardine, Schmitt, and Vasoli are suggesting that an interest in the study of logic and especially of the "pure" Aristotelian texts continued well beyond the close of the Middle Ages and had great influence on the philosophy of the seventeenth century.

The pioneering work of Maier and others on the history of science in the late medieval period received powerful support, especially in Great Britain and the United States, with the compilation by Dr. Weisheipl of his Oxford doctoral thesis (1957) on the Merton "scientists" of the fourteenth century and his subsequent publication in article form of much of this material. The Merton School, its contemporaries and subsequent influence especially in Renaissance Italy, have inspired a great number of books and articles of which we have indicated only the most significant produced in recent years. Research seems now to be moving toward a close study of the fate of this scientific "school" in the seventeenth century. Here the brilliant paper by Charles Schmitt, "Philosophy and Science in the Sixteenth Century Universities: Some Preliminary Comments" (1975) is an outstanding introduction to this complex subject. Interest seems to be shifting from Renaissance classical scholarship toward an attempt to evaluate the humanist response to the scientific progress of the later medieval period. Scholars are attempting to discover the true origins of the great advance in scientific knowledge that seems to characterize the last decades of the seventeenth century. Here Charles Webster's *The Great Instauration* (1975) is a perceptive and stimulating survey of the background to the early scientific enlightenment, and *New Perspectives on Galileo* (1978) contains some valuable and pointed suggestions.

Recent works on other subjects studied within the faculty of arts, which we have summarized under the general heading of "philosophy," again have a much wider audience than students of university history alone. Their relevance to academic organization is perhaps best seen in the "via" controversy, or *wegestreit*, that affected many faculties of arts and theology at the close of the medieval period. Here *Antiqui und Moderni* (1974) presents a collection of essays that adds greatly to our understanding of this controversy. Again, research seems to be concentrating on an attempt to evaluate the continuity or otherwise of medieval philosophical traditions into the renaissance and reformation. A number of collected papers and essays by such scholars as Kristeller, Michalski, and Moody has thrown considerable light on aspects of late medieval and Renaissance philosophy; Oberman has suggested some modifications (1977) to the conventional view of the relationship between academic Ockhamism and sixteenth-century thought in his study *Werden und Wertung der Reformation* (revised edition 1979, translated and abridged as *Masters of the Reformation* 1981). There are some signs of a movement away from a concern with the major figures of the late medieval and Renaissance period towards an interest in the lesser and perhaps more typical academics. The impact of the humanistic philosophy in Europe is being studied by scholars interested primarily in university history as an attempt to introduce new studies and new methods into the curriculum. Most studies, that of Jardine for Cambridge for example, investigate the reaction of one university to these reforming criticisms, but such scholars as Nauert (1973) and Boehm (1976) have attempted a broader analysis of this problem.

Work on the history of the three higher faculties has naturally been concerned with the life and work of the great controversialists of the period: we have, for example, new studies of Gabriel Biel, Arminius, Linacre, and Hotman. The Faculty of Theology at Louvain has now been studied in detail in a series of papers concerned with its history 1432–1797. For the academic study of law, major

335

works have been produced in Germany and in Italy. Professor Coing's *Handbuch* (1972–) is a valuable introduction to legal literature, and among the many important works relating to Italy, the study by Bellomo, *Saggio sull 'Universita nell' Eta del Diritto Comune* (1979), is a clear and comprehensive survey with much information on the teaching of law in Italian universities. The study of the history of theology, law, and medicine within the universities has perhaps suffered from the understandable concentration by scholars on the content of works produced by theologians, lawyers, and physicians rather than on their academic background. Interesting efforts, however, to understand the interaction of medical and arts studies within the Italian universities have been made by Siraisi and Schmitt, and Dr. Fletcher has published an account of the establishment of the Linacre lectureships in medicine at Oxford and Cambridge in *Linacre Studies* (1977). There is, however, ample scope for further research on the organization of the university higher faculties, especially in the later medieval, Renaissance, and seventeenth-century periods.

Research into the history of universities during this period as shown by publications during the past twelve years seems to be, therefore, in a flourishing state. The new techniques of sociological inquiry, despite the reservations expressed by some scholars, are producing fresh information relating to the structure of the universities. We now know far more about the "personnel" of the universities than we did ten years ago, although much further work is needed before we can attempt a general survey of the careers, status, obligations, and responsibilities of masters and students. Similarly, there has been considerable progress in our understanding of the content of university studies, especially in logic, grammar, and the sciences. However, scholars cannot afford to be complacent. Many major figures of this period can only be studied from unsatisfactory editions or from unedited manuscripts; much source material, especially from the German universities, remains available only in manuscript form. In some areas, the plethora of article material seems to indicate that the time is appropriate for at least a temporary synthesis to be made. Too many scholars still concentrate on a narrow field, working often on the history of one university. It is perhaps fitting that this short introduction should end with a plea to all scholars working in the field to support those international efforts now being made to bring together university historians and to publicize their work. Such a task of cooperation would be worthy of the subject it is designed to illuminate.

BIBLIOGRAPHY

BIBLIOGRAPHIES

Abe, H. R. "Zwanzig Jahre 'Beitr. zur Gesch. der Univ. Erfurt 1392–1816' mit einem Verzeichnis der Autoren und ihrer Veroffentlichungen." *Beitr. Zur Gesch. der Univ. Erfurt 1392–1816* 18 (1977):247–63.

Ashworth, E. J. *The Tradition of Medieval Logic and Speculative Grammar from Anselm to the end of the 17th Century. A Bibliography from 1836 onwards.* Toronto, 1978.

Baumgart, P., ed. *Bibliographie zur Gesch. der Univ. Wurzburg 1575–1975.* Wurzburg, 1977.

Bibliographie Internationale de L'Hist. des Universities, 1. Spain, Louvain, Copenhagen, Prague, Geneva, 1973.

⸺, 2. Portugal, Leyden, Pecs, Franeker, Basel, Geneva, 1976.

Coing, H., ed. *Handbuch der Quellen und Literatur der neueren Europaischen Privatrechtsgeschichte.* Munich, 1972–.

Flaschendrager, W. et al. *Forschungen zur Wissenshaftgeschichte, zur Gesschichte der Akademien, Universitaten und Mochschulen der DDR (1970–1979).* Berlin, 1980.

Fletcher, J. M., ed. *The History of European Universities. Work in Progress and Publications.* Birmingham, 1978–. An annual publication available from The Dept. of Mod. Langs., Univ. of Aston, Birmingham, England.

Gabriel, A. L. *Summary Bibliography of the Hist. of the Universities of Great Britain and Ireland up to 1800. Covering Publications between 1900–1968.* Notre Dame, 1974.

Garcia y Garcia, A. "Bibliografia de Hist. de las Universidades Espanolas." *Repert. de His. de las Ciencias Eclesiasticas en Espana* 7 (1979):599–627.

Guenee, S. *Bibliographie de l'Hist. des Universites Francaises des Origines a la Revolution*, 2, D'Aix en Provence a Valence et Academies Protestantes, Paris, 1978; 1, *Generalites. Universite de Paris*, 1981.

Hassinger, E. *Bibliographie zur Universitatsgeschichte. Verzeichnis der im Gebiet der Bundesrepublik Deutschland 1945–71 Veroffentlichten Literatur.* Freiburg, 1974.

Melanova, M. and M. Svatos. *Bibliografie k dejinam prazske univerzity do roku 1622 (1775–1975).* Prague, 1979.

Rossetti, L. "Bibliografia dell'Univ. di Padova," *Quaderni per la Storia dell' Univ. de Padova* 9–10 (1976–77):293–354.

Schmitt, C. B. *Critical Survey and Bibliography of Studies on Renaissance Aristotelianism 1958–69.* Padua, 1971.

Seck, F. et al. *Bibliographie zur Geschichte der Universitat Tubingen.* Tubingen, 1980.

Straube, M. and W. Flaschendrager. "Forschungen zur Gesch. der Universitaten, Hochschulen und Akademien der D.D.R.," *Zeitschrift fur Geschichtswissenschaft* 18 (1970), Sonderband:187–209.

Zanella, G. *Bibliografia per la Storia dell' Univ. di Bologna, Origini–1945.* Bologna, 1976

GENERAL WORKS

Baldwin, J. W. and R. A. Goldthwaite, eds. *Universities in Politics. Case Studies from the Late Middle Ages and Early Modern Period.* Baltimore, 1972. Contains essays relating to Bologna, Paris, Prague, Oxford, and Cambridge.

Bernhard, M., ed. *Goswin Kempgyn de Nussia: Trivitia Studentium. Eine Einfuhrung in das Universitatsstudium aus dem 15. Jahrhundert.* Munich, 1976.

Boehm, L. "Humanistische Bildungsbewegung und mittelalterliche Universitatsverfassung" in *Festschrift P. Acht.* Edited by P. Herde and W. Schlogl. Kallmunz, 1976: 311–33.

_____. "Libertas Scholastica und Negotium Scholare. Entstehung und Socialprestige des Akademischen Standes im Mittelalter." *Universitat und Gelehrtenstand 1400–1800*. Edited by H. Rossler and G. Franz, Limburg, 1970: 15–61.

Cobban, A. B. *The Medieval Universities: Their Development and Organisation*. London, 1975

Fletcher, J. M. "Change and Resistance to Change. A Consideration of the Development of English and German Universities during the Sixteenth Century." *History of Universities* 1 (1981): 1–36.

Gabriel, A. L., ed. *The Economic and Material Frame of the Mediaeval University*, Notre Dame, 1977. Contains essays relating to Orleans, Cracow, and the Universities of the Midi, France, and England.

_____. *Garlandia: Studies in the Hist. of the Mediaeval University*. Frankfurt a. M., 1969.

Garin, E. *L'Educazione in Europa 1400–1600*. Rome, 1976.

Genese et dubuts du Grand Schisme d'Occident. Paris, 1980. Contains some studies relating to university history.

Grane, L. *University and Reformation*. Leyden, 1981.

IJsewijn, J. and J. Paquet, eds. *The Universities in the late Middle Ages*. Louvain, 1978.

L'Histoire des Universites. Problemes et Methodes. Warsaw, 1980.

Maschke, E. and J. Sydow, eds. *Stadt und Universitat im Mittelalter und in der Fruhen Neuzeit*. Sigmaringen, 1977.

Paquet, J. "Recherches sur l'Universitaire 'pauvre' au Moyen Age." *Rev. Belge de Philologie et d'Hist.* 56 (1978):301–53.

Pedersen, O. *Studium General*. Aarhus, 1979.

Pollard, G. "The Pecia System in the Medieval Universities." *Medieval Scribes, Manuscripts and Libraries. Essays presented to N. R. Ker*. Edited by E. B. Parkes and A. G. Watson. London, 1978.

Radcliff-Umstead, D., ed. *The University World. A Synoptic View of Higher Education in the Middle Ages and Renaissance*. Pittsburgh, 1973.

Ridder-Symoens, D. de. "Universiteitsgeschiedenis als Bron voor de Sociale Geschiedenis." *Tijdschrift voor Sociale Geschiedenis* 10 (1978): 87–115.

Swanson, R. N. *Universities, Academics and the Great Schism*. Cambridge, 1979.

Verger, J. *Les Universites au Moyen Age*. Paris, 1973.

Zimmermann, A. *Antiqui und Moderni. Traditionsbewusstsein und Fortschrittsbewusstsein im spaten Mittelalter*. Berlin-New York, 1974.

AREA STUDIES

Belgium and the Netherlands

De Jonge, H. J. "The Study of the New Testament in the Dutch Universities." *History of Universities* 1 (1981):113–29.

Ekkart, R. E. O. *Athenae Batavae. De Leidse Universiteit*. Leyden, 1975.

_____. *Frieslands Hogeschool en het Rijksatheneum te Franeker*. Franeker, 1977.

Lunsingh Scheurleer, T. H. and G. H. M. Posthumus Meyjes, eds. *Leiden Univ. in the 17th Century. An Exchange of Learning*. Leyden, 1975.

Meijer, T. J., ed. *Album Promotorum Academiae Franekerensis 1591–1811*. Franeker, 1972.

Paquet, J. "La Ville et l'Univ. de Louvain en 1461." *Rev. Hist. Eccles.* 64 (1969): 5–22.

_____. "Statuts de la Fac. des Arts de Louvain 1567–8 (?)." *Bull. de la Comm. Roy. d'Hist.* 136 (1970): 179-271.

Posthumus Meyjes, G. H. M. *Geschiedenis van het Waalse Coll. te Leiden 1606–69*. Leyden, 1975.

Witkam, H. J. *De Dagelijkse Zaken van de Leidse Univ. 1581–96*. Leyden, 1970–75.

_____. *Immatriculatie en Recensie in de Leidse Univ. 1575–81*. Leyden, 1975.

_____. *Introductie tot de Dagelijkse Zaken van de Leidse Univ. 1581–96*. Leyden, 1969.

Woltjer, J. J. "De Positie van Curatoren der Leidse Univ. in de 16. Eeuw." *Tijdschrift voor Rechtsgeschiedenis* 38 (1970):485–96.

The British Isles

Aston, T. H. "Oxford's Medieval Alumni." *Past and Present* 74 (1977):3–40.

———— et al. "The Medieval Alumni of the Univ of Cambridge." *Past and Present* 86 (1980):9–86.

Bennett, J. A. W. *Chaucer at Oxford and at Cambridge.* Oxford, 1974.

Cant, R. G. *The Univ. of St. Andrews.* Rev. ed., Edinburgh, 1970.

Cobban, A. B. *The King's Hall within the Univ. of Cambridge in the Later Middle Ages.* Cambridge, 1969.

Duncan, A. A. M. "The Old and New Foundations." *College Courant* 29 (1977):14–20.

Durkan, J. "The Early Hist. of Glasgow Univ. Library 1475–1710." *Bibliothek* 7 (1977):102–26.

———— and J. Kirk. *The Univ. of Glasgow 1451–1577.* Glasgow, 1977.

Emden, A. B. *A Biographical Register of the Univ. of Oxford A.D. 1501 to 1540.* Oxford, 1974.

————. "Oxford Academical Halls in the Later Middle Ages." *Medieval Learning and Literature.* Edited by J. J. G. Alexander and M. T. Gibson. Oxford, 1976:353–65.

Fletcher, J. M. *Registrum Annalium Collegii Mertonensis 1521–67.* Oxford, 1974.

————. *Registrum Annalium Collegii Mertonensis 1567–1603.* Oxford, 1976.

Hackett, M. B. *The Original Statutes of Cambridge Univ.: The Text and its History.* Cambridge, 1970.

Hammer, C. I. "Patterns of Homicide in a Medieval Univ. Town. Fourteenth Century Oxford." *Past and Present* 78 (1978):3–23.

Jardine, L. "Humanism and Dialectic in 16th Century Cambridge: A Preliminary Investigation," in *Classical Influences on European Culture A.D. 1500–1700.* Edited by R. R. Bolgar. Cambridge, 1976:141–54.

————. "The Place of Dialectic Teaching in 16th Century Cambridge." *Studies in the Renaissance* 21 (1974):31–62.

Kearney, H. *Scholars and Gentlemen. Universities and Society in Pre-Industrial Britain 1500–1700.* London, 1970.

Logan, F. D. "The Origins of the so-called Regius Professorships. An aspect of the Renaissance in Oxford and Cambridge." *Renaissance and Renewal in Christian Hist. Studies in Church Hist.* Oxford, 1977: 271–78.

McConica, J. K. "Humanism and Aristotle in Tudor Oxford." *English Hist. Rev.* 94 (1979):291–317.

_____. "The Social Relations of Tudor Oxford." *Trans. of Roy. Hist. Soc.* 27 (1977):115–34.

Pantin, W. A. *Oxford Life in Oxford Archives.* Oxford, 1972

_____ and W. T. Mitchell, eds. The Register of Congregation 1448–63. Oxford, 1972.

Rich, E. E., ed. *St. Catherine's College, Cambridge, 1473–1973.* Cambridge, 1973.

Russell, E. "The Influx of Commoners into the Univ. of Oxford before 1581. An Optical Illusion." *English Hist. Rev.* 92 (1977):721–45.

Scotland, J. *The Hist. of Scottish Education.* London, 1969.

Smith, W. H. "Some Humanist Libraries in Early Tudor Cambridge." *The Sixteenth Century Journal* 5 (1974):15–34.

Stone, L., ed. *The Univ. in Society. 1. Oxford and Cambridge from the 14th to the Early 19th Century.* Princeton, 1975.

Tyacke, N. "Science and Religion at Oxford before the Civil War," in *Puritans and Revolutionaries.* Edited by D. Pennington and K. Thomas. Oxford, 1978.

Underwood, M. "The Structure and Operation of the Oxford Chancellor's Court from the 16th to the Early 18th Century." *Soc. of Archivists' Journal* 6 (1978): 18–27.

Watt, D. E. R. *A Biographical Dictionary of Scottish Graduates to A.D. 1410.* Oxford, 1977.

Weisheipl, J. A. "Repertorium Mertonense." *Mediaeval Studies* 31 (1969):174–224.

Eastern Europe

Beranek, K. ed. *Manual rektora se jmeny studentu zapsanych v ztracene matrice Univerzity, Karlovy v Praze v letech 1560-1582. Poznamenani jmen professaruv a jinych preceptoruv v uceni prazskem z roku 1604.* Prague, 1981.

Betts, R. R. "The Univ. of Prague: The First Sixty Years." *Essays in Czech Hist.*, pp. 13–28. London 1969.

Bohacek, M. "Prazska universitni statuta a jejich bolonsky vzor." *Studie o Rukopisech*, pp. 11–64. Prague, CSAV, 1969.

Cepenas, P. *Lietuvos Universitetas 1579–1803–1922.* Chicago, 1972.

Gabriel, A. L. *The Mediaeval Universities of Pecs and Pozsony.* Frankfurt am Main, 1969.

Kadlec, J. and R. Zeleny. "Ucitele pravnicke fakulty a pravnicke univ. prazske v dobe predhusitski 1349–1419." *Acta Univ. Carol.: Hist. Univ. Carol. Prag.* 18, fasc. 1 (1978):61–106.

Kavka, F. "Zur Frage der Statuten und Studienordnung der Prager theologischen Fak. in der vorhussitischen Zeit." *Folia Diplomatica* 1, pp. 129–43. Brno, 1971.

Kejr, J. *Kvodlibetni Disputace na Prazske Univ.* Prague, 1971.

Kolta, J. "Fejezetek a Pecsi Felsooktatas Tortenetebol." *Universitas* 1 (1972). Various articles.

Kowalczyk, M. *Krakowskie Mowy Uniwersyteckie z Pierwszej Polowy 15w.* Wroclaw-Warsaw-Cracow, 1970.

Michalewicz, J. and M. Michaelewiczowa. *Liber beneficiorum et benefactorum Universitatis Iagellonicae in seculis 15–18 (2): Fundationes pecuniariae Universitatis Iagellonicae saec. 15–18.* Cracow, 1980.

Molnar, A. A. debreceni foiskolara 1590–1610 kozott beiratkozott hallgatok tovabbi sorsa. *Diakkor dolgozatok 1977–1979*, pp. 201–27. Budapest, 1980.

Navratil, J., ed. *Kapitoly z Dejin olomoucke Univ. 1573–1973.* Ostrava, 1973.

Pesek, J. "Nektere otazky dejin univ. prazske Jagellonskeho obdobi 1471–1526." *Acta Univ. Carol.: Hist. Univ. Carol. Prag.* 18, fasc. 1 (1978):129–71.

Praha-Vilnius Sbornik praci k 400 vyroci zalozeni univerzity ve vilniusu. Prague, 1981.

Rabikauskas, P. *The Foundation of the University of Vilnius 1579.* Rome, 1979.

Rak, J. "Karlova Universita v provomoci defensoru 1609-22." *Acta. Univ. Carol.: Hist. Univ. Carol. Prag.* 17, fasc. 1 (1977):33–46.

Rakova, I. "Prehled rektoru a dekanu jednotlivych fak. prazske univ. v.

obdobi 1654-1773." *Archivni Zpravy Archivu Univ. Karlovy* 2 (1977):31-68.

Sandblad, H. "Om Dorpats Univ. under dess aidsta Skede 1632-56." *Lychnos*, 1975-76:211-35.

Triska, J. *Studie a prameny k retorice a k univ. literature.* Prague, 1972.

_____. *Retoricky styl a prazska univ. literatura ve stredoveku.* Prague, 1977.

_____. *Vybor ze starsi prazske univ. literatury.* Prague, 1977.

Vaclavu H. "Pocet graduovanych a negraduovanych studentu na prazske artisticke fak. v letech 1367-98 a jejich rozdeleni podle puvodu do universitnich narodu." *Acta. Univ. Carol.: Hist. Univ. Carol. Prag.* 17, fasc. 1 (1977):7-32.

Vetulani, A. *Poczatki Najstarszych Wszechnic Srodkowo-Europejskich.* Wroclaw-Cracow, 1970.

_____. *Z Badan nad Kultura Prawnicza w Polsce Piastowskiej.* Wroclaw-Warsaw-Cracow-Danzig, 1976.

Zathey, J. *Indeks Studentow Uniwersytetu Krakowskiego w Latach 1400-1500.* Wroclaw, 1974.

France

Bernstein, A. E. *Pierre d'Ailly and the Blanchard Affair. University and Chancellor of Paris at the beginning of the Great Schism.* Leyden, 1978.

Brockliss, L. W. B. "Medical Teaching at the Univ. of Paris 1600-1720." *Annals of Science* 35 (1978):221-51.

_____. "Patterns of Attendance at the Univ. of Paris 1400-1800." *Historical Journal* 21 (1978):503-44.

_____. "Philosophy Teaching in France, 1600-1740." *History of Universities* 1 (1981):131-68.

Feenstra, R. "De Univ. van Orleans in de Middelleeuwen. Centrum van Europese Rechtswetenschap en Kweekschool van Nederlandse Juristen." *Samenwinninge,* Zwolle, 1977.

Frijhoff, W. "L'Album Inclytae Nationis Belgicae de l'Univ. de Dole en Frache-Comte 1651-74."*Lias* 5 (1978):87-151.

Gabriel, A. L. "The Conflict between the Chancellor and the University of Masters and Students at Paris during the Middle Ages." *Die*

Auseinandersetzungen an der Pariser Univ. im 13. Jahrhundert pp. 106–54. Edited by A. Zimmermann. Berlin-New York, 1976.

Harris, P. R., ed. *Douai College Documents 1639–1984*. London, 1972.

Illmer, D. "Die Statuten der Deutschen Nation an der Alten Univ. Orleans von 1378 bis 1596." *Ius Commune* 6 (1977):10–107.

Pillorget, R. "L'Univ. de Bourges au 16ᵉ siecle." *Ethno-psychologie. Rev. de Psychologie des Peuples*. 2/3 (1977):117–33.

Ridderikhoff, C. M.; H. de Ridder-Symoens; and D. Illmer. *Premier Livre des Procurateurs de la Nation Germanique de l'ancienne Univ. d'Orleans 1444–1546. 1ᵉ partie. Texte des Rapports des procurateurs. 2ᵉ partie. Biographies des Etudiants*. Leyden, 1971–.

Saint-Louvent, F. de. "Les Facultes de Droit et de Droit Canonique a L'Univ. de Caen." *Mel. Offerts a P. Andrieu Guitrancourt*, 1973:833–55.

Sanderlin, D. *The Mediaeval Statutes of the College of Autun at the Univ. of Paris*. Notre Dame, 1971.

Talazac-Landaburu, A. *La Nation de France au Sein de l'Univ. de Paris d'apres le Livre de ses Procureurs*. Paris, 1975.

Verger, J. "Le Recrutement Geographique des Universites Francaises au Debut du 15ᵉ siecle." *Melanges d'Archeologie et d'Hist.* 89 (1970):855–902.

———. "Le Role Social de l'Univ. d'Avignon au 15ᵉ Siecle." *Bib. d'Humanisme et Renaissance* 33 (1971):489–504.

———. "Les Universites Francaises au 15ᵉ Siecle: Crise et Tentatives de Reforme." *Cahiers d'Histoire* 21 (1976):43–66.

Vidor-Borricand, M. *Une Universite Meconnue: l'Univ. d'Orange*. Avignon, 1977.

Viguerie, J. de. "L'Universite dans la Cite. L'exemple de l'Univ. d'Angers au 16ᵉ siecle." *Ethno-psychologie. Rev. de Psychologie des Peuples*, 2/3 (1977):135–46.

The German Empire

Abe, H. R. "Die Univ. Erfurt und der Deutsche Bauernkrieg 1524–5." *Beitr. zur Gesch. der Univ. Erfurt 1392–1816* 18 (1977):21–6.

Andritsch, J. *Die Matrikel der Univ. Graz* 1, 1586–1630. Graz, 1977.

Angerbauer, W. *Das Kanzleramt an der Univ. Tubingen und seine Inhaber 1590-1817.* Tubingen, 1972.

Arndt, K.-H. "Due Pestepidemie von 1682-83 und ihre Auswirkungen auf Stadt und Univ. Erfurt." *Beitr. Zur Gesch. der Univ. Erfurt 1392-1816* 18 (1977):27-89.

Baumgart, P. "Die Anfange der Univ. Helmstedt im Spiegel Ihrer Matrikel." *Braunschweig* 50 (1969):5-32.

Benrath, G. A. "Die Deutsche Evangelische Universitat der Reformationszeit." *Universitat und Gelehrtenstand 1400-1800*, pp. 63-83. Edited by H. Rossler and G. Franz. Limburg, 1970.

Boehm, L. and J. Sporl, eds. *Die Ludwig-Maximilians Univ. in Ihren Fakultaten.* Berlin, 1972.

Decker-Hauff, H. M., ed. *Beitr. zur Gesch. der Univ. Tubingen 1477-1977.* Tubingen, 1977.

―――― and W. Setzler, eds. *Die Univ. Tubingen von 1477 bis 1977.* Tubingen, 1977.

Duchhardt, H., ed. *Die Altesten Statuten der Univ. Mainz.* Wiesbaden, 1977.

Elsener, F., ed. *Lebensbilder zur Gesch. der Tubinger Juristenfakultat.* Tubingen, 1977.

Evans, R. J. W. "German Universities after the Thirty Years War." *History of Universities* 1 (1981):169-90.

Festschrift Univ. Salzburg 1622-1962-1972. Salzburg, 1972.

Finke, K. K. *Die Tubinger Juristenfakultat 1477-1534.* Tubingen, 1972.

Fletcher, J. M., ed. *The Liber Taxatorum of Poor Students at the Univ. of Freiburg im Breisgau.* Notre Dame, 1969.

Gall, F. et al. *Die Matrikel der Univ. Wien.* Graz-Vienna-Cologne, 1954-.

Goossens, J. "De Oudste algemene Statuten van de Universiteiten van Keulen en Leuven. Een vergelijkende tekstanalyse." *Arch. et Bibliotheques de Belgique* 48 (1977):42-78.

Grossmann, M. *Humanism in Wittenberg 1485-1517.* Nieuwkoop, 1975.

Haensel, W. *Catalogus Professorum Rintellensium. Die Professoren der Univ. Rinteln und des Akademischen Gymnasiums zu Stadtlagen 1610-1810.* Rinteln, 1971.

Heath, T. "Logical Grammar, Grammatical Logic and Humanism in Three German Universities." *Studies in the Renaissance* 18 (1971):9-64.

Heinemeyer, W; T. Klein; and H. Seier, eds. *Academia Margurgensis. Beitr. zur Gesch. der Philipps-Univ. Marburg.* Marburg, 1977.

Hubner, H., ed. *Gesch. der Martin-Luther-Univ. Halle-Wittenberg 1502-1977.* Halle, 1977.

Jauernig, R. and M. Steiger, eds. *Die Matrikel der Univ. Jena, 2, 1652-1723.* Weimar, 1977.

Kausch, W. *Gesch. der Theologischen Fak. Ingolstadt im 15. und 16. Jahrhundert 1472-1605.* Berlin, 1977.

Kleineidam, E. *Universitas Studii Erffordensis. Uberblick uber die Gesch. der Univ. Erfurt im Mittelalter (1392-1521).* Leipzig, 1964-69; *Die Zeit der Reformation und Gegenreformation (1521-1632).* Leipzig, 1980.

Kuhn, W. *Die Studenten der Univ. Tubingen Zwischen 1477 und 1534. Ihr Studium und ihre spatere Lebensstellung.* Goppingen, 1971.

Kurrus, T. *Die Jesuiten an der Univ. Freiburg im Br. 1620-1773.* Freiburg, 1977.

Mathy, H. *Die Univ. Mainz 1477-1977.* Mainz, 1977.

Muller, R. A. *Universitat und Adel. Eine Soziostrukturelle Studie Zur Gesch. der Bayerischen Landesuniv. Ingolstadt 1472-1648.* Berlin, 1974.

Muller, W., ed. *Freiburg in der Neuzeit.* Buhl, 1972.

Olechowitz, K. F. *Gesch. der Univ. Rostock 1419-1959, 1 (1419-1789),* s.1., 1970.

Overfield, J. H. "Nobles and Paupers at German Universities to 1600." *Societas: A Review of Social Hist.* 4 (1974): 175-210.

Rintelen, F. "Die Medizinische Fak. der Univ. Basel." *Basler Stadtbuch* (1970): 164-81.

Roegele, O. B. and W. R. Langenbucher, eds. *Ludwig-Maximilians-Univ. Munchen 1472-1972. Gesch., Gegenwart, Ausblick.* Munich, 1972.

Rosen, J. "Die Besoldung der Basler Professoren im Mittelalter. Finanzen und Salare an der Basler Univ. 1460 bis 1532." *Basler Nachrichten* 172 (1969).

Seifert, A. *Die Univ. Ingolstadt im 15. und 16. Jahrhundert. Texte und Regesten.* Berlin, 1973.

Seifert, A. *Statuten-und Verfassungsgesch. der Univ. Ingolstadt 1472-1586.* Berlin, 1971.

Steiger, G. and W. Flaschendrager, eds. *Magister und Scholaren. Professoren und Studenten.* Leipzig/Jena/Berlin, 1981.

Teufel, W. *Universitas Studii Tuwingensis. Die Tubinger Universitatsverfassung in vorreformatorischer Zeit, 1477–1534.* Tubingen, 1977.

Uiblein, D., ed. *Die Akten der Theologischen Fakultat der Universitat Wien 1396–1508.* 2 vols. Vienna, 1978.

Wackernagel, H. G. et al. eds. *Die Matrikel der Univ. Basel 1666/67–1725/ 26.* Basel, 1975.

Weber, H., ed. *Tradition und Gegenwart. Studien und Quellen zur Gesch. der Univ. Mainz, 1, Aus der Zeit der Kurfurstlichen Universitat.* Wiesbaden, 1977.

Wolff, H. *Gesch. der Ingolstadter Juristenfakultat 1472–1625.* Berlin, 1973.

Italy

Arnaldi, G. "Il Primo Secolo dello Studio di Padova." *Storia della Cult. Veneta. 2. Il Trecento*, pp. 1–18. Vicenza, 1976.

Bellomo, M. *Saggio sull' Universita nell' Eta del Diritto Comune.* Catania, 1979.

Brizzi, G. P., A. d'Alessandro, and A. del Fante, *Universita, Pricipe, Gesuiti, La politica farnesiana dell' istruzione a Parma e Piacenza (1515–1622).* Rome, 1980.

Brucker, G. A. "Florence and its University 1348–1434." *Action and Conviction in Early Modern Europe.* Edited by T. K. Rabb and J. E. Seigel. Princeton, 1979.

Ceccuti, C. "Alle Origini della Univ. Fiorentina: L'Istituto di Studii Superiori." *Rass. Storica Toscana* 23 (1977):177–203.

Clough, C. H. "Cardinal Gil Albornoz, the Spanish Coll. in Bologna, and the Italian Renaissance." *Studia Albornotiana* 12 (1972):225–38.

Colliva, P., ed. *Statuta Nationis Germanicae Universitatis Bononiae 1292–1750.* Bologna, 1975.

Di Simone, M. R. *La Sapienza romana nel Settecento.* Rome, 1980.

Ermini, G. *Storia dell' Univ. di Perugia.* 2d ed. Florence, 1971.

Fasoli, G. *Per la Storia dell' Univ. di Bologna nel Medio Evo.* Bologna, 1970.

Fletcher, J. M. "The Spanish College. Some observations on its Foundation and Early Statutes." *Studia Albornotiana* 12 (1972):73–91.

Griffiths, G. "Leonardo Bruni and the Restoration of the Univ. of Rome 1406." *Renaissance Quarterly* 26 (1973):1–10.

Gualazzinni, U. *Corpus Statutorum Almi Studii Parmensis.* Milan, 1978.

Matsen, H. J. "Students' 'Arts' Disputations at Bologna around 1500." *History of Education* 6 (1977):169–81.

Mor, C. G. "Momenti e Figure della Fac. Giuridica Modenese." *Rass. per la Storia della Univ. di Modena* 7 (1977):113–21.

Piana, C. "Nuove Documenti sull' Univ. di Bologna e sul Coll. di Spagna." *Studia Albornotiana* 26 (1976).

––––––. *La Fac. Teol. dell' Univ. di Firenze nel Quattro e Cinquecento.* Rome, 1977.

Schmitt, C. B. "The Faculty of Arts at Pisa at the Time of Galileo." *Physis* 14 (1972):243–72.

Siraisi, N. G. *Arts and Sciences at Padua. The Studium of Padua before 1350.* Toronto, 1973.

Svatov, M. "Studenti z Cexkych zemi na Univ. v Perugia 1579–1727." *Arch. zpravy Arch. Univ. Karlovy* 2 (1977):89–105.

Verde, A. *Lo Studio Fiorentino 1473–1503. Richerche e Doc., 3. Studenti 'Franciulli a Scuola' nel 1480.* Pistoia, 1977.

Portugal and Spain

Ajo Gonzalez de Rapariegos y C. J. M. Sainz de Zuniga. *Hist. de las Univ. Hisp. Origenes y desarrollo desde su Aparicion hasta nuestros dias.* Avila, 1957–.

Beltran de Heredia, V., ed. *Cart. de la Univ. de Salamanca 1218–1600.* Salamanca, 1970.

Esteban Mateo, L. "Catedraticos ecles. de la Univ. Valenciana del s. 16." *Rep. de Hist. de las Cien, Ecles. en Esp.* 6 (1977):349–439.

Garcia Oro, J. "Las Reformas Pretridentinas en los Col. Relig. de Salamanca." *Studia Hist.-Eccles.* Edited by I. Vazquez. Rome, 1977.

Hernandez, R. "Algunos Aspectos de la Crisis de la Univ. de Salamanca a Finales del s.16 y Principios del s.17." *Estudios* 34 (1978):67–98.

Jimenez, A. *Hist. de la Universidad Espanola.* Madrid, 1971.

Kagan, R. L. *Students and Society in Early Modern Spain.* Baltimore and London, 1974.

_____. "Universities in Castile 1500–1700." *Past and Present* 49 (1970):44–71.

Lopez Rodriguez, A. *El Real Col. de Cirugia de Cadiz y su Epoca.* Seville, 1969.

Monumenta Henricana. Coimbra, 1960–73.

Robles, L. "La Univ. de Valencia." *Temas Valencianos* 7 (1977):1–24.

Sa, A. Moreira da, ed. *Chartularium Universitatis Portugalensis 1288–1537.* Lisbon, 1966–.

_____. "La Foundation de l'Univ. a Lisbonne en 1288 et son Role dans le Developpement de la Culture Port. Jusqu'au Milieu de 15ᵉ siecle." *Rev. de Fac. de Letras de Lisboa* 3:12 (1971).

Sanchez, M. S. R. *Hist. del Real Col. de Estudios Mayores de la Purisima Concepcion de Cabra (Cordoba) 1679–1847.* Sevile, 1970.

Sandin Calabuig, M. *El Col. Mayor de Arzob. Fonseca en Salamanca.* Salamanca, 1977.

Sommaia, G. da. *Diario de un Estudiante de Salamanca 1603–7.* Edited by G. Haley. Salamanca, 1977.

Terrero, A. R. *Proyeccion Historico-Social de la Univ. de Salamanca a traves de sus Colegios (siglos 15 y 16).* Salamanca, 1970.

Torre, A. De La, Y Del Cerro. *Documentos para la Hist. de la Univ. de Barcelona.* Barcelona, 1971–.

Scandinavia

Acta Universitatis Upsaliensis. Stockholm, 1976–. A series of volumes relating to the history and organization of the Univ. of Uppsala. The first eleven volumes are concerned with the history of the different faculties, the twelfth with the univ. library, and the thirteenth with with univ. orchestra: "fran 'chorus musicus' till symfonisk samverkan."

Lindroth, S. *A History of Uppsala Univ. 1477–1977.* Stockholm, 1976.

Malmstrom, A. *Juridiska Fak. i Uppsala Studier till Fak. Hist.,* 1, Den medeltida fac. och dess hist. bakgrund. Stockholm, 1976.

Mornet, E. "Pauperes Scholares. Essai sur la Condition Materielle des Etudients Scandinaves dans les Universites aux 14ᵉ et 15ᵉ Siecles." *Le Moyen Age* 84 (1978):53–102.

Plitz, A. *Studium Upsalense. Specimens of the Oldest Lecture Notes taken in the Mediaeval Univ. of Uppsala.* Stockholm, 1977.

Rosen, J. *Lunds Univ. Historia, 1, 1668–1709.* Lund, 1978.

Sallander, H. *Uppsala Universitet Akademiska Konsistoriets Protocoll 1688–.* Stockholm, 1976–.

Stybe, S. E. *Copenhagen University: 500 Years of Science and Scholarship.* Copenhagen, 1979.

STUDIES OF THE FACULTIES

Faculty of Arts: Grammar and Rhetoric

Bartlett, K. "The Decline and Abolition of the Master of Grammar: an early Victory of Humanism at the Univ. of Cambridge." *History of Education* 6 (1977):1–8.

Bursill-Hall, G. L. *Speculative Grammars of the Middle Ages. The Doctrine of Partes Orationis of the Modistae.* The Hague, 1971.

————, ed. Thomas of Erfurt. *Grammatica Speculativa. An ed. with Trans. and Commentary.* London, 1972.

Miller, J. M.; M. H. Prosser; and T. W. Benson, eds. *Readings in Medieval Rhetoric.* Bloomington and London, 1973.

Monfasani, J. *George of Trebizond. A Biography and a study of his Rhetoric and Logic.* Leyden, 1976.

Murphy, J. J., ed. *Three Medieval Rhetorical Arts.* Berkeley, 1971.

Faculty of Arts: Logic

Ashworth, E. J. *Language and Logic in the Post-Medieval Period.* Dordrecht-Boston, 1974.

————. "Some Notes on Syllogistic in the 16th and 17th Centuries." *Notre Dame Journal of Formal Logic* 11 (1970):17–33.

Buridanus, Johannes, *Sophismata.* Critical Edition with an Introduction by T. K. Scott. Stuttgart-Bad-Cannstatt, 1977.

_____. *The Logic of*: Acts of the 3rd European Symposium on Medieval Logic and Semantics. Edited by J. Pinborg. Copenhagen, 1976.

Enders, H. W. *Sprachlogische Traktate des Mittelalters und der Semantikbegriff. Ein historische-systematischer Beitrag zur Frage der semantischen Grundlegung formaler Systeme.* Munich, 1975.

Henry, D. P. *Medieval Logic and Metaphysics.* London, 1972.

Maieru, A. *Lo "speculum puerorum sive Terminus est in quem" di Riccardo Billingham.* Spoleto, 1970.

_____. *Terminologia Logica della tarda Scolastica.* Rome, 1972.

Markowski, M. "Logik und Semantik im 15. Jahrhundert an der Univ. Krakau." *Medievalia Philosophica Polonica* 21 (1975):73–84.

Munoz Delgado, V. *La Logica Nominalista en la Univ. de Salamanca (1510–30).* Salamanca, 1972.

_____. "Logica Hispano-Portuguesa hasta 1600. Notas bibliograficodoctrinales." *Repertorio de Hist. de las Ciencias Ecles. en Espana* 4 (1972):9–122.

Nuchelmans, G. *Theories of (the) Proposition. Ancient and Medieval Conceptions of the Bearers of Truth and Falsity.* Amsterdam and London, 1973.

Peter of Spain (Petrus Hispanus Portugalensis). *Tractatus afterwards called Summulae Logicales.* First critical edition from the MSS. with an introduction by L. M. de Rijk. Assen, 1972.

Pinborg, J. *Logik und Semantik im Mittelalter. Ein Uberblck.* Stuttgart-Bad-Cannstatt, 1972.

Rijk, L. M. de. "Logica Cantabrigiensis. A Fifteenth Century Cambridge Manual of Logic." *Rev. Internationale de Philosophie* 29 (1975):297–315.

Spade, P. V. *The Medieval Liar: A Catalogue of the Insolubilia-Liberature.* Toronto, 1975.

Vasoli, C. "La Logica Europa nell' Eta dell' Umanesimo e del Rinascimento," *Atti del Convegno di storia della Logica (Parma, 1972),* pp. 61–94. Padua, 1974.

Faculty of Arts: Scientific Subjects

Butts, R. E. and J. C. Pitt, eds. *New Perspectives on Galileo.* Dordecht/Boston, 1978.

Eagles, C. M. "David Gregory and Newtonian Science." *British Journal for the Hist. of Science* 10 (1977):216–25.

Grant, E. *Physical Science in the Middle Ages.* New York, 1971, reissued by Cambridge University Press, 1977.

_____., ed. *A Source Book in Medieval Science.* Cambridge, Mass., 1974.

Molland, A. G. "The Geometrical Background to the 'Merton School.' " *British Journal for the Hist. of Science* 4 (1968–9):105–25.

Poppi, A. *Introduzione all' Aristotelismo Padovano.* Padua, 1970.

Rose, P. L. "Erasmians and Mathematicians at Cambridge in the early 16th Century." *Sixteenth Century Journal* 8, 2 (1977):47–59.

_____. *The Italian Renaissance of Mathematics.* Geneva, 1975.

Schmitt, C. B. "Philosophy and Science in 16th Century Universities: Some Preliminary Comments." *The Cultural Context of Medieval Learning,* pp. 485–537. Edited by J. E. Murdoch and E. D. Sylla. Dordrecht, 1975.

Seck, F., ed. Wilhelm Schickhard (1592–1635). *Astronom, Geograph, Orientalist, Erfinder der Rechenmaschine.* Tubingen, 1977.

Wallace, W. A. "The 'Calculatores' in Early 16th Century Physics." *British Journal for the Hist. of Science* 4 (1969):221–32.

Webster, C. *The Great Instauration: Science, Medicine and Reform 1626–60.* London, 1975.

Weisheipl, J. A., ed. *Albertus Magnus and the Sciences: Commemorative Essays 1980.* Toronto, 1980.

Faculty of Arts: Philosophy

Kristeller, P. O. *Medieval Aspects of Renaissance Learning.* Durham, N.C., 1974.

Kuksewicz, Z. *Albertyzm i Tomizm w 15 wieku w Krakowie i Kolonii.* Wroclaw, 1973.

_____. "La Philosophie au 15ᵉ siecle a l'Univ. de Cracovie. Tendances principales et lignes de developpement." *The Late Middle Ages and the Dawn of Humanism outside Italy.* Edited by G. Verbeke and J. IJsewijn. Louvain, 1972.

Leff, G. *William of Ockham. The Metamorphosis of Scholastic Discourse.* Manchester, 1975.

Markowski, M. *Burydanizm w Polsce w Okresie Przedkopernikanskim.* Wroclaw, 1971.

Michaeski, K. *La Philosophie au 14ᵉ Siecle.* Collected Essays. Edited by K. Flasch. Frankfurt, 1969.

Moody, E. A. *Studies in Medieval Philosophy, Science and Logic.* Collected Papers 1933-69. Berkeley, 1975.

Oberman, H. A. *Werden und Wertung der Reformation.* Tubingen, 1977. Rev. ed. 1979. Trans. and abridged as *Masters of the Reformation.* Cambridge, 1981.

Paque, R. *Das Pariser Nominalistenstatut zur Entstehung des Realitatsbegriffs der neuzeitlichen Naturwissenschaft: Occam, Buridan und Petrus Hispanus, Nikolaus von Autrercourt und Gregor von Rimini.* Berlin, 1970.

Schmitt, C. B. "Towards a Reassessment of Renaissance Aristotelianism." *Hist. of Science* 11 (1973):159-93.

Senko, W. *Les Tendances Prehumanistes dans la Philosophie Polonaise au 15ᵉ Siecle.* Wroclaw, 1973.

Una Juarez, A. *La filosofiadel Siglo 16. Contexto Cultural de Walter Burley.* Madrid, 1978.

Humanism and Classical Studies

Camporeale, S. *Lorenzo Valla: Umanesimo e Teologia.* Florence, 1972.

Erasmus en Leuven. Louvain, 1969. Catalogue of an exhibition with important notes.

Green L. C., "The Bible in the 16th Century Humanist Education." *Studies in the Renaissance* 19 (1972):112-34.

IJsewijn, J. "Henricus de Oesterwijck, the First Latin Poet of the Univ. of Louvain (ca. 1430)." *Humanistica Lovaniensia* 18 (1969):7-23.

Jardine, L. "Humanism and the 16th Century Cambridge Arts Course." *Hist. of Education* 4 (1975):16-31.

Martinek, J. "Prispevek k poznani vlivu university na rosvoj humanisticke literarni cinnosti v ceskych zemich." *Acta Univ. Carol.: Hist. Univ. Carol. Prag.* 10, fasc. 2 (1969):7-16.

Nauert, C. G. "The Clash of Humanists and Scholastics: An Approach to Pre-reformation Controversies." *The Sixteenth Century Journal* 4 (1973):1–18.

Oberman, H. A. and T. A. Brady, eds. *Itinerarium Italicum. The Profile of the Italian Renaissance in the Mirror of its European Transformations. Dedicated to Paul Oskar Kristeller on the Occasion of his 70th Birthday.* Leyden, 1975.

Pfeiffer, R. *History of Classical Scholarship from 1300–1850.* Oxford, 1976.

Porter, H. C. *Erasmus and Cambridge.* Toronto, 1970.

Rueda, J. L. *Helenistas Espanoles del Siglo 16.* Madrid, 1973.

Schmitt, C. B. *Cicero Scepticus: A Study of the Influence of the Academica in the Renaissance.* The Hague, 1972.

Watervolk, E. H. "Rodolphus Agricola, Desiderius Erasmus en Viglius van Aytta. Een Leuvens triumviraat." *Scrinium Erasmianum* 1 (Leyden, 1969):129–50.

Faculty of Theology

Andres, M. *La Teologia Espanola en el s. 16.* Madrid, 1977.

Bangs, C. *Arminius. A Study in the Dutch Reformation.* Nashville and New York, 1971.

Crahay, R. "Les conflits entre Erasme et la Fac. de Theologie (de Louvain)." *Erasme et la Belgique*, pp. 50–69. Brussels, 1969.

Ehrle, F. *Gesammelte Aufsatze zur englischen Scholastik.* Edited by F. Pelster. Rome, 1970.

Eijl, E. J. M. van, ed. *Facultas S. Theologiae Lovaniensis 1432–1797. Contributions to its History.* Louvain, 1977.

Ernst, W. *Gott und Mensch am Vorabend der Reformation: Eine Untersuchung zur Moralphilosophie und -theologie bei Gabriel Biel.* Leipzig, 1972.

Gargan, L. *Lo Studio Teologico e la Biblioteca dei Domenicani a Padova nel Tre- e Quattrocento.* Padua, 1971.

Nuttall, G. F. "Cambridge Nonconformity 1660–1710. From Holcroft to Hussey." *United Reformed Church Hist. Society Journal* 1, 9 (1977):281–88.

Schuling, H. *Caspar Ebel (1595–1664). Ein Philosoph der Lutheranischen Spatscholastik an den Universitaten Marburg und Giessen.* Giessen, 1971.

356

JOHN M. FLETCHER AND JULIAN DEAHL

Faculty of Law

Burmeister, K. H. *Das Studium der Rechte im Zeitalter des Humanismus im deutschen Rechtsbereich.* Wiesbaden, 1974.

Elsener, F. *Die Schweizer Rechtschulen vom 16. bis zum 19 Jahrhundert.* Zurich, 1975.

Gabriel, A. L., "Les Colleges Parisiens et le Recrutement des Canonistes." *L'Annee Canonique* 15 (1971):233–48.

Kelley, D. R. *Francois Hotman: A Revolutionary's Ordeal.* Princeton, 1973.

Kisch, G. "Die Univ. Basel und das Romische Recht im Funfzehnten Jahrhundert." *Civilta dell' Umanesimo.* pp. 117–24. Florence, 1972.

Kuttner, S., ed. *Proceedings of the Third International Congress of Medieval Canon Law: Strasbourg, 3–6 September 1968.* Vatican City, 1970.

Smith, J. A. C. *Medieval Law Teachers and Writers, Civilian and Canonist.* Ottawa, 1975.

Veen, T. J. *Recht en Nut. Studien over en naar Aanleiding van Ulrich Huber 1636–94.* Zwolle, 1976.

Vergottini, G. de *Scritti di Storia del Diritto Italiano.* Milan, 1977.

Faculty of Medicine

Demaitre, L. E. *Doctor Bernard de Gordon. Professor and Practicioner.* Toronto, 1981.

O'Malley, C. D. *The History of Medical Education.* Berkeley, 1970.

Maddison, F.; M. Pelling; and C. Webster, eds. *Linacre Studies. Essays on the Life and Work of Thomas Linacre c. 1460–1524.* Oxford, 1977.

Temkin, O. *Galenism. Rise and Decline of Medical Philosophy.* Ithaca, New York and London, 1973.

.

NOTES ON CONTRIBUTORS

Heiko A. Oberman is Professor Ordinarius für Kirchengeschichte and Direktor des Instituts für Spätmittelalter und Reformation of the University of Tübingen. His many publications include *The Harvest of Medieval Theology* (Cambridge, Mass., 1963) and *Werden und Wertung der Reformation. Vom Wegestreit zum Glaubenskampf* (Tübingen, 1977).

Lewis W. Spitz is William B. Kennan, Jr., Professor of History at Stanford University. He is the author of many books and articles on humanism, the Renaissance, and the Reformation, including *The Religious Renaissance of the German Humanists* (Cambridge, Mass., 1963) and *The Renaissance and Reformation Movements* (Chicago, 1971).

Edward Grant is professor of history and of the history and philosophy of science at Indiana University. He is the editor, translator, and commentator on three basic texts of Nicole Oresme, the author of many articles on scientific thought in the late Middle Ages and Renaissance and *Physical Science in the Middle Ages* (New York, 1971).

William J. Courtenay is professor of history at the University of Wisconsin. He is coeditor of *Canonis Misse Expositio Gabrielis Biel*, 4 vols. (Wiesbaden, 1963–67), the author of numerous articles on fourteenth-century thought and of *Adam Wodeham. An Introduction to his Life and Writings* (Leiden, 1978).

John M. Fletcher is reader in the history of European universities at the University of Aston in Birmingham. He is the British representative on the International Commission for the History of Universities, editor of the annual publication *History of European Universities: Work in Progress and Publications*, joint editor of *Studies in the History of European Universi-*

ties, and associate editor of the new journal *History of Universities*. His many publications include editions of the statutes of the Faculty of Arts at Freiburg, of the *Freiburg Liber Taxatorum*, and of the *Registrum Annalium Collegii Mertonensis*. He is contributing chapters to the first three volumes of the official history of the University of Oxford.

Paul W. Knoll is associate professor of history at the University of Southern California. He is the author of *The Rise of the Polish Monarchy. Piast Poland in East Central Europe, 1230–1370* (Chicago, 1972) and of numerous articles on Polish intellectual life during the late Middle Ages and Renaissance.

Guy Fitch Lytle is assistant professor of history at the University of Texas. He is the author of several articles on Oxford University from the late Middle Ages through the Reformation.

James H. Overfield is an associate professor of history at the University of Vermont. He has published articles on various aspects of the late medieval German universities, in particular humanist-scholastic relations and the make-up of student populations.

M. A. Screech is Fielden Professor of French Language and Literature at University College London, the editor of several Rabelais texts and most recently the author of *Rabelais: La Pantagruéline Prognostication* (Geneva and Paris, 1975) and *Rabelais* (London, 1979).

Julian Deahl has been working for the past five years with John M. Fletcher on a study of the teaching of logic in Europe, and especially at Oxford and Prague, during the late medieval period. He is at present assistant secretary to the editors of the planned *Encyclopedia of the Middle Ages, Renaissance and Reformation* to be published by E. J. Brill of Leiden. He is joint editor of *Studies in the History of European Universities*.

NAME INDEX

Abelard, 164
Accursius, 165
Agricola, Rudolph, 49; *De inventione dialectica*, 9
Ailly, Pierre d', 142f, 145 n.6, 202
Albert I, Duke of Prussia, 55
Albrecht, Archbishop of Mainz, 30
Alhazen: *Optics*, 70, 72
al-Khwarizmi: *Algebra*, 70
Altdorf, University of, 63
Amsdorf, Nicholas, 63
Anglicus, Robertus: *Tractatus quadrantis* (*Treatise on the Quadrant*), 71
Appulby, William, 231
Aquila, Peter of, 118, 152 n.53
Aquinas, Thomas, 5, 37, 58, 271, 297
Arezzo, Bernard of, 135
Aristotle, 7–8, 24, 42, 49, 51–52, 53–54, 58, 69–71, 78ff, 81, 86ff, 109, 143, 148 n.20, 164; *Nicomachaean Ethics*, 52
Ascham, Roger, 51
Augustine, 54, 127, 296, 303–4, 308, 310–11, 319; *De musica*, 73
Aureol, Peter, 133
Aurifaber, John, 142
Aurillac, Gerbert of, 77. *See also* Sylvester II, Pope
Autrecourt, Nicholas of, 121–24, 136, 155 n.70
Averroes, 69
Avicenna, 53, 70, 76

Bacon, Roger, 72–75
Baduel, Claude, 51
Baldus, 45
Basel, John of, 137
Basel, Council of, 27–29, 48, 198ff, 202–4
Basel, University of, 36, 55

Batmanson, John, 228
Baysham, John, 230
Beauchamp, Richard, Earl of Warwick, 230
Beckmann, Otto, 50
Béda, Noel, 8, 293, 314f
Bede (Venerable), 69
Bekynton, Thomas, 226
Bellays, du, 315
Bertuccio, 76
Biel, Gabriel, 33, 276 n.49; *Collectorium*, 34
Billingham, Richard, 106
Boethius, 20, 69, 73, 95 n.22; *Arithmetica*, 73, 78; *Musica*, 73
Bolney, Bartholomew, 228
Bologna, University of, 62, 75–76, 97 n.42, 135f, 141, 165–66, 170, 173, 184, 275 n.27; anatomical dissection at, 76; secessions from, 179, 184
Borzynów, Derslaw of, 198f, 200
Bradwardine, Thomas, 103, 110, 114, 131f, 148 n.19, 149 n.32; *Arithmetica speculativa*, 95 n.22
Brassikan, Johannes, the Younger, 34
Brecknock, William, 232
Brześć, Lutek of, 199
Buridan, John, 85f, 87f, 118f
Burley, Walter, 110, 114, 116, 151 n.47
Bury, Richard de, 244
Busche, Hermon von, 50

Cajetan, Cardinal, 35
Calcagnini, Celio, of Ferrara, 318
Calvin, John, 59
Cambridge, University of, 176–78, 181f, 186f, 268; King's Hall College, 225
Camerarius, Joachim, 55
Campsale, Pseudo-, 105
Canisius, 58

NAME INDEX

Capella, Martianus, 69
Casimir the Great, King, 191
Casimir the Jagiellonian, King of Poland, 204
Cassiodorus, 69
Caxtone, Robert, 227
Ceffons, Peter, 133, 135
Celtis, Conrad, 35, 49, 274 n.26
Cesena, Michael of, 119
Chaderton, Edmund, 231
Chalcidius, 69
Charles V, King of France, 75
Charles VII, King of France, 183
Chartres, School of, 69
Chatton, Walter, 105, 130–32, 147 n.7
Chauliac, Guy de, 76
Chytraeus, David, 56
Cicero, 20, 50, 54
Ciołek, Stanislaw, of Poznań, Bishop, 199
Clement V, Pope, 294
Coimbra, University of, 185
Cologne, *studia generalia*, of the mendicant orders, 139–140,144
Cologne, University of, 36, 48, 50, 161 n.144, 205, 271; matriculation records, 262–65, 279–80
Constance, Council of, 27, 32, 191–93, 266
Copenhagen, University of, 47, 55
Cracow, University of, 2, 5, 16, 104, 191ff, 208 n.6
Crathorn, 130
Cremona, Gerard of, 164f

Dillingen, University of, 37, 58
Dobra, John of, 200
Dudley, Edmund, 227
Dumbleton, John, 106, 110
Durham, diocese of, benefices of, 245

Eberhard, Graf, 171
Eberhart the Bearded, Count, 28
Eck, Johannes, 30, 32, 35, 57
Eckhart, Meister, 119
Edward III, King of England, 185ff
Edward IV, King of England, 230
Elgot, John, 201–2
Erasmus, 2, 8–9, 15, 22, 34, 36, 50, 60, 244, 266, 293–94, 295ff, 314, 317, 319; *Adages*, 301; *Annotations in Novum Testamentum*, 296–97, 300, 301ff, 306, 313, 319; *Collo-*

quies, 296, 310; *De Ratione concionandi*, 301; *Enchiridion Militis Christiani*, 296, 301; On Psalm 33, 310f; On Psalm 41, 305; On Psalm 83, 311; *Praise of Folly*, 60, 298, 309, 310
Erfurt, studium of, mendicant, 139–40, 143–44
Erfurt, University of, 24–25, 33, 48–49, 52, 104, 166, 202, 205; matriculation records, 260f, 263, 281
Etaples, Lefevre d', 305f
Euclid: *Elements*, 69, 71, 73
Eugenius IV, Pope, 198, 203
Eyb, Gabriel von, 30

Faber, Felix, 256–57, 260
Falkenberg, John, 197
Felix V, Pope, 28, 200–203, 205
Ferdinand I, Emperor, 55
Ferdinand II, Emperor, 11, 62
Ferrara, University of, 46
Fiennes, Thomas, 224
Fitzralph, Richard, 106
Florence, city of: business schools, 96 n.23
Florence, University of, 46, 62, 168
Francis I, King of France, 293–94
Frankfurt-on-the-Oder, University of, 55–56, 254, 264, 286
Frederick II, Emperor, 184
Frederick the Wise, Elector, 8, 28, 35, 50f
Freiburg-im-Breisgau, University of, 9, 271; matriculation records, 263f, 284f
Fuggers, the, 30
Fuld, Jesuit College of, 58

Galen, 53, 70, 76
Galileo, 91
Gemmingen, Uriel of, 256
Geneva, University of, 36
George, Duke of Saxony, 55
Giessen, University of, 56
Gikatilia, Joseph ben Abraham: *Gate of Light*, 300
Gratian: *Decreta*, 294
Gratius, Ortuinus, 316, 318
Greenhurst, Ralph, 228
Greifswald, University of, 50, 55, 181, 262; matriculation records, 264, 284
Groote, Geert, 33
Grosseteste, Robert, 73–74; *On Lines, Angles, and Figures*, 74

Grunwald (Tannenbeg), Polish victory at, 192

Hales, Alexander, 73
Halifax, 131–32, 143, 148 n.19
Hasselbach, Thomas, 276 n.48
Heidelberg, University of 24, 50, 55–57, 104, 273 n.12; matriculation records, 262–63, 265, 278–79
Helmstedt, University of, 55f
Hesse, Benedict, 201–2
Heytesbury, William, 106, 110, 142, 149 n.23
Hippocrates, 53, 70
Holocot, Robert, 103, 106–7, 111, 130, 132, 143, 147 n.11; Sapientia Commentary, 23
Honorius III, Pope, 176
Hostiensis, 195
Humphrey, Duke of Gloucester, 230
Hus, John, 193
Huswyfe, Roger, 229

Ingolstadt, University of 28–30, 57–58, 61; matriculation records, 263f, 269, 285; theologians at, 270–71

Jena, University of, 55–56
Jerome, Saint, 296, 301, 303–5, 308–9, 311
John, King of England, 181f
John XXII, Pope, 119
John Frederick, Elector of Saxony, 55

Kaisersberg, Geyler von, 267
Kent, Thomas, 229
Kilvington, Richard, 110, 114, 149 n.32
Königsberg, University of, 55
Kozłowski, Nicholas, 199
Kyngesmyll, John, 228

Lancaster, Duchy of: administrators, 230
Langenstein, Henry of, 276 n.48
Lang, Johannes, 50
Łaskarz of Poznan, Andrew, 193
Lasocki, Nicholas, 199
Lauffen, Battle of, 33
Leipzig, University of, 47, 49, 53, 55, 174, 205; matriculation records, 264, 269, 276 n.45, 282
Lille, Alan of, 77
Lombard, Peter, 20, 36–37, 54, 83; Sentences, commentaries, 112, 114–16, 121f, 125–27,

131, 133, 135–36, 140, 143f, 270; Sentences, questiones literature, 83f
Lombardi, Bernardus, 118
Louvain, Collegium Trilingue, 36
Louvain, University of, 9, 28, 63, 168
Ludwig the Rich, Duke of Bavaria, 28
Ludzisko, John of, 200, 210 n.38
Luther, Martin, 2, 3, 8–9, 12, 22, 30, 32–33, 34f, 36f, 42, 46, 50–51, 54, 57, 59, 271; Babylonian Captivity of the Church, 52–53; Disputatio contra scholasticam theologiam, 52; Heidelberg disputation, 52
Lutterell, 105, 131–32
Lyra, Nicholas of, 297

Macrobius, 69
Magdeburg, studium of, mendicant, 139
Mainz, University of, 30
Marbach, Johannes, 10–14
Marburg, University of, 25, 53f
Marchia, Francis of, 115
Marschalk, Nicolaus, 50
Martin V, Pope, 28, 197
Martyn, Richard, 226f
Massa, Michael of, 116–17
Maximilian I, Emperor, 49
Maximilian II, Emperor, 11, 56
Mayronis, Francis, 115
Medici, Lorenzo di, 46
Meinhardi, Andreas: Dialogus, 50
Melanchthon, Philip, 6, 9, 35, 51–53, 54f, 58–59, 63, 271, 293; De corrigendis adolescentia studiis, 51
Merseburg, Otto of, 143
Mirecourt, John of, 133–35
Moerbeke, William of, 70
Mondeville, Henri de, 76
Montpellier, medical studies at, 75, 176
More, Thomas, Saint, 227
Mosellanus, Peter, 49, 51
Munich, Franciscan convent at, 141
Muris, Johannis de: Ars nove musice (Art of the New Music), 73; Musica speculativa secundum Boetium, 73

Nemore, Jordanus de: Arithmetica, 95 n.22; Tractatus de ponderibus (Treatise on Weights), 71f
Newport, John, 228
Nicholas V, Pope, 204–5

Niger, Monachus, 143
Nipeth, Conrad of, 142

Ockham, William of, 103, 105–6, 107–10, 112, 115–18, 121f, 123f, 126, 129f, 131f, 141–45, 146 n.6, 147 n.7, 148 n.14, 148 n.17, 151 n.41, 151 n.47, 155 n.73, 155 n.75, 158 n.113
Oleśnicki, Zbigniew, Bishop, 198, 203–4
Olivi, Peter John, 119
Oresme, Nicole, 74
Origen, 308, 311
Orleans, University of, 180
Orosius, 53
Orvieto, Hugolino of, 133–35
Osiander, Lucas, 13f
Oxford, University of, 70–71, 103, 105–7, 108, 111-12, 115–16, 119–20, 136, 141, 166–67, 169, 175ff, 181f, 213ff, 237, 268; All Souls College, 225; Balliol College, 220; Merton College, 166; New College, 216, 218, 220, 221–23, 225, 228, 237, 245; Oriel College, 186; Queens College, 220; relations of Oxford with Paris, 119ff; Winchester College, 221

Padua, University of, 62
Paltz, John of: Supplementum Coelifodinae, 33
Pappus, Johannes, 13ff
Paradyż, James of, 201, 203, 207, 210 n.38
Paris, College of Royal Lecturers, 36
Paris, Sorbonne, 62, 314–16
Paris, University of, 5, 21, 27, 70–71, 75, 78–79, 85, 88, 104, 112, 115, 116ff, 119–20, 121-22, 124, 133, 135ff, 138, 140–41, 145, 153 n.62, 166, 174, 176, 178, 180, 183, 205, 293, 314; Condemnation of 1277, 86–88; Condemnation of 1347, 134–36; Oath of 1272, 85f; relations of Paris with Oxford, 117ff, 136
Paul, 301
Pavia, University of, 45
Pecham, John, 72
Perugia, Paul of, 135
Petrarch, Francesco, 7f
Pfefferkorn, 300
Philipp of Hesse, Prince, 53
Piacenza, University of, 45
Pisa, Council of, 27
Pisa, University of, 45, 62, 168

Pius II (Aeneas Silvius Piccolomini), Pope, 6, 199
Plato: Republic, 309; Timaeus, 69
Poitiers, University of, 183
Porte, William, 231–32
Potman, William, 231
Prague, Franciscan convent at, 143
Prague, studium of, mendicant, 139–41, 144
Prague, University of, 23f, 39 n.8, 136, 173f, 180
Ptolemy, 72; Almagest, 69, 72
Pythagorus, 301

Rabelais, 2, 8, 15, 294, 312ff, 319; Gargantua, 316; Pantagruel, 313, 315; Pantagrueline Prognostication, 313; Quart Livre de Pantagruel, 314, 317; Tiers Livre, 314, 316–17
Racibórz, Lawrence of, 201–2
Ravenna, Peter of, 50
Reading, John of, 105, 111
Regensburg, Frederick of, 143
Reisch, Gregor: Margarita Philosophica, 20
Reuchlin, Johann, 8, 35, 57, 296, 300, 303; Augenspiegel, 316; De Verbo magnifico, 301
Ricci, Paul, 300, 302–3, 312
Rimini, Gregory of, 122, 125, 126ff, 134–35, 154 n.66, 156 n.87, 156 n.88, 157 nn.98, 99, 100, 101; 159 n.129
Ripa, Jean de, 131, 133
Rodington, John, 106, 124
Rostock, University of, 47, 50, 55, 180; matriculation records, 264, 283
Rudolf II, Emperor, 62
Rufus, Mutianus, 49
Rydon, Robert, 227

Sacrobosco, John of: Algorismus vulgaris, 73, 95 n.23; De sphaera, 72; Theorica planetarum (Theory of the Planets), 72
Salerno, medical studies at, 75
Salisbury, John of, 77, 164; on dialectic, 5, 8
Scheurl, Christoph, 30, 50
Schippower, Johann, 256–57
Scotus, John Duns, 116–17
Sevenoaks School, 237
Seville, Isidore of, 69
Sigismund, Emperor, 191
Stamford, secession of, from Oxford, 175ff, 182, 185ff
Stamford, town of, 169

Stapledon, Bishop, 226
Strasbourg, Thomas of, 118, 127
Strasbourg, city of, 12, 14f
Strasbourg, Gymnasium, Academy, University of, 10f, 14–15, 29, 36
Strzempiński, Thomas, 199, 201–3
Sturgeon, Richard, 228
Sturm, Johannes, 10ff, 51
Sutton, William, 106
Sylvester, II, Pope, 77. *See also* Aurillac, Gerbert of

Tempelfeld, Nicholas, 199
Tiptoft, John, 224
Totting of Oyta, Henry, 144
Toulouse, University of, 62
Trappe, Nicholas, 228
Trent, Council of, 57, 271
Trithemius, Johann, 257; *Institutio vitae sacerdotalis*, 256
Trutvetter, Jodocus, 50
Tübingen, University of, 13, 28–29, 30, 33f, 36, 49–50, 55, 57, 171; matriculation records, 259, 263, 269, 285–86
Tyngilden, Henry, 227

Ulrich, Duke, 33
Urbach (Auerback or Frebach), John, 196
Urban V, Pope, 75, 236

Valencia, Gregor of, 58
Valla, Lorenzo, 7, 8
Vargas, Alfonsus, 133, 135
Varignana, Bartolommeo da, 76

Vercelli, city of, 184
Vienna, College of Poets and Mathematicians, 49
Vienna, Council of, 30
Vienna, studium of, mendicant, 139
Vienna, University of, 49, 104, 205, 254, 263, 271; matriculation records, 277–78
Virgil, 50
Visconti, Giangalleazzo, 45
Vladimiri, Paul, 17, 20, 21, 24; *Ad aperiendam*, 196; *Iste tractatus*, 197; *Opinio Ostiensis*, 195; *Quoniam error*, 196; *Saevientibus*, 195

Wakefield, Robert, 296
Wales, Thomas of, 119
Wallopp, Richard, 228
Westphalia, Peace of, 56
Whitstones, James, 230
Wimpheling, Jacob, 256–57, 267
Wittenbeg, city of, 34
Wittenberg, University of, 25, 28–29, 33, 48, 50f, 52–53, 54–56, 61, 264, 271, 286; reform of, 51
Władysław III (Warneńczyk), King, 200
Władysław Jagiełło, King, 191–94, 197–98
Wodeham, Adam, 103, 106–7, 111–12, 124, 128, 130f, 132, 144, 148 n.13, 148 n.19, 151 n.41
Wolfram of Lwów, Peter, 193f
Würzberg, University of, 58
Wykeham, William of, Bishop of Winchester, 216, 220, 223, 225, 238

Zasius, Ulrich, 9

SUBJECT INDEX

anatomy (dissection), 76
anticlericalism, 236, 255
arithmetic, in university curriculum, 73–74, 84, 96 n.24, 96 n.30
arts course curriculum, 58–59, 83, 85–86, 269–70
astronomy, in university curriculum, 72, 74–75, 97 n.31
Augsburg Confession, 11

Bible, in university curriculum, 270ff
Bible, New Testament, 296–99, 301–6, 312, 319
Bible, Old Testament, 298–99, 306–7, 308f, 310, 312, 317, 319
bishops, university graduates as, 239ff

cabala, cabalists, 296–97, 300–303, 312, 313f, 316–17
Chaldaeans, 317
clergy, careers of, 218, 221, 225, 230–31, 249 n.12, 267
clergy, education of, 214, 216, 238–43
clergy, educational status of, 255f, 257–58, 260, 265ff
clergy, terms of identification of, 261f
clericus, 262f
colleges, at universities, 171
conciliar movement, 3, 5, 27, 29–30, 32, 47, 190, 198, 201, 203–4, 206
Concordat of 1516, 29
Confessionalism, and universities, 36–37, 56–57, 61, 62
corpus christianum, 27

devotio moderna, 33, 35
dialectic, 5, 7
dropouts, from universities, 223, 234f

emperor, authority of, 194–95
Epistolae obscurorum virorum, 316

The Forme of Curry, 227
Formula of Concord, 13

geometry, in university curriculum, 71, 73, 94 n.13
German Concordat of 1418, 266
government positions, Oxford graduates in, 224ff, 226ff
graduates, university: standard of living, 243ff
Greek studies, 42, 51, 294, 313, 319

Hebrew studies, 42, 53, 293ff
history, in university curriculum, 53, 59
humanism, humanists, studia humanitatis, 6–9, 12, 14–15, 18 n.13, 24, 34–36, 37, 41 n.30, 45, 46, 48–49, 50, 51, 58, 59f, 61, 63, 103, 201–2, 293

Indulgence Controversy, 8

Jesuits, 37, 57f, 59, 271

Letters of Obscure Men, 22, 31
libraries, at universities, 166, 171
Logica Anglicana, 108ff, 113, 126, 142–43, 148 n.20
logica antiqua, 108
logica modernorum, 108

marranos, 296, 312, 315, 322 n.57
marriage, as a reason for leaving the university, 232f
Master of Arts degree, 218, 269, 276 n.42

matriculation records, 217, 258f, 260ff, 269, 272 n.1, 274 n.26, 277ff
medicine, in university curriculum, 75
mendicants, 33
music, in university curriculum, 73, 75

natural philosophy, 70f, 75, 78–79, 83–86, 88
Neo-Judaism (legalism), 297f, 309–11
nominalism, 103–5, 129, 134, 137–38, 143, 145, 146 n.5, 146 n.6. See also Ockhamism

Observantism, 28, 32
Ockhamism, 4, 103–5, 111, 130, 134, 137, 143, 145, 147 n.11. See also nominalism
Ockhamists, 123
ordination, educational standards for, 269, 271

papal authority, 47, 194–95, 202–3
Pelagian Crisis, 131ff
philology, as necessary for Scripture, 305–6
philosophia Christi, 295–98, 318
Platonism, in fifteenth century Italy, 300
Prisca theologia, 300

quadrivium, 20, 36, 71, 77, 93 n.9
questiones technique, 80ff, 88–90, 100 n.58

reformatio moderna, 35
Reformatio Sigismundi, 256
Reformation, affect of, on universities, 23–25, 37, 42ff
repetitiones technique, 98 n.46
rithmomachia, 77f

scholasticism, 20, 34, 49, 60, 81ff
secession, from a university, 163, 167, 169, 170ff

secundum imaginationem, acts of God, 84
seminaries, Catholic, 271–72
seminaries, Lutheran, 271
semi-Pelagianism, 107, 132
Sentences of Peter Lombard, commentaries on, 112–16, 121f, 125–27, 131, 133, 135–36, 140, 143–44, 270
Sodalitas Staupitziana, 30
sophismata, 109–10, 134, 142
students, university, careers of, 213ff
studia generalia, mendicant, 120, 125–26, 138, 139, 140ff, 145, 249 n.12
studium generale, 2, 21, 27, 32, 181
supposition theory, 108ff, 270

Talmud, 312, 314
Talmudistes, 317
territorial interests, in founding universities, 28f, 48, 62, 191
Teutonic Order, 191f, 194ff
Theologia Anglicana, 111ff, 126, 137, 143f
theology, theologians, 51f, 57, 59–61, 83, 85, 106f, 114, 117, 118ff, 124, 126ff, 137ff, 138, 213, 218, 240, 269, 271, 314, 316
tonsure, first, 223, 263
translations, of the twelfth and thirteenth centuries, 68ff, 91, 93 n.3, 164
trivium, 20, 36, 59

universities, Iberian peninsula, special character of, 184f
universities, purpose of, 52, 54, 213, 216, 223, 226

Veritas Hebraica, 296, 302–4, 305, 319
via antiqua, 20, 29, 37, 50, 160 n.144
via moderna, 20, 29, 33, 37, 50, 104, 138, 146 n.5, 160 n.144